Communication

Research

Strategies and Sources

Fifth Edition

Communication
Research
Strategies and Sources

Fifth Edition

Rebecca B. Rubin
Kent State University

Alan M. Rubin
Kent State University

Linda J. Piele
University of Wisconsin–Parkside

Ⓦ **Wadsworth**
Thomson Learning™

Australia • Canada • Denmark • Japan • Mexico • New Zealand • Philippines
Puerto Rico • Singapore • South Africa • Spain • United Kingdom • United States

Executive Editor: *Dierdre Cavanaugh*
Associate Development Editor: *Megan Gilbert*
Editorial Assistant: *Dory Schaeffer*
Marketing Manager: *Stacey Purviance*
Project Editor: *Marlene Vasilieff*
Print Buyer: *Mary Noel*

Permissions Editor: *Joohee Lee*
Production: *Ruth Cottrell*
Copy Editor: *Betty Duncan*
Cover Designer: *Lisa Delgado*
Compositor: *Ruth Cottrell Books*
Printer/Binder: *Webcom Ltd.*

Printed in Canada.
  2 3 4 5 6 03 02 01 00

**Library of Congress
Cataloging-in-Publication Data**

Rubin, Rebecca B.
    Communication research : strategies and
sources / Rebecca B. Rubin, Alan M.
Rubin, Linda J. Piele.—5th ed.
        p.   cm.
    Includes bibliographical references and
    indexes.
    ISBN 0-534-56169-1
    1. Communication—Research—
Methodology. I. Rubin, Alan M.,
II. Piele, Linda J. III. Title
P91.3.R83 1999
302.'2. 072—dc21   99-16080

**For more information, contact
Wadsworth/Thomson Learning
10 Davis Drive
Belmont, CA 94002-3098
USA
www.wadsworth.com**

International Headquarters
Thomson Learning
290 Harbor Drive, 2nd Floor
Stamford, CT 06902-7477
USA

UK/Europe/Middle East
Thomson Learning
Berkshire House
168-173 High Holborn
London, WC1V 7AA,
United Kingdom

Asia
Thomson Learning
60 Albert Street #15-01
Albert Complex
Singapore 189969

Canada
Nelson/Thomson Learning
1120 Birchmount Road
Scarborough, Ontario M1K 5G4
Canada

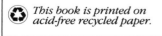

Contents

Foreword

Communication Research: Strategies and Sources is designed to acquaint students with research and the vast array of information sources available in communication. It describes the strategies involved in selecting, refining, and researching communication topics. It is a guide to the literature, explaining the content and utility of significant and representative communication research sources. It is also a communication research manual, providing an opportunity for students to use and become familiar with communication research materials. Throughout the book, we stress the overall strategy of searching the literature for information on a particular topic.

This book provides a comprehensive overview of the necessary steps to begin communication research and describes on-line and published sources that are available in or accessible through most medium-sized college and university libraries. The works that are described are used when conducting documentary, archival, or library research. This type of research is necessary before any other research methodology is attempted.

Communication is a broad discipline in which researchers are interested in many subject areas. Thus, we explain the structure of the communication field and the types of research done by students of communication, and focus on the basics of documentary and library research. These basics include developing and refining research questions, writing and organizing, beginning investigation of a topic, and acquiring the tools that make the research process more efficient. We also describe each type of communication research source that is available for accomplishing a research goal.

This text is beneficial for both undergraduate and graduate students who need to become acquainted with the variety of available communication research resources and procedures. We introduce students to sources in interpersonal, group, organizational, public, and mass communication and to common research strategies. Because the book is designed as a supplemental text, there is a fair amount of flexibility in its use—from one or two students working independently, to a module within a theory course, to an entire class focused on communication research. Any undergraduate or graduate communication course that requires students to use the literature of the field is an appropriate vehicle for offering instruction in researching topics.

For example, this text is a helpful introduction to research procedures and the communication literature in Introduction to Graduate Studies classes as well as in undergraduate and graduate Communication Theory and Research classes. It is appropriate for a variety of introductory-level undergraduate classes in which it is desirable to acquaint students with the literature and research procedures of the field. In addition, instructors may select from among the many sources cited those that are pertinent to their specific courses, such as Freedom of Speech, Media Law, Organizational Communication, Investigative Reporting, Interpersonal Communication, and Media Research. This book is also a useful manual to aid research-paper writing and development by students working on independent studies. It is most helpful for graduate student preparation of thesis and dissertation proposals and for the literature reviews required in many undergraduate and graduate courses.

Students unfamiliar with the library will need some general orientation instruction. The library staff will be able to clarify such matters as the use of the library catalog, location of periodicals, electronic media, and any special location symbols used in the library.

Some chapters include exercises that require students to use several annotated sources. Generally, these questions hypothetically place students in a specific course and present a need to acquire information for a specific project. For example, "You are preparing to lead a discussion on the effects of cartoon violence on children in your Group Communication class. . . ." These assignments lead students to important communication research sources and provide perspective on how the sources are useful in a variety of courses and situations. Questions reiterate points made in the text of the chapter and show how the sources can be used to build a comprehensive bibliography on a chosen communication topic. Answers to the Exercise questions for Part 2 are available to instructors from the authors. Chapters in other sections of the book include exercises for classroom discussion.

Users of previous editions will notice major changes in the chapters devoted to searching the Internet and electronic databases. We have also updated all sources, adding new ones and eliminating some older materials, and have changed several Exercise questions. At the end of most chapters we now include a boxed example of student projects and explanation about how some students have used chapter information for these projects. There have been some additions to the APA style since the last edition, namely, how to cite Internet sources. We include these changes in Appendix A.

We have always been uncomfortable updating this text because we know that by the time it is published, some new important sources will appear or new editions will appear. To counter this trend, we have developed a website for this text that will contain new sources and Internet sites, updated materials that have been published, and additional information for students. This site can be accessed through Wadsworth's Communication Café at:

<http://communication.wadsworth.com>

As usual, we are grateful for the comments and suggestions of the many students, teachers, and scholars who have helped us refine our ideas throughout our five editions: Sherilyn Marrow Ferguson, University of Northern Colorado; Janie M. Harden Fritz, Duquesne University; Mike Hemphill, University of Arkansas at Little Rock; Susan A. Holton, Bridgewater State College; Sandra M. Ketrow, University of Rhode Island; Alan C. Lerstrom, Luther College; and Roger Smitter, North Central College.

R.B.R.
A.M.R.
L.J.P.

Introduction

We believe that university students actively seek to master the available tools when learning about the field of communication. The library contains many of these communication research tools. Our aim is to introduce these tools to you and to explain how they can be used to help increase your knowledge of communication. How much effort you give to this learning process will determine how much you personally gain.

OVERVIEW

This book is divided into three main parts. In Part 1 we explain why and how communication research is done. After surveying the field of communication, we look at the research process, selecting and narrowing research topics and questions, searching the literature, and using computers to search databases and access information on computer networks.

In Part 2 we explore the available types of communication research sources or reference materials. We consider general communication research sources such as subject handbooks, textbooks, encyclopedias, and annual reviews. These materials are helpful in defining subjects or topics you may wish to investigate. We also examine access tools such as bibliographies, guides to the literature, indexes, and abstracts. These tools are needed to locate sources and materials. In the next two chapters we discuss more specific communication research sources, namely, communication periodicals (scholarly journals and professional magazines) and information compilations (collections, statistical compendia, government publications, yearbooks, directories, dictionaries, and manuals). These periodicals and compilations are important for finding primary and factual data and for developing research projects.

In Part 3 we explain how to design and conduct research investigations and how to complete literature reviews and other projects. The final chapter ties together the ideas presented throughout the book.

Because we try to highlight a representative sample of references in each chapter, not all works important to the study of communication can be discussed at length. Numerous sources, though, are listed at the ends of the chapters and are indexed at the end of the book. The sources we have selected do not constitute an exhaustive list. We chose them because they represent the many diverse areas of communication research, they are written in or translated into the English language, and they are available at many college and university libraries. We also identify some specific sources, such as archival and legal references, which are available via specialized libraries, because they are accessible and of particular utility to communication researchers.

As with any book, materials become dated, and new or revised sources become available between the time a book is written and is available for use. Visit our new website at <**http://communication.wadsworth.com**> for new and updated sources. You will undoubtedly uncover other important bibliographic tools in your literature searches. As you do, just add them in the chapters and to the source index for quick reference in the future.

We mentioned earlier that a major goal is to introduce and explain bibliographic tools that are available for investigating communication topics. In so doing, we hope we will accomplish a secondary goal of reducing the anxiety many students feel when researching a communication topic for the first time or when confronted with so much information that they don't know where to start. We anticipate that this book will be a useful starting point and a reference guide and that it will assist you in learning about communication.

HELPFUL HINTS

Students who have used earlier versions of this book have offered some helpful hints. These tips make a lot of sense.

First, get to know the physical layout of the library you will be using. Find the reference section, the reserve desk, the library catalogs, and the computer stations. Discover how books and periodicals are arranged in your library. This information is usually available in printed form when you enter the library. Ask about the availability of CD-ROM databases, on-line databases, and accessibility of the Internet. Consult a reference librarian or staff member at an information desk if you have a question, any question.

Second, complete the Exercises at the ends of the chapters. Be sure to read each chapter thoroughly before trying to answer the questions. In fact, we constructed the Exercises so that reading the chapter first will be an enormous aid to completing the questions. Students who were looking for shortcuts in the past became frustrated. Your amount of effort will actually be reduced by reading the chapters before trying to answer the questions.

There are no trick questions in the Exercises. Each reference source you are asked to use is explained in the chapter text. Read the annotations carefully. The sources that are annotated or described in detail in the text sometimes provide clues for answering the questions. When you locate reference sources that are new to you, examine them carefully. Explore the table of contents, examine the preface and introduction, and look for an index. In so doing, the sources themselves may provide you with a more efficient method of use. If you find yourself spending more than 15 minutes on any one question, your approach to the problem may not be the best. Ask a reference librarian for advice. Also, ask for help when you cannot find a source you need. It may be shelved in a different location in the library.

Third, if you are working on a research paper, literature review, or research prospectus as you read this book, keep in mind the sources you examine as you develop a research topic or question. You might find it advantageous to return to the materials discussed in earlier chapters for a more thorough examination. For instance, the Exercises in Part 2 will sometimes ask you to look at only one volume of a multivolume work. Once you have solidified your own research topic, you might want to go back to the other volumes to see if they can help lead you to additional references. Because you already will be familiar with how these sources are used, it will require little effort to check them for pertinent information.

In a similar vein, if you have a clear-cut topic in mind as you progress through the chapters, do not hesitate to examine each source thoroughly as you use the guide. This will save you time in the future. You can easily compile a thorough bibliography as you proceed through the chapters of this book.

Fourth, update the references in this book whenever possible. Students in the past have found that they misplace additional or updated references if they do not add them when they are first located. Update and add your new references at the ends of the chapters and in the index. You may also want to augment the annotations and citations with your own notes on using the materials. In this way, the book will become an even more useful and comprehensive collection of communication research materials.

part one

Communication Research Strategies

T he essence of strategy is careful planning. Accordingly, communication research requires a comprehensive plan of action. Part 1 focuses on conventional search procedures used to investigate communication topics.

In Chapter 1 we discuss the types of research projects students typically undertake and then describe the general structure of the communication discipline. Next, in Chapter 2 we outline search procedures and provide an orientation to library research. In Chapter 3 we explain what the Internet is and how to use it for communication research. In Chapter 4 we explain the strategies used to search computerized bibliographic databases and the World Wide Web.

Part 1 of the book, then, is an orientation to the process of communication research. We include end-of-chapter exercises to help you formulate a strategy—a plan of action—for completing research projects. If you are using this text in a college course, you will find it worthwhile to ask your instructor for feedback about how well you understand the research strategies by discussing your answers to the exercises.

chapter 1

Studying Communication

W hy should we study communication? Those who do will tell you that their work is driven by a need to know more about human interaction and the communication process. Communication professionals need to develop skills for acquiring and using information throughout their professional lives.

Research is often defined as systematic inquiry into a subject. The key word in this definition, *systematic*, points to the need to examine topics methodically rather than to plunge haphazardly into sources. Two major goals in this book are to acquaint you with this step-by-step procedure of inquiry and to provide guidance for following these generally accepted principles and practices of research.

In this chapter we explain how communication students and professionals become involved in the research process. First, we explore the profession and how the discipline is organized. This will give you an idea of the interdisciplinary nature of communication and a sense of what interests communication researchers. Then we look at the types of projects that require systematic inquiry in the communication discipline.

THE COMMUNICATION DISCIPLINE

Communication is how people arrive at shared meanings through the interchange of messages. Although *communication* has been defined in a variety of ways, when we define it as the process through which meaning and social reality are created, many things become communication events. Political scientists, educators, business executives, linguists, poets, philosophers, scientists, historians, psychologists, sociologists, and anthropologists—to name but a few—are concerned with communication within their specific areas of inquiry. It is little wonder that no other discipline of knowledge is quite as broad as communication.

Communication researchers examine the processes by which meanings are managed—in other words, how people structure and interpret messages and use language and other symbol systems in several contexts: interpersonal, group, organizational, public, and mass. Thus, the focus of communication inquiry is broad, and the contexts in which the communication process is examined are diverse and interrelated.

Communication is a time-honored and yet modern field of inquiry. The Greek philosopher Aristotle (384–322 B.C.) devoted much thought to examining the constituent elements of *rhetoric*, or the available means of persuasion. From 1600 through the early 1900s, speech theorists focused on effective delivery of the spoken word. Early students of mass communication were intrigued by the effects of media-delivered messages. Contemporary communication researchers have also expanded their interests to interpersonal, group, and organizational communication contexts and to the processes that occur during communication. In examining the flow of information and the interchange of messages between individuals in a variety of contexts, researchers today are also probing the uses and effects of modern communication technologies in a world where societies and people are linked by instantaneous transmissions via satellites and computers.

Communication has a rich history, so rich that we couldn't do justice to it here. For more information on the history of the communication discipline, consult the following sources:

Benson, T. W. (Ed.). (1985). *Speech communication in the 20th century*. Carbondale: Southern Illinois University Press.

Cohen, H. (1994). *The history of speech communication: The emergence of a discipline, 1914–1945*. Annandale, VA: National Communication Association.

Crowley, D., & Heyer, P. (Eds.). (1991). *Communication in history: Technology, culture, society* (2nd ed.). New York: Longman.

Delia, J. G. (1987). Communication research: A history. In C. R. Berger & S. H. Chaffee (Eds.), *Handbook of communication science* (pp. 20–98). Newbury Park, CA: Sage.

Rogers, E. M. (1994). *A history of communication study: A biographical approach*. New York: Free Press.

Schramm, W. (1980). The beginnings of communication study in the United States. *Communication Yearbook, 4*, 73–82.

Schramm, W. (1997). *The beginnings of communication study in America: A personal memoir*. S. H. Chaffee & E. M. Rogers (Eds.). Thousand Oaks, CA: Sage.

Schramm, W. L. (1988). *The story of human communication: Cave painting to microchip*. New York: Harper & Row.

Because communication is studied in several allied disciplines, you may sometimes find it difficult to focus on one particular research topic and to find all the available literature about that topic. And, because communication is of interest to the social and behavioral sciences, the arts, and the humanities, many research sources exist in these disciplines. With so much information available, determining which sources are most pertinent becomes difficult.

For example, if you are interested in organizational communication, you will find pertinent reference materials in health education, business management, sociology, psychology, personnel, and other communication-related sources. However, the differences in the language and vocabulary used might make understanding the works in these disciplines somewhat difficult for someone not in those fields. As a communication scholar, you are thus faced with learning about the communication process within one of several traditionally defined communication contexts, while also trying to integrate knowledge about the process generated in other disciplines.

STRUCTURE OF THE FIELD

As a result of this breadth and diversity, the communication literature includes a variety of subjects that define the field. Knowledge of these subjects will help you discover the most appropriate sources for your research. We have grouped these subjects into six major content categories: interpersonal communication, small-group communication, language and symbolic codes, organizational communication, public communication, and mass communication. The study of communicators and their messages is common to all areas of communication. What differentiates one subject area from another is the focus on different settings or dominant modes of interaction.

1. *Interpersonal communication* involves the study of people and their interactions or relationships. Researchers in this area study the use of verbal and nonverbal messages in developing and maintaining relationships between people. Some topics they find interesting are interpersonal competence, impression formation, spousal conflict, interpersonal attraction, communication apprehension, and relational communication.
2. *Small-group communication* covers communication in groups of three or more persons. Researchers often study how groups emerge, accomplish their goals, and solve problems and how group leaders function. Topics in small-group communication include small-group effectiveness, cohesion, conflict, group roles, consensus, productivity, group culture, and family communication.
3. *Language and symbolic codes* is concerned with verbal and nonverbal codes of communication. When examining these codes, researchers focus on how language and nonverbal symbols are transmitted, are received, and come to have meaning for people of the same or different cultures. Topics cover issues such as text or discourse, language intensity, proxemics, language development in children, conversational flow, listening, nonverbal immediacy, and relational power.
4. *Organizational communication* is concerned with the processing and use of messages between and within organizations. It focuses on the complexities of communication in formal structures where many interpersonal and group relationships already exist. Researchers look at organizational networks,

systems, conflict, negotiation, superior/subordinate relationships, and other aspects of organizational life.

5. *Public communication* covers communication in nonmediated public settings and focuses mainly on one-to-many communication. Primary topics include rhetoric, public address, analysis and delivery of speeches, persuasion, argumentation, and debate. Research focuses on speaker credibility, ethics, interpreting literature, propaganda, political campaigns, and communication education.

6. *Mass communication* focuses on communication from a source or organization to many people via mediated channels such as television or newspapers under conditions of limited feedback. Those who study mass communication are concerned with how such mediated messages are formulated and received and how they affect individuals and society, as well as the control of power in society. They are often interested in media effects, history, ethics, formation of public opinion, policy and regulation, international broadcasting, and critical or textual analysis of messages.

These six subject areas are listed below, along with terms that describe subareas of study relevant to each of the larger topics. These subareas may be useful when deciding on a research topic or locating materials in a library. Naturally, many of the subareas could be placed under two or more of the broader headings because of the interdisciplinary and fluid nature of communication inquiry.

Interpersonal Communication

Conflict management
Dyadic communication
Gender and communication
Instructional communication
Interpersonal influence
Interpersonal perception
Intrapersonal communication
Relational communication

Small-Group Communication

Decision making
Family communication
Group dynamics
Intergenerational communication
Leadership
Problem solving

Language and Symbolic Codes

Developmental communication
Discourse analysis
Intercultural communication

Linguistics
Nonverbal communication
Semantics
Semiotics
Textual analysis

Organizational Communication

Business and professional speaking
Health communication
Human communication technology
Negotiation and mediation
Organizational behavior
Socialization and assimilation
Training and development

Public Communication

Argumentation
Communication pedagogy
Debate
Environmental communication
Freedom of speech
Legal communication

Public Communication (cont'd.)

Performance studies
Persuasion and attitude change
Political communication
Public address
Rhetorical theory and criticism
Voice and diction

Mass Communication

Advertising
Broadcasting and
   telecommunications

Comparative media systems
Criticism and culture
Economics of media industries
Film and cinema
Journalism
Media effects
Media ethics
New technologies
Policy and regulation
Popular culture
Public relations

These topics help us see how diversified the communication discipline is. Students have many avenues of scholarship available to them. Scholars often need to know about more than just one topic, so they conduct research on many, often overlapping topics during their careers. This interest in multiple areas influences scholars' memberships in professional communication organizations. Many members of the communication discipline belong to several organizations or to several divisions within one or more organizations. Professional communication associations, then, reflect the many interests of their members.

STRUCTURE OF PROFESSIONAL COMMUNICATION ORGANIZATIONS

Because of the diversity of their members' interests, major professional communication organizations have developed classifications for interest groups in the field. For example, the National Communication Association (NCA) has several divisions: applied communication; argumentation and forensics; Asian/Pacific American communication studies; basic course; critical and cultural studies; ethnography; family communication, feminist and women studies; gay, lesbian, bisexual, transgender studies; group communication; health communication; instructional development; international and intercultural communication; interpersonal communication; language and social interaction; Latina/ Latino communication studies; mass communication; organizational communication; performance studies; political communication; public address; public relations; rhetorical and communication theory; theatre; and training and development. For additional information about the organization, its publications, divisions, conventions, and affiliated associations, visit the association's home page at <**www.natcom.org**>. NCA recently changed its name from the Speech Communication Association; keep this in mind when you see references to the Speech Communication Association throughout publications listed in this text.

The International Communication Association (ICA) has similar divisions: communication and technology, feminist scholarship, health communication, information systems, instruction and developmental communication, intercultural and development communication, interpersonal communication, language and social interaction, mass communication, organizational communication, philosophy of communication, political communication, popular communication, and public relations. The subject-area divisions of the ICA are reflected in earlier volumes of the *Communication Yearbook*, first published in 1977. This source, along with *Communication Abstracts*, first published in 1978, provides important access to and integration of communication knowledge. Both publications are constantly updated and are valuable sources for those who study communication, as is the more recent addition of *ComIndex* and *CommSearch* computerized databases. These sources are described in more detail in later chapters. For additional information about the association, divisions, conventions, and publications, visit ICA's home page at <**www.icahdq.org**>.

Mass-communication organizations also have specialized divisions that reflect several concerns and content areas. The Association for Education in Journalism and Mass Communication (AEJMC) has the following divisions: advertising, communication technology and policy, communication theory and methodology, history, international communication, law, magazine, mass communication and society, media management and economics, minorities and communication, newspaper, public relations, qualitative studies, radio-television journalism, scholastic journalism, and visual communication. The Broadcast Education Association (BEA) also contains several divisions: communication technology; courses, curricula and administration; gender issues; history; international; law and policy; management and sales; multicultural studies; news; production aesthetics and criticism; research; student media advisors; two-year/small colleges; and writing.

Thus, the discipline of communication can be partitioned into more specific topical areas, even though the work of researchers in the various divisions is often relevant to researchers in other areas. For example, health communication researchers, as well as those who study computer-mediated communication, may find information on interpersonal, organizational, and mass communication pertinent to their own studies.

■ ACTIVITIES

Among other activities, professional communication associations publish journals and hold yearly conventions around the country. The papers presented at these conventions represent the most current concerns of communication researchers and may be helpful in your research projects. Some of these papers are submitted to the Educational Resources Information Center (ERIC) for inclusion in the Resources in Education (RIE) system (see Chapter 6). This system places the papers on microfiche, and many libraries receive the entire collection. Some of these papers are collected in proceedings, which are published by the association, or are available on-line.

Other authors may choose to submit their papers for publication in a scholarly journal. Unfortunately, there could be a 2-year delay (or longer) between the time the paper is first submitted and the time it is published. It is often possible, though, to receive a copy of a paper by attending the convention, by writing to the author (see the discussion of professional association directories, pp. 171–173), by downloading it from a database, or by having paper copies made from the microfiche (for a small fee).

■ Publications

Professional organizations also publish many materials of interest to communication scholars. The NCA, for example, publishes monographs, tapes, books, reports, and bibliographies. The NCA newsletter, *Spectra,* is sent to members monthly to inform them of new developments in the field; fellow members' promotions, grants, and new appointments; and job openings in communication. Issues also contain reports on publications and conventions that are of interest to members. NCA also manages a weekly listserv (electronic newsletter), CRTNET, which distributes to subscribers information on jobs and grants, discussion of relevant issues, and questions or requests for assistance or information.

Both the ICA and the AEJMC publish general newsletters with news of issues, events, people in the field, and job listings. The BEA publishes *Feedback*, its official communicator of association news (in addition to essays and articles). The BEA also sends members electronic mailings and occasional packets of materials (including news; grant, paper, and scholarship announcements; and job openings). Several divisions of these four organizations also have listservs and their own newsletters, which are sent to members of those divisions. All organizations publish directories. These may be helpful if you wish to contact researchers directly about their work.

For more information about these professional organizations, contact them directly:

> Association for Education in Journalism and Mass Communication, 121 LeConte College, University of South Carolina, Columbia, SC 29208 <**www.aejmc.sc.edu**>
>
> Broadcast Education Association, 1771 N Street NW, Washington, DC 20036 <**www.beaweb.org**>
>
> International Communication Association, PO Box 9589, Austin, TX 78766 <**www.icahdq.org**>
>
> National Communication Association, 5105 Backlick Road, Bldg. F, Annandale, VA 22003 <**www.natcom.org**> (*Note*: NCA expects to move to Washington, DC, in the near future, so contact the organization for a current address.)

■ Types of Associations

The associations in the preceding list are national scholarly associations. We encourage graduate and undergraduate students to join them. Although most members are academic faculty and professional communicators, they offer special student memberships. Meetings of regional and state communication associations also provide valuable opportunities for students to attend their conferences and to present their research. Four regional associations that are affiliated with the NCA follow. Because the executive secretaries (and thus the addresses) change often, check the associations' websites for current addresses.

Eastern Communication Association (ECA) <**www.easterncommunication. org**>
Central States Communication Association (CSCA) <**www.bsu.edu/csca/**>
Southern States Communication Association (SSCA) <**www.ssca.net/**>
Western States Communication Association (WSCA) <**www.csufresno. edu/speechcomm/wsca.htm**>

An organization that affiliates with some of the preceding organizations is the World Communication Association (WCA). It publishes a journal and meets every 2 years in countries around the world. For information, contact WCA at <**http://ilc2.doshisha.ac.jp/users/kkitao/organi/wca/**>.

Some professional organizations focus on the practical activities of their members' careers. Such organizations also distribute newsletters, hold annual conventions, and compile directories of members. They differ from the more scholarly organizations in their emphasis on information and techniques for dealing with practical problems and situations arising in practitioners' lives. Many have student chapters. Contact the following organizations for more information:

American Association of Advertising Agencies, 405 Lexington Ave., New York, NY 10174. <**www.commercepark.com/aaaa**>
American Marketing Association, 250 S. Wacker Dr., Suite 200, Chicago, IL 60606 <**www.ama.org**>
International Association of Business Communicators, One Hallidie Plaza, Suite 600, San Francisco, CA 94102 <**www.iabc.com**>
National Association of Broadcasters, 1771 N Street NW, Washington, DC 20036 <**www.nab.org**>
Public Relations Society of America, 33 Irving Place, New York, NY 10003-2376 <**www.prsa.org**>
Radio-Television News Directors Association, 1000 Connecticut Avenue NW, Suite 615, Washington, DC 20036 <**www.rtnda.org**>
Society of Professional Journalists, 15 S. Jackson St., Greencastle, IN 46135-0077 <**www.spj.org**>
Women in Communications, Inc., 3717 Columbia Pike, Suite 310, Arlington, VA 22204-4255 <**www.wici.org**>

Several additional organizations are affiliated with NCA; check NCA's home page for additional information on membership and services for:

American Forensic Association
International Listening Association
Lambda Pi Eta
National Forensic Association

Pi Kappa Delta
Religious Communication Association
Chinese Communication Association

COMMUNICATION RESEARCH PROJECTS

Throughout a college career, a communication student faces a wide variety of assignments requiring the use of research tools and skills:

Compiling bibliographies
Completing take-home exams
Conducting audience or consumer surveys
Conducting original research investigations
Giving speeches or oral readings
Investigating and writing news stories
Leading seminars
Preparing advertising or public relations campaigns
Preparing debate cases or group discussions
Writing abstracts, research reports, theses, or dissertations
Writing television, radio, or film scripts, or critiques
Writing term papers, seminar papers, or literature reviews

Although there are many different types of student assignments or projects, many have similar characteristics. For example, projects typically could have a persuasive, informative, or combined *goal*. This means the student might be attempting to change the audience's mind, convince them of something or alter their beliefs. Or the goal could be informational in nature, attempting to impart new knowledge to others through description and explanation. Sometimes, after considering the information available, students might take a stand and defend it with relevant information.

The *scope* of the project could be narrow, moderate, or broad. A narrow project is one that is limited by time or space (for example, a 3-minute speech or a 5-page paper). A broader project might be limited by the amount of information that is available (for example, a dissertation is expected to include all relevant sources).

The *audience* might be as narrow as a college classroom or as broad as the general public. Often, the audience is an academic one, so the language may be scholarly and technical. At other times, a project will have an applied focus, so it will have a very specific work group in mind. The level of language that is used should be adjusted to the audience.

To complete all assignments effectively, we need to know the methods and materials of communication research—the tools within and outside the library that provide the needed information. We also need to know how to use these tools.

Class assignments require locating and documenting facts and finding pertinent supporting materials. Sometimes instructors suggest that you read a specific study (for example, McCroskey and McCain's 1974 article on interpersonal attraction, Hart and Burks' 1972 essay on rhetorical sensitivity, or Horton and Wohl's 1956 discussion of parasocial interaction). How would you go about finding these with such limited information? One way would be to consult an index (see Chapter 6) to find complete bibliographic citations for journal articles.

Sometimes you will just want to explore the scholarly journal literature for research on a particular idea or topic of interest. You may find the topic interesting or relevant to your life and wonder what scholars actually know about it. At other times, you may need specific facts—the current number of employees in the television or newspaper industry or the most recent decision of the Federal Trade Commission about advertising, for example. You may need to choose a method of running a meeting in a particular organization. Or you may read articles to find out what questions are of interest and how to phrase your own questions.

■ ACADEMIC PURSUITS

Preparing a term paper, literature review, research study, or thesis or dissertation prospectus requires extended use of the communication literature and the library. Also, students often conduct their own research investigations, where research questions are asked, a study is designed, and data are collected and analyzed. These projects require you to examine and understand past research in the area so that you can determine what important communication problems still need to be addressed. This process will also help you determine whether your research question has already been satisfactorily answered by others. It gives you a solid foundation on which to build the investigation or to generate hypotheses about how the communication concepts or ideas are related to one another.

For example, suppose you decide to conduct a research investigation and you conclude, after browsing through the literature, that you want to study the variable "eye contact" (which may vary from a great deal of eye contact to very little—thus the term **variable**). After reading some more of the literature, you decide to examine the effect of eye contact on a second variable, the "length of conversation" during an interpersonal interaction (which may vary from a few seconds to many minutes). You will need to give a reason for proposing this study (why it is important) and a question or prediction about how the variables (eye contact and length of conversation) might be related. The first section of a research proposal summarizes and analyzes the findings of research studies that have previously examined these variables, and the **hypotheses**, educated or informed guesses about the relationships between the variables, are the end product of this exhaustive literature search.

Sometimes there is not enough research to allow an educated guess, so a research question is posed that will guide the study. Or perhaps your method is first to observe many people's eye contact with others while interacting and then to arrive at an explanation about the role of eye contact in interpersonal interaction. This latter method is more *inductive* than *deductive* in nature; that is, we reason from specific observations to a general principle. We will discuss the different approaches to conducting a research study in Chapter 9.

■ PROFESSIONAL PURSUITS

The need to seek information and the importance of knowing what information is available are certainly not limited to the academic world. Communication professionals use and refer to many of these materials on a daily basis. For example:

Film critics search past film reviews for references to particular directors.

Public relations specialists consult directories for names and addresses of organizations.

Television producers check current statistical sources to ascertain that a documentary is current.

Communication consultants use abstracts and indexes to learn about new teaching or training methods.

Advertising or media researchers search scholarly studies for relevant communication research.

Political speech writers examine collections of speeches and editorials for themes and issues.

Journalists check grammatical usage or news style by consulting a wire service handbook.

Professors keep abreast of the field by reading professional and scholarly periodicals.

Being able to answer questions systematically and knowing what materials are available and how to find and use them are essential in any career. These materials are the tools of the trade.

The projects and assignments given in your classes help you understand how communication researchers satisfy their need to know more about communication. Such assignments teach you the systematic methods of searching for knowledge. In effect, your link to the communication discipline is through your participation in scholarship.

In the Examples that follow, we present five typical projects or assignments students complete in communication classes. In several later chapters we'll show you how these students used the information in the chapter for their projects.

SUMMARY

Communication research, like all research, must be systematic to be effective. Communication researchers study the processes through which meaning and social reality are created. Researchers examine the flow of information and the interchange of messages between individuals in several contexts. Although the study of communication is broad based and interdisciplinary, the field can be divided into several major areas of focus. Professional communication associations publish scholarly journals, organize conventions and conferences, and produce materials and newsletters to keep their members informed. Students complete a variety of assignments in their classes, which differ in scope, purpose, audience, and goal.

REFERENCES

Hart, R. P., & Burks, D. M. (1972). Rhetorical sensitivity and social interaction. *Communication Monographs, 39*, 75–91.

Horton, D., & Wohl, R. R. (1956). Mass communication and para-social interaction: Observations on intimacy at a distance. *Psychiatry, 19*, 215–229.

McCroskey, J. C., & McCain, T. A. (1974). The measurement of interpersonal attraction. *Communication Monographs, 41*, 261–266.

EXAMPLES

CHRIS is taking a basic public-speaking class. One assignment in the class is to prepare and deliver a persuasive speech. "Ethics" has always been a topic of interest, so pursuing a topic in communication and ethics seems to be worthwhile at this time. This assignment seems to have the following characteristics:

> GOAL: Persuasion—Take a stand and defend it
> SCOPE: Narrow
> AUDIENCE: General (college students)
> SIMILAR PROJECTS: Debate case, critical essay, editorial, opinion paper

FELECIA has an ongoing interest in new technologies and how they complement interpersonal communication. Recent experiences with the college's new voice-mail system cause her to wonder about whether this asynchronous form of communication is better than the former alternative. A journalism assignment—to write a newspaper article about this new system—provides a good opportunity to learn more about it. This assignment seems to have the following characteristics:

> GOAL: Information—Describe and explain
> SCOPE: Narrow
> AUDIENCE: General (college students)
> SIMILAR PROJECTS: Newspaper article, broadcast story, documentary, magazine article, informative speech

MARIA is taking the beginning communication theory class in which a variety of theories are discussed and explained. Students in the class must choose one theory and (a) write a 5-page paper that explains what the theory is about and (b) lead a 10-minute discussion of the theory in class. Maria has always been interested in how we get to know others, so "attribution theory" seems like a good choice. This assignment seems to have the following characteristics:

GOAL: Information—Describe and explain
SCOPE: Moderate
AUDIENCE: Academic (professor and students)
SIMILAR PROJECTS: Term paper, seminar paper, take-home exam, classroom report

ORLANDO is a taking a senior/graduate seminar in interpersonal and mediated communication. Students are expected to conduct a thorough review of the literature on a specific topic and to propose several possible research directions. So far, exciting topics include talk radio, portrayals of relationships on television, and parasocial interaction. Orlando's first step is to find out if these topics have sufficient research support to write the 20- to 25-page assignment. This assignment seems to have the following characteristics:

GOAL: Combined—Describe research findings within a strong thesis
SCOPE: Limited by demands of the project
AUDIENCE: Academic (scholars)
SIMILAR PROJECTS: Research prospectus, senior thesis, thesis, dissertation

KAT, **CALVIN**, **ROCKY**, and **MICHELLE** are taking organizational communication. One project is to develop a training module that can be used in any organization. The group is supposed to develop and pilot test the module this semester in class. Naturally, it takes the group quite a while to decide on a good topic, but when it starts to develop, everyone seems to think that "conflict resolution at work" would be appropriate and interesting. This assignment seems to have the following characteristics:

GOAL: Informative/instructional—Teach others new skills
SCOPE: Narrow, focused
AUDIENCE: Specific and applied
SIMILAR PROJECTS: Group discussion, campaign

EXERCISES

1. Describe two situations in your anticipated career that would require you to have knowledge of communication research. To help, speak to a professional in the area and ask about communication research in that profession.

2. Identify three key terms or headings in the communication subject areas listed in this chapter that now interest you. Explain how these key terms can be applied to projects you plan to complete in the near future, such as a literature review, speech, news story, group discussion, or term paper.

3. Indicate the main subject area described in this chapter with which you most closely identify at this point in your education. Find a national scholarly communication organization that has a division in that area. Contact the organization for information about the division.

4. Examine some newsletters from the professional associations identified in this chapter. What issues are currently of concern to members? What functions do these newsletters serve for members?

5. Locate the home page of a professional association listed in this chapter. How is the site organized? What would you have to do to join this organization?

chapter 2

Searching the Communication Literature

The process of conducting library research for communication projects is fairly standard, no matter what sort of project you are attempting. Literature reviews, research reports, thesis or dissertation prospectuses, debates, speeches, group discussions, interviews, news editorials, and feature articles all begin in the same way. You will need to select and refine a topic, identify core concepts and search terms, locate and read background information, decide what types of sources you will need to support your topic, select and use appropriate **databases** and other **access tools**, and locate and obtain the needed publications and documents. It's really a pretty straightforward process.

Throughout this process you will also need to continue to adjust your topic, evaluate carefully the citations and materials you retrieve, and identify additional search terms and important authors to recycle into your searches of print and electronic sources. Once you've assembled your sources, you may identify some gaps in your research and have to head back to the library. In fact, although the search process has starting and ending points, it can seem at times to be more a circular than linear process. Effective research usually entails recycling through some of the intermediary steps. We strongly recommend that you document your research with careful and complete notes as you go along. This all takes time, although our experience tells us that it is time well spent and will save you time and frustration in the end.

Those new to conducting research in a college or university library frequently fall into the trap of underestimating the amount of time needed to conduct library research. They reason that, thanks to computers, all they need to do is pick a general topic, go to the library (or access it electronically), type in the first search terms that come to mind, pull up and print their results, and head home to write their project. After all, everything is **on-line**, right? Because the whole process shouldn't take more than a few hours, why not wait until a week (or a few days) before the project is due to get started?

Unfortunately, "everything" is not on-line, and computers neither read minds nor evaluate the suitability of materials for a particular purpose. Furthermore, short time frames don't allow time for adjusting topics, learning to use unfamiliar databases, refining electronic searches, asking librarians for help, recalling books that are checked out, tracking down off-the-shelf periodicals, and sending for that "perfect" sounding book or article through interlibrary loan—let alone to read, evaluate, and digest resources as the search progresses. Once home, we find that quickly compiled materials make for difficult-to-write projects. We may have found 10 or 20 sources—or whatever was stipulated in the assignment—but these sources just don't hang together or have a clear focus. The result is anxiety, frustration, and disappointed instructors. Therefore, the time to get started on any research project is immediately after it's assigned. Instructors allow lead time for projects because they know from personal experience that it's necessary.

In this chapter we describe in some detail the steps involved in the research process. Remaining chapters will flesh out many of the concepts presented. For example, in this chapter we need to refer briefly to some characteristics of electronic databases and procedures for searching them, even though we won't thoroughly explain these until Chapter 4. We also need to refer to different types of access tools and publications that are covered in detail in Part 2. For this reason, we suggest that you read this chapter now, to set the stage, and then review it after you've finished reading Part 2.

To conduct library research, you'll need to have a basic familiarity with your library and its services. Many students will have gained this basic knowledge through library instructional programs offered to freshman classes. But if not, the following section is for you. Terms that are in **bold print** are defined in the Glossary (Appendix C), which you may want to bookmark for quick referral as you read this section.

BECOMING FAMILIAR WITH YOUR LIBRARY AND ITS SERVICES

Many libraries conduct drop-in orientation sessions or offer self-guided tours and handouts for new users. Take advantage of these if offered, because the basic information and tips you will learn will save you much confusion and frustration. Lacking such an orientation, the best approach when using a library new to you is simply to find the reference desk and ask a **reference librarian** some basic questions. He or she will be happy to help you find your way around and may be able to offer you instructional handouts on using the catalog and other resources. By the way, never feel reluctant to ask for such help from a librarian. That's why the reference desk is there.

Find out where the **book stacks** (library term for "bookshelves") are located and how they are arranged. Most college and university libraries are arranged by Library of Congress (LC) call numbers (a mixture of letters and numbers), although a few use the Dewey Decimal System you're probably accustomed to from your school and public libraries.

Library of Congress Call Number	Book Title	Dewey Call Number
HD30.3 .G656 1998	Corporate Communications for Executives	658.45 G653 C822 1998

About all you need to know about Library of Congress call numbers is that the first one or two letters designate broad disciplines. For example, as a communication researcher, you'll find that many of the sources and tools you use fall into sections beginning with these letters:

BF	Psychology	JK	Political science
H	Social sciences (general)	K	Law
HD, HF	Business management	L	Education
HM	Sociology	P, PN	Communication

You'll also need to ask where the current and **bound periodicals (magazines, journals**, and newspapers) are housed. If a periodical is on **microfilm** or **microfiche**, is it housed in a separate location? How can you tell which periodicals the library subscribes to and where they are located? Are they arranged alphabetically by title, by call number, or by a different subject arrangement? How can you tell which **full-text periodicals** the library subscribes to? Where are the computer workstations that provide access to the library **catalog, periodical indexes** that the library has licensed, and the **World Wide Web**? How is the menu arranged? Will that menu also tell you about specialized databases available only on **CD-ROM**? Is it possible to access the electronic resource menu from other on- and off-campus locations? What sort of printing is available? Will you need a special card?

Almost all libraries maintain collections of **reference** materials (for example, **encyclopedias, handbooks, dictionaries, yearbooks,** and **almanacs**). **Reference books**, which are meant to be consulted rather than read cover to cover, generally are part of a **noncirculating collection (**that is, they cannot be checked out of the library). Find out where the **reference collection** is located and how these materials are identified in the catalog. Many libraries also have separate sections that house **government documents.** Find out if these materials are listed in the main catalog and, if not, what access tools are available to identify and locate them. Most libraries with separate government-document collections arrange materials using Superintendent of Documents (SuDocs) numbers. These numbers classify materials by the issuing agency, rather than by subject.

If the library doesn't own some of the books or **periodical** articles you identify, you may want to order them from another library using your library's **interlibrary loan system**. Requests for such loans are usually filled out at the reference desk, the circulation desk, or the interlibrary loan department. The normal loan period for books is about 2 weeks. Photocopies of articles are yours to keep.

An item requested through interlibrary loan may take 2 or more weeks to arrive—this is one reason why you need to begin research projects early in the semester. If you do end up short on time, a library in your region may own the work. You will probably be able to access the individual catalogs of other libraries in your region through the Internet. Or, perhaps there is a state or regional **union catalog**, which lists the holdings of multiple libraries. Such catalogs may or may not tell you if the item is checked out or kept in noncirculating reference collections. You can also use OCLC's *WorldCat,* a national union catalog, to determine which libraries own the materials. Unfortunately, *WorldCat* cannot tell you if the materials have been checked out. Ask at the reference desk about the availability of regional catalogs and *WorldCat.*

Interlibrary loan helps overcome one complication that may arise when the journal issue you want is "at the bindery." If you know what journal article you want (as opposed to just wanting to browse through an issue), it should be possible to request a paper copy through interlibrary loan.

Library policies and procedures differ, library by library. You need to be aware of the different protocols followed in the libraries you use. If a book has been checked out, some libraries may allow you to put a "hold" on it when it is returned or to recall the book from the borrower. If the catalog indicates that an item is owned but it is missing from the shelf, see if you may have it "searched." The library will notify you if the item is located. (Don't expect this to happen overnight; it may take several weeks.) Or perhaps your library has "sorting shelves" that users can peruse. Because libraries' protocols differ, inquire about specific procedures at the main information desk of the library. For basic guidelines on using research libraries, see:

Beasley, D. R. (1988). *How to use a research library*. New York: Oxford University Press.

As you go about using the library for your research and completing the exercises in this book, you will inevitably come up with many additional questions. Never hesitate to ask reference librarians to help you. They realize that libraries are somewhat complicated to use and that students will have many questions. When they go to an unfamiliar library, they have to ask questions, too.

■ SEARCH STRATEGY OUTLINE

So you've figured out where things are, and you're ready to tackle a communication research project. At this point, we're going to outline a general **search strategy**. Remember that, although this may appear as a list of steps, expect it occasionally to be a circular process. By this we mean that, as you start retrieving and examining citations, examining bibliographies, and reading materials, you will come across additional terms and authors that can be recycled back into your search. You will find yourself looping back to repeat one or more steps. Expect to test, evaluate, and adjust. Be flexible. And know when to stop.

- Select, narrow, and adjust your topic.
- Identify types of sources needed.
- Select appropriate databases and other access tools.
- Decide what types of searches to do and then formulate searches.

- Examine and evaluate the citations retrieved.
- Identify additional access points (key words, subject headings, authors, titles) and reformulate search queries to narrow, broaden, or improve focus, as needed.
- Evaluate citations retrieved, selecting items worth locating.
- Examine bibliographies for additional leads.
- Evaluate and summarize information.
- Read materials thoroughly, taking careful notes.
- Systematically document everything.
- Decide when to stop!

THE TOPIC

■ SELECTING, NARROWING, AND ADJUSTING A TOPIC

Select a Topic

Often the most difficult part of the research process is selecting a topic and defining the research area. You need to identify a topic that is suitable for the project at hand and for which you will be able to find previous research. It's easy to pick a topic that is too broad, such as "interpersonal communication." On the other hand, picking a topic that is too narrow may give you problems, too. There are no easy answers because it's not a mechanical process. You can't type a few terms into the computer, for example, and expect the computer to come up with a topic, but many strategies can help. One is to find an appropriate starting place.

Your starting point should be determined by your familiarity with the structure and terminology of the field. If it is generally unfamiliar to you, you will want to step back and start with a source that can provide a comprehensive picture of the entire **discipline** (for example, communication) or subfield (for example, groups). For example, for your first research projects in communication, you would do well to find and browse through some general sources that will acquaint you with the various facets of communication and its terminology. Some of the sources described in Chapter 5 of this book— handbooks, textbooks, subject encyclopedias, and annual reviews—can serve this purpose.

You may get ideas for possible research topics by examining the textbooks used in your courses. Browsing in handbooks and subject encyclopedias in communication and related disciplines may also help you find a topic that interests you. Specific topic areas may also be found in annual reviews, periodical indexes, and abstracts (which list articles published in scholarly and professional journals; abstracts generally give paragraph-long summaries of research studies). These sources are helpful in narrowing a general topic to a specific research area because they identify subtopics or research problems that are particular to the research topic and list the current studies in these subtopics. Bibliographies and guides to the literature can also be used when defining and refining a problem area for investigation. These communication research sources are discussed in Chapters 5 and 6.

If your project is a debate, speech, interview, or newspaper editorial or article, you may need to find starting points that fall outside the communication literature, but the general strategy remains the same. For example, if you are thinking of giving a speech on some aspect of the social welfare system in the United States, you could start by identifying a subject encyclopedia that covers the sociology discipline. You could identify one by going to Chapter 5, where we list subject encyclopedias for communication and related disciplines, along with general search strategies for locating additional subject encyclopedias. Browse the table of contents, article titles, and the index. The purpose is to get an overview and to come up with some broad topic ideas.

A simple but effective way to find reference sources is simply to browse in the reference collection, taking advantage of its Library of Congress subject arrangement. For example, you know that sociology materials are generally classified in the HMs (their **Library of Congress classification**). Go to that section of your library's reference collection and browse. You will probably find some useful subject encyclopedias and handbooks.

But let's say you want to give a speech that has something to do with bioethics, and you don't know under what section of the Library of Congress classification that would fall. Why not make a librarian's day by going to the reference desk and asking for help in locating such a source? (Reference librarians know how useful these reference sources are, and their underuse by students is a continuing source of frustration.)

Narrow the Topic

Once you have chosen a general topic or research problem, the next step is to narrow it so that you can formulate a specific research question. By constructing a specific research question, you narrow the focus of your research, and you can channel all your energies into a productive purpose. The research question also provides a theme that helps you unify disparate elements and eliminate or reduce nonproductive efforts. A specific research question sets a goal for your efforts and helps you save time. We often develop specific research questions by thinking about a topic, talking to and brainstorming with others, and most of all, reading about the topic or research problem in the literature of the field.

For example, let's imagine that you are interested in both mass communication and organizational communication and you want to investigate the interface of these two general areas. At this point, your broad topic might be "The Use of Media in Organizations." By examining some textbooks and bibliographies, you find such subtopics as advertising, in-house publications, public relations, organizational training programs, institutional media, corporate television, and so on. This may start you thinking, conversing with others, seeking out past research, and reading about the experiences of those people in organizations who must communicate with the public by working with journalists. Your initial research may cause you to ask whether these organizational professionals receive any training in dealing with the press or reporters. At this point, you have identified a more specific research problem and can formulate a preliminary question to examine, such as "What types of training programs in media relations

and public interviews do organizations provide for their management personnel?" This is a viable question that is sufficiently narrow in focus to study and
discuss in a research paper. Another possible research question would be "Which
type of media training program is the most effective for management personnel?"

Identify Key Concepts and Search Terms

Start by underlining the significant terms in your search question. For example:

> What types of <u>training programs</u> in <u>media relations</u> and <u>public interviews</u>
> do <u>organizations</u> provide for their <u>management personnel</u>?

Then try to identify the two or three basic concepts represented by these terms.
In this example, we might identify three basic concepts:

> training programs
> media relations/public interviews
> management personnel

We drop "organizations," because it seems less critical and is probably implied
in "management personnel." Next, look for synonyms for these concepts. One
way of doing this is to investigate the **subject headings** assigned to your concepts in the library catalog.

Virtually all catalogs in academic libraries use Library of Congress (often
abbreviated **LC**) subject headings. These headings are an ideal place to begin
the subject-headings list we recommend you maintain for your research project.
(See the later section on documenting your research.) Most computerized
library catalogs provide cross-references that allow you to investigate subject
headings while searching the catalog itself. For example, a subject-heading
(rather than key-word) search for "management personnel" in a library catalog
will get zero results. We must assume that this term is not a Library of Congress
subject heading. We might guess that the appropriate subject heading is "managers." A subject-heading search for "managers" results in this message:

> MANAGERS
>
> Search under: EXECUTIVES

In other words, "managers" is not a Library of Congress subject heading, but we
do find a cross-reference, which refers us to the correct heading for this
concept: "executives." We now have these terms for this concept:

> management personnel
> managers
> executives (LC)

If we do a subject-heading search for "executives," we find this cross-reference:

> EXECUTIVES
>
> Search also under:
>   GOVERNMENT EXECUTIVES
>   HEALTH SERVICE ADMINISTRATORS

LIBRARY ADMINISTRATORS
MIDDLE MANAGERS
SOUND RECORDING EXECUTIVES AND PRODUCERS
WOMEN EXECUTIVES

We now have still more terms to consider adding to our list. Notice that cross-references can also be useful for those still seeking ideas for narrowing or broadening a search. Some topics, for example, might appropriately be narrowed to "middle managers" or "women executives."

We include all three terms on the subject-heading list because one of the alternate terms may be used in another tool. Also, we may want to use **keyword searching** in some tools, in which case a list of **natural language** synonyms would be needed. Follow a similar process to investigate appropriate terms for each concept in your research question.

Another convenient tool for investigating subject headings (some prefer it) is the printed guide to Library of Congress subject headings:

> Library of Congress. (1910-). *Library of Congress subject headings* (4 vols.). Washington, DC: Author.

Figure 2-1 shows a Library of Congress heading for one topic. The *precise subject heading* in this example is "Communication in Management." The information listed directly below it (in this example, May Subd Geog and HD30.3) is of interest primarily to librarians who catalog library materials. Several abbreviations are used to refer library users to related headings and synonymous terms. UF, which stands for "use for," tells the researcher that the terms listed after it are synonymous with the precise subject heading but are not Library of Congress subject headings. Thus, they will not be used in library catalogs, although they might appear in periodical indexes or abstracts. Next, related headings are listed. These are either broader terms (BT) or narrower terms (NT). These terms are Library of Congress subject headings and are used in library catalogs. By searching under

---

Communication in management
  (May Subd Geog)
    [HD30.3]
    Here are entered works on the role of communica-
    tion in effective management. Works on the various
    forms of oral and written messages used by a business
    in the conduct of its affairs are entered under Busi-
    ness communication.

    UF   Communication Industry
    BT   Management
    NT   Automatic data collection systems
            Management—Comunication systems

Figure 2-1 Library of Congress Subject Heading

the subject heading "Communication in Management" in the library's catalog, you would find a **record** like the one shown in Figure 2-2.

All subject headings under which a particular book can be searched are listed in the subject **field** at the bottom of the catalog record. It may be appropriate to search one or more of them for related sources. Consider adding them to your subject-headings list.

Note the fields included on the record: author, title, location, call number, publisher, and publication date. Most if not all of these fields will be **access points** for searching the catalog. In other words, you will be able to search by author, title, subject, and so forth. And you may be able to limit your search to a particular library location, publication year, or format. The record also notes that this book contains an index and bibliographic references. As we stress later, examining books (and other publications) that have bibliographies in order to obtain references to other useful sources is one of the most important components of an effective search strategy.

Test and Adjust the Topic

Once you have decided on a specific preliminary research question and have identified key concepts and preliminary search terms, the next step is to do some testing. You might simply select an appropriate periodical index described in Chapter 6 and try a preliminary search using the search terms you've already developed. You are trying to get an idea of the available literature related to that preliminary question. In other words, what is the status of published research and information about your topic? If the subject area is still too broad, you'll find yourself doing extraneous work and feeling uncertain about what to include. If you find it difficult to choose pertinent sources, reexamine your research question and try to limit it further. In the preceding example, for instance, you may decide to exclude government and other nonprofit organizations from

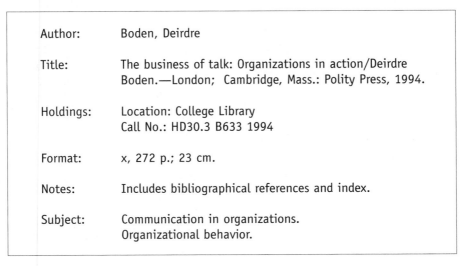

Author:	Boden, Deirdre
Title:	The business of talk: Organizations in action/Deirdre Boden.—London; Cambridge, Mass.: Polity Press, 1994.
Holdings:	Location: College Library Call No.: HD30.3 B633 1994
Format:	x, 272 p.; 23 cm.
Notes:	Includes bibliographical references and index.
Subject:	Communication in organizations. Organizational behavior.

Figure 2-2 Library of Congress Subject-Heading Record

consideration and to focus on commercial organizations. Naturally, you don't want to go to the other extreme and make the research question too narrow, or you will have very little information to examine.

How will you know whether your question is sufficiently narrow in focus? Your examination of the literature should tell you. If the topic area is too broad, your treatment of it may be too superficial, and there may be too many sources with which to deal. But if the topic is too narrow, the answer to the question may be obvious or insignificant.

Adjusting a question to a manageable size also depends on the scope of the assignment or your personal goal for the project. If you are working on a literature review or on a thesis or dissertation proposal, the amount of literature you will consult will be greater than if you are completing a 10-page research report.

This notion of adjusting a research question as the **literature search** progresses is difficult for a beginning researcher. Discussions with instructors, advisers, and librarians can prove helpful in this process.

THE SEARCH

■ PREPARING FOR THE LITERATURE SEARCH

Determine Types of Sources Needed

At this point it will help you to clarify your next steps if you take some time to decide just what types of sources you need to support your topic. That is, what types of sources do you want to cite in the bibliography of your paper or other project? Naturally, the sources needed will depend on the type of project you are undertaking. For example, if you are doing a paper for your Communication Research Methods class, you know that you'll need to cite books and journal articles written by scholars. It may also be appropriate to cite certain types of reference works (such as subject encyclopedias, handbooks, or annual reviews).

In terms of currency, you will need to include up-to-date studies, but older works may still be pertinent, as well. And you may decide that you need to cite appropriate statistical data. If you're preparing a 5-minute speech on a current topic, on the other hand, you may be able to limit yourself to newspapers, statistical data, government documents, or magazines published within the last 2 years.

Select Appropriate Databases and Other Access Tools

Once you have clarified the type of publications and other sources you need to support your topic, deciding the types of access tools needed will be relatively straightforward. As you work your way through Chapters 5 and 6, you'll learn about the scope and purpose of many electronic periodical indexes and abstracts and other access tools (including print ones). For example, if you need to identify newspaper articles, you'll use one of the newspaper indexes we describe. To locate scholarly articles in psychology, you will learn in Chapter 6 that *PsycINFO* would be the most appropriate database. To find books, you would use your library's catalog and regional/national union catalogs. But you can also identify books through book-length bibliographies and through bibliographies appended to articles or other books, annual reviews, and yearbooks. Additionally, you'll learn that some periodical indexes and abstracts also index books, book chapters, and book reviews.

One handy way of planning a search is to list types of sources you plan to use and the access tools you plan to search, updating these as the search progresses. We've found it useful to complete a search strategy sheet (Figure 2-3 on page 28). Here you can identify the main reference sources and access tools you think will be useful for your topic. As you read through Chapters 5 and 6, you'll notice sources that are very much related to your topic and others that are not related. List the related ones on the search strategy sheet and use the sheet when you visit the library. It will also help you keep track of sources you have consulted and those that remain.

Students may fall into the trap of relying too heavily on the access tool with which they are most comfortable, perhaps the library catalog, full-text periodical databases, or the World Wide Web. Each of these tools has an important place but should be used appropriately.

The Library Catalog The library catalog is the most obvious and well-known part of a library and may be the first access tool to which students turn. There are problems, however, with relying on the library catalog. Most catalogs provide detailed subject access only to books, and only to those books owned by the library. Books provide only one type of information, and the information is often dated because the lag between the time a work is written and the time it is published is often considerable. When writing a research paper, you should support material from sources with more recent information, usually that found in journal articles.

Furthermore, libraries have to be selective about what books they purchase. No college library can own every book that has been published, so library catalogs do not truly represent all the materials available to a researcher. By limiting yourself to the holdings of one particular library, you will miss some important sources and perhaps use sources that are not entirely relevant to the topic. Finally, the catalog does not help you judge the relative authority or relevance of books on your topic. For this reason, a **selective topical bibliography**, such as those found at the end of articles in encyclopedias, handbooks, and textbook chapters, is often a more efficient starting place for research projects.

Full-Text Databases We usually find full-text periodical databases easy to use, and the convenience of simply pushing a button to print an article or send it to an e-mail address is hard to resist. These can be wonderful tools, providing quick access to periodicals to which the library doesn't subscribe. Unfortunately, we may be tempted to ignore the existence of better, more pertinent articles that would take a bit of effort to retrieve and copy. Relying on these tools can also cause students to forget about books as good sources of background and analysis.

The World Wide Web The World Wide Web poses similar problems. Typing a **query** into a search engine is easy; getting results of some kind is almost

Name:
Research question: What do researchers know about . . . ?
Key Concepts:
Relevant subject headings and synonymous terms:

Sources needed:
Reference books: __encyclopedias __handbooks __yearbooks
　　 __dictionaries __annual reviews
Books: __textbooks __by scholars __journalists __lay experts
　　 __series __other:
Articles: __journal __professional/trade __newspaper
　　 __newsmagazine __opinion/commentary __book review
　　 __literature review
Factual information: __statistical data __biographical data
　　 __case/statutory laws __administrative regulations
　　 __government reports __other factual information:
　　 __WWW pages:

　　 Other:

Time period: __current month/year __5 years __10 years
　　 __can include older items

Access tools to check:
Library catalogs:
　　　　 My library:
　　　　 Regional/national:
Guides to the literature:
Annual reviews:
Bibiographies:
Electronic periodical indexes/abstracts:
　　　　 Newspaper:
　　　　 Interdisciplinary:
　　　　 General purpose:
　　　　 Communication:
　　　　 Related disciplines:
　　　　 Citation:
　　　　 Book review:
　　　　 Government publications:
　　　　 Full-text:
Print indexes/abstracts:
Finding aids for statistics:
Directories:
WWW subject directories:
WWW search engines:

Figure 2-3 Search Strategy Sheet

guaranteed, and most pages can easily be printed. Unfortunately, it has become a truism that almost anyone can and does put almost anything on the Web. So material found here must be carefully evaluated. (You'll read more about this important issue later in this chapter and in Chapter 3.) In addition, you'll be much more successful searching for *published* materials, such as journals, using the periodical indexes and abstracts licensed by libraries. However, students should plan to use the Web for most projects. It is an especially appropriate source for certain types of information: current or recent news, government publications, and business information, for example. The number of publications and valuable text, audio, and image archives being made available is growing rapidly.

■ DECIDING WHAT TYPE OF SEARCH TO DO

Consider your strategy in broad terms first. With some assignments, a general-to-specific search strategy is most beneficial. When little is known about the topic or when the assignment involves a comprehensive overview of the literature, it is best to begin with general sources such as encyclopedias, annual reviews, and handbooks (see Part 2). Next, move to bibliographies, guides, and periodical indexes and abstracts. Then, complete the literature search by examining the original journal articles, books, or media. With this search strategy, we limit the topic as we continue through the search, rather like the strategy used in searching **computerized databases** (see Chapter 4).

Key words are combined to enlarge the search (for example, adding "radio" to "television" to find out more about the broadcast media). Key words are separated to limit the number of sources we will find (for example, removing "radio" from the descriptors examined).

In other situations, we may find it advantageous to use a specific-to-general search strategy. For example, if we have found a key reference or article, we will want to enlarge the search beyond that one reference. Again, indexes, abstracts, and bibliographies provide additional information. Citation indexes are particularly helpful in locating related studies. (These are all discussed in Chapter 6.)

Sooner or later you will need to confront the capabilities of the electronic databases available to you. Most databases offer a variety of access points. You may choose to search by subject heading, key word, author, or title, at a minimum. In some databases, subject searching is facilitated by an excellent on-line **thesaurus** (an organized list of subject headings, also known as **descriptors**), making it easy to identify and use appropriate subject headings. In this case, subject searching is generally the option of choice. Other databases may have such poorly designed subject-heading listings that they encourage searchers to start with key-word searches. A popular and effective strategy is to start with a key-word search, examine the subject field of the pertinent records retrieved, and select appropriate subject headings. Then redo the search as a subject search. Of course, you might need to do a key-word search if your topic is unusual or not used as a subject heading. At this point, subject searching on the Web is limited to a key-word search.

You may want to do an author search if you've identified a prominent author who writes on your topic. Maybe you need to do a title search because someone gave you a title to an article, but you don't know what journal it's in or when it was published. Often you will find a combination of search types to be most successful. When you first connect to a database, you will see what your options are.

Formulate Searches

In Chapter 4 you will learn how to put together the subject headings and terms on your subject-headings list to construct effective searches, most often using the **operators** AND, OR, and NOT. Because database **interfaces** differ from one another and change rapidly, concentrate on learning the concepts of database searching. Students who are familiar with these will have little difficulty adjusting systematically to the rapidly changing information environment, particularly if they learn to use the Help function available for each database.

Examine the Results and Modify the Search

Once you have a list of articles, take a good look at the items and decide if they will help you on your project. It would be surprising if you did a perfect search on your first attempt, but you can probably find a few items that are at least close to what you are looking for. Look carefully at the records that look promising. What you are looking for are additional access points: subject headings, key words, and key authors. Using this information, reformulate your search query to narrow or broaden it or just generally to improve its focus. Repeat this process until you are satisfied that you have retrieved all of the most appropriate records for your topic.

Evaluate Citations Retrieved, Selecting Items Worth Retrieving

Students are often too quick to hit the print button at this point. Don't print a bunch of citations before you have taken the time to do some preliminary evaluation. You can tell quite a bit about a source just from its record. First, is the item really on your topic? The fact that a key word you typed appears someplace in the record is no guarantee of this. Read the abstract carefully and examine the subject headings assigned. Do you need scholarly articles? You can make some determination about whether an article is scholarly in nature from the journal title as well as from the article title. (Scholarly articles tend to be long and explicit; they sometimes include a colon followed by a subtitle.) Other clues to look for include article length, publication date, and publisher. You'll find other things to look for in the "Evaluate the Sources" section below.

Now is the time to get your hands on the actual articles, book chapters, books, and other sources. In most cases you will need to check your library catalog to see if the library owns the book or subscribes to the journal, magazine, or newspaper in question. If it's a periodical article, be sure to look in the catalog for the title of the periodical (not the title of the article).

If the library does not have what you need, there are other options. First, check with a librarian to make sure that the periodical in question is not available electronically in full text. (Some full-text periodicals may not be listed in the library catalog.) Full-text articles present a variety of delivery options (e-mail, cut and paste, different file formats, and the like), which we will explore in Chapter 3. **Document delivery services**, which deliver articles—for a fee—via fax, are also a viable option. And, of course, you can usually order what you need from another library in your region using your library's interlibrary loan service.

Examine Bibliographies for Additional Leads

As you retrieve published works, be sure to examine the bibliographies or "reference lists." They can provide you with additional access points to search. Let's say the bibliography lists what appear to be some key books on your topic. Does your library own any of them? Does it own other books by the same author(s)? If you find entries in the catalog, what subject headings have been assigned to them? Do these subject headings fit your topic? Following up with a subject search on these headings will help you find more recent books on the topic.

THE RESULTS

■ EVALUATING AND SUMMARIZING INFORMATION

Scholarship is not of uniform quality. Some research studies and books are of greater substance than others. Not all authors engage in flawless research. The scholar who is conducting a literature review is expected to know and to evaluate the quality of the work in addition to summarizing the findings. To evaluate a scholarly journal article, you must understand the research process and its conventions. We will discuss these in Chapter 9. Rules guide research investigations, and breaking these rules can result in research of lower quality. By conducting a systematic review process, most scholarly journals prevent publication of articles that have major or serious flaws. Occasionally, though, dubious practices are not uncovered or are overlooked in the review process and result in published articles that cause one to question the validity of the findings. As beginning scholars in the communication discipline, you must learn about research conventions and rules and be able to evaluate research articles and books with a critical eye.

Evaluate the Sources

Just because a book has been published and acquired by a library or an article has been published in a scholarly journal doesn't mean it is a quality source. Many complex factors determine a book's or an article's worth or quality. Here are some suggested criteria for judging quality. Note that some of these are relevant for Internet sources as well, although we'll discuss Internet materials more specifically in the next chapter.

Examine the Book's Front Matter The preface and introduction should indicate why the work was written. Was the purpose to inform, interpret, explain, or share new discoveries? Also, determine the intended level of audience (high school students, college seniors, other researchers). Books such as textbooks that are intended as **secondary sources**—ones that summarize previously reported research or contain opinion essays—may help you understand the field better but may not be works you would want to cite in a literature review. Literature reviews should contain findings from **primary sources** (scholarly books and journal articles). Sometimes, authors of journal articles intend to summarize published literature in an area or to comment on that literature. Such articles mostly serve the purpose of a secondary source, yet they may contain new conclusions or a research agenda that you'd want to cite. Journal articles that are primary sources seek to add new knowledge or insights.

However, all primary research is not of even quality. Sometimes the author's purpose is to test or to develop a new theory or research procedure. If such research is published in a top-tier national or international journal in the discipline (see Chapter 7), it is likely to be highly regarded, even if the theory is controversial. At other times, an author's purpose may be (a) to replicate previous studies looking for similar or contrasting results, (b) to revise or to adapt a scale or other research measure, or (c) to test a small aspect of an existing theory. These studies are important and well regarded but will typically fall below the level of regard for research that breaks new ground about theory and measurement. The purpose of the article or book, then, can tell you the scope of the study and its potential value.

Critique the Book or Article's Methodology and Data The methodology should be clearly detailed. The **data** should be accurate. The work that went into producing the study should be apparent. Also, determine how recent the research is. Have environmental or social conditions changed since the data were collected in a way that might cause you to question the results? Sometimes you may not be expert enough to critique a work's validity and reliability. If not, consult reviews for others' opinions about books. Book reviews, too, are of uneven quality, but there may be agreement among several reviews about the book you're evaluating. Another indicator of quality is if the book or article has received an award from a national association. Directories or association websites may contain this information.

Explore the Author's Background and Qualifications Try to check the author's publication track record. What else has the author written in the area? Who else has cited his or her writings in their own work? Authors should be experts in the area, and their qualifications should tell you if they are. If their qualifications are not printed in the book, look them up in relevant directories to see if they belong to national professional organizations and what their work affiliation is. If authors are in communication, you can examine their research records in *ComIndex* or in the *Index to Journals in Communication Studies* (see Chapters 3 and 6). You can search a convention program on-line to identify their current research interest. Or you can look in *Social Sciences Citation Index* or *Arts and Humanities Citation Index* to see who else has cited their research (see Chapter 6).

Investigate the Reputation of the Publisher National and international journals with high rejection rates tend to publish consistently high-quality articles. Readers can generally trust editorial boards and editors to scrutinize the articles prior to publication. Regional journals are also respected, although often below the level of the national or international journal. State and local journals, and those with lower rates of rejection, often have somewhat lower standards and publish articles that may have some minor flaws or are of interest to a specific population. Book-publishing companies also have reputations. Some have editors and editorial boards in charge of reviewing texts or scholarly books for possible publication; these tend to have higher standards. At the other end of the continuum are publishers who are paid by authors to publish their work. These "vanity" presses might publish books of lower quality.

Examine the Back Matter A book that contains an **index** can be used as a reference source. If it lacks an index, the use of the book may be limited. The footnotes and bibliography indicate the breadth and depth of research that went into the book and the author's authoritative knowledge of the field. It is possible, though, that innovators may not have many works to cite or may be restricted to citing their own work because of the recency of the topic. If few original books and articles are cited or if major works in the field are not mentioned, there may be reason to question the value of the book as a reputable source. Also, expect some works cited in the bibliography to be 1 or 2 years older than the copyright date of the book itself. For instance, this edition of this book was completed in mid-1999, but because of the publication process the copyright date is 2000. We have included, however, sources that were available through late 1998 (and even 1999 and 2000 in some cases). Had we not included recent sources, you could suspect that we hadn't done our homework. Visit this book's home page for updated sources!

Read Materials Thoroughly

Some articles and books are easier to read than others. Historical, critical, and qualitative research reports (see Chapter 9 for explanations of these research forms) typically contain verbal descriptions of findings; the results are presented in everyday language or common communication jargon. Empirical research, which relies on observation or experimentation, often contains statistical data and tables, which students often skip over when reading. If you are not familiar with statistics, this may be the only way you can read the article. Here are some pointers on how to read a research article, chapter, or book:

- *Look at the title.* Often the main features can be identified from the title. Also, take a look at who the authors are and their backgrounds.
- *Read the abstract* (if provided). The abstract gives you a short synopsis of the work and prepares you to read it.
- *Read the introductory material and review of research.* This tells you why the study was done and what prior research led up to this present research

project. This is a good time to create new bibliography cards for important sources that you may have missed.

■ *Read the method section*. Here you will find how the study was actually performed, who was involved in it, and what instruments or techniques were used to perform it. This section will reveal the soundness of the empirical choices made by the authors.

■ *Read the results*. This is the meat of the research article. Most of your notes about this research report will come from this section because it contains the actual findings. Look at the tables and figures to see what was found. If the results are full of numbers and statistics that you can't understand, read past the numbers to the conclusions drawn by the authors. Don't give up!

■ *Read the discussion*. The authors typically summarize the results in less technical terms here. Authors sometimes inflate the actual importance of the findings, but some journal editors temper these exaggerations. Try to identify here the most important findings in the study, the meaning or implications of these findings, and the limitations of the study. Authors also offer good ideas for future research projects.

■ *Scan the bibliography* for sources that may be useful but you have not yet encountered.

Careful reading of research takes energy and concentration. The reading is much more difficult than textbook prose, and you should be prepared for it. Keep a communication, statistics, or general dictionary handy so you can look up terms you don't understand (see Chapter 8).

Take Careful Notes

New scholars sometimes find it difficult to take notes on what they read, either because the material contains too much information or because they are unfamiliar with the techniques of abstracting. Abstracting helps you synthesize the information you read and distinguish the most important parts of the article, book, or chapter. In effect, abstracting helps you become more critical of what you read because it forces you to understand the research thoroughly. We explain some of the basic steps involved in abstracting in Chapter 11. For additional guidance, consult the following source:

Cremmins, E. T. (1996). *The art of abstracting* (2nd ed.). Arlington, VA: Information Resources Press.

When taking notes from books or research articles, be sure to summarize the materials in your own words, or you might fall prey to inadvertent **plagiarism**. If you summarize the material in your own words, you will be certain that what you will write later will be your own words, not those of the original author. If you find that certain passages are so well stated that you couldn't do justice to them yourself, copy the direct quote (using quotation marks) and the page number for future reference in a footnote or bibliographic citation. But as a rule of thumb, try to understand what the author is saying and then translate it into your own words.

Scholars who take careful notes during the literature search can proceed to the writing stage without having to reexamine sources already read. When typing the bibliography, you will find that having these citations on 3-inch by 5-inch index cards (or already entered into a bibliography management program) is helpful.

■ DOCUMENTING THE SEARCH PROCESS

As we have said, library or **documentary research** is much easier to conduct if it is done systematically. Disorganized researchers find that they waste much time searching for and consulting sources that were previously located but forgotten. You can simplify the organizing effort in any research project if you construct bibliography cards (or records, if you choose to use a computer for this purpose), prepare a subject-headings list, and keep a search record.

Keep Bibliography Cards or Electronic Records

A **bibliography card** or record holds complete information for each source examined. It lists a complete and accurate citation, as well as where the source is found. It should also include a capsulized summary of the pertinent contents of the source. Bibliography cards or electronic records serve three major purposes:

- They furnish a complete current record of sources for later use in compiling a bibliography or citing references.
- They eliminate the practice of repeating or retracing steps by allowing recently located sources to be checked against what was previously examined.
- They provide a record of needed sources that have yet to be found in the research process.

Cards are suggested here, instead of notebook paper, because they are handy, sturdy, and easy to organize and alphabetize. Figure 2-4 shows an example of a bibliography card.

Note-taking programs are now available for home and portable computers, and students with these resources will find them useful to prepare bibliography records. Those beginning extensive research projects may want to invest in **bibliography-management programs**, such as EndNote, Reference Manager, and ProCite. These timesaving tools, which can be set up to accept citations downloaded directly from a growing number of periodical indexes, offer the ultimate in convenience. Once installed, they work as an integral part of standard word processing programs. Stored citations can be formatted automatically to print in all standard bibliographic styles, including APA, MLA, and Chicago.

People have found a variety of note-taking styles useful for summarizing what has been read. You should use the system that works best for you. We suggest you use a citation format similar to the one shown in Figure 2-4. This is a modification of the style used by the American Psychological Association (APA), which is explained later in this book. This modified style for the bibliography card begins with full information on the author(s), the year (and month) of publication, and the title of the article. Then the publication name, volume number (both under-lined), and inclusive page numbers follow. This modification is necessary because, although the APA style does not require authors' first names or the journal issue (if each issue does not begin with page 1), some other bibliographic styles do. By including this information here you may save much time in the future should you use the information in a project requiring a different style or if you need to use a masculine or feminine pronoun to refer to his or her work.

The *Publication Manual of the American Psychological Association* gives the details of bibliography form and provides a quick reference guide for writing style, editorial style, typing and submitting manuscripts, and proofreading.

Rubin, Alan M. (Winter 1983). Television uses and gratifications: The interactions of viewing patterns and motivations. <u>Journal of Broadcasting</u>, <u>27</u>, 37–51.

TV uses and gratifications study. Qs: (1) What are the interactions among TV motives, behaviors, & attitudes? (2) What TV motive pattern can explain viewing attitudes & behaviors? Survey sample—464 adults, ages 18 to 89; secondary analysis. Findings: TV motives—pass time/habit, information/learning, entertainment, companionship, escape. Motives interrelated.

[Card 1 of 2]

Rubin ('83). <u>JOB</u>. #2

Canonical roots: (1) entertainment & pass time motives with TV affinity, viewing levels, & realism: (2) information & nonescape with news, talk, game shows & viewing levels. Predictors: entertainment, pass time, companionship, & information motives predict viewing levels and affinity; information & entertainment motives predict realism. Discussion: TV dependence emphasizes the medium, not content; "...heavy users of television are not necessarily motivated by a desire to escape from reality." (p. 49)

[Card 2 of 2]

Figure 2-4 Bibliography Card

Communication researchers often use it when they prepare final versions of papers. You should, however, use one style during the entire research process. It is unnecessarily time-consuming to convert references written on bibliography cards or records in one format to another format for the paper. Learning a style early can save time in the future.

We use the APA format throughout this book because it is used in most major communication journals. Use our citations as guides for your own bibliographic citations. However, be aware that typed references will have a slightly different format from those printed in this book. When typing, you indent the first line, like a normal paragraph. When it is typeset, it takes the form of an indented overhang, where the first line is flush with the left margin and all other lines are indented three spaces.

Students often find photocopying or printing out full-text articles preferable to sitting in the library and taking notes. Keep in mind, though, that this practice can be very costly and more time-consuming than it may first appear. Often you scan a newly discovered article first to see if it is relevant to your topic and make some initial judgment about the article's worth. This means you are preparing yourself to take notes on a bibliography card, but stop short. Later, you'll have to reread the article and repeat this preparatory process. Also, by stopping at this point and filing the photocopy of the article for later use, you are not making full use of the article's reference list for other places to search. Finally, by photocopying everything, you tend to put off reading the articles to just before writing, so writing is delayed and hurried. By reading articles and taking notes immediately, you're ready to organize and write once all sources have been found. So, you may be tempted to photocopy or print everything, but doing so can add extra time and costs to the search and writing processes.

Maintain a List of Subject Headings

You should develop a subject-headings list and keep it current throughout the research process. Include in this list all possible headings and synonyms related to the topic that you may use when consulting the library catalog, bibliographies, and periodical indexes and abstracts. For example, information on the topic "Audiovisual Aids" may be found under many headings (Figure 2-5). The more topical categories you include in the subject-headings list, the more likely it is that you will find most of the possible references to that topic.

Use Search Records

When undertaking lengthy research projects, it is wise to note all sources you've consulted to prevent redoing research work or missing valuable sources. Search records indicate which access tools or sources (indexes, abstracts, bibliographies, and so forth) you have already examined and what portions of these sources you inspected. Index cards are most convenient for this purpose, although search records can also be entered in notebook computers. One card, which includes relevant subject headings and dates searched, should be used for each source. Figure 2-6 is an example of such a search record. In addition, a

```
┌─────────────────────────────────────────────────────────────────┐
│                       AUDIOVISUAL AIDS                            │
│                                                                   │
│        Film                            Television                 │
│        Multimedia                      Visual aids                │
│        Recordings                      Graphics                   │
│        Radio                           Photography                │
│        Educational media               Instructional media        │
│                                                                   │
└─────────────────────────────────────────────────────────────────┘
```

Figure 2-5 Subject-Heading List

general search-record card, which lists all sources that have been examined, should be prepared for quick reference (Figure 2-7).

■ TIPS ON SEARCHING THE LITERATURE

Keep in mind three main points when searching the literature. First, don't let yourself get bogged down. Read completely only those articles that are relevant and note other interesting articles for future reading. It is sometimes tempting to browse through a multitude of new sources, but all you will be doing is delaying the inevitable task of pursuing your research.

Second, don't entertain the illusion that you can exhaust all possible sources related to your topic. It is of course important to be as thorough as possible. It is also important to start your research early. Remember, some sources may not be in the library, and you will need to order them through an interlibrary loan. You will never find all possible references, so you must set a research stopping point and at that time start writing. You will learn to realize that you've exhausted all the pertinent, available sources when newly found bibliographies list sources you've already seen and have nothing new for you to examine.

Third, remember to practice good note-taking skills when you are conducting your library research. To take notes on the content of the material, you will need to abstract, or condense, what you read. Windows Notepad offers the opportunity to take notes while reading on-line material. You will also need to have a complete and accurate bibliographic citation (one that is legibly written). We summarize proper format for bibliographic citations in Appendix A, "APA Style Basics." You may want to refer to that section as you proceed through this book.

■ WRITING

We emphasize throughout this book how essential it is that you thoroughly examine the literature before you start the writing process. That means all library work should be done before you begin to write. As you pursue your search, find a topic that is interesting and related to the project. Through exploratory reading of general sources, narrow the topic to a manageable size.

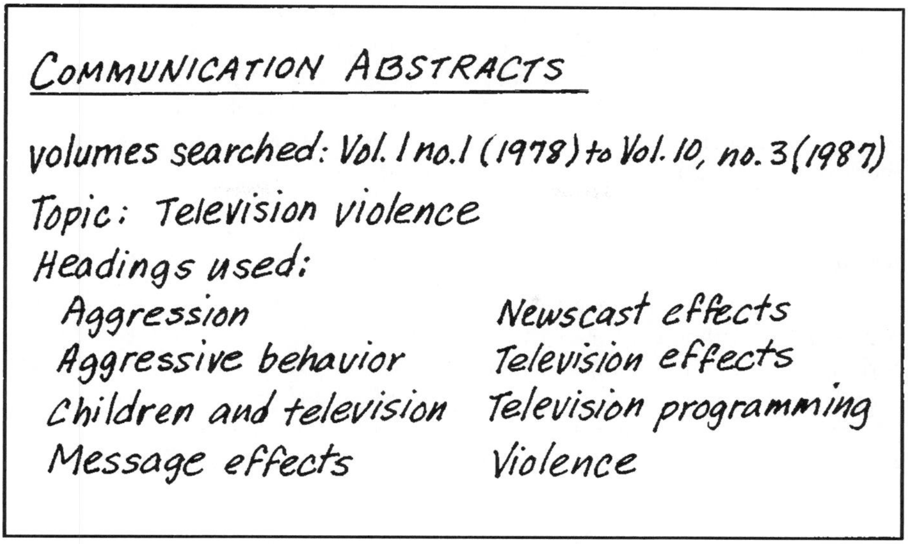

COMMUNICATION ABSTRACTS

volumes searched: Vol. 1 no.1 (1978) to Vol. 10, no. 3 (1987)
Topic: Television violence
Headings used:
  Aggression   Newscast effects
  Aggressive behavior   Television effects
  Children and television   Television programming
  Message effects   Violence

Figure 2-6 Search Record Card

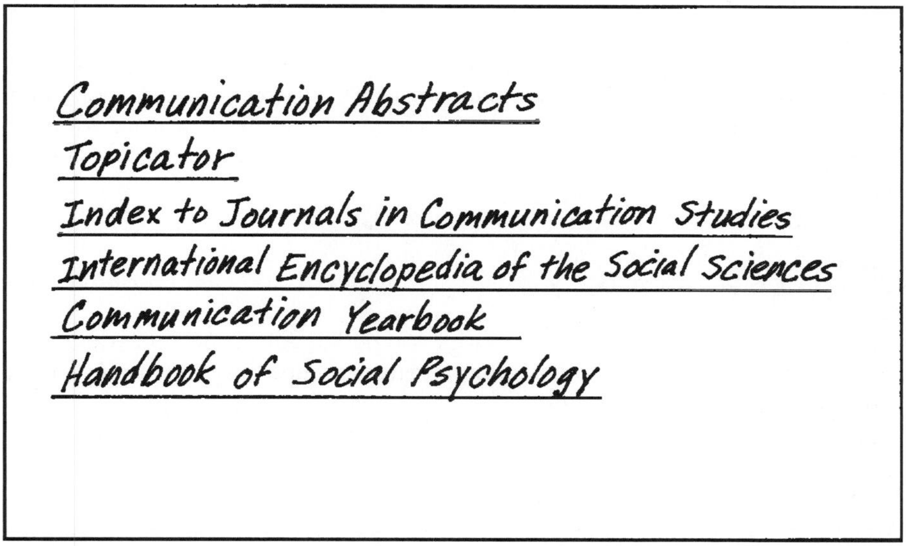

Communication Abstracts
Topicator
Index to Journals in Communication Studies
International Encyclopedia of the Social Sciences
Communication Yearbook
Handbook of Social Psychology

Figure 2-7 General Search Record Card

One or more research questions should emerge at this point. These questions guide the rest of the literature search, your evaluation of what you read, and the writing process.

After exhausting all relevant sources, you will need to consider how best to organize the materials you've found into a meaningful review of the literature.

Even if your research goal is something other than a research paper (for example, a speech, group discussion, broadcast script, debate case, feature article, seminar, critique, review, or exam), the process is similar. You will need to make sense of the information, organize it into a coherent pattern, and select the best method of presentation. To do this, you must keep your specific research question and the goal of your research endeavor clearly in mind.

Develop an Outline

Complete an initial outline at this time to help decide which specific sources to examine. An outline organizes the subtopics or subthemes found in the literature and guides the arguments you will make in your review. Once you have found all the materials you need, expand and develop your original outline. Always check your outline along the way to ensure it conforms to the thesis statement or research questions. Standard word processing programs often include a handy outlining function that can be worth trying.

Edit

Write from the outline. Then set the written review aside for a day or two before editing and revising it into final form. We suggest you set this final form aside for another day or two, then edit again. Once the final copy is typed, proofread it carefully for typographic errors. Don't rely on your word processing program to find all your spelling and grammatical errors. Details on writing, proofreading the parts of the literature review, and summarizing strategies are found in Chapters 10 and 11. Be sure to take a look at these chapters before you begin writing.

SUMMARY

The research process relies on how well you define your topic and your awareness of the many possible sources of information. Research into topic areas is necessary for most assignments communication students encounter and for many tasks communication professionals face in their daily routines. Being able to identify a research topic and to clarify specific questions for investigation are essential skills for all communication researchers. These skills simplify the research process by providing an efficient, organized direction.

Selecting a topic and defining the research problem are often the most difficult parts of searching the literature. Once a topic is chosen and a specific research question is formulated, a researcher concentrates on finding and reviewing the available literature related to that preliminary question. Often the topic must be adjusted (narrowed or broadened) during the search process. Lists of citations retrieved should be carefully reviewed to make sure that the most appropriate terms are being used. Particular care should be placed on effectively utilizing the subject headings or descriptors available for each database searched.

Researchers must be familiar with the library and understand the workings of the library catalog, interlibrary loan, and systematic procedures for library searching. These procedures include bibliography cards or records, subject-headings lists, and search-record cards. Tips for conducting a literature search include reading only relevant materials, setting a stopping point for the search, and practicing good note-taking strategies such as abstracting. Researchers also must understand and evaluate what they read before they begin writing.

In general, researchers must be organized and approach library or documentary research tasks systematically. Not only does having a search plan save time and energy, but it also results in a better, more coherent product.

REFERENCES

Beasley, D. R. (1988). *How to use a research library*. New York: Oxford University Press.

Bolner, M. S., & Poirier, G. A. (1997). *The research process: Books and beyond* (Rev. ed.). Dubuque, IA: Kendall/Hunt.

Cooper, H., & Hedges, L. V. (Eds.) (1994). *The handbook of research synthesis.* New York: Russell Sage Foundation.

Cremmins, E. T. (1996). *The art of abstracting* (2nd ed.). Arlington, VA: Information Resources Press.

Katz, W. A. (1997). *Introduction to reference works* (7th ed., 2 vols.). Hightstown, NJ: McGraw-Hill.

List, C. (1998). *An introduction to information research*. Dubuque, IA: Kendall/Hunt.

Roth, A. J. (1999). *The research paper: Process, form, and content* (8th ed.). Belmont, CA: Wadsworth.

U.S. Library of Congress. (1910–). *Library of Congress subject headings* (4 vols.). Washington, DC: Author.

EXAMPLES

CHRIS'S topic, "Ethics," is too broad for a 5-minute persuasive speech. By talking about the topic, thinking about why the topic was interesting in the first place, and looking at some general references, the topic is starting to become more narrow. Chris finds subtopics dealing with ghostwriting, and because this is a speech class, this direction seems promising. One first step is to check the Library of Congress subject-headings list for related topics. When logging onto the Library of Congress site, Chris chooses "Online Catalogs" and then "Browse Search" to find the subject headings. By typing "ghostwriting" as a subject, various subject headings appear.

Here are the results:

Ghostwriter (television program)
Ghostwriters
  NARROW: Women Ghostwriters
  BROAD: Authors
Ghostwriting
  NARROW: Speechwriting
  BROAD: Authorship—Collaboration

FELECIA'S news article assignment on the new campus voice-mail system is sufficiently narrow. A chance exists, though, that few sources will be found, even with the best search, because of the multiple terms that have been used in the literature. A good first step is to start identifying all those possible key words: "voice mail," "v-mail," "answering machines," and "telephone information systems." She must also consider which type of reference materials would be most worthwhile. The following seem relevant: professional/trade journals, newspapers, newsmagazines, World Wide Web, periodical indexes, statistics, and interviews with relevant people. Only sources within the last 5 years are relevant.

MARIA'S communication theory paper on attribution is proving to be a nightmare. She decided to test the topic and selected a periodical index, *PsycINFO*, to see how many articles were published during the 1990s. Searching for this term in the subject heading (descriptor) field results in 5811 hits. A similar search for "interpersonal interaction" resulted in 5916 hits. Combining these terms and looking at only those focusing on humans and written in English from 1990 to 1999 resulted in 50 hits. Because this is a communication class, adding this term (in a title or abstract) reduced the number to 6 hits. If these were supplemented with books, chapters, or annual review materials, this number might be reasonable. Broadening the above search to 1980–1999 adds 4 additional sources. So the key words to use seem to be "attribution," "interpersonal interaction," and "communication."

ORLANDO'S literature review on parasocial interaction seems to be one that can be handled in 20–25 pages, or so the databases suggest. To identify other access tools that will result in relevant literature, Orlando will use a general-to-specific strategy by reading through Chapters 5–8 of this text and picking out relevant sources. But a specific-to-general strategy is also possible because everyone seems to cite Horton and Wohl's article (see the citation at the end of Chapter 1) as the origination of the term. By using the *Social Sciences Citation Index* (described in Chapter 6), Orlando will have double-checked that all literature has been found.

KAT, CALVIN, ROCKY, and MICHELLE are tossing around ideas about their training module on conflict resolution. After identifying several key words, they decide to divide the labor and each search different sources. They promise to keep full search records to share with one another so that all can be assured that the sources were searched as expected. Kat takes the on-line research databases and library catalogs. Calvin plans a full Internet search, including relevant search engines and communication metasites. Rocky uses directories to find organizational consultants to interview. And Michelle scans professional and trade journals for references to training programs.

EXERCISES

1. Choose an area of communication that you identified as being of interest to you in Chapter 1 and describe a general research topic you would like to pursue further.
2. Formulate three specific research questions about this general research topic.
3. Complete a search strategy sheet for one of these three research questions. Examine each of these general sources and complete bibliography cards for each source you find. The bibliography should include a sufficient number of sources to support a 20-page research report. The bibliography should be listed on 3-inch by 5-inch index cards and entries should follow the style used in this chapter.
4. As your bibliography progresses, complete the following additional records:

   a. Subject-headings/key-word list. Keep a record on a 3-inch by 5-inch index card of all headings and key words that pertain to your topic.

   b. Search-record cards. Keep both a general card, listing by title all sources used, plus an individual card for each finding tool (for example, index or abstract), using the format in this chapter.

5. Answer the following questions as a way of tracking your literature search progress.

   Topic

   - Have you selected a topic? What is it?
   - Does it need to be narrowed? What is the narrowed topic?
   - How can you adjust the topic to one that is manageable? What is the topic now?

   Search

   - Have you selected a search strategy appropriate for this topic? Which one is best? Have you completed your search strategy sheet?
   - Have you toured the library? Do you know how to use the library catalog? Do you know how to order material through interlibrary loan?

Do you know where reference materials, government documents, and statistical materials are located?

- Have you set up a system for searching the literature? Do you have a 3-inch by 5-inch bibliography card system developed? Do you have a subject-headings list? Do you have search-record cards for each reference source? Do you have a general search-record card for all sources?

Results

- Have you evaluated the sources you plan to use? Are they reliable?
- Have you read the materials carefully?
- Are your notes in your own words? Did you use quotation marks around materials you had to quote, and did you record the page numbers for these quotes?

Writing

- Are you ready to write? What is the thesis of the work? Have you constructed an outline? What are its main points or divisions?
- After you wrote, did you revise the paper two or three times to make sure it made sense? Did you edit the manuscript and proofread carefully for typographic errors and misspellings?

6. Narrow a topic by completing the following steps:
   a. Pick a broad topic in which you are interested.

   Topic: ⎯⎯⎯⎯⎯⎯⎯⎯⎯⎯⎯⎯⎯⎯⎯⎯⎯⎯⎯⎯⎯⎯⎯⎯⎯⎯

   b. What is a research question you might pose about this topic?

   Question: ⎯⎯⎯⎯⎯⎯⎯⎯⎯⎯⎯⎯⎯⎯⎯⎯⎯⎯⎯⎯⎯⎯⎯⎯⎯⎯

   ⎯⎯⎯⎯⎯⎯⎯⎯⎯⎯⎯⎯⎯⎯⎯⎯⎯⎯⎯⎯⎯⎯⎯⎯⎯⎯ ?

   c. Now identify two or three key concepts in your question.

   ⎯⎯⎯⎯⎯⎯⎯⎯⎯⎯⎯⎯⎯⎯⎯⎯⎯⎯⎯⎯⎯⎯⎯⎯⎯⎯

   ⎯⎯⎯⎯⎯⎯⎯⎯⎯⎯⎯⎯⎯⎯⎯⎯⎯⎯⎯⎯⎯⎯⎯⎯⎯⎯

   ⎯⎯⎯⎯⎯⎯⎯⎯⎯⎯⎯⎯⎯⎯⎯⎯⎯⎯⎯⎯⎯⎯⎯⎯⎯⎯

   d. Provide synonyms for each of the concepts you identified.

   ⎯⎯⎯⎯⎯⎯⎯⎯⎯⎯⎯⎯⎯⎯⎯⎯⎯⎯⎯⎯⎯⎯⎯⎯⎯⎯

   ⎯⎯⎯⎯⎯⎯⎯⎯⎯⎯⎯⎯⎯⎯⎯⎯⎯⎯⎯⎯⎯⎯⎯⎯⎯⎯

For help in finding synonyms, (1) identify and consult a reference source that provides an overview of the discipline or general subject and (2) test your concepts and terms in the library catalog or a periodical index.

Reference source I used: ─────────────────────────────

I tested it in: ──────────────────────────────────────

e. Now reformulate your question, using the information you have gained. Your reformulated question should use some of the new terms you identified and should be narrower and more focused.

New question: ────────────────────────────────────

─── ?

chapter 3

Using the Internet for Communication Research

Increasingly, the resources used for communication research are stored on computers. In fact, most of the access tools (such as catalogs and periodical indexes), large numbers of periodicals, and selected reference sources described in this book have made the transition from print to electronic format and are residing in a computer someplace. But they would lead an isolated existence without the Internet. The **Internet** can be thought of as the communication utility—really a network of networks—connecting all those computers that store all those resources.

The **World Wide Web** (WWW) is the interface that allows us practically seamless access to it all. You'll carry out much of your research seated at a computer using a web **browser** to search periodical indexes, consult reference works, and read periodical articles. You'll use the same web browser to search library catalogs and various types of **websites**. And, carrying this integration one step further, your library's catalog may well have expanded its role to serve as the interface that integrates access to many, or even all, of these different types of resources. These changes reflect a fundamental shift in the role of the library. Instead of simply being repositories of materials that they own, libraries have become gateways to information resources available electronically.

Some dangers lurk in this convenience and integration. One is that students may fail to differentiate between the types of resources they are using and to value them appropriately. An article in a scholarly journal may physically resemble a document put up on a homegrown website, and you may use similar search procedures to find both. At a basic level they're both "on the Web." In this situation your ability to evaluate the quality of resources and the necessity of doing so becomes more critical than ever. Also dangerous is the tendency to get ahead of reality, concluding that "everything is on the Internet." Wishful thinking doesn't make it so, and acting under this false assumption will lead you to miss whole categories of information.

46

All these developments started in a remarkably undirected way. About 30 years ago, researchers wanting to share data thought it would be useful to connect their networks. The government financed the project, and from this the Internet grew. All sorts of resources on computers came to be shared over the Internet, but the systems and commands necessary to do so were not particularly friendly or easy to use. The WWW more or less solved the problem. Developed by Tim Berners-Lee at CERN, the European Laboratory for Particle Physics, the WWW provided a way to access many different types of resources through one interface. It is that collection of resources we mean when we refer to the WWW.

One web innovation was to use hypertext to link resources. **Hypertext** is simply regular text that includes connections, or **hyperlinks**, within the text to other documents. Thus, hypertext documents allow you to move from one document to another by selecting links. Links can be an icon rather than text, and they can also connect to other types of media, including images, video, and sound recordings. Because of the promise of this new technology for sharing information, many text resources were converted into **html** (hypertext markup language) format to be readily accessible through the WWW. Web pages are written in this relatively simple format, though they may include links to documents formatted in more sophisticated ways to resemble, for example, the actual printed pages of a journal article.

It is important to understand that no one person or organization is in charge of the Internet. In other words, no one started this enterprise by first devising an overall organizational structure, and no one exerts overall control of what is made available in terms of content, quality, or format. It has become a truism that anyone can publish a **web page**, and anyone does. The result is a collection that includes both valuable gems and worthless fakes, and everything in between. Quality control is established only at the level of a particular resource or site. Therefore, we stress again that one of your jobs as a researcher will be to evaluate web resources to determine which have established such control and can claim credibility. We include in this chapter a section on the special challenges posed by evaluating web resources.

RESEARCH AND THE WORLD WIDE WEB

As already mentioned, many traditional types of scholarly, research-oriented resources are accessible through the WWW: library catalogs, periodical indexes and abstracts, scholarly journals, government publications, bibliographies, dictionaries, encyclopedias, almanacs, directories, statistical compendia, and other types of reference works, for example. Even books, particularly important works in the public domain, are increasingly available. Many, though by no means all, of these types of resources are available to researchers only through licensing arrangements made by their libraries.

In addition, there is that vast and somewhat hard-to-define category: other types of websites. Many are of potential interest to communication researchers. Important categories include:

- Collections of primary sources (print, audio, video, and images). These include important electronic archives of political speeches, press releases, and historical documents. Transcripts and video archives of many news broadcasts are available, for example. We identify several of these in Chapter 8.
- Research so recent that it has not yet been formally published (or even evaluated for possible publication).
- News and current events.
- Biographic information about scholars and other communication professionals, maintained on personal or professional home pages.
- Statistical information from many sources. The U.S. Census Bureau, for example, now issues most census reports on the WWW rather than in print.
- Publications issued by nongovernment agencies, including everything from brochures to research reports.
- Educational sites. There seems to be a tutorial for everyone, no matter what the level or topic. Examples include tutorials on such topics as: how to do library research; how to write a research paper; how to write an annotation; how not to plagiarize; how to give an effective speech or presentation; how to cite sources in APA-, MLA-, or Chicago-style format; how to search the WWW; how to find statistical information; and how to use a particular database.
- Departments of communication at universities around the world. These websites include information about departmental programs and faculty, as well as links to other communication-related sites.
- Professional associations. Many associations try to make these useful to members by including listings of employment opportunities, research bibliographies, convention activities, and links to other important research-related sites in the field. See Chapter 1 for a listing of communication associations with web addresses.
- On-line communities. The WWW is of course not only a repository of information but also a communication medium. Communication researchers often find electronic discussion groups in their particular fields of interest to be useful.
- The WWW as a broadcast medium. You can, for example, view the nightly news on the websites of news organizations, either in real time or at your convenience.

GAINING ACCESS TO THE INTERNET

Students normally access the Internet through **client** workstations in the library or in computer labs. On most campuses you'll be able to find workstations with a browser installed that will allow you to access resources on the WWW. To use e-mail, it's necessary to obtain an e-mail account on a university computer. If you don't already have an account, ask at your computer center for information about getting one.

From home, you currently have two basic options. One is to access the Internet by dialing into your e-mail account from off-campus, using a microcomputer equipped with **communications software** and a **modem**. To access the WWW, you'll need to do so through a connection that is somewhat specific to your institution. Your computer center can provide directions. Connecting to the Internet through your university offers a significant advantage to researchers. When you attempt to connect to periodical indexes and other databases that your library has licensed, database vendors will automatically recognize you as an authorized user and permit you to access them. (They will actually recognize the university's **Internet protocol**, or IP, **address**.) You can also access the Internet via a local or national Internet service provider (ISP), such as AT&T, or through commercial on-line services such as *America Online*.

■ INTERNET ADDRESSES

When you get an e-mail account, your Internet address will look something like those of the authors of this book:

Rebecca Rubin:	rrubin@kent.edu
Alan Rubin:	arubin@kent.edu
Linda Piele:	pielel@uwp.edu

The symbol @ ("at") is used to separate the name of an individual (on the left) from his or her **domain** (to the right). In the first two cases above, the domain, **kent.edu**, refers to a mainframe computer at Kent State University. In the third, the domain is a computer at the University of Wisconsin–Parkside. You'll use addresses like these to send electronic mail to people.

Each website also has an address, as does each page (or file) on that site. Web addresses are called **uniform resource locators** (or URLs). Published references to Internet resources supply their URLs, and they must be included in APA citations. The URLs of the websites of the institutions above, for example, are:

<http://www.kent.edu>
<http://www.uwp.edu>

Breaking down this address into its component parts, we have:

http://	**hypertext transfer protocol**, which is the WWW protocol
www	host computer name
kent	second-level domain name
edu	top-level domain name

The following domain-name extensions (or top-level domains) are commonly used at the present time, though there are proposals to expand and change them. Extensions provide useful information about various Internet addresses. You are likely to encounter these extensions:

edu	educational sites in the United States
com	commercial sites (companies or corporations) in the United States
gov	government institutions
net	an administrative site for a network
org	nonprofit organizations that don't fit elsewhere

Below is a bit more complicated example, the URL for the WWW version of the Communication Studies Instructional Web Site at Kent State University:

<**http://www.library.kent.edu/commstudies/Genpublic/generalframe.htm**>

The additional components tell your browser the complete path to a particular file:

commstudies/	**directory name**
Genpublic/	**subdirectory name**
generalframe.htm	**file name**

Another piece of general information that you can glean from an Internet address is the country of origin. Each country has been assigned a two-letter code. For example, **.fr** refers to France, **.it** to Italy, **.ch** to Switzerland, **.us** to the United States, **.ca** to Canada, and **.de** to Germany. If there is no country designation, the location is the United States.

You may also see addresses, termed IP addresses, that are entirely numerical. These addresses, which consist of four numbers connected by periods, are assigned to each machine on the Internet. A typical IP address is 137.113.10.35. Actually, each Internet domain address has a corresponding IP address, which is how the address is actually transmitted over the Internet.

■ BROWSER BASICS

When you access the Web you do so through a browser. Popular examples include Netscape and Microsoft's Internet Explorer. A **browser** is a computer program that enables you to use your computer to view and capture WWW documents, taking advantage of hypertext links, images, sound, motion, and other features. To take full advantage of multimedia, a browser usually needs to have additional programs installed, called plug-ins or helper applications. These develop and change rapidly, so you'll need to refer to current information to find out about them. The websites maintained by your browser are often the best sources of information about these. They can be accessed through links provided in your browser's Help function.

One helper application used frequently for textual information is Adobe Acrobat. This desktop publishing program is employed to create many print publications, such as scholarly journals, government documents, and forms. Acrobat creates pdf (portable document format) files rather than html files (the basic WWW text format). When publications created using Acrobat are made available on the Internet, the publisher may choose to do so in the original pdf format. This format offers the advantage of making the on-line version of a document identical to the way it looks in print. Researchers often appreciate seeing original charts, graphs, photographs, and page numbering, for example. One disadvantage is that the Adobe Acrobat "reader" must be installed on the computer you are using to view pdf documents. However, the reader is available free of charge and is easily downloaded and installed, so this should not be a serious impediment. As you use full-text periodical databases, you may be given a choice of viewing a given document in either html or pdf format. Try both to see which will meet your particular needs. Additional formats are being developed to facilitate the publication of journals electronically, and you may encounter one of these as well.

Browsers regularly incorporate additional functions and features and have become very powerful tools. You may use a browser to handle your e-mail, to participate in Usenet newsgroups (discussed later in this chapter), to participate in a real-time meeting, or to compose text in html. To take full advantage of these capabilities, seek out training opportunities at your university.

To use a browser as an access tool for research, however, you need to perform only a few tasks. Learning how to do the following will enable you to carry out research effectively and efficiently. If you like to figure out things by yourself, the Help function on your browser may suffice. Or go through the list with a Net-savvy friend. You should be able to:

- Type in a URL to go directly to a website.
- Use the Back button to go to the previous page visited.
- Use the Stop button to stop a slow page from loading.
- Elect to load pages without graphics, if so desired, for speedier retrieval.
- Reload a page that was not completely retrieved the first time.
- Adjust the font size of a page. (Sometimes the default size may be either too small or too large for comfortable viewing or efficient printing.)
- Adjust the colors of a page. (They may be impossible or uncomfortable to view or print.)
- Use the Find in Page feature to locate a particular term or phrase in a web document. This is particularly useful when viewing full-text journal articles and other long documents.
- Print either entire documents or only specified pages.
- Use the Print Preview feature to help you see the paging for a long document, allowing you to determine which pages you want to print.
- Send a web page or a web-page address to your e-mail account.
- Use your Cut-and-Paste feature to save retyping URLs, article titles you wish to paste into a search box, and the like. You should also be able to cut and paste to a word processor.
- Use the Search History feature to go back to sites visited previously.
- Maintain personal lists of Favorites or Bookmarks (websites you may want to visit again).

■ TROUBLESHOOTING

As you use the World Wide Web, you are sure to encounter the frustrating problem of links that do not work. You may get an error message that the **server** housing that resource is down or that the URL doesn't exist. Servers do go down, sometimes for a short period and sometimes for longer. In this case, you have no choice but to try again later.

The nonexistent URL could indicate one of several things. First, it may mean simply that the network is busy. Often, you will be successful on your second or third attempts. Second, if you typed it in directly, check your typing. Make sure that each space and character is correct. URLs are case sensitive, so use lowercase unless part of the address you are typing is in uppercase. If you are working from an on-line source, cut and paste the URL instead of typing it in. Finally, if mistyping was not the problem, consider other possibilities. Is this the type of site that is likely to be short-lived or transient? Is it conceivable that the individual maintaining it simply decided to remove it? Or was it located on the type of site that would seem to be more stable, perhaps one sponsored by a university, government agency, organization, or company?

If you determine that you're probably dealing with an *address change* rather than a page *disappearance*, there are some simple things to try. First, attempt to go to the home of the site: the university, agency, organization, or company **home page**. You could simply work from the URL that is displayed, erasing the file name and successive directories. You may ultimately get to a Web page with a directory that will allow you to find the page you are seeking. You may even find a search engine for the site. If this approach fails, try searching for the page using a web search engine (discussed in Chapter 4), using the title of the site plus any additional information you may have.

■ EVALUATING INTERNET SOURCES

Our ability to find information quickly on the WWW sometimes leads us to forget that our goal is not just *some* information, but the *best* information. We can easily forget to slow down to evaluate carefully what we find and to make sure that it meets our needs. As we discussed earlier, evaluation is particularly important in the case of a self-publishing medium such as the Web. Some websites are mounted by an expert or group of experts, others by laypersons or amateurs. The latter may be perfectly appropriate for some purposes, but a research paper by a university professor must be distinguished, for example, from a term paper submitted for a classroom project by an undergraduate student. Some websites are carefully maintained and regularly updated. Others are one-time efforts that quickly become outdated.

Of course, evaluating sources has always been an important part of doing research. We discussed criteria for evaluating traditional sources in Chapter 2. Many of the points addressed there apply equally to the evaluation of websites. In fact, if the source you are using on the Web is a traditional print source that has simply changed format, the criteria suggested in Chapter 2 should be used to evaluate it. A scholarly journal that appears in print and electronic forms is no different on the Web than in print format. Often, however, websites prompt us to give a new twist to standard evaluation criteria. Learn to ask yourself questions such as these when you use a website for research purposes:

■ Is the author or sponsor readily identifiable, and, if so, can you determine his or her background and credentials from the web page (or by following a link from the page)? Is information provided to enable you to contact the author?
■ Should you assume that the material is presented from a particular point of view, given the author's background, the sponsor, or other evidence?
■ Is the tone objective, analytical, reflective, emotional, or subjective?
■ Is the purpose to inform, persuade, or promote?

- Are conclusions clearly supported by evidence? Does the author himself or herself identify points that are less well supported?
- Does the page use facts and figures that you can check? Do they agree with information you've already learned? Are sources provided for these data?
- Are conclusions consistent with other materials you have gathered?
- What can you tell about the intended audience? Is the material directed at a general audience, students (what level?), professionals in the field, or scholars and researchers?
- When was the site last updated? Can you tell? Is currency important for your purpose?
- Is a bibliography included? Does it include sources that support only a particular point of view? Is it outdated? Does it include authors you have identified elsewhere as authorities in the field?
- Given what you have learned, does this source meet your needs?

If you are not satisfied with some of the answers to these questions, consider turning to external sources for evidence. Names of individuals and organizations can quickly be checked in one of the comprehensive, interdisciplinary periodical indexes described in Chapter 6, for example. If an initial search doesn't turn up anything, be sure to search the full text of articles, as well. You can use a web search engine to see what other web pages might reveal. The name might also turn up in a search of the archives of Usenet newsgroups, which are described later in this chapter. Perhaps the site itself has been evaluated and rated. Check the special web directories that rate websites; we discuss these later in this chapter.

■ FINDING RESOURCES ON THE WORLD WIDE WEB

As discussed previously, many of the most important research resources you use on the Web will be licensed by your library for the use of students and faculty at your university. Most libraries list the periodical indexes, collections of full-text periodicals, reference works, directories, and statistical sources that they provide on a web page linked to their home page. Often these listings are arranged by broad subjects. Of course, they may also be listed in the library catalog. These are the primary tools that you will use as you pursue most of the steps in the search strategy presented in Chapter 2. When you are ready to go beyond these sources to see what is available on assorted websites, you'll turn to web directories and web search engines.

Web Directories

Web directories are subject listings, sometimes annotated, of selected websites. *Yahoo!* is the most familiar example of such a directory. You will find web directories variously titled as virtual libraries, webliographies, gateways, clearinghouses, subject directories or guides, metaindexes, and metasites. Expect them to vary in quality, currency, and comprehensiveness. Most web directories are arranged hierarchically by broad subject and are searched by browsing, although larger sites usually include the ability to search them by key word. Use web directories when you want to find recommended sites, still at a broad level.

Besides general-purpose, comprehensive directories such as Yahoo!, specialized web directories, often maintained by academic departments or by professional associations, service academic fields. They may be initiated and maintained by a single person in the field. Several useful web directories are available for the communication field. Browsing these is a good way to get a feel for the types of assorted web resources that are available to communication researchers. The URLs listed were current as of early 1999 but may well change. If so, use the troubleshooting tips described earlier in this chapter to locate them.

University of Iowa. (1998). *Links to communication studies resources.* [On-line]. Available: http://www.uiowa.edu/~commstud/resources/index.html (1999, April 25).

■ This comprehensive site, based at the University of Iowa Department of Communication Studies, lists websites under these categories: advertising, cultural studies, digital media, film studies, gender and race, journalism and mass communication, media studies, rhetorical studies, social science resources, and speeches and speechmakers. The listings include evaluative **annotations**.

CIOS. (1999). *Communication Institute for Online Scholarship* [On-line]. Available: http://www.cios.org (1999, April 25).

■ Anyone may search this site, but the links will not be active for the ComWeb MegaSearch unless your institution is an affiliate of CIOS or unless you subscribe to the service. If so, the site provides full-text searches for communication, journalism, speech, and rhetoric-related websites and resources.

American Communication Association. (1999). *ACA Center for Communication Research* [On-line]. Available: http://www.americancomm.org/ (1999, April 25).

■ This site provides links via its electronic reference desk to publishers, professional associations and departments, on-line books, libraries and archives, research centers, and writing skills resources.

University of Wales. (1999). *MCS: The Media and Communications Studies Site* [On-line]. Available: http://www.aber.ac.uk/~dgc/media.html (1999, April 25).

■ Subtitled "Constructivism at Work," this site originates from the Department of Education at the University of Wales. Admitting to a British focus, it covers global resources as well. The site is well organized and updated. Resources are listed under broad categories that include gender, ethnicity and class, advertising, media education, textual analysis, film studies, media influence, active interpretation, TV and radio, pop music/youth, and the written and spoken word.

Wadsworth Publishing Company. (1999). *The Communication Café* [On-line]. Available: http://communication.wadsworth.com (1999, April 25).

■   This site provides links to communication associations, student resources, instructor resources, and links to websites of interest, in such areas as public speaking, interpersonal and group communication, business and professional communication, intercultural communication, rhetoric, political communication, media law and ethics, mass communication, advertising and public relations, and radio, television, and film. A link to this book's website is found here also.

World Communication Association. (1999). *Home page* [On-line]. Available: http://ilcz.doshisha.ac.ip/users/kkitao/organi/wca/ (1999, April 25).

■   This website of the World Communication Association contains access to Internet resources for communication studies, including communication programs, organizations, conferences, journals, publishers, and other resources.

Additional web directories are devoted to subfields of communication. Examples include *Douglass: Reference Links for Students of Public Address* **<http://douglass.speech.nwu.edu/comsrces.htm>** and *Advertising World* **<http://advweb.cocomm.utexas.edu/world/>**. One well-organized example of such a more narrowly focused directory is CMC Information Sources.

December, J. (1997). CMC information sources [On-line]. Available: http://www.december.com/cmc/info/ (1999, April 25).

■   This list provides links to information sources about computer-mediated communication. Its stated purpose is "to collect, organize, and present information describing the Internet and computer-mediated communication technologies, applications, culture, discussion forums, and bibliographies." The communication subsection of its application section includes links to resources in interpersonal, group, organizational, and mass communication.

Many other specialized web directories for communication and related areas can be identified through the Department of Communication Studies site at the University of Iowa. In addition, communication-related sites can be browsed by following the links in the *Communication WebRing*. Web rings can be thought of as a type of on-line community, in which sites focused on a narrow topic are linked together in a loop. Starting at any site in the loop, you can browse to see what sites have linked themselves to the ring. Eventually, you will return to your starting place. *The Communication Ring*, maintained by Dan Oetting, is "dedicated to the study and teaching of communication, rhetoric, and related topics." You may find the web-ring directional commands (forward, back, or random) at the bottom of various communication sites you visit. For example, the World Communication Association Home Page and MCS: The

Media and Communications Studies Site, described above, are on the Communication Ring.

Communication researchers should also be aware of major interdisciplinary web directories. The best of these are selective, well organized, and searchable. Annotations are evaluative, and sites are often rated. They can save researchers much time. The communication field often gets significant coverage in these tools. These directories will also help you identify the best sites in related disciplines and will point you in the direction of the best sites for research using a particular type of source (government and statistical sites, for example).

Argus Associates. (1999). *The Argus Clearinghouse* [On-line]. Available: http://www.clearinghouse.net (1999, April 25).

■ Scholarly sources are the focus of this searchable database of "value-added topical guides." Specialists who compile lists in specific areas submit them for evaluation and rating by Argus staff. Fewer than 10% of those submitted meet the selection criteria. Communication, 1 of the 13 broad subject categories, includes these subdivisions: communications and media studies, journalism and writing, libraries and information science, news media, publishing, and television and radio.

University of California, Riverside, Library. (1999). *Infomine: Scholarly Internet resource collections* [On-line]. Available: http://infomine. ucr.edu (1999, April 25).

■ Librarians from all nine campuses of the University of California, as well as Stanford University, participate in selecting, annotating, and indexing databases, web directories, textbooks, conference proceedings, and journals. Many access points are provided for searching, including government information, instructional resources, Internet-enabling tools, and social sciences and humanities. As of 1999 more than 14,000 resources were indexed.

Other selective, annotated, searchable web directories with a less scholarly focus are also useful for research purposes. Some of the best available guides or indexes to the Internet include the *Librarians' Index to the Internet* <**http://sunsite.berkeley.edu/InternetIndex/**> and *Britannica*, the *Encyclopedia Britannica's* Guide to the Internet <**http://www.ebig.com**>. The latter includes site ratings.

Search Engines

Search engines are access tools that allow key-word searching of many websites. Several comprehensive search engines are available, and new ones appear regularly. As of early 1999 some of the most popular search engines were AltaVista, HotBot, Infoseek, Excite, Lycos, Webcrawler, and Northern Light. The trend has been for search engines to develop into commercial web **portals**, offering more and more services, along with more advertising.

Because search engines take different approaches to indexing and searching websites, it is usually recommended that searches be run in more than one engine. You will often retrieve quite different results. **Metasearch engines** greatly facilitate this process by making it possible to run a search through multiple search engines at one time. They are a good place to start a search, to test the waters, and to get a feeling for what is available on a topic. Metasearch engines are best searched with simple search syntax and a limited number of terms. If necessary, you can follow up with more complex searches using the syntax of a particular search engine. Popular metasearch engines include MetaCrawler, Dogpile, and Inference Find. These and many others can be found on the All-in-One Search Page, <**http://allonesearch.com**>.

Be aware that there's a lot of material on the WWW that search engines can't identify, at least at the level of individual documents. For example, they cannot search web databases, including those licensed by libraries. Databases, including archival collections, must be searched using an internal search system. At the website of the *Christian Science Monitor*, for example, you can find archives for the newspaper that extend back to 1980. Although these are freely available, they can be retrieved only by searching the database at that site.

In addition to general search engines, there are many specialized ones, which focus on particular types of information. Scour.Net <**http://www. scour.net**>, for example, searches multimedia files on the Web. You can use it to find still images and audio or video recordings. GovBot <**http://ciir2.cs.umass. edu/Govbot/**> searches only government sites and can be used to trace legislation, regulations, and court cases. Disinformation <**http://www.disinfo.com/**> bills itself as "the subculture search engine."

How does one keep all this straight? Learning about and remembering all the possible approaches and tools, especially given the frequency with which new tools arrive on the scene, can seem overwhelming. You may be tempted to limit your web search to typing some terms into a comprehensive search engine. Instead, turn to The Internet Sleuth to get you started. It attempts to bring together in one place many of your search options: web directories, search engines, and databases.

> iSleuth.com. (1995–1999). *The Internet Sleuth* [On-line]. Available: http://www.isleuth.com (1999, April 25).
>
> ■   The home screen for The Internet Sleuth presents various starting points, including some of the web directories listed above. In addition, it maintains an index of specialized databases. It's very important to realize that your initial goal when using this tool is to identify appropriate databases, so you should try to think only in terms of broad categories when you search The Internet Sleuth itself. These are listed and can be browsed. You can then do a specific search in the databases you select, often right from The Internet Sleuth screen.

This field is very competitive, with strong pressure to improve the effectiveness and efficiency of search engines. These tools have a daunting task.

Each search engine must visit each site on the Web to create and regularly update its own version of a web database, containing millions of sites. Then it must attempt to devise an easy-to-use and effective search system that will be able to identify and retrieve any document in its database rapidly, all without benefit of human indexing. We should not be surprised when the search engine does not distinguish between a fifth-grade report on climate change and a study written by a panel of geologists. Because of the difficulties involved, it may take more preparation and ingenuity to search the Web effectively than it does to search other databases. However, many of the principles involved are similar. In Chapter 4 we will describe tools and strategies for searching all types of databases, along with some particular tips for using search engines.

COMMUNICATING ON THE INTERNET

■ E-MAIL

You probably send mail to people, groups, and organizations—perhaps even to yourself—using the **e-mail** system that your college or university provides. These systems vary so much that we won't bother to provide instructions here. Documentation is probably available either on-line or at a service or help desk in your computer center. You'll find it necessary to use e-mail for various research-related activities, such as subscribing to electronic discussion groups or retrieving documents from periodical indexes. These documents can be e-mailed to yourself.

■ ELECTRONIC DISCUSSION GROUPS

Another important way researchers use e-mail is to participate in electronic discussion groups. You may want to join a group because you have an ongoing interest in the topic about which it discusses and shares information. Or, perhaps, you have a research project that would benefit from locating an expert in the field and getting some advice. Although discussion groups can be used for this purpose, you should be warned that a blatant request for information needed for a classroom project, if the information is readily available elsewhere, will seldom be successful. But it is often possible to search the archives of discussion groups, allowing you to see what information might have been shared about a particular topic. Electronic discussion groups are of two distinct types: e-mail discussion lists (often called listservs), and Usenet newsgroups.

Because it was the software first used for this purpose, **listserv** has become the generic term for electronic discussion lists that share messages through e-mail. Many lists continue to use listserv, but you may also come across discussion lists using other software programs such as ListProc, Majordomo, and Lyris. The commands for using these programs are similar.

These programs facilitate the sharing of e-mail messages among members by automatically forwarding to the entire mailing list any message addressed to the group. Messages are received by group members in their individual mail boxes, at their home e-mail sites. Such a system facilitates ongoing discussion of research and professional topics of common interest. Listservs have become a popular way to share information in many fields. The list software also makes it a simple matter to join or resign from groups.

Listservs are available for most communication fields. A listing of many can be found on the web directory maintained at the University of Iowa Department of Communication Studies:

<http://www.uiowa.edu/~commstud/resources/index.html>

Others can be located by searching one of the directories of discussion groups available: *The Directory of Scholarly and Professional E-Conferences* **<http://n2h2.com/KOVACS/>** and Liszt **<http://www.liszt.com>** are both useful. Both directories provide a short description of each group and tell you whether archives are available. Examples from these lists include:

CARR-L: computer-assisted research and reporting
EMPATHY: teachers of interpersonal communication
JOURNET: journalists and journalism educators
FOI-L: Freedom of Information Act discussions
SCREEN-L: research in film and television
H-FILM: film history and scholarly study of media
CRTNET: communication research and theory network

Let's say you decide to participate in SCREEN-L. The description you found in *The Directory of Scholarly and Professional E-Conferences* tells you that it's "for all who study, teach, theorize about, or research film and television—mostly in an academic setting, but not necessarily so." Two addresses are listed for the group:

<listserv@ua1vm.ua.edu> and **<SCREEN-L@ua1vm.ua.edu>**

The first is the address you use to subscribe to the group. The second is the address you use to send a message that you want to share with the entire group. It's very important not to confuse the two, if you want to avoid clogging the mailboxes of your new electronic colleagues with extraneous and annoying messages.

To subscribe, you would send an e-mail message to the listserv address: **<listserv@ua1vm.ua.edu>**. Leave the subject line blank. Type a one-line message, as follows:

subscribe screen-l FirstName LastName

For example:

subscribe screen-l Jane Doe

This model can be used to subscribe to most listservs. You'll quickly receive a message welcoming you to the group, describing its mode of operation, and giving you instructions for, among other things, canceling your subscription. It's important to save this message, as you may decide at some point that this particular group is not for you or that you want to suspend your subscription during a vacation period. Naturally, all messages about your subscription should be sent to the listserv address, not to the group address. The instructions will also tell you how to search the group's archives, if available.

Communication Research and Theory Network (CRTNET) is a listserv in communication. It is moderated at the National Communication Association (NCA). A list like this might be of interest to graduate students in the field. If you would like to subscribe, you'd send a message like the one above to <**listserv@list.psu.edu**>. CRTNET provides discussions of issues relevant to all aspects of the subject and discipline of communication. It also includes announcements posted from the national office of the NCA, job listings, and texts of recent political speeches. To contribute to the list, you would send e-mail to <**crtnet@natcom.org**>.

■ USENET NEWSGROUPS

Newsgroups are discussion groups on **Usenet**, a network of thousands of groups available on most campus networks. Instead of receiving e-mail in your mailbox, you use special software to read and participate in the newsgroups in which you're interested. Unlike listservs, you do not need to subscribe actively to a newsgroup. The current messages of all groups are available for anyone to read, so you can check into what is going on in any group at any time. Students usually select a few groups that they might read regularly, or irregularly. Those newsgroups then automatically come up whenever they access the **newsreader** software.

Although many newsgroups are strictly recreational in nature, others serve professional and scholarly purposes. In fact, some listservs are also available as Usenet newsgroups, providing an alternative and convenient method for participating in them. (Some may prefer to access listservs through Usenet to avoid dealing with an overabundance of messages in their e-mail boxes.) Inquire at the computer center on your campus about your campus access to Usenet.

Many discussion groups have developed FAQs, or frequently asked questions, a compilation of questions that newcomers and visitors to the group often pose. Sometimes a group effort, they include useful information on the group topic and may become used by a wider audience. Newcomers to newsgroups are expected to read a group's FAQs before participating in it actively (it's considered to be very bad form to ask a group a question that is answered on its FAQ). One website <**http://www.faqs.org**> attempts to compile and maintain a comprehensive list of discussion group FAQs.

Newsgroup messages usually stay on a university system for only a few days. But archives exist, and some search engines offer the option of searching these. In fact, you may find newsgroup messages popping up unexpectedly among your results when you use a search engine. A special search engine, DejaNews, is designed specifically for the purpose of searching newsgroup archives.

The need to evaluate information sources critically is important in this venue, as well, particularly when dealing with information gathered in Usenet newsgroups. Listservs tend to be associated with academic institutions, and participants often include scholars and professionals. Topics discussed are often scholarly and professional. Newsgroups, on the other hand, cover topics that range far beyond academe, and the expertise of participants varies widely. As always, try to establish the author's credentials and point of view, check the validity of "facts," and look for underlying assumptions.

■ CIOS/COMSERVE

Comserve is an on-line service provided by the Communication Institute for Online Scholarship (CIOS) that provides access to news services (position announcements, new books, news, new research), electronic journals, syllabi, bibliographies, research articles, and hot lines (electronic discussion groups in the many different areas of the discipline). Communication scholars join hot lines to discuss issues relevant to many specialty interests—for example: computer-mediated, family, gender, health, intercultural, interpersonal, mass, organizational, and political communication; history; magazine journalism; philosophy; research methods; rhetoric; speech disorders; and speech education. Students may join ComGrads, a hot line for students to exchange ideas about graduate school, teaching, and research.

Students attending universities that are affiliates of CIOS may download unlimited numbers of files and join as many hot lines as they wish, whereas students at nonaffiliated universities and the general public have limited access. If the university is an associate, students, faculty, and others connected to the university can conduct global searches of CIOS/Comserve's Journals Indexes and do searches in the resource library. CIOS charges students and faculty extra fees to access abstracts and full-text article databases.

CIOS/Comserve is an important electronic service, one designed especially for communication scholars. You can access it at <**www.cios.org**>. It's a way to become involved in the discipline, to see what topics are of interest to faculty and fellow students, and to search the communication literature.

ETHICAL ISSUES

WWW sites are so easily accessed and inviting that students sometimes get the mistaken impression that the documents they find there can be freely used. They can be, up to a point. The authors have placed them there to be consulted by a wide audience. But, whether or not web pages include an explicit copyright notice, they are copyrighted and can be used only to the extent allowed by fair-use provisions of the copyright law. Documents and multimedia obtained through the WWW should be treated with the same respect as books or journal articles. Anything you quote or paraphrase must be properly attributed, with a standard citation. Anything else is plagiarism. Appendix A includes examples of the APA format for citing Internet resources.

Downloading documents is something that you will naturally want to do because it is so much more convenient than photocopying. You may then be tempted simply to copy and paste material into your project, with the intention of paraphrasing and citing later. If you follow this practice, you run the risk of making a mistake and forgetting exactly which are your words and which are someone else's. Or you may lose track of which quotation came from which

source. To avoid this problem, anticipate it. Develop a system to keep track of where everything came from. Anytime you paste something in, change the font, or the font size. Or convert it to all caps. Devise an abbreviation for each publication (for example, the first four letters of the author's name and first four letters of the title) and put this in front of each piece of text you paste. The same caution applies to images and multimedia files. Downloading a portion of a speech, for example, to use as an audio or visual aid in your own speech might constitute "fair use" as an educational aid. But downloading several speeches and then selling that CD would surely violate fair-use principles.

SUMMARY

The Internet is a network of networks that connects computers worldwide. The World Wide Web functions as an interface to the Internet and facilitates access to materials in electronic format. Traditional library access tools, selected reference sources, and large numbers of periodicals are now accessed through a web browser, and libraries serve as gateways to all types of web-based resources.

Students should learn to differentiate between different types of web-based resources. Asking evaluative questions about resources they encounter is particularly important in the case of assorted websites. Quality control on the Internet can be exercised only at the local level, so students must take responsibility for checking the authority of website authors and sponsors and the validity of factual information. They must learn to detect unsupported assumptions and to be cognizant of points of view and possible bias.

Many valuable sources of potential interest to researchers are available on a wide assortment of websites. Collections of primary sources (print, audio, video, images), government publications, statistical data, news, and current events are particularly important for researchers.

Researchers find materials on the Internet by browsing web directories (for broad subjects), using search engines (for specific topics), and taking part in electronic discussion groups. Discussion groups are of two types: e-mail discussion lists, to which one subscribes, and Usenet newsgroups, which one may access and read with few formalities.

Almost all web documents are copyrighted and must not be used without acknowledgment. The presence or absence of a copyright notice is irrelevant. The speed and ease with which material may be accessed and downloaded requires that students make special efforts to avoid plagiarism and to read carefully and think critically about the sources they use.

REFERENCES

Barker, J. (Maint.). (1997/1999). Finding information on the Internet: A tutorial. In *UC Berkeley Library Internet Resources* [On-line]. Available: http://www.lib.berkeley.edu/TeachingLib/Guides/Internet/FindInfo.html (1999, April 25).

Branscomb, H. E. (1998). *Casting your net: A student's guide to research on the Internet.* Boston: Allyn & Bacon.

Cohen, L. (Maint.). (1999, April). *University at Albany Libraries Internet Tutorials* [On-line]. Available: http://www.albany.edu/library/internet/ (1999, April 25).

Courtright, J., & Perse, E. M. (1998). *Communicating online: A brief guide to the Internet.* Mountain View, CA: Mayfield.

Gale Guide to Internet Databases (5th ed.). (1998). Farmington Hills, MI: Gale Research.

Jones, S. G. (1998). *Doing Internet research.* Thousand Oaks, CA: Sage.

Kaye, B. K., & Medoff, N. J. (1999). *The World Wide Web: A mass communication perspective.* Mountain View, CA: Mayfield.

Kovacs, D. K. (Ed.). (1998/1999). Directory of scholarly and professional e-conferences [On-line]. Available: http://www.n2h2.com/KOVACS/ (1999, April 25).

EXAMPLES

CHRIS'S topic is starting to take shape. He decides to check if the Internet has any information available on this topic. But, rather than type this term into a search engine (and come up with more hits than could be managed), he visits Wadsworth Publishing's Communication Café and its Speech Communication links for possible sites. The <**www.Douglass.speech.nwu.edu**> site leads him to the text of many different speakers on various issues. After looking through some of these, he wonders if the speakers actually wrote the speeches themselves or if someone else did. This direction seems to be promising, especially because his instructor stressed that his speech must be original and *not* written by anyone else.

FELECIA'S interest in voice mail is a prime candidate for the Internet. She chooses Yahoo! and enters "voice mail" as a phrase. Results indicated one category (with not much in it) and 218 sites. Most of the sites are voice-mail companies, some of which explain their products and services. This provides a little background information. By doing an advanced search and limiting it to "exact-phrase match" as a search method, selecting "Yahoo! Categories" as a search area, and limiting the search to "new listings added during the past 6 months," Felicia finds 12 site matches. The first one (on 2/14/99) is Golden Voice, a voice-mail service for small businesses, individuals, and start-up companies.

MARIA'S interest in interpersonal communication and attribution is starting to take shape. Because her college is an affiliate of CIOS, she checks to see if its database has any information on attribution theory. At CIOS she searches the demonstration indexes, specifically *Human Communication Research;* four articles and their abstracts are retrieved. They provide a little more information on the topic.

ORLANDO'S topic on parasocial interaction, being a mass-communication topic, might be searchable in *Links to Communication Studies Resources*. After looking at the Journalism and Mass Communication page (no references to "parasocial") and the Radio, TV, and Media page (no way to search it), Orlando turns to General Resources and decides that a better way to approach this is to look at one of the professional organization's sites. At the National Communication Association, he uses the search engine and finds five references to "parasocial." One of these provides some interesting background information.

KAT, CALVIN, ROCKY, and MICHELLE, for their conflict-resolution training program, decide to see if there are relevant sites in The Communication Ring, so they enter the site at the National Communication Association. The first relevant site of interest is the American Communication Association site, where there is a separate page for Conflict and Communication. Unfortunately, most of the links provided are not updated, including one to the Mediation Center. Although it moved, it gave its forwarding address. At this site, the group finds books, other sites of interest, and a video store. They decide to look into renting videos instead of purchasing them.

EXERCISES

1. Go to the Links to Communication Studies Resources Web Site <**http://www.uiowa.edu/~commstud/resources/index.html**>. Find a link to Content Analysis Resources. Explore that page. Who is the webmaster? What are the webmaster's credentials for maintaining a website in this subject area?
2. Go to Disinformation <**http://www.disinfo.com/**> and select one of the sites indexed under the category "propaganda." Referring to the section on evaluating web resources in this chapter, write a paragraph evaluating the site you selected.
3. You have heard that the soc.college newsgroup publishes a useful FAQ about financial aid. To find this FAQ you use the Usenet FAQ Archives <**http://www.faqs.org**>. Select the link to the soc hierarchy.

a. In the list of soc FAQs by newsgroup, find the link to the soc.college newsgroup and select it. Find information about the college/financial-aid-faq.

b. Find a link to the URL of the FAQ home page. On the FAQ home page, find a link to Common Myths. What is one common myth about financial aid?

5. Go to the Communication Studies Instructional Web Site at Kent State University <**www.library.kent.edu/commstudies/**> and find the Internet Basics section. Review the main features of Internet searching, newsgroups, e-mail, and web-page creation. Try some of the tutorials to improve your skills.

chapter 4

Using Computers to Search Electronic Databases

A s we saw in Chapter 3, most of the access tools that you will use in communication research—especially library catalogs and periodical indexes—will be available only as electronic **databases**. Catalogs and indexes are bibliographic databases, one of the types of databases that we discuss in this chapter. You will also need to search other types of databases: directories, statistical sources, and the full text of reference books, newspapers, journals, and other periodicals. The World Wide Web itself can be thought of as a database—either one large database or a number of smaller, more specialized databases.

A researcher who is reluctant to use computers to find information or who does not know how to do so effectively will be severely handicapped. Fortunately, learning to search databases well involves learning some basic concepts and standard searching procedures that can then be applied in many different situations. The search interfaces used by different database **vendors** usually offer only slight variations of these concepts and procedures. Once you understand the basic concepts and get some practice on the procedures, you will be able to search many different types of databases effectively. In this chapter we introduce you to the different types of computerized databases and explain the process and concepts involved in searching them.

DIFFERING TECHNOLOGICAL ENVIRONMENTS

The electronic environment you find on your campus might vary considerably from that at another university. This is partly because technology has provided libraries with many options for delivering electronic information. Thus, on one campus, the electronic equivalent of *Psychological Abstracts* may be offered through the WWW, searchable not only from the library but also from offices, residence halls, or any modem-equipped microcomputer. On another campus it may be available only on CD-ROM work-stations in the library itself. At still another it may be available only through a statewide system. If it is available on a campus network, the searching procedures may be identical to those used to search the library's own **on-line catalog**, the same as the procedures used to search CD-ROM indexes in the library, or quite different from either.

Students may become confused by all these options, but they need not be. Libraries usually provide a browser-based menu that serves as a gateway to the electronic databases provided, no matter what their origin or format. If you have questions, ask the reference librarian for advice and assistance. Librarians can help you find out what electronic sources are available and how you can access and use them effectively.

VARIETIES OF COMPUTERIZED DATABASES

A database is information stored in such a way that it can be retrieved. Card catalogs and periodical indexes—in fact, all the reference sources discussed in this book—are examples of databases. They are organized so that you can easily find what you're looking for. A **computerized database** is simply information stored electronically, to be retrieved via a computer terminal or a microcomputer. Such databases greatly increase the flexibility for retrieving information. Databases can be categorized broadly in many different ways. One way is to think of them as either bibliographic, directory, or source databases, although many combine aspects of more than one of these types. It is important to distinguish between electronic *databases*, which are fully searchable, and electronic *publications* whose text can be retrieved, but not searched, electronically. Many resources now available, though, are a combination of the two.

■ BIBLIOGRAPHIC DATABASES

Bibliographic databases consist of citations to published literature, often with **abstracts**, or short summaries. They correspond to print periodical indexes and abstracts. Computerized library catalogs are also examples of bibliographic databases. At the conclusion of their search, users of these databases will usually still need to locate the actual publications cited, although many periodical indexes now include on-line the full text of at least some of the publications they cite.

Most of the periodical indexes and abstracts described in Part Two of this book were initially print publications that are now available both on-line and on CD-ROM as bibliographic databases. Those of major interest to communication researchers are: *ERIC* (Educational Resources Information Center), the computerized equivalent of the printed indexes *Resources in Education* and *Current Index to Journals in Education*; *PsycINFO* and *PsycLIT* (*Psychological Abstracts*); *Sociofile* (*Sociological Abstracts*); *Wilson Business Abstracts* (*Business Periodicals Index*); *Social Sciences Abstracts* (*Social Sciences Index*); *Humanities Abstracts* (*Humanities Index*); and *Education*

Abstracts (*Education Index*). Most of these databases correspond closely to their print counterparts in scope and journal coverage. A major difference, however, is the number of years available for retrospective searching. Just a few databases were available on-line before the 1970s, and the coverage of most starts after 1980.

Other bibliographic databases do not correspond to any printed index and are available only in computerized form. A potentially useful example for communication researchers, particularly those in organizational communication, is *ABI/Inform*, which indexes and abstracts periodical literature in business and management. More interdisciplinary, comprehensive indexes include *Expanded Academic Index* (IAC/InfoTrac), *Periodical Abstracts* (UMI/ProQuest), and *Academic Search* (EBSCOhost). These and other bibliographic databases are described in detail in Chapter 6.

■ DIRECTORY DATABASES

Directory databases, also called referral databases, correspond to printed directories and contain references to organizations, people, grants, archives, research projects, and so on. Although some directory databases contain summaries or abstracts, researchers most often use these databases to locate a primary information source. A directory database of possible interest to communication researchers is the *Encyclopedia of Associations*.

■ SOURCE DATABASES

In contrast, **source databases** contain such complete information that after consulting them you may not need to continue the search for information. This category includes statistical, full-text, image, and multimedia databases.

Statistical databases consist primarily of statistical or other numeric data and are somewhat equivalent to statistical compendia such as yearbooks and almanacs. They may also contain some textual information. Many libraries received 1990 census data as statistical databases on CD-ROMs produced by the U.S. Bureau of the Census. Data from the 2000 census will largely be distributed through the WWW. The searching **protocols** for statistical databases may allow the user to create, correlate, and retrieve personally defined sets of data that might take many hours to assemble from printed publications. Many statistical sources available over the WWW are not true databases in the sense that their data can be manipulated. Statistical compendia are often published on-line simply as text documents, in which the data are consulted in tabular form, much as one would view the pages of a printed volume.

Full-text databases contain the complete text of publications such as journals, newspapers, wire service stories, court decisions, books, encyclopedias, almanacs, and other reference works. In true full-text databases, every word of the entire text can be searched interactively on-line. For example, if a person's name, hometown, street address, or occupation appeared as incidental information in a newspaper article, the article could be retrieved by searching for any of those words or phrases. This capability distinguishes full-text databases from electronic publications available merely for on-line perusal. Be warned, however, that the term *full text* is used loosely and may be applied to one or both types of products. *Contemporary Authors* (Gale Research) is an example of an extensive series of print reference volumes that is now available (by subscription) and searchable full text through the WWW. Full-text searching capability in this database allows one, for example, to identify authors with a particular first name, who were born in a particular town or country, who graduated from a particular university, and so on.

Image databases consist of graphic images, such as photographs, representations of works of art, and textual material. Textual material available in this manner is simply a reproduction of the printed page and cannot be searched interactively. Many periodicals are now available as part of image databases. Examples available in university libraries include the ProQuest Direct products produced by University Microfilms International (UMI): *ABI/Inform* and *Periodical Abstracts*. An advantage of image databases for reproducing text is that, in contrast to full-text databases, they include illustrations and photographs as they appeared in the printed publication. The pagination will also be identical, which makes it possible to cite them more accurately and completely. As discussed in the previous chapter, *full-image* textual databases store documents in file formats that require special "helper applications" for viewing (for example, Adobe Acrobat or RealPage). In contrast, *full-text* publications available on the WWW are usually web pages written in the standard web language, **html**. The WWW is a rich repository of many other types of image databases. Photographs, manuscripts, representations of artworks, illustrations, and other images have been collected and are searchable at their website of origin. Some may be searched through specialized search engines.

Multimedia databases include, in addition to text and graphics, audio and video components. Several multimedia databases are now available through the WWW, including important collections of broadcasting archives (we discuss these in Chapter 8).

We discuss each type of database in Part Two. The *Gale Directory of Databases* attempts to list comprehensively those available commercially either on-line or on CD-ROM, magnetic tape, and floppy disks. Many web-based databases are listed in web subject directories. Some can be identified with such tools as *The Internet Sleuth*, described in Chapter 3.

HOW TO SEARCH COMPUTERIZED DATABASES

Computerized databases can be deceptively easy to search. When novice searchers type the first topical word or phrase that occurs to them into a bibliographic database and retrieve some citations to articles on their topics, they may be satisfied with the results. They may not, however, realize that they have failed to identify many other, sometimes more appropriate, articles. Or they may spend hours browsing through hundreds of citations, not realizing that they could easily have narrowed their search and obtained more manageable results. Such problems tend to be compounded when using search engines to search the WWW.

In this section we describe some basic features of search systems. Mastering these concepts will help you search effectively, making your searches as precise or as comprehensive as you wish. Of course, it will be necessary to combine this general information with specific information about the features of the databases you are searching. Fortunately, such specific information is readily available. Most databases include on-line tutorials and ample Help screens. Such tutorials are well worth the small amount of time that it takes to go through them. Manuals with sample searches and detailed information are often available, as well. Web search engines also include on-line help documentation, and a variety of websites offer excellent tutorials in the use of search engines. Once the basic concepts of searching computerized databases are understood, the Help screens provided by on-line sources can be much more easily understood and used.

STANDARD SEARCH FEATURES

The search features that we describe next are so widely used that they can be termed "standard." Their implementation varies from one system to another, but the concepts involved remain the same.

■ CONTROLLED VOCABULARY VERSUS KEY-WORD SEARCHING

Most databases allow the user to enter **search statements** simply by typing in everyday words or phrases. The system then retrieves those citations whose records contain the words or phrases entered. The citations retrieved may have found matches in almost any field: title, journal title, abstract, or subject heading. Searching in this way, using natural language, is searching by **key word**.

Key-word searching, also called **free-text searching**, is often effective in locating citations on a topic, but it does have drawbacks. First, because language is imprecise, it is likely that at least some records retrieved will match the words entered but will not actually be on the topic intended. At the same time, the searcher may miss a number of citations that were about this topic but that did not happen to contain the term used. Perhaps the citation contained a synonym instead.

For these reasons, almost all bibliographic databases have established a **controlled vocabulary** that is used in a systematic way to describe the subject of articles and books. Subject terms (called **subject headings** or **descriptors**) are assigned to each **record** and are listed in the subject (or descriptor) field for each item. The example in Figure 4-1 is a record from the *Social Sciences Abstracts* database, using the WilsonWeb system. Notice that three descriptors were assigned to this article.

If we had done a key-word search for the term "attribution" in *Social Sciences Abstracts*, we would have retrieved the record in Figure 4-1 because this term occurs in the record in one or more fields, in this case the abstract field and the descriptors field. If we had specified that we wanted to do a subject

<table>
<tr><td>TITLE</td><td>Yours, mine, and ours: mutual *attributions* for non-verbal behaviors in couples' interactions</td></tr>
<tr><td>PERSONAL AUTHOR</td><td>Manusov, Valerie; Floyd, Kory; Kerssen Griep, Jeff</td></tr>
<tr><td>SOURCE</td><td>Communication Research. v. 24 June '97 p. 234-60.</td></tr>
<tr><td>ABSTRACT</td><td>A study was conducted to test the contention that nonverbal cues act very similarly to other behaviors in provoking *attribution* making in couples' interactions. Findings from a sample of 60 couples indicated that negative behaviors were more likely to be noticed than were positive nonverbal cues, that satisfaction was associated with *attributions* for positive behaviors, that mutual *attributions* for the same behaviors differed significantly, and that self-other *attributional* differences were improved by relational satisfaction. These findings extend previous applications of *attribution* theory by presenting some validation for the use of *attribution* theories with nonverbal behaviors and by demonstrating that *attribution* making happens in a manner that reflects the mutually occurring, dyadic level of interpersonal communication.</td></tr>
<tr><td>DESCRIPTORS</td><td>*Attribution* Social psychology; Interpersonal communication; Nonverbal communication.</td></tr>
</table>

Figure 4-1 A Social Sciences Abstracts Record [italics added]

search, our search would have been limited to the descriptor field. In this case we would have retrieved the record with either method.

You are probably already familiar with the concept of a controlled vocabulary and the use of subject headings because their use is essential for all printed indexes and catalogs. And, you are probably familiar with the **Library of Congress subject headings**, which are used in almost all college and university library catalogs. **Database producers** usually publish lists of subject headings or descriptors (often called a **thesaurus**). Even better, many products have incorporated this thesaurus into their search system. Thus, when searching these databases, it is possible to query the on-line thesaurus to determine if a particular term is a subject heading. The on-line thesaurus allows the user to move easily between cross-references, and terms may be selected and entered directly from the screen. The most common mistake that new searchers make is to ignore a database's controlled vocabulary, relying exclusively on key-word searching.

Of course, some concepts are so new that they have not yet been incorporated into the controlled vocabulary, and key words must be used. As they gain experience, searchers will find that it is effective to use both key words and subject headings. In fact, a common and often effective strategy is to start by doing a key-word search, then to review the displayed citations. If you find citations on your topic, the subject headings assigned to that record are usually an excellent source of headings that can be entered to make the search more effective. Locating subject headings in this way is sometimes called *lateral* or *sideways searching*, and search systems are usually designed to facilitate it. In web-based search systems, subject headings assigned to records are usually links that can be searched simply by clicking on them. This is the case in the example record from WilsonWeb shown in Figure 4-1.

■ BOOLEAN OPERATORS

Operators are special terms that allow searchers to connect or combine words and concepts. The most widely used operators—AND, OR, and NOT—are sometimes called **logical**, or **Boolean, operators**.

AND This operator retrieves only those citations that include all the combined search terms. In Figure 4-2 , "television AND radio" are terms contained in bibliographic records that the computer is searching. The computer is being asked to "AND" the sets of records together. The shaded area represents those records that the computer is being asked to retrieve. It includes only those records in which *both* words, "television" and "radio," appear.

OR When we "OR" the sets of records together (Figure 4-3), we get all records to which at least one of these descriptors has been assigned—either "television OR radio." They need not necessarily both be assigned to the same document. Thus, many more records will be found with the OR operator than with the AND operator. This operator is generally used to combine synonyms, related terms, alternate spellings, and acronyms.

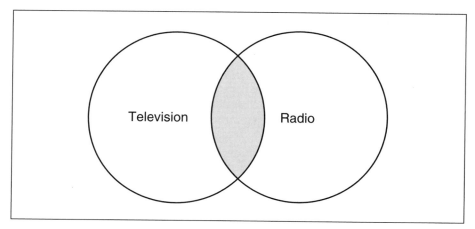

Figure 4-2 Television AND Radio

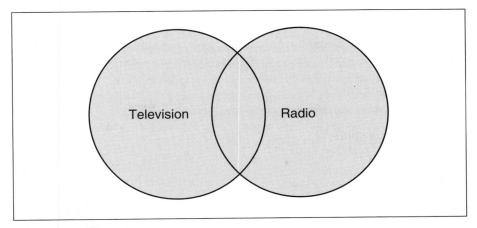

Figure 4-3 Television OR Radio

NOT (sometimes called AND NOT or BUT NOT) This operator excludes
a particular term from your search results. For example, "television
NOT radio" (Figure 4-4) excludes all records that include the term
"radio." This operator is used much less often than AND and OR,
and it should be used with care. In the example in Figure 4-4, we
may be excluding desirable articles that contain valuable information on television, simply because they also mention radio.

In conducting searches, we often group together with the OR operator all
synonyms and related terms that represent each separate concept we wish to
search. The resulting sets of records, which tend to be large, are then "AND-ed"
together to produce a much smaller set. Simply stated: *Synonyms are "OR-ed,"
then the resulting sets, representing concepts, are "AND-ed."* Using a form such
as the one in Figure 4-5 when preparing a search can clarify the relationships
between *concepts* and *terms*.

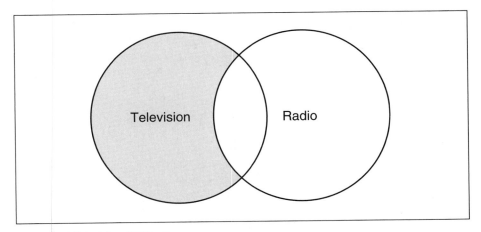

Figure 4-4 Television NOT Radio

■ PARENTHESES

When searches are entered into a search system, parentheses are used to indicate how we want to group the terms we have selected. Typically, the synonyms for each concept are enclosed in parentheses and then the concepts are AND-ed together. For example:

(radio OR television)   AND   (advertising OR commercials)

If we fail to use parentheses, we lose control of how the computer will interpret and process our search statement.

Search systems for web-based databases often include guided search screens that allow us to enter terms in separate search boxes and specify which operator (AND, OR, or NOT) should be used to combine them. This saves us from having to use parentheses. Unfortunately, it can make it difficult to specify the order in which we want the terms to be processed. One way of getting around this is to enter all the synonyms for each concept in a single search box, connected with OR. Then, make sure that AND will combine the results of the search boxes. For example:

radio OR television

AND

advertising OR commercials

Topic: ——————————————————————————

——————————————————————————————

	Concept 1	AND	Concept 2	AND	Concept 2
S y n o n y m s	————		————		————
	OR		OR		OR
	————		————		————
	OR		OR		OR
	————		————		————

Figure 4-5 Search Preparation Form

■ ALTERNATIVES TO BOOLEAN OPERATORS

Some search systems use Boolean concepts without resorting to the operators AND, OR, or NOT. For example, you might enter search terms into a search box and then be asked to specify whether you wish to search for:

- "all of these terms" or "must contain the terms" (equivalent to AND).
- "any of these terms" or "can contain the terms" or "should contain the terms" (equivalent to OR).
- "must not contain the terms" or "should not contain the terms" (equivalent to NOT).

Another popular alternative is to use symbols (+ and –) in place of AND and NOT. These are sometimes called **implied Boolean symbols**. The plus symbol (+) is placed in front of terms that *must* be included, and the minus symbol (–) is used to exclude terms. Thus, "+" is somewhat equivalent to AND, and "–" to NOT. If you want to retrieve articles (or websites) that deal with radio commercials exclusively, for example, you might enter this search:

> +radio +commercials –television

Notice that, in order to be retrieved by this search, records must contain *both* the words "radio" and "commercials," but any records that also happen to include the word "television" will be eliminated. As with the NOT operator, use extreme caution when using "–."

What is less clear to many searchers is that *no* symbol—that is, simply a space—means something, too. In most search engines, for example, a space between two search terms usually *implies* OR. Thus, if you want to retrieve items about *either* radio or television, you could enter:

> radio television

Unfortunately, for those of us trying to keep it all straight, in a few systems (FirstSearch, as well as a few web search engines) the space between two terms implies AND rather than OR. This will make a big difference in your results, so consult the Help function of the system you are using to determine how spaces are interpreted.

■ PROXIMITY OPERATORS

Other operators frequently available for use with search systems are called **proximity operators**. These operators allow the searcher to specify the physical proximity of the terms being searched. Unfortunately, not much standardization exists among search systems in terms of proximity operators. Those used in OCLC's FirstSearch system are only one example of how these operators may be used:

w (with):	Two words must be adjacent and in the specified order.
	EXAMPLE: communication w research
n (near):	Two words must be adjacent but can be in any order.
	EXAMPLE: communication n research

Another common proximity operator is "adj" (adjacent). It is used like "w" and "n" to indicate that two terms must be immediately adjacent. Often, it is possible to specify that two terms must be separated by no more than a specified number of words. Thus, "television n3 commercials" would retrieve records in which these two words were close but not immediately adjacent. To determine which, if any, proximity operators are available in a particular database and how they are defined, you must check the on-line Help function. In another database, for example, "with" might mean that the two terms must be in the same sentence, and "near" might mean that they must be in the same paragraph.

■ PHRASE SEARCHING

You will often want to search for a phrase rather than for a single word. The search systems for most bibliographic databases assume that two adjacent words constitute a phrase. For example, if you enter "television commercials" in a search box, you will normally retrieve records in which those two words appear together and in that order. But you cannot take this practice for granted because most search engines interpret a space as OR. Thus, "television commercials" would retrieve articles with either term in them. And, just to make things complicated, as we mentioned, some systems, including FirstSearch, interpret the space as an AND. Thus, in FirstSearch, you will need to insert "w" between the words to search a phrase. (Otherwise, FirstSearch may retrieve records in which both words appear, but in different parts of the record.)

An increasingly common way of forcing a phrase search is to enclose the phrase in quotes: "television commercials." This method of phrase searching is the common practice in web search engines. It is coming into practice in search systems for bibliographic databases, as well.

■ FIELD-SPECIFIC SEARCHING

The information in each database record is organized in fields (author, title, subject headings, and so on). The fields available, and the terms used to designate them, vary from one database to another. Some databases include many fields with a great deal of information that can be used by the searcher to narrow and broaden searches. To search most effectively, searchers should familiarize themselves with the fields used in the database they are searching. Often, this requires seeking help via the Help screens for the *database* itself (for example, *PsycINFO*) rather than the Help screens for the *search system* (for example, FirstSearch, Ovid, EBSCOhost, SilverPlatter).

The record in Figure 4-6 from the *ERIC* database on OCLC's FirstSearch system illustrates the relatively wide variety of fields available in this database. Notice that this *ERIC* record is for the same article shown in Figure 4-1 as it appears in the *Social Sciences Abstracts* database. Compare the fields available and the descriptors assigned by each database. Notice that *ERIC* has a special category of controlled vocabulary, called **identifiers**. Identifiers are not listed in the *ERIC* thesaurus but are highly specific subjects that are useful for subject retrieval.

```
ERIC NO:       EJ550439
AUTHOR:        Manusov, Valerie; Floyd, Kory; Kerssen-Griep, Jeff
TITLE:         Yours, Mine, and Ours: Mutual Attributions for Nonverbal
               Behaviors in Couples' Interactions.
YEAR:          1997
SOURCE:        Communication Research (v24 n3 p234–60 Jun 1997)
PUB TYPE:      Journal article; Research/technical report
LANGUAGE:      English
ABSTRACT:      Argues that nonverbal cues act much like other behaviors in
               triggering attribution-making in couples' interactions. Finds
               that negative behaviors were more likely than positive non-
               verbal cues to be noticed; satisfaction was related to attribu-
               tions for positive behaviors; mutual attributions for the same
               behaviors differed significantly; and self/other attributional
               differences were enhanced by relational satisfaction. (SR)
MAJOR DESC:    Attribution Theory; Interpersonal Communication; Interper-
               sonal Relationship; Nonverbal Communication
MINOR DESC:    Communication Research; Higher Education
IDENTIFIERS:   Communication Behavior
CLEARINGHOUSE NUMBER: CS753990
```

Figure 4-6 An *ERIC* Record [italics added]

ERIC also has two classes of descriptors: major (used for the primary focus) and minor (used for peripheral subject areas). Notice that the broad term *Communication Research* is assigned as a minor descriptor to this record. Because this practice is followed consistently by *ERIC* indexers, you can use this descriptor to narrow searches to the literature of this discipline. *ERIC* has document-type, year, and language fields; you can restrict your search to certain types of documents, publications in a particular language, and items published in a specified year or range of years.

When searching bibliographic databases, you may specify the field or fields to be searched. This gives you many possible access points and a great deal of flexibility. For example, you may elect to search only the title field, only major descriptors, a combination of title-abstracts-descriptors, and so on. Furthermore, in some databases you may specify whether you want to search a given field as an *exact phrase* or by *key word*. The difference can be significant. If you search the term "television" in the major descriptors field as an exact phrase, for instance, you would retrieve only records to which the descriptor "television" had been assigned. If, however, you searched "television" as a key word in the major descriptors field, you would retrieve all records in which "television" appeared as part of a descriptor, including these descriptors: "television commercials," "television curriculum," "television research," "television surveys," and "television viewing." Which way you elect to go—key word or exact phrase—will depend on what you are looking for and whether you wish to broaden or narrow your search. Web-based search interfaces typically offer guided Search screens that facilitate field-specific searching. Figure 4-7 shows what this type of screen would look like for an "attribution" key-word search.

■ TRUNCATION

When entering key-word terms, you may find that you want to enter several words that have the same root (for example, adolescent, adolescents, adolescence). It is possible to do this simply by typing each word connected with the OR operator, but it is a bit faster to truncate (shorten) the word to its root. Most search systems allow you to use a symbol to indicate that you wish to truncate a word. Here are some examples: adolescen*, adolescen?, adolescen$.

Check Help screens to see which truncation symbol a particular database uses. Of course, you must use truncation with caution. If you truncate a root too short, you will retrieve many irrelevant terms. For example, "auto" would retrieve not only "auto," "automobile," and "automotive," but also "automatic," "autobiography," and so on. It is almost always a good idea to use truncation to search for both the singular and plural form of terms. Another way of searching for alternate forms of terms is to use the *Word Index feature* of your search system.

■ WORD AND PHRASE INDEXES

Many databases have an Index feature that allows you to browse and select terms from an alphabetized list of words and phrases contained in the database

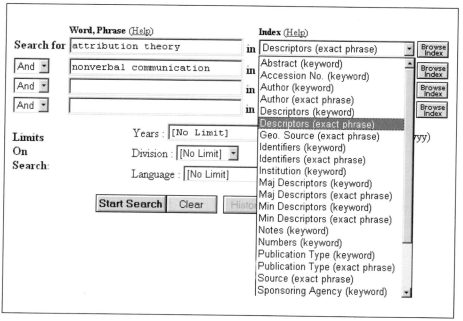

Figure 4-7 An *ERIC* Search Screen

as a whole or in a particular field. This is usually an as-is list: Don't be surprised when you find typos and misspellings. You can often use this feature to browse and select subject headings. Searching the names of authors can be particularly troublesome, due to the variation of first names and initials. Using the Browse feature can solve this problem.

■ CREATING AND REUSING SETS

As you enter search terms into some search systems, the results are displayed on the screen in numbered **sets** of records, or **hits**. For example, if you have separately entered the terms "television," "children," and "violence," the results displayed might look something like this:

set 1   6709   TELEVISION
set 2   2171   VIOLENCE
set 3   54547   CHILDREN

It is then possible to refer to these sets by set numbers and to combine them using AND, OR, and NOT operators. For example, if we AND-ed the preceding sets, we would receive the following result:

set 4   95   #1 and #2 and #3

The resulting set, #4, could then be modified and combined with other sets, as desired. We might, for example, limit our search to English-language books and journal articles published since 1990.

Other search systems might take you directly to a display of brief records, rather than to a listing of sets. Often these systems offer a History feature that allows you to review sets already created and to combine them in various ways using Boolean operators.

Of course, sets can also be created using parentheses to group terms connected by operators, as they are entered:

(sex-bias OR sex stereotypes) AND (television OR TV)

This search will give us only listings of records in which the terms "sex-bias" or "sex-stereotypes" appear that also mention "television OR TV."

SEARCH STRATEGIES: BOOLEAN SEARCHING

A well-designed **search strategy** will use several of these search options to search efficiently and effectively. Start by investigating the controlled vocabulary to see if there are descriptors for your concepts. If you have several from which to choose, pick the most specific available, enter them as search statements, and appropriately combine them with AND and OR operators. Then review the results. Depending on your objective, you may be able to stop here. If you retrieved too few citations, you will need to broaden your search. If you have located too many, you will want to narrow it. In either case, you have many options.

To narrow a search:

- Use the AND operator to add additional concepts, one at a time.
- Use field-specific search statements and the AND operator to limit your search (for example, by year, language, age groups, publication type).
- Consult the thesaurus and choose a more specific descriptor.

To broaden a search:

- Consult the thesaurus and choose a broader search descriptor.
- Use the OR operator to add synonyms.
- Reduce the number of concepts that are AND-ed.

As you attempt to refine your search, take full advantage of the interactive nature of computerized searching systems. By examining the records you retrieve, together with the assigned descriptors, you can determine whether you should drop or add search terms to achieve either a more precise or a more complete set of results.

As a sample search to illustrate these strategies, we'll search the *ERIC* database, using FirstSearch, to find reports dealing with the effects of television on children. This database includes records from 1966. Naturally, if we were to do a comprehensive search on this topic, we would need to search other databases in the field of communication and the social sciences, as well. If we followed our own advice, we would start by using *ERIC*'s Browse Index feature to investigate possible descriptors. To make this search closer to the way many students, researchers, and librarians actually behave, however, we'll plunge in with a key-word search statement. We enter our search statement on the initial search screen, using the "Subject (keyword)" option:

television AND children

The result is 3323 records retrieved.

Wow! We don't want to look through 3323 records, so it's time to narrow this search. One way to do so is to restrict the terms we used, "television AND children," to the descriptor field. (The "Subject keyword" option searches additional fields, such as title.) This should eliminate items that are only peripherally related to the topic, but we don't know what the exact descriptors are, so we'll search the descriptor field in key-word mode:

television AND children   in   "descriptors"

The result is 1351 records retrieved.

That's better, but it's still far too many citations to browse through. Perhaps we can narrow one of the descriptors. Let's look at some of the records we retrieved to find one that's right on the topic and then see which descriptors were assigned to it. After examining several records, we decide that the descriptor "television viewing" comes closest to our intent. We also notice that "children" is itself a descriptor, but that a narrower term, such as "kindergarten children," is often assigned to a record instead. This means that we should continue to use the "descriptors" key-word search rather than opting for the "descriptor exact phrase" search, in order not to miss many pertinent records. So, we enter:

television viewing AND children   in   "descriptors"

The result is 790 records retrieved.

More progress, but it looks as though this topic was just too broadly conceived to begin with. It's time to do some serious thinking about how to narrow it. We move to the Advanced Search screen, which will make it easier to use the FirstSearch Index Browse feature to investigate possible descriptors. We come up with these alternatives:

- Add another concept ("academic achievement" or "violence" are two possibilities).
- Narrow the "children" concept by restricting it to "young children."
  The results of each option:

television viewing AND children AND academic achievement in "descriptors (keyword)"

Results: 23

television viewing AND young children   in   "descriptors (keyword)"

Results: 105

television viewing AND children AND violence in "descriptor (keyword)"

Results: 130

The first result is puzzling: Only 23 records were retrieved for our search "television viewing AND children AND academic achievement." There must be more published on that topic in the education literature. Looking at our search, we realize that the term "children" is somewhat redundant. It may seem odd, but this term would not automatically be assigned to every publication that relates to children. Let's take it out. When we do so, our search retrieves 142 records. That sounds better, but we would have to examine some records to decide for sure. We'll let you decide which of these options you would choose.

As you can see, there are many different ways to proceed in virtually every search. Furthermore, at any point you could opt to limit your search by language, year, or document type. Limiting an *ERIC* search to the document type "research/technical report" would be particularly useful if you were looking only for research studies.

■ NATURAL LANGUAGE SEARCHING

Natural language searching is the basic search option for many search engines, as well as for the *Encyclopedia Britannica*. It is also available as an option for an increasing number of bibliographic search systems as well.

In a natural language mode, searchers are encouraged simply to type in words, phrases, and even entire questions that relate to their topic. The system interprets what we enter and retrieves what often seems like an impossibly large set of results, ranked by relevancy (see below).

Such an approach is of course a complete departure from the Boolean methods usually used to search bibliographic databases, which involve a much more structured approach. A natural language query entered in a standard bibliographic search system would usually retrieve no records at all. A Boolean search system takes everything entered literally, so it can't cope with extraneous words (*is, what, where, be, interested, find*, and so on). A natural language search, on the other hand, will just ignore what it can't use and will attempt to interpret what is entered.

Which system is better? The answer depends on many factors. It seems that both systems can work well, and one type of searching might be better than another in particular situations. For comprehensive results, it's advantageous to try both. For many topics, relevant results will be retrieved with both approaches, with surprisingly little overlap. That was the conclusion of librarians at Colorado State University, who systematically compared the results of traditional Boolean and natural language searches done in EBSCOhost's *Academic Search* database (Tomaiuolo & Packer, 1998).

■ SEARCH STRATEGIES FOR THE WORLD WIDE WEB

Many of the strategies and tools traditionally used to search bibliographic databases are also applicable to searching the World Wide Web. You have already learned about the basic tools. Boolean operators, adjacency operators, and truncation can be used in most search engines, often on their Advanced Search screens. Implied Boolean operators (+, –) and phrase searching using double quotes have become standard features of search engines (and are now used in some bibliographic databases). But the WWW differs in important ways from bibliographic databases. Different approaches are necessary.

Every search engine creates its own version of a web database. This process is usually carried out automatically, using "robots" and "spiders" that search the Web automatically and build the database specified by a particular search engine. For example, some search engines index only certain parts of a web page, whereas others index the entire page. Some index images, such as photographs, in more useful ways. Others strive for comprehensiveness and include many more documents than others. When you are deciding which engine to search, you should take these characteristics into account. It's also important to realize that the database you are searching is not the Web as it exists at the moment. It's the version created at an earlier moment (days or weeks earlier), when the spiders and robots last made their rounds. Of course, no human indexer is involved in the process of building these databases, and a controlled vocabulary is not available (although web-page creators themselves may include key words as metatags, to help retrieval). Key-word searching is required, so the liberal use of synonyms pays off.

Many search engines create records with the equivalent of the fields we have seen in bibliographic database records. Fields typically include title (the "official" page title that appears at the top of your browser), domain (*edu, com, gov,* for example), and other parts of the URL (host, file names, directories). Some search engines allow field-specific searching, which can be helpful in narrowing results.

Search engines sort results by their **relevancy**, as determined by the search engine. Many factors are used to determine relevancy. Where does the search term appear (title, body, URL, and the like)? How many of the terms in the search statement appear in the document? How often do they appear? How close are they to one another? A ranking algorithm (particular to each search engine) takes the answers to these and many other questions into account and, in a somewhat mysterious way, comes up with a ranked listing. The items at the top of the list should, in theory, be highly relevant, whereas those at the bottom may include only one of the search terms. Thus, a huge number of results is normal and should not be dismaying. It's assumed that only the results near the top will be of interest. The searcher's challenge is to ensure not just that documents be retrieved, but that those most wanted appear near the top of the list. These tips can help:

- Use several synonyms (including variant spellings) for the most important concept. This will give more weight to that concept.
- Enter the most important concepts first. They are weighted more heavily than terms at the end of a statement.
- Use terms specific to your topic. If possible, include unique terms (distinctive names, abbreviations, acronyms).
- Avoid broad terms.
- Always enclose phrases in double quotes.
- In general, use lowercase, although using the uppercase of proper nouns can be helpful in some search engines.
- Truncate terms.
- Use the implied Boolean operators (+, –) to indicate terms and phrases that must be included or excluded.
- Use Boolean operators (AND, OR, NOT) and parentheses when possible, often from an advanced search option. As usual, use OR to combine synonyms; use AND to combine concepts. (Some search engines allow Boolean; others do not.)

The bottom line is that search engines vary a great deal. They offer different features and capabilities. To use them most effectively, it pays to look at their documentation and become aware of their peculiarities. Fortunately, websites are available that attempt to do that for you. Going to one of these sites can help you decide which search engines to use for a particular purpose and alert you to particular syntax used by each. Two academic sites that keep track of and present the features of most popular search engines are those maintained at the University of Albany Libraries

<**http://www.albany.edu/library/internet/**>

and at the University of California, Berkeley Teaching Library

<**http://www.lib.berkeley.edu/TeachingLib/Guides/Internet/FindInfo.html**>

If you run your search in different search engines, you will invariably get different results. Therefore, it pays to use more than one. Metasearch engines, which search several search engines at once, are helpful here. They are especially useful at the beginning of a search, to see what types of things are readily retrieved on your topic. Popular examples (in 1999) include MetaCrawler, Dogpile, All4one, Inference Find, and Profusion. Because these tools send a search out to a variety of engines with varying syntax, it works best to use a simple search statement, probably combining two concepts, with one of them being a phrase in double quotes.

USING YOUR SEARCH RESULTS

The final product of most searches is a printed list of sources. If the databases you've searched have included full-text documents, you have probably printed a number of these. You have a couple of other options, as well. The first is to e-mail the results to yourself. Many web-based search systems allow this. Another option is to save your results to your computer's hard drive or to a floppy disk. If you have an appropriate bibliography-management program, such as EndNote, ProCite, or Reference Manager, you can add the citations you've retrieved to others you've located and entered in the database, either manually or through **downloading**. In this way, you can create your own personal on-line database.

A bibliography-management program should allow you to add not only your own descriptors and notes to individual records but also sort your records, selectively retrieve and print them, use them with a word processing program, and so on. Of course, such downloading practices do raise questions of copyright, and database vendors and producers have varying policies about downloading, which you should explore. It also raises the possibility of plagiarism, either from the original article or from the abstract. These abstracts are written by others and are copyrighted, so you cannot use sections of the abstract without using quotation marks and citing the abstract as the source.

Citing abstracts in this manner, though, is not typically done. The abstract itself is incomplete and merely provides a summary of someone else's interpretation of the original publication. In other words, the abstract should help you identify a publication as being relevant to your project, but you then must locate and read the actual publication (for example, journal article) if you are going to use it in your own literature review or research project.

As with other search aids, then, the final step in using a bibliographic database is retrieving the actual documents. After exploring the resources of your library to determine which publications are readily available, you will probably want to use your library's interlibrary loan service to obtain any other sources you need that your library does not have. Many records for journals will include a special number, called an ISSN (International Standard Serial Number). This number may help your library staff quickly identify and retrieve the document you need. Citations may also provide other useful numbers. Ask the interlibrary loan staff which numbers to include on your request.

Another convenient avenue for retrieving materials is available for those library users fortunate to live in states that have created statewide on-line systems that allow users access to the on-line catalogs of all or most of that state's college and university libraries, as well as to various periodical databases. These systems may allow users to initiate transactions on-line to borrow materials from other libraries, thus eliminating the need to fill out interlibrary-loan-request cards. Often, materials can be delivered using these systems in a matter of days.

Many database producers and distributors offer an additional service to help you secure publications not owned by your library. Called document delivery services, they allow you to order publications on-line for delivery by fax or through the mail. CARL's UnCover and many of OCLC's (**Online Computer Library Center**) FirstSearch databases provide such document delivery services. The fees charged for such services, which include a copyright charge, may often be charged to a credit card.

MEDIATED SEARCHING

Although most libraries now make a variety of electronic databases available to their users to search on their own at workstations within and outside the library, hundreds of more databases are available for remote searching through such vendors as DIALOG. Libraries may, for example, opt to provide access to databases that are not widely used on their campuses only through mediated searching because it is much less expensive to pay a per-search fee than to license a database for unlimited use. Using these databases often requires special training, so they are made available through a mediated **on-line search service**. In this situation, you would relate your needs to the librarian searcher who would enter your request, discuss the results with you, revise the request, and so on. Typically, users will make an appointment with a librarian to discuss their search topics and will be present while the librarian performs the search. Students may be asked to pay some or all of the on-line fees associated with such searches. If you have questions about the availability of additional computerized databases, ask the reference librarian about this service.

SUMMARY

Methods used by communication professionals to conduct documentary research are changing rapidly. Using computer-based sources has become essential. Many necessary tools for communication research are available only in electronic formats and through electronic networks. A computerized database stores information on a magnetic or optical storage medium so that the information can be retrieved via a microcomputer or a computer terminal. Databases may be classified as being bibliographic, directory, statistical, or source.

To use computerized databases effectively, researchers must understand basic searching concepts and acquire skill in using controlled vocabularies, key words, field-specific searching, word and phrase indexes, and logical and proximity operators. They should understand the differences between Boolean searching and natural language searching and be able to use them both for comprehensive retrieval.

Documentation should be used to gain familiarity with the structure of databases and the features of search systems. On-line Help screens, tutorials, and printed manuals are usually available. A few minutes spent exploring such documentation will save time in the long run and help you retrieve more relevant search results.

In general, the most effective search strategy is to start with the most specific descriptors available, examine the results, and add search statements to broaden or narrow the search as necessary. To narrow a search, add additional concepts, one at a time, using the AND operator. You can also limit search results by publication year, language, document type, and so on. To broaden a search, use a less specific descriptor and/or add synonymous terms using the OR operator. Computer databases help researchers identify pertinent publications, but the actual document must then be located and fully examined before it is used in a research project.

Using search engines to search the World Wide Web poses special challenges. Search engines vary in terms of search features, size, speed, comprehensiveness, indexing, and the algorithms used to rank results. Boolean search strategies can often be used from advanced Search screens. Searchers should adjust their search strategies to an environment in which results will be ranked by relevancy. Most searches should be run in more than one search engine, and the use of metasearch engines is recommended at initial stages.

REFERENCES

Barker, J. (Maint.). (1997/1999, January 25). Finding information on the Internet: A tutorial. In UC Berkeley Library Internet Resources [On-line]. Available: http://www.lib.berkeley.edu/TeachingLib/Guides/Internet/FindInfo.html (1999, April 25).

Cohen, L. (Maint.). (1999, April). *University at Albany Libraries Internet tutorials* [On-line]. Available: http://www.albany.edu/library/internet/ (1999, April 25).

Gale Directory of Databases (2 vols.). (1993–). Detroit: Gale Research.

Tomaiuolo, N. G., & Packer, J. (1998). Maximizing relevant retrieval. *Online, 22*(6), 57–59.

EXAMPLES

CHRIS uses information in this chapter to prepare for database searching. The best strategy seems to be to AND the term "ethics" with a group of speech terms: "speech," "speaking," "speechwriting," "speechwriters," "ghostwriting," and "collaboration" (these latter terms will be OR-ed together). Some of the terms could be truncated to simplify things and make sure he doesn't miss anything (for example, speech*, ghostwrit*, ethic*).

FELECIA'S initial investigation of voice mail tells her that the two words must be considered together, as a phrase, because "voice" or "mail" produces too many bad hits. The topic, being relatively new, might allow her to search selectively in the literature of the last 5–10 years.

MARIA has now read several summary articles about attribution and the term seems to be used consistently in the literature. Because many articles point to Heider as the originator of the term, this information might come in handy when needing to narrow the term in upcoming searches.

ORLANDO'S paper on parasocial interaction will be using the upcoming access tools and databases extensively. Because it is spelled in different ways, Orlando makes a note of the variations found: "para-social" and "parasocial." Also, references to the first use of the term by Horton and Wohl in 1956 will be important when searching the journal indexes.

KAT, CALVIN, ROCKY, and **MICHELLE'S** training idea in the area of conflict resolution results in too many different terms for conflict: *fighting, arguing, conflict management, conflict resolution, disagreements,* and so on. They keep a running list of these and make a note to use a thesaurus whenever they can in searching databases to identify the relevant subject headings/descriptors for each.

EXERCISES

1. When a descriptor is not available for your topic and key words must be used, take care to find all possible alternative phrasings and spellings. For each of the following concepts, make a list of at least 10 synonymous key words or phrases: *role playing, executives, news media, press interviews, minorities,* and *gender*.
2. In your research paper, you want to investigate the relationship between teachers' communication styles, gender or ethnic background of students, and student performance. You have decided to limit your research to middle schools. You have entered a number of terms and now have the following sets:

#1	minorities	#10	gender differences
#2	educational performance	#11	student performance
#3	teachers	#12	middle schools
#4	blacks	#13	ethnic groups
#5	females	#14	males
#6	native americans	#15	african americans
#7	junior high school	#16	mexican americans
#8	communication styles	#17	academic achievement
#9	hispanics	#18	asian americans

Assuming that you wish to use all these terms in your search, write a single search statement that will incorporate them all. Use set numbers to refer to each term, connecting sets as appropriate with AND and OR operators. Use parentheses to group terms, for example: (#1 OR #2 OR #7) AND (#6 OR #8) AND (#11 AND #15).

If you retrieve too many citations, how could you narrow this search? If you retrieve too few citations, how could you broaden it?

3. Now plan searches for the topic in Exercise 2 in each of the following databases: *PsycLIT* (or *PsycINFO*), *ERIC*, and *Sociofile*. Use the thesaurus for each database to identify relevant descriptors and list search statements in the order in which you would enter them.

4. Try one or more versions of the search statement that you developed in Exercise 3 in a comprehensive, interdisciplinary periodical database licensed by your library. Examine the first 10 records you retrieve and adjust your search accordingly. How did you change your search statement? Compare the results you retrieved with your previous results.

5. Complete the following Search Preparation Form for your topic.

Topic: _____

_____

	Concept 1	AND	Concept 2	AND	Concept 3
S					
y	———	———	———	———	———
n	OR		OR		OR
o					
n					
y	———	———	———	———	———
m	OR		OR		OR
s					
	———	———	———	———	———

6. What type of resources relevant to your topic might be available on web-sites? Think in terms of particular organizations, types of organizations, people, programs, government reports, archival materials, and so on. Make a list of terms you could use in a search engine to retrieve web documents. Select an appropriate metasearch engine and two individual search engines, at least one of which accepts search statements written with Boolean operators and parentheses. Search your topic in all three, adjusting your search strategy. What was your initial search statement? What was your final search statement? Compare the results you retrieved from the three search engines.

part two

Communication
Research Sources

In this part of the book, we identify current, important, and useful communication and communication-related sources in print or available electronically. In the next four chapters, we discuss a variety of general and specific research sources. We describe handbooks, textbooks, encyclopedias, and annual reviews in Chapter 5. These are useful for defining, refining, and developing a research topic. The bibliographies, guides, and indexes described in Chapter 6 can help further develop the research topic or question. In Chapter 7 we discuss the periodical literature of communication: scholarly journals and professional or trade magazines. The articles found in these publications present current conceptual and practical knowledge. Finally, in Chapter 8 we describe specific, factual information sources such as collections, statistical sources, government publications, yearbooks, directories, dictionaries, and manuals.

In each chapter we annotate several sources. We consider these to be some of the more important, useful, or representative sources of the type discussed. The end-of-chapter exercises refer you to some of these sources and ask you to use them. Clues to their use are found in the annotations or in the questions themselves.

The annotated sources certainly do not constitute the totality of sources of that genre. Many additional and valuable sources are listed at the end of each chapter and on our home page. Several of these can help you select, refine, and develop an interesting research topic and project. Add new sources in the book margins and at the ends of chapters when your find especially useful ones. You'll then be able to refer to these sources whenever you undertake a research project in the future.

chapter 5

General Sources

In the preceding chapters you've become acquainted with the multi-faceted nature of communication and with systematic research search strategies to address communication topics. Now it's time to examine more closely the various communication sources that are available in or accessible from most college and university libraries.

You may be working on a literature review or research project and have not yet fully identified a specific topic or research question. To gain an understanding of topics that others find interesting or relevant, browse through some general sources, which may help you formulate or develop your own research topic. If you already know the topic you wish to investigate, these general reference works often have useful bibliographies that can lead you to sources specifically related to your research question.

After you examine these sources, list them on bibliography and search-record cards as a reminder that you've already searched through them for references to pertinent materials. As we have stressed, this action can save much time, especially because there will be so many sources that are potentially valuable to your research goal.

Just like many other disciplines, communication is a rapidly evolving field. New research results, new applications, and changes in professional practices often make it difficult to get a grasp of the state of generally accepted knowledge in a given field. Even the vocabulary keeps changing. To alleviate this problem, authorities in all disciplines create handbooks, subject encyclopedias, and subject dictionaries. These sources summarize generally accepted findings or practices in a field at a particular time. In so doing, they provide a useful reference point when you begin researching a subject area.

HANDBOOKS

The term **handbook** is often used to categorize two distinctive types of publications. One type, a manual, is a compact book of facts. We will discuss manuals in Chapter 8 when we deal with other compilations of information. The other type of handbook, the scholarly or subject handbook, is more general in nature and helps orient communication scholars to current issues and topics.

Scholarly handbooks provide a comprehensive summary of past research and thematic viewpoints in a particular discipline. They are generally broad based and treat a great number of topics. It is difficult for the editors of these volumes to keep them current because of the breadth of topics covered and the delays in publication time. Thus, handbooks are soon dated, although they provide important background information about knowledge and development of many relevant topics.

One handbook outside the communication discipline that communication researchers find valuable for background information, even though they must always look for other sources to give perspective on new developments, is:

Gilbert, D. T., Fiske, S. T., & Lindzey, G. (Eds.). (1994). *The handbook of social psychology* (4th ed., 2 vols.). Boston: McGraw-Hill.

■   Two volumes contain independent articles (each with a lengthy bibliography) summarizing the state of the art in social psychological theory and research. Volume 1 provides a historical perspective, explains theories and models of social psychology (for example, attitude change, motivation, child development, and gender), and reviews research methods, including attitude measurement, quantitative methods, experimentation, survey methods, and data analysis.

Volume 2 contains articles on altruism, aggression, small groups, language use and social behavior, personality, attraction, intergroup relations, organizations, social influence and conformity, health behavior, social movements, psychology and law, opinion and politics, and cultural psychology. Indexes appear at the end of each volume.

A somewhat older handbook examines several aspects of the field of communication: ·

Berger, C. R., & Chaffee, S. H. (Eds.). (1987). *Handbook of communication science.* Newbury Park, CA: Sage.

■   This handbook synthesizes research in communication. It is divided into five sections: overviews, levels of analysis, functions, contexts, and conclusions. Topics include interpersonal, family, marital, organizational, mass, campaign, and cross-cultural communication, as well as language, nonverbal signals, persuasion, conflict, children, health care, and public opinion. The overview chapters provide an introduction to the communication field.

Similar handbooks concentrate on more specific content areas. Sometimes these handbooks are onetime works; others may be revised and reissued. One recent useful handbook examines organizational communication:

Jablin, F. M., & Putnam, L. L. (Eds.). (2000). *The new handbook of organizational communication*. Newbury Park, CA: Sage.

■   This handbook offers a multidisciplinary view of organizational communication issues, contexts, structures, and processes. The 21 chapters cover such topics as communication technologies, culture, networks, collaborative work, leadership, identity, conflict, decision making, assimilation, and power. There are also chapters on quantitative and qualitative research and interaction analysis.

Another handbook updates writings in political communication. It intends to move research beyond traditional ways of looking at the persuasion of voters to newer contexts and views of political communication:

Swanson, D. L., & Nimmo, D. D. (Eds.). (1990). *New directions in political communication: A resource book.* Newbury Park, CA: Sage.

■   This handbook examines the role of communication in politics. Besides an introductory chapter that considers the present state and future directions of research, nine other chapters are divided into four sections: foundations of political communication, understanding political messages, the institutional perspective on political communication, and recent political communication research. Each essay contains a series of references. The last section provides a selective bibliography of research published within the last 10 years.

Handbooks have been developed for several areas of the discipline. One handbook examines dimensions of intercultural communication:

Gudykunst, W. B., Newmark, E., & Asante, M. K. (Eds.). (1994). *Handbook of international and intercultural communication* (2nd ed.). Newbury Park, CA: Sage.

■   Communication specialists, psychologists, and anthropologists review the state of research in international and intercultural communication. They attempt to provide a framework for future work in the field. The essays provide overviews and address processes, effects, and contexts. An index provides access to subjects and authors.

Another communication handbook provides an overview of group communication:

Frey, L. R. (Ed.), Gouran, D. S., & Poole, M. S. (Assoc. Eds.). (1999). *The handbook of group communication theory and research.* Thousand Oaks, CA: Sage.

■   Communication specialists and researchers review the present state of research in group communication. They attempt to provide a framework for future work in the field. The essays are arranged in six sections: Foundations, Individuals and Group Communication, Task and Relational Group Communication, Group Communication Processes, Group Communication Facilitation, and Contexts and Application. An index provides access to subjects and authors.

Another handbook in the communication discipline is a revised edition of a specialized handbook in interpersonal communication:

Knapp, M. L., & Miller, G. R. (Eds.). (1994). *Handbook of interpersonal communication* (2nd ed.). Thousand Oaks, CA: Sage.

■   This handbook summarizes the development and state of theory and research in interpersonal communication. The authors discuss approaches to basic issues in studying interpersonal communication, fundamental units, processes and functions, and contexts. Chapters cover such topics as language, communicator characteristics, nonverbal signals, power, influence, competence, and communication in work, social, health, and family contexts. Each essay contains a lengthy list of references.

Communication researchers, particularly those in organizational communication, advertising, and public relations, often find subject handbooks from business to be useful. These handbooks usually offer a practical, rather than scholarly, approach to their subjects. Although they may lack extensive bibliographies, their concise explanations of accepted practices, procedures, and concepts in a given area are useful when you start a research paper or other communication project. Among the handbooks available in marketing, advertising, and public relations is:

Dilenschneider, R. L., Forrestal, D. J., & Darrow, R. W. (1994). *The Dartnell public relations handbook* (3rd ed., Rev.). Chicago: Dartnell.

■   This handbook describes different aspects of the public relations profession, the work of public relations professionals in various fields, and methods of internal communication. A special section is devoted to the health-care field. Many chapters offer short case studies of exemplary public relations campaigns. A detailed subject index is provided.

We list other scholarly and subject handbooks from communication and related disciplines at the end of this chapter. These handbooks are valuable for selecting and refining research topics. Their content also provides specific information for developing a literature review, research paper, or prospectus.

TEXTBOOKS

Textbooks are handy aids when defining and refining research questions. They seek to survey information about a field of study and to present the fundamentals of a subject in an easy-to-understand manner. Some textbooks are edited collections of writings in a subject area and are quite similar to handbooks. In fact, it is sometimes not an easy task to distinguish some textbooks from scholarly handbooks. At times, instructors may even use handbooks as class texts.

In basic textbooks the authors offer a brief summary of existing knowledge along with their conclusions about the essential points derived from communication theory and research in that area. The bibliographies at the ends of chapters can be helpful for locating useful books and articles about the subject. However, these bibliographies are often limited in scope. When using textbooks, keep in mind that, as with all printed materials, there is a gap between the time the book is written and the time it is printed. As secondary sources, it is usually best to use textbooks to acquire an overview or general orientation to a topic and to gather a few reference sources.

Several communication-related textbooks are listed at the end of this chapter. The list is quite selective and by no means represents the multitude of communication-related textbooks published each year.

ENCYCLOPEDIAS

Encyclopedias are all-embracing compilations of information that provide a multifaceted approach to a subject. The essays within encyclopedias generally have bibliographies that can be used to find other general sources about the topic. These bibliographies may also identify specific sources that can give background for narrower aspects of the topic. It may not be too helpful, though, to consult general encyclopedias like the *Encyclopedia Britannica* unless you initially know very little about your topic.

Subject encyclopedias contain overview articles summarizing what is known about topics in a specific discipline. The first communication subject encyclopedia was published in 1989 and has been a useful source over the last decade:

> Barnouw, E. (Ed.). (1989). *International encyclopedia of communications* (4 vols.). New York: Oxford University Press.
>
> ■   This encyclopedia contains over 500 articles on various facets of communication. It provides interdisciplinary and international coverage. Major topics include advertising and public relations, animal communication, arts, communication research, computer era, education, international communication, journalism, language and linguistics, media, motion pictures, music, nonverbal communication, photography, political communication, radio, speech, television, theater, and theories of communication. Articles are illustrated and include bibliographies of general books and textbooks. A comprehensive index lists concepts, terms, names, and titles.

A legal encyclopedia is another type of subject encyclopedia. It is a useful source when you are researching topics of communication law, freedom of speech, and debate. Legal encyclopedias are typically written in narrative form and are nonevaluative in approach. They best serve as case finders and starting points in searching the law. They generally include a statement of the applicable law, citations to appropriate cases, and analytical and subject indexes. Good encyclopedias also have frequent supplements.

The two principal legal encyclopedias of national scope are *Corpus Juris Secundum* and *American Jurisprudence Second* (second series). State and local legal encyclopedias are also available.

When first reading the literature of an academic discipline, you may encounter a whole new language. The words may be familiar, but many times the meanings seem to be different. Although we discuss most dictionaries in Chapter 8 as largely being information manuals, a **subject dictionary** can be an abbreviated type of subject encyclopedia. Subject dictionaries may help clarify your understanding of new or unique terms and lead you to important references.

Subject dictionaries list and define basic and specialized terms in a particular field. They also provide meanings for abbreviations, jargon, and slang. Most disciplines (for example, education, psychology, and political science) have comprehensive dictionaries that define terms used in those fields. Although somewhat dated, one dictionary that provides broad coverage of communication terms is:

DeVito, J. A. (1986). *The communication handbook: A dictionary.* New York: Harper & Row.

■   This is perhaps the only dictionary that addresses several areas of communication. Besides providing brief definitions for communication terminology, it gives over 100 essays for major communication areas such as interpersonal communication, language, mass media, nonverbal communication, organizational communication, persuasion, public speaking, and small-group communication. The dictionary gives references to seminal articles and books for additional information.

ANNUAL REVIEWS AND SERIES

Besides handbooks and encyclopedias, other general sources will help you find information or define a research question more clearly. Communication, like many other disciplines, is experiencing a surge in research activity. This expansion is so rapid that keeping abreast of what others in the various specialty areas are researching is sometimes difficult. **Annual reviews** provide yearly summaries of current research activities. They are useful for selecting and refining a research topic or question, finding information and sources, and updating bibliographies. Because some of the sources cited in annual reviews may be outside your usual reading area, reading annual reviews helps to broaden your search strategy.

Annual reviews, then, are vehicles for gauging the level of research activity in various areas of communication. They also update research and are helpful later in the research process when you're looking for recent information and bibliographic citations.

Some annual reviews provide updates of current research and thinking in a variety of content areas. Others focus on one particular content area that changes each year. One annual review of the former type is *Communication Yearbook*. It contains current research and writings in several related content areas.

Communication Yearbook. (1977–). Thousand Oaks, CA: Sage.

■ This annual review is an official publication of the International Communication Association (ICA). Volumes before 1988 presented two different types of articles: reviews and commentaries, covering general communication topics, and selected studies, including research papers in each subfield (for example, interpersonal, organizational, and mass communication), competitively selected and presented at the annual meeting of the ICA. Early editions also included overviews of developments within the subfields during that year. From 1988 to 1994 the *Yearbook* offered original essays and commentaries reflecting conceptual developments across the communication discipline. Starting in 1995 the *Yearbook* refocused to feature reviews of the literature.

Reviews and research studies contain valuable bibliographic sources. Examine the table of contents to determine the broader chapter topics and use the subject index at the back to locate references to narrower topics. There is also an index by author.

Another annual review focuses on information systems, communication uses and effects, and control of communication and information:

Progress in Communication Sciences. (1979–). Stamford, CT: Ablex.

■ Each annual volume contains 7 to 10 review essays on topics in most subareas of communication. Over the years, essays have focused on broadcast regulations, grapevines, communication networks, children's television, political campaigns, nonverbal communication, communication competence, gender, statistics, telecommunications, persuasion, intercultural communication, ethnography, and many other topics too numerous to list here. Each volume has a subject and author index.

Series examine new topics each year, focus on research related to those specific subjects, and often have different titles. The articles in each volume are reports of original research or theoretical pieces. Sage Publications has published a series (which it calls an "annual review") of communication research. These volumes are helpful in identifying research topics, finding contemporary information, and broadening your search strategy.

Sage Annual Reviews of Communication Research, which ceased publication in 1994, contained many useful volumes. Topics ranged from mass and political communication to persuasion, interpersonal, and nonverbal communication. More recent volumes focused on media audiences, critical perspectives on narrative, negotiation, culture, information campaigns, and message effects.

Other series that may contain helpful reference sources are listed at the end of this chapter. Several of these series, including *Sage Annual Reviews of Communication Research, Media and Society, LEA's Communication Series,* and Guilford's *Communication Series*, are known as publishers' series. This means volumes in the series have different titles and may not appear regularly. Because many libraries list these works only by the title of the individual volumes and not by the series title, identifying and locating the specific volumes that make up a particular series can be difficult. If you wish to find individual works in a series, check *WorldCat* (see Chapter 6) for series titles.

These sources, then, provide a general understanding of the communication field, as well as specific interests, concerns, and methodologies of communication researchers. They are most helpful when identifying a specific area within communication that may be of interest for a term paper, literature review, or research prospectus. In many instances, handbooks, yearbooks, and annual reviews can also serve as vehicles for widening a search strategy and locating additional and, in some cases, recent sources about a chosen communication topic.

SELECTED SOURCES

■ HANDBOOKS

Andersen, P. A., & Guerrero, L. K. (1998). *Handbook of communication and emotion: Research, theory, application, and contexts.* San Diego: Academic Press.

Berger, C. R., & Chaffee, S. H. (Eds.). (1987). *Handbook of communication science.* Newbury Park, CA: Sage.

Christ, W. G. (Ed.). (1994). *Assessing communication education: A handbook for media, speech, and theatre educators.* Hillsdale, NJ: Erlbaum.

Clegg, S. R., Hardy, C., & Nord, W. R. (1996). *The handbook of organization studies.* Thousand Oaks, CA: Sage.

Cragan, J. F., & Wright, D. W. (1996). *Theory and research in small group communication* (2nd ed.). Edina, MN: Burgess.

Craig, R. L. (1996). *The ASTD training and development handbook: A guide to human resource development* (4th ed.). New York: McGraw-Hill.

Dervin, B., Grossberg, L., O'Keefe, B., & Wartella, E. (Eds.). (1989). *Rethinking communication* (2 vols.). Newbury Park, CA: Sage.

Dilenschneider, R. L., Forrestal, D. J., & Darrow, R. W. (1994). *The Dartnell public relations handbook* (3rd ed., Rev.). Chicago: Dartnell.

Duck, S. (Ed.). (1997). *Handbook of personal relationships: Theory, research and interventions* (2nd ed.). New York: Wiley.

Dunnette, M. D., Triandis, H. C., & Hough, L. M. (1994). *Handbook of industrial and organizational psychology* (2nd ed., 4 vols.). Palo Alto, CA: Consulting Psychologists Press.

Frey, L. R. (Ed.), Gouran, D. S., & Poole, M. S. (Assoc. Eds.). (1999). *The handbook of group communication theory and research.* Thousand Oaks, CA: Sage.

Garnett, J. L., & Kouzmin, A. (1997). *Handbook of administrative communication.* New York: Marcel Dekker.

Gehring, W. D. (Ed.). (1988). *Handbook of American film genres.* New York: Greenwood Press.

Gilbert, D. T., Fiske, S. T., & Lindzey, G. (Eds.). (1994). *The handbook of social psychology* (4th ed., 2 vols.). Boston: McGraw-Hill.

Giles, D., & Robinson, W. P. (1992). *Handbook of language and social psychology* (2nd ed.). Chichester, UK: Wiley.

Goldhaber, G. M., & Barnett, G. A. (Eds.). (1988). *Handbook of organizational communication.* Norwood, NJ: Ablex.

Goodin, R. E., & Klingemann, H. (Eds.). (1996). *A new handbook of political science.* New York: Oxford University Press.

Gudykunst, W. B., Newmark, E., & Asante, M. K. (Eds.). (1994). *Handbook of international and intercultural communication* (2nd ed.). Newbury Park, CA: Sage.

Hare, A. P., Blumberg, H. H., Davies, M. F., & Kent, M. V. (1994). *Small group research: A handbook.* Norwood, NJ: Ablex.

Hargie, O. (1997). *A handbook of communication skills* (2nd ed.). London: Routledge.

Hess, B. B., & Ferree, M. M. (Eds.). (1987). *Analyzing gender: A handbook of social science research.* Newbury Park, CA: Sage.

Higgins, E. T., & Kruglanski, A. W. (Eds.). (1996). *Social psychology: Handbook of basic principles.* New York: Guilford Press.

Hurst, B. (1996). *The handbook of communication skills* (2nd ed.). London: Kogan Page.

Inge, M. T. (Ed.). (1989). *Handbook of American popular culture* (2nd ed., 3 vols.). New York: Greenwood Press.

Jablin, F. M., & Putnam, L. L. (Eds.). (2000). *The new handbook of organizational communication.* Newbury Park, CA: Sage.

Jonassen, D. H. (Ed.). (1996). *Handbook of research on educational communications and technology.* New York: Macmillan Library Reference.

Knapp, M. L., & Miller, G. R. (Eds.). (1994). *Handbook of interpersonal communication* (2nd ed.). Thousand Oaks, CA: Sage.

Kreps, G. L., & O'Hair, D. (Eds.). (1995). *Communication and health outcomes.* Cresskill, NJ: Hampton Press.

Landis, D., & Bhagat, R. S. (1996). *Handbook of intercultural training* (2nd ed.). Thousand Oaks, CA: Sage.

Lesly, P. (Ed.). (1998). *Lesly's handbook of public relations and communications* (5th ed.). Lincolnwood, IL: Contemporary Books.

Levy, S. J., Frerichs, G. R., & Gordon, H. L. (Eds.). (1994). *The Dartnell marketing manager's handbook* (3rd ed.). Chicago: Dartnell.

March, J. G., & Brief, A. P. (Eds.). (1987). *Handbook of organizations.* New York: Garland.

Medhurst, M. J. (Ed.). (1999). *A rhetorical history of the United States: Significant moments in American public discourse* (10 vols.). East Lansing: Michigan State University Press.

Miller, J. L., & Eimas, P. D. (Eds.). (1995). *Handbook of perception and cognition* (2nd ed.). San Diego: Academic Press.

Noth, W. (1990). *Handbook of semiotics.* Bloomington: Indiana University Press.

Nussbaum, J. F., & Coupland, J. (Eds.). (1995). *The handbook of communication and aging research.* Mahwah, NJ: Erlbaum.

Phillips, G. M., & Wood, J. T. (Eds.). (1990). *Speech communication: Essays to commemorate the 75th anniversary of the Speech Communication Association.* Carbondale: Southern Illinois University Press.

Ruch, W. (1989). *International handbook of corporate communication*. Jefferson, NC: McFarland.

Smelser, N. J. (Ed.). (1988). *Handbook of sociology*. Newbury Park, CA: Sage.

Spitzberg, B. H., & Cupach, W. R. (1989). *Handbook of interpersonal competence research*. New York: Springer-Verlag.

Swanson, D. L., & Nimmo, D. D. (Eds.). (1990). *New directions in political communication: A resource book*. Newbury Park, CA: Sage.

Swanson, J. L. (Ed.). (1998). *First Amendment law handbook*. St. Paul, MN: West.

Vangelisti, A. L., Daly, J. A., & Friedrich, G. W. (Eds.). (1999). *Teaching communication: Theory, research, and methods* (2nd ed.). Mahwah, NJ: Erlbaum.

Wells, A. (1997). *World broadcasting: A comparative view*. Stamford, CT: Ablex.

■ TEXTBOOKS

Agee, W. K., Ault, P. H., & Emery, E. (1997). *Introduction to mass communications* (12th ed.). New York: Longman.

Alexander, A., Owers, J., & Carveth, R. (Eds.). (1998). *Media economics: Theory and practice* (2nd ed.). Mahwah, NJ: Erlbaum.

Allen, R. C. (1992). *Channels of discourse, reassembled: Television and contemporary criticism* (2nd ed.). London: Routledge.

Allen, R. C., & Gomery, D. (1993). *Film history: Theory and practice* (2nd ed.). New York: McGraw-Hill.

Barge, J. K. (1994). *Leadership: Communication skills for organizations and groups*. New York: St. Martin's Press.

Beebe, S. A., & Masterson, J. T. (1995). *Family talk: Interpersonal communication in the family* (2nd ed.). New York: McGraw-Hill.

Bettinghaus, E. P., & Cody, M. J. (1994). *Persuasive communication* (5th ed.). Ft. Worth, TX: Harcourt Brace.

Borisoff, D., & Merrill, L. (1998). *The power to communicate: Gender differences as barriers* (3rd ed.). Prospect Heights, IL: Waveland Press.

Bryant, J., & Zillmann, D. (Eds.). (1994). *Media effects: Advances in theory and research*. Hillsdale, NJ: Erlbaum.

Burgoon, J. K., Buller, D. B., & Woodall, W. G. (1996). *Nonverbal communication: The unspoken dialogue* (2nd ed.). New York: McGraw-Hill.

Carbaugh, D. (Ed.). (1990). *Cultural communication and intercultural contact*. Hillsdale, NJ: Erlbaum.

Carter, T. B., Franklin, M. A., & Wright, J. B. (1996). *The First Amendment and the fifth estate* (4th ed.). Westbury, NY: Foundation Press.

Carter, T. B., Franklin, M. A., & Wright, J. B. (1997). *The First Amendment and the fourth estate* (7th ed.). Westbury, NY: Foundation Press.

Cherwitz, R. A. (Ed.). (1990). *Rhetoric and philosophy*. Hillsdale, NJ: Erlbaum.

Christians, C. G., Fackler, M., & Rotzoll, K. B. (1998). *Media ethics: Cases and moral reasoning* (5th ed.). New York: Longman.

Daniels, T. D., Spiker, B. K., & Papa, M. J. (1997). *Perspectives on organizational communication* (4th ed.). Madison, WI: Brown & Benchmark.

Denton, R. E., Jr., & Woodward, G. C. (1998). *Political communication in America* (3rd ed.). Westport, CT: Praeger.

DeVito, J. A. (1998). *The interpersonal communication book* (8th ed.). New York: Longman.

Eastman, S. T., & Ferguson, D. A. (Eds.). (1996). *Broadcast/cable programming: Strategies and practices* (5th ed.). Belmont, CA: Wadsworth.

Ellis, D. G. (1992). *From language to communication*. Hillsdale, NJ: Erlbaum.

Foss, S. K., Foss, K. A., & Trapp, R. (1991). *Contemporary perspectives on rhetoric* (2nd ed.). Prospect Heights, IL: Waveland Press.

Gudykunst, W. B., & Kim, Y. Y. (1997). *Communicating with strangers: An approach to intercultural communication* (3rd ed.). New York: McGraw-Hill.

Harris, R. J. (1999). *A cognitive psychology of mass communication* (3rd ed.). Mahwah, NJ: Erlbaum.

Head, S. W., Sterling, C. H., & Schofield, L. B. (1998). *Broadcasting in America: A survey of electronic media* (8th ed.). Boston: Houghton Mifflin.

Infante, D. A., Rancer, A. S., & Womack, D. F. (1997). *Building communication theory* (3rd ed.). Prospect Heights, IL: Waveland Press.

Jamieson, K. H., & Campbell, K. K. (1997). *The interplay of influence: The mass media and their publics in news, advertising, and politics* (4th ed.). Belmont, CA: Wadsworth.

Jandt, F. E. (1998). *Intercultural communication: An introduction* (2nd ed.). Thousand Oaks, CA: Sage.

Kreps, G. L., & Thornton, B. C. (1992). *Health communication: Theory and practice* (2nd ed.). Prospect Heights, IL: Waveland Press.

Leeds-Hurwitz, W. (1993). *Semiotics and communication*. Hillsdale, NJ: Erlbaum.

Littlejohn, S. W. (1999). *Theories of human communication* (6th ed.). Belmont, CA: Wadsworth.

Matsen, P. P., Rollinson, P. B., & Sousa, M. (Eds.). (1990). *Readings from classical rhetoric*. Carbondale: Southern Illinois University Press.

Moore, R. L. (1998). *Mass communication law and ethics* (2nd ed.). Mahwah, NJ: Erlbaum.

Newsom, D., Turk, J. V., & Kruckeberg, D. (1996). *This is PR: The realities of public relations* (6th ed.). Belmont, CA: Wadsworth.

O'Keefe, D. J. (1990). *Persuasion: Theory and research*. Newbury Park, CA: Sage.

Pearson, J. C., West, R. L., & Turner, L. H. (1995). *Gender and communication* (3rd ed.). Madison, WI: Brown & Benchmark.

Perloff, R. M. (1997). *Political communication*. Mahwah, NJ: Erlbaum.

Rogers, E. M. (1995). *Diffusion of innovations* (4th ed.). New York: Free Press.

Severin, W. J., & Tankard, J. W. (1997). *Communication theories: Origins, methods, and uses in the mass media* (4th ed.). New York: Longman.

Sherman, B. L. (1995). *Telecommunications management: Broadcasting/cable and the new technologies* (2nd ed.). New York: McGraw-Hill.

Sloan, W. D. (1991). *Perspectives on mass communication history*. Hillsdale, NJ: Erlbaum.

Smith, C. A. (1990). *Political communication*. San Diego: Harcourt Brace Jovanovich.

Sterling, C. H., & Kittross, J. M. (1990). *Stay tuned: A concise history of American broadcasting* (2nd ed.). Belmont, CA: Wadsworth.

Tedford, T. L. (1997). *Freedom of speech in the United States* (3rd ed.). State College, PA: Strata.

Teeter, D. L., Jr., Le Duc, D. R., & Loving, B. (1998). *Law of mass communications* (9th ed.). Westbury, NY: Foundation Press.

Trent, J. S., & Friedenberg, R. V. (1995). *Political campaign communication: Principles and practices.* Westport, CT: Praeger.

Van Evra, J. P. (1997). *Television and child development* (2nd ed.). Mahwah, NJ: Erlbaum.

Williams, F. (1992). *The new communications* (3rd ed.). Belmont, CA: Wadsworth.

Wolvin, A. D., & Coakley, C. G. (1993). *Perspectives on listening*. Norwood, NJ: Ablex.

Wood, J. T. (1999). *Gendered lives: Communication, gender, and culture* (3rd ed.). Belmont, CA: Wadsworth.

Yerby, J., Buerkel-Rothfuss, N., & Bochner, A. P. (1998). *Understanding family communication* (2nd ed.). Boston: Allyn & Bacon.

■ ENCYCLOPEDIAS

Alkin, M. (Ed.). (1992). *The encyclopedia of educational research* (6th ed., 4 vols.). New York: Macmillan.

American Jurisprudence Second (82 vols.). (1962–). Rochester, NY: Lawyers Cooperative.

Amey, L., & Rasmussen, R. K. (1997). *Censorship* (3 vols.). Pasadena, CA: Salem Press.

Argyris, C., & Cooper, C. L. (1998). *The concise Blackwell encyclopedia of management.* Oxford, UK: Blackwell.

Barnouw, E. (Ed.). (1989). *International encyclopedia of communications* (4 vols.). New York: Oxford University Press.

Bessette, J. M. (1996). *American justice* (3 vols.). Pasadena, CA: Salem Press.

Borgatta, E. F., & Borgatta, M. L. (Eds.). (1992). *Encyclopedia of sociology* (4 vols.). New York: Macmillan.

Bouissac, P. R. (Ed.). (1998). *Encyclopedia of semiotics*. New York: Oxford University Press.

Britannica Online [On-line]. (1996). Britannica Advanced Publishing. Available: http://www.eb.com

Clark, B. R., & Neave, G. R. (Eds.). (1992). *The encyclopedia of higher education* (4 vols.). Oxford, UK: Pergamon Press.

Cole, R. (Ed.). (1998). *The encyclopedia of propaganda* (3 vols). New York: Sharpe.

Colman, A. M. (Ed.). (1994). *Companion encyclopedia of psychology* (2 vols.). London: Routledge.

Cooper, C. L., & Argyris, C. (1997). *The Blackwell encyclopedia of management* (12 vols.). Oxford, UK: Blackwell.

Corpus Juris Secundum (100 vols.). (1936–). St. Paul: West.

Corsini, F. J., & Auerbach, A. J. (1998). *Concise encyclopedia of psychology* (2nd ed.). New York: Wiley.

Corsini, R. J. (Ed.). (1994). *Encyclopedia of psychology* (2nd ed., 4 vols.). New York: Wiley.

DeVito, J. A. (1986). *The communication handbook: A dictionary*. New York: Harper & Row.

Duffy, B. K., & Ryan, H. R. (Eds.). (1987). *American orators before 1900: Critical studies and sources*. New York: Greenwood Press.

Duffy, B. K., & Ryan, H. R. (Eds.). (1987). *American orators of the twentieth century: Critical studies and sources*. New York: Greenwood Press.

Enos, T. (1996). *Encyclopedia of rhetoric and composition: Communication from ancient times to the information age*. New York: Garland.

Findlay, M. S. (1998). *Language and communication: A cross-cultural encyclopedia*. Santa Barbara, CA: ABC-Clio Press.

Gall, S. B., Berns, B., & Feldman, A. (Eds.). (1996). *Gale encyclopedia of psychology*. Detroit: Gale Research.

Gardner, R., & Shortelle, D. (1997). *From talking drums to the Internet: An encyclopedia of communications technology*. Santa Barbara, CA: ABC-Clio Press.

Husen, T., & Postlethwaite, T. N. (Eds.). (1994). *The international encyclopedia of education* (2nd ed., 12 vols.). Oxford, UK: Pergamon Press.

Kuper, A., & Kuper, J. (Eds.). (1996). *The social science encyclopedia* (2nd ed.). New York: Routledge.

Lewis, R. (1997). *Communication: Print, images, sounds, and the computer* (Rev. ed.). New York: Macmillan Reference.

Manstead, A. S. R., & Hewstone, M. (1995). *The Blackwell encyclopedia of social psychology*. Cambridge, MA: Blackwell.

Maurer, J. G. (Ed.). (1995). *Encyclopedia of business* (2 vols.). Detroit: Gale Research.

Miller, D. (1996). *The Blackwell encyclopaedia of political thought* (2nd ed.). Oxford, UK: Blackwell.

Muller, N. J. (1998). *Desktop encyclopedia of telecommunications*. New York: McGraw-Hill.

Muller, N. J. (1999). *Desktop encyclopedia of the Internet*. Boston: Artech House.

Ramachandran, V. S. (Ed.). (1994). *Encyclopedia of human behavior* (4 vols.). San Diego: Academic Press.

Reed, R. M., & Reed, M. K. (1992). *The encyclopedia of television, cable, and video*. New York: Van Nostrand Reinhold.

Sills, D. L. (Ed.). (1968–1991). *International encyclopedia of the social sciences* (19 vols.). New York: Macmillan.

Squire, L. R. (Ed.). (1992). *Encyclopedia of learning and memory*. New York: Macmillan.

Sterling, C. H. (1998). *Focal encyclopedia of media* [CD-ROM]. Woburn, MA: Butterworth Heinemann.

Warner, M. (Ed.). (1996). *International encyclopedia of business and management* (6 vols.). New York: Routledge.

Wolman, B. B. (Ed.). (1996). *The encyclopedia of psychiatry, psychology, and psychoanalysis*. New York: Holt.

■ ANNUAL REVIEWS

Advances in Experimental Social Psychology. (1964–). San Diego: Academic Press.
Advances in the Study of Behavior. (1965–). San Diego: Academic Press.
Annual Review of Anthropology. (1972–). Palo Alto, CA: Annual Reviews.
Annual Review of Applied Linguistics. (1980–). New York: Cambridge University Press.
Annual Review of Psychology. (1950–). Palo Alto, CA: Annual Reviews.
Annual Review of Sociology. (1975–). Palo Alto, CA: Annual Reviews.
Annual Review of the Institute for Information Studies. (1990–). Falls Church, VA: Institute for Information Studies.
Communication Yearbook. (1977–). Thousand Oaks, CA: Sage.
Current Research in Film. (1985–1991). Norwood, NJ: Ablex.
Free Speech Yearbook. (1961–). Carbondale: Southern Illinois University Press.
International and Intercultural Communication Annual. (1974–). Thousand Oaks, CA: Sage.
Progress in Communication Sciences. (1979–). Stamford, CT: Ablex.
Research in Consumer Behavior. (1985–). Greenwich, CT: JAI Press.
Review of Marketing. (1987–). Chicago: American Marketing Association.
Syntax and Semantics. (1972–). San Diego: Academic Press.

■ SERIES

Advances in Semiotics. (1976–). Bloomington: Indiana University Press.
Communication and Human Values. (1988–). Thousand Oaks, CA: Sage.
Communication and Society. (1994–). New York: Routledge.
Communication Concepts. (1991–). Thousand Oaks, CA: Sage.
Communication Series. (1989–). New York: Guilford Press.
Communication Series. (1992–). Cresskill, NJ: Hampton Press.
Contemporary Studies In Communication, Culture & Information. (1996–). Stamford, CT: Ablex.
Contemporary Studies in International Political Communication. (1998–). Stamford, CT: Ablex.
Contributions to the Study of Mass Media and Communications. (1983–). Westport, CT: Greenwood Press.
Critical Studies in Communication. (1992–). Boulder, CO: Westview.
Information and Behavior. (1985–). New Brunswick, NJ: Transaction.
Interpersonal CommTexts. (1990–). Thousand Oaks, CA: Sage.
LEA's Communication Series. (1985–). Hillsdale, NJ: Erlbaum.
Medhurst, M. J. (Ed.). (1998–). *A rhetorical history of the United States.* East Lansing: Michigan State University Press.
Media and Society. (1987–). Westport, CT: Praeger.
Media Culture & Society. (1987–). Thousand Oaks, CA: Sage.
Media Studies Series. (1992–). Somerset, NJ: Transaction.
New Media Cultures. (1997–). Thousand Oaks, CA: Sage.
Organization-communication: Emerging Perspectives. (1986–). Stamford, CT: Ablex.

Praeger Series in Political Communication. (1990–). Westport, CT: Praeger.

Sage Annual Reviews of Communication Research. (1972–1994). Thousand Oaks, CA: Sage.

Sage Series in Written Communication. (1993–). Thousand Oaks, CA: Sage.

Series in Interpersonal Communication. (1983–). Thousand Oaks, CA: Sage.

Series in Public Communication. (1981–). New York: Longman.

Studies in Culture and Communication (1990–). New York: Routledge.

Studies in Rhetoric and Communication. (1989–). Tuscaloosa: University of Alabama Press.

Studies in Rhetoric/communication. (1984–). Columbia: University of South Carolina Press.

SUNY Series in Communication Studies. (1998–). Albany: State University of New York Press.

SUNY Series in Human Communication. (1985–). Albany: State University of New York Press.

SUNY Series in Speech Communication. (1991–). Albany: State University of New York Press.

EXAMPLES

CHRIS decides to check out the meaning of the term *ghostwriting* by looking in *The Communication Handbook: A Dictionary.* The one-sentence definition found here wasn't much help, although other terms clearly have larger entries. So, the next step is to check *New Directions in Political Communication: A Resource Book* for additional information. The index leads Chris to a discussion of political speeches of presidents, but it doesn't help much with specifics on ghostwriting.

FELECIA'S topic, voice mail, is very new and specialized, so many of the general sources will not be useful. In looking through the encyclopedia list at the end of this chapter, however, one recent volume seems possible, *From Talking Drums to the Internet: An Encyclopedia of Communications Technology.* This volume is not in Felecia's library, so she orders it via interlibrary loan. She also looks it up in the *International Encyclopedia of Communications,* but there is no listing for "voice mail," only "telephone and telecommunications networks"; these provide some background information on the industry.

MARIA hits the jackpot in *The Communication Handbook: A Dictionary* for her attribution theory topic. There are two full pages of explanation of the theory and references to the original articles where the theory was developed. Because this topic is an interpersonal one, several other sources are pertinent here: *Handbook of Communication Science, Handbook of Interpersonal Communication,* and *The Handbook of Social Psychology*. These sources will provide more than enough information for the class report. The index to Volume 1 of *The Handbook of Social Psychology,* for instance, leads Maria to a three-page summary of attribution theory and its origins.

ORLANDO'S parasocial interaction topic receives only brief treatment in some textbooks or handbooks, but there is one volume of *Sage Annual Reviews of Communication Research* (Vol. 16: *Advancing Communication Science: Merging Mass and Interpersonal Processes*) that might be useful. Unfortunately, the volume lacks an index, and the table of contents doesn't contain listings that would be helpful. This topic is better approached through indexes (Chapter 6).

KAT, CALVIN, ROCKY, and **MICHELLE** look for handbooks on organizational conflict and find *The New Handbook of Organizational Communication,* Vol. 20 of the *Sage Annual Reviews (Communication and Negotiation), The ASTD Training and Development Handbook: A Guide to Human Resource Development,* the *Handbook of Group Communication Theory and Research,* and *The Handbook of Organization Studies*. They divide the labor, and each looks for relevant sources. *The New Handbook of Organizational Communication* has some relevant sections.

EXERCISES

1. For your Group Communication class, you have decided to write a report on some aspect of group conformity, but you still need to narrow your topic further. To get some background on research that has been done on various aspects of this subject, you consult the *Handbook of Group Communication Theory and Research*. Turning to the chapter (11) that looks most promising, you find a reference to a publication by Allen.

   a. On which page does the first reference to this article appear?

   b. By referring to the bibliography at the end of this essay, you find the piece is a chapter in which edited book?

2. You are a member of a small group in your Organizational Communication class that must plan a presentation on the culture within organizations. Your group decides to focus on organizational culture and turns to Jablin and Putnam's *The New Handbook of Organizational Communication* to find out more about it. In what chapter would this topic be explained for you?

3. To begin a research paper on propaganda, you consult a subject encyclopedia covering all the social sciences, the *International Encyclopedia of Communications*, to find an introductory essay. You find that an essay is devoted to this topic.

   a. In what volume and on what page does the essay begin?

   b. What is the title of the first book in the bibliography at the end of the essay?

4. While researching a topic for a course in new communication technologies, you come across *subscription TV*, a term with which you are not familiar. You turn to an appropriate dictionary, *The Communication Handbook: A Dictionary*, for help.

   a. To what does this term refer?

   b. What other term is related to this one?

5. You are preparing for a classroom discussion on social control and obedience in the workplace. You decide to examine one publisher's series described in this chapter, *Sage Annual Reviews of Communication Research,* for an up-to-date survey of research in this area. It appears that one recent volume might be most appropriate for your topic.

   a. What is the title of the article in this volume that seems most closely related to your topic?

   b. An essay by Bormann in 1983 is mentioned in this article. On which page is the first reference to this study found in the article?

   c. In what book was the Bormann essay originally published?

6. You're doing a literature review in your advanced interpersonal communication class on interpersonal communication competence. One handbook, the *Handbook of Interpersonal Communication*, has a chapter that relates to your topic.

   a. On what page does the chapter begin?

   b. As you read through the chapter, what are three components of most definitions of *competence*?

7. Identify some situations in which a researcher would consult an edited textbook when doing communication research.

8. Browse though recent volumes of *Communication Yearbook*. What themes are prevalent? What questions are researchers asking?

9. List five articles from the *International Encyclopedia of Communications* that you find interesting. Skim through each and identify five potential research topics you'd like to pursue. Choose one of these for a literature review.

10. Identify sources you discovered in this chapter that would be helpful in searching a communication topic and list them on your search strategy sheet.

chapter 6

Access Tools

The general sources identified in Chapter 5 should help you develop a precise research topic. Do not be concerned, though, if you find that you need to reword or refine the topic as your research progresses. This is normal. The more you learn about your topic, the more precisely you can state the research question.

By this time our example topic, "The Use of Media in Organizations," might have been narrowed to a research question: "What types of public interview training programs do organizations provide for their management personnel?" It is likely that we would once again alter this question, if only slightly, as we continue our search for additional sources of information.

In this chapter we focus on tools that provide access to additional information sources. If you are writing a research paper and have already found a bibliography pertinent to your topic in a handbook or annual review, you are well on the way to identifying sources to consult for more information on your topic. If you have not yet found a bibliography, this chapter should lead you to helpful ones. At this point in your research, you will want to start using your library's catalog to determine which books listed in the bibliographies you have found are owned by your library. You will also want to locate items published after these bibliographies were compiled. Note that following this search strategy will mean your first approach to the library catalog will be by the authors or titles of works you have already identified, rather than by subject.

In addition to books, you have probably identified periodical articles as one type of information source you need to obtain. Do you need articles in scholarly journals, trade or professional journals, newsmagazines, or newspapers? Perhaps you would like to find reviews of the books you've already located. At this point you've probably already identified some pertinent articles through careful review of bibliographies, but you'll no doubt need more.

In this chapter you learn about the different types of periodical indexes available and how they can help you identify particular types of articles. We describe access tools devoted to communication journals, those for related disciplines, general and interdisciplinary tools, and media indexes. We also cover a special type of tool, citation indexes, in which the primary access point is a "cited author" rather than a subject heading or key word. Most periodical indexes are now available either on-line or on CD-ROM, so you will get a lot of practice using the electronic search strategies you learned about in Chapter 4.

Sources such as media indexes (covered later in this chapter) and government publications (see Chapter 8) concentrate on specialized access tools, those dealing with original media sources (such as newspapers, television, and film) and documents of the U.S. government. Not all research topics, of course, would benefit from including the sources found using the specialized finding tools for media and government sources. For example, there would be few government publications on "Eye Contact in Initial Interactions." However, research on other topics, such as "The Effect of Television Violence on Children" or "The Impact of Government Regulation on the Operation of Cable Television," would be incomplete without these specialized sources.

By the time you have examined and used the sources listed in this chapter, you will have a fairly comprehensive list of sources (books, articles, and so on) that you should consult in the research process and consider including in a research paper bibliography.

BIBLIOGRAPHIES

The idea of a **bibliography** as a list of citations to sources needs little introduction, particularly for those of you who are currently compiling such a list. Your final product will probably fit the definition of a **selective topical bibliography**. This is a carefully chosen list of materials on a given topic. Like many (but by no means all) bibliographies, yours will include several types of sources, such as books, periodical articles, and government documents, which you have identified using many types of references. Because each of your citations will include complete bibliographic information, another researcher could use and build upon the work you have done.

You will want to use bibliographies to take advantage of the work others have already done in selecting and compiling sources relevant to your topic. As we saw in Chapter 2, tracking down the leads provided by bibliographies to find additional sources is a crucial research strategy. Other authors may even have provided the additional service of annotating their bibliographies—that is, giving a brief summary of the content of the article or book and possibly commenting on its quality.

Selective topical bibliographies, such as those compiled for research papers and literature reviews, are often **appended bibliographies**—that is, they are attached to the end of an article, chapter, or book. The bibliographies found in encyclopedias, handbooks, and yearbooks are also examples of appended bibliographies. Such bibliographies in other publications may be more difficult to find, but the *Bibliographic Index* does provide a systematic and efficient way of locating both appended and book-length bibliographies. Although this bibliography of bibliographies is searchable on-line, it is not widely available in this format. More libraries subscribe to the semiannual printed index.

Some book-length bibliographies are similar to appended bibliographies in that they are topical (devoted to one specific topic, such as nonverbal communication), whereas others are general. A **general bibliography**, such as the following one, may be more useful at the beginning of the search process, when you are still choosing and narrowing a topic.

> Blum, E., & Wilhoit, F. (1990). *Mass media bibliography: An annotated, selected list of books and journals for reference and research* (3rd ed.). Urbana: University of Illinois Press.

> ■ This annotated bibliography of 2100 sources in mass communication serves as a reference tool for locating research materials. The entries identify mass communication sources on such topics as theory, structure, economics, and effects. Annotated entries are arranged according to media: general (two or more media); broadcast (radio and television); print (newspapers, books, and periodicals); film; and advertising and public relations. The source includes lists of mass-communication bibliographies, annuals, journals, and indexes. There are author–title and subject indexes that refer users to entry numbers.

Many valuable general book-length and **topical bibliographies** are published for communication researchers. A listing of several additional bibliographies, which represent a variety of subject areas and have been published within the past 15 or so years, is at the end of this chapter.

The bibliographies described thus far are known as **retrospective bibliographies**. This means they appear at a particular point in time and are not updated. The type of bibliography that appears in *The Handbook of Social Psychology*, for example, includes sources (such as books, research articles, and government documents) that have appeared since the topic was first investigated. Retrospective bibliographies, then, lend historical perspective to the research area.

In contrast, **current bibliographies** are published regularly—monthly, **semiannually**, or yearly. Each issue lists books and sometimes articles that have been published since the previous issue. Current bibliographies lead you to contemporary investigations and writings.

Not many current bibliographies are published specifically for communication, although bibliographies appended to **review articles** on regularly recurring topics in the annual editions of *Communication Yearbook* sometimes fulfill this function. One useful current annotated bibliography, which is published **quarterly**, is the following:

> *Communication Booknotes Quarterly.* (1998–). Mahwah, NJ: Erlbaum.

> ■ This quarterly, annotated bibliography of new publications in mass communication describes in each issue about 50 books, periodicals, reports, government documents, and reference sources from the United

States and abroad. Coverage includes advertising and public relations, communications technology, electronic media, general communication, history, information industry, international communication, journalism, law and policy, mass communication, motion pictures, popular culture, and telecommunications. Contributors periodically annotate communication sources of additional countries. The publication was titled *Mass Media Booknotes* from 1969 to 1981 and *Communication Booknotes* from 1982 to 1997.

Communication researchers working in some subject areas may find it useful to check the current bibliographies of related disciplines. A listing of some of these is provided at the end of this chapter.

Locating satisfactory bibliographies on your topic may sometimes be difficult. An option available in this case is to seek out the most comprehensive of bibliographies—those of national libraries. The Library of Congress attempts to collect copies of all significant publications available in the United States. It contributes its cataloging records to a national **union catalog**, *WorldCat*, maintained by OCLC, and available through its FirstSearch collection of databases. Besides the records contributed by the Library of Congress, *WorldCat* includes cataloging records from most academic and public libraries in the United States. Searching *WorldCat* is an effective way of updating information sources you have located in retrospective bibliographies, such as Blum and Wilhoit's (1990) *Mass Media Bibliography*.

Ask your reference librarian to find out what type of access the library provides to this and other large union catalogs. Keep in mind, though, when using comprehensive bibliographies, that works are included, not because they are necessarily authoritative or important, but because they exist. Before going to some trouble (using interlibrary loan, for example) to obtain a copy of a book you have identified through this catalog, it would be wise to determine its relative worth (see Chapter 2).

GUIDES TO THE LITERATURE

One particularly useful type of bibliography is called a guide. **Guides to the literature** are broad bibliographies made up primarily of reference works and periodicals available in a given subject field or fields. Many guides also list and describe organizations that can lead you to sources of information outside of libraries. Guides describe the basic organization of the field's literature and the processes and techniques of literature searches peculiar to that field. Thus, they can orient you to the literature of fields with which you are not familiar.

As you become acquainted with different types of reference works and their uses, you will probably realize at some point in a literature search that you need a particular type of reference work—a dictionary of statistics or an annual review of psychology, for example. A guide to the literature can often help you identify such a source. A general guide that covers the literature of many subject fields is the following:

Balay, R., Carrington, V. F., & Martin, M. S. (1996). *Guide to reference books* (11th ed.). Chicago: American Library Association.

■   You can use this source and its supplements to locate a listing and evaluation of reference works. The reference works are arranged under these broad headings: general reference works, the humanities, social science, history and area studies, and pure and applied sciences. Within each of these groups, the listings are broken down by narrower subject fields and by type of publication (such as bibliography or dictionary). An index provides access by title, author, and subject.

The following guide is a good introduction to the literature of the social sciences:

Herron, N. L. (1996). *The social sciences: A cross-disciplinary guide to selected sources* (2nd ed.). Englewood, CO: Libraries Unlimited.

■   One chapter of this guide is devoted to the general reference literature of the social sciences and one chapter to statistics and demography. Each of the remaining 12 chapters covers the literature of a particular discipline (including communication). Other disciplines covered are political science, economics and business, history, law and legal issues, anthropology, sociology, education, psychology, and geography. Essays on the nature of each discipline and its literature introduce each chapter, followed by fully annotated listings of reference works.

If you're trying to find topics for speeches, Congressional Quarterly publishes a weekly guide to topics of interest:

CQ Researcher. (1992–). Washington, DC: Congressional Quarterly.

■   This guide identifies, in each issue, a topic of national concern faced in the United States. The issue is thoroughly discussed, background is provided, the current situation explained, and a bibliography of sources is provided. These are published weekly and are compiled in a loose-leaf binder, with annual bound cumulations. Cumulative indexes cover the five most recent years. Check in the reference area of the library. This source is available on-line as part of *CQLibrary*.

Other guides deal with a specific field of study. For example, Cates's (1997) *Journalism: A Guide to the Reference Literature* identifies sources and writing methods helpful for those conducting research in journalism. This work and a few of the other guides available for disciplines related to communication are listed at the end of this chapter. In addition, the following work has several uses, one of which is to serve as a guide to research in mass communication:

Sterling, C. H., Bracken, J. K., & Hill, S. M. (1998). *Mass communications research resources: An annotated guide.* Mahwah, NJ: Erlbaum.

■ This work presents selected publications and research sources in mass communication. Its 10 chapters describe bibliographic and selected secondary resources in: general reference areas, such as bibliographies, dictionaries, databases, indexes, and abstracts; history, including archives and libraries; technology, such as patents and technical standards; industry and economics, including associations, organizations, and annual reports; content, such as secondary resources; research and audiences, including research organizations and media education; policy and regulation, including government sources and policy; international arenas, such as international satellites and United Nations agencies; periodicals, including international and legal sources; and audiovisual resources, including technology, and industry and economics. Two appendixes describe how to find library materials and to read Library of Congress subject headings.

■ LEGAL RESEARCH

Legal research poses some interesting complexities to communication students. Students of debate, mass-communication policy and regulation, and freedom of speech, among others, often need to consult the legal literature in their research endeavors. Just as the field of communication is constantly changing, so are the everyday legal decisions that affect the operations of communication organizations, the expression of ideas in a society, and the formulation of public policy.

Like the literature of other fields, the legal literature consists of primary sources, secondary sources, and finding tools. Primary sources include legislative statutes, court decisions, executive orders, administrative agency decisions and rules, and treaties. These are the enforceable rules of a society. Secondary sources include legal textbooks, dictionaries, and encyclopedias (some of which we listed at the end of Chapter 5), as well as commentaries, periodicals, restatements, and document sourcebooks. Their purpose is largely to describe and explain the law. Finding tools ease access to the many legal statutes and court decisions. Bibliographies, citators (that is, citation indexes for legal cases), computerized search services such as LEXIS and Westlaw, indexes, law digests, looseleaf services (see Chapter 8), and legal research guides provide the means of locating primary sources.

Although further explanation of legal research is beyond our scope, there are several legal research guides you can consult. These guides focus on primary, secondary, and finding-tool sources. They describe the legal process and the procedure of legal research, as well as standard legal and citation forms. They often include identification of legal abbreviations and a glossary of legal terms. They serve not only as guides to the literature but also as manuals for conducting legal research. Several of these guides are listed at the end of this chapter. One especially useful legal research guide is the following:

Jacobstein, J. M., Mersky, R. M., & Dunn, D. J. (1998). *Fundamentals of legal research* (7th ed.). New York: Foundation Press.

■   The guide accomplishes three purposes. First, it explains the legal process and research procedures. Second, it details primary sources (such as federal court decisions, federal legislation, and administrative law), secondary sources (such as legal periodicals and legal encyclopedias), and finding tools (such as court report digests, annotated law reports, looseleaf services, and citators). Third, it describes international law, English legal research, federal tax research, and computers in legal research. Among the appendixes are a glossary of legal abbreviations, state guides to legal research, state reports, and coverage of the national reporter system. There is a subject–source index.

ON-LINE SEARCH STRATEGIES: FINDING ADDITIONAL BIBLIOGRAPHIES AND GUIDES

We list many book-length bibliographies and literature guides at the end of this chapter, but new ones appear each year. You can search for these using library catalogs and *WorldCat*. The Library of Congress (LC) subject heading "bibliography" is usually assigned as part of the subject heading for both bibliographies and guides to the literature. Sometimes the subject heading "reference books" is also assigned. For example, these LC subject headings were assigned to *Journalism: A Guide to the Reference Literature:*

Journalism–Bibliography
Reference books–Journalism

You can also do key-word searches combining "bibliography" and/or "reference books" with broad subject areas or narrower topical terms. For example:

communication AND bibliography   mass media AND reference books
telecommunications AND bibliography   radio AND bibliography
television violence AND bibliography

If the catalog you are using allows you to restrict terms to particular fields (as *WorldCat* does), you may want to try restricting your search for "bibliography" to the subject-headings field. As always, examine the subject headings of any records you retrieve to find additional access points (more specific or broader subject headings, authors, and so on).

BIBLIOGRAPHIES ON THE WORLD WIDE WEB

Scholars and students frequently "publish" bibliographies on the World Wide Web. Although they vary in length and quality and must be evaluated carefully (see Chapters 2 and 3), some may be very useful. Identifying them may be difficult. One place to look is on websites maintained by associations, journals, and academic institutions. For example, the website maintained by the Poynter

Institute <**http://www.poynter.org/**> includes bibliographies on several broad journalism-related topics, including broadcast journalism, politics and the press, media ethics, new media, presidential debates, and many others. Some attempt is made to update them. The website also provides links to other journalism-related websites.

Search engines can also be used to find bibliographies, rather easily using the following method. Assuming you've already found several good citations, start by selecting one that appears to be substantial. Ideally, the author may be one you've already identified as being important, and the article should have a distinctive title. Longer titles will work better than shorter ones. Enter the article title in the search box, enclosing it in quotes. If you've chosen well, you are likely to get hits of documents that cite that article. There's a good chance that they include a bibliography that is at least peripherally related to your topic.

PERIODICAL INDEXES

The primary purpose of **periodical indexes** is to provide access to articles in journals, magazines, and newspapers. A few include other types of publications as well, such as government reports, dissertations, and book chapters.

Though many began publication in print format, most periodical indexes are now available either on-line or on CD-ROM. The electronic versions of these tools incorporate many features and conveniences that greatly increase their efficiency, scope, and power. They usually offer the searcher at least these standard access points: subject heading, key word, author, article title, and periodical title. Thus, although you will most often search indexes by subject or key word, indexes offer other options that often come in handy. In addition, most searches can be limited by publication year and language. Of course, fewer access points are available for printed indexes, most of which can be searched only by subject and author.

Records in these databases typically include these fields: author, title, subject headings, periodical title, volume, date of publication, and page numbers. Periodical indexes also usually include abstracts, or summaries, of each article, allowing you to see whether the original source is relevant to your topic. We now include in the category "periodical indexes" many access tools that started off as a type of tool known as an **abstracting service** or, simply, an **abstract**. At that time, periodical indexes did not provide summaries, and one had to turn to abstracting services to find them. Now the distinction between the two types of tools has faded. A few abstracting services useful for communication researchers do, however, continue to be published only in print format, and we will describe them in this chapter.

Abstracts provide a valuable service. By supplying condensed versions of articles, they allow you to find relevant sources efficiently. It is important, though, not to rely on abstracts at the expense of the original works. The original sources contain essential information about the research problem, procedures, findings, and conclusions. You need to read and review these fully, especially if you are going to list these sources in bibliographies, literature reviews, or research reports.

An increasing number of periodical indexes are moving beyond abstracts to include the full text of a significant portion of the articles indexed. Such **full-text databases** can be a real boon to the researcher, providing the ultimate in convenience. But "full text" can mean several different things. It often means that the article text can be easily viewed and printed, using your browser's Print function, but that accompanying graphics (such as photographs, illustrations, charts, and graphs) will be missing. If the graphics are included, the databases are said to be **full image** (or **image databases**). Viewing and printing full-image database searches may be a bit more complicated, often requiring Adobe Acrobat or another program.

The full-text articles included in periodical databases may or may not be searchable. In other words, if you're searching a full-text searchable database and you enter the search term "asynchronous," you will retrieve any article that includes that term anywhere in the article, even if it is not included in the subject headings, abstract, or title. This capability can come in handy on those occasions when you want to find articles that mention something too obscure to be included as a subject heading or mentioned in an abstract.

There are differences between a database, a database producer, a database interface, and a database vendor. For example, if your instructor asks you to report on which databases you used in your research, you don't want to give the name of the vendor or its interface rather than the name of the database. When you are looking for a particular database, you shouldn't be confused by the prominently displayed name of the vendor.

Some companies produce databases, some develop a proprietary search interface and distribute (or vend) databases, and some do both. Databases are often distributed by multiple vendors. In Table 6-1 we identify some vendors, interfaces, databases, and producers. This is not meant to be a comprehensive listing of vendors, but it does include many of those you're likely to come across. You should assume that the details (interface names, database names, who offers what) will change from year to year.

Table 6-1 Some Database Vendors

Vendor	Interface	Sample Databases	Database Producers
SilverPlatter	WebSPIRS	PsycINFO	APA
		ERIC	ERIC
		Sociofile	Sociological Abstracts
OCLC	FirstSearch	Business & Industry	Responsive Data Technologies
		PsycFIRST	APA
		Social Sciences Abstracts	H. W. Wilson
Ebsco	EBSCOhost	Academic Search	Ebsco
		PsycINFO	APA
		ERIC	ERIC
UMI	ProQuest	ABI/Inform	UMI
		Periodical Abstracts	UMI

Table 6-1 Some Database Vendors (*Continued*)

Vendor	Interface	Sample Databases	Database Producers
		Social Sciences Abstracts	H. W. Wilson
IAC	SearchBank (InfoTrac)	*Expanded Academic Index*	IAC
		ERIC	ERIC
H. W. Wilson	WilsonWeb	*Social Sciences Abstracts*	H. W. Wilson
		Humanities Abstracts	H. W. Wilson
		Education Abstracts	H. W. Wilson
Ovid Technologies	Ovid	*Sociofile*	Sociological Abstracts
		PsycINFO	APA
		Education Abstracts	H. W. Wilson

What difference does this make to you? You may become accustomed to and prefer a particular vendor's search interface. This might lead you to seek out databases from that vendor. But, because libraries have to limit the number of vendors they can use, you will probably have limited choices. In any case, you should be a knowledgeable consumer and focus on the quality and characteristics of the underlying database rather than the vendor and the names they have chosen to market their products.

Notice that many of the statements above are qualified by terms such as *many*, *most*, and *usually*. Databases differ, and you need to be aware of these differences in order to select the right database for the job. For starters, you need to know the subject area, type of periodicals indexed, and time period.

There are several questions to consider when choosing a database. For example, if you're looking for something recent, how often is the database updated? What access points are available? In what ways can searches be limited? Does the search interface offer special features that will be useful to you? If you're looking for something that is extremely specific, you may want to select a database with searchable full text.

As you search, learn to evaluate the subject headings used in different databases critically. Some have excellent, specific subject headings and assign them consistently. Others use broad subject headings with little apparent consistency. Consider how many headings are assigned to each record. Some databases don't add subject headings at all, so you'll need to develop complete lists of synonyms. These factors must be taken into account as you decide how to formulate your search. Don't use a cookie-cutter approach. A search that works well in one database should be adjusted when you search another database. One source that might be helpful for selecting terms to use when searching communication literature is:

Knapp, S. D. (1993). *The contemporary thesaurus of social science terms and synonyms: A guide for natural language computer searching.* Phoenix: Oryx Press, 1993.

As you search and retrieve items, remember that you're going to be following through on these parts of the search strategy outlined in Chapter 2:

- Examine and evaluate the citations retrieved.
- Identify additional access points (key words, subject headings, authors, titles) and reformulate search queries to narrow, broaden, or improve focus, as needed.
- Evaluate citations retrieved, selecting items worth retrieving.
- Examine bibliographies for additional leads.

■ DISCIPLINE-BASED PERIODICAL INDEXES

Indexes devoted to the periodical literature of specific disciplines are often more useful for research papers and literature reviews because they list the articles published in the scholarly journals read by professionals in that field. Unfortunately, no one index covers all communication and communication-related journals, but *ComIndex*, which is available on diskette or on-line to users from member institutions from Communication Institute for Online Scholarship (CIOS), indexes most communication-related journals but provides no abstracts. Users must search *ComIndex* by author name, journal name, or word in the title, which limits its use. Also available through CIOS membership is access to *ComAbstracts*, a database of abstracts for over 40 communication journals, which can be searched by key word. Users from member institutions can access this database at <**www.cios.org/www/abstract.htm**> and search for key words, but they need to have individual memberships (in addition) to retrieve the abstracts for the citations provided.

CommSearch, a CD-ROM index, and its print version, *Index to Journals in Communication Studies Through 1995,* index many of the major journals in the field and provide full text for several recent journal editions. (A discussion of some major communication journals, including identification of where they are indexed, is in Chapter 7.)

National Communication Association. (1997). *CommSearch* [CD-ROM] (2nd ed.). Annandale, VA: Author.

■ This CD-ROM provides basic access to 24 communication journals from their inception through 1995. Access points are title, author, and key word. In addition, abstracts are available from their inception for the six journals published by the National Communication Association: *Communication Education, Communication Monographs, Critical Studies in Mass Communication, Journal of Applied Communication Research, Quarterly Journal of Speech,* and *Text and Performance Quarterly*. The full text of these six journals is available for the years 1991–1995. Both the abstracts and full text of the six journals are searchable by key word. Other journals indexed are *Argumentation and Advocacy, Communication Quarterly, Communication Reports, Communication Research, Communication Research Reports, Communication Studies, Communication Theory, Howard Journal of Communications, Human Communication Research, Journal of Broadcasting & Electronic Media, Journal of Communication, Journal of Communication and Religion, Journal of the Association for Communication Administration, Journalism Quarterly, Philosophy and*

Rhetoric, Southern Speech Communication Journal, Western Journal of Speech Communication, and *Women's Studies in Communication.* A brief users' guide to searching *CommSearch* is available at the association's website: <**http://www. natcom.org/publications/**>.

CommSearch is based on a printed index, which appears at 5-year intervals:

> Matlon, R. J., & Ortiz, S. P. (Eds.). (1997). *Index to journals in communication studies through 1995* (2 vols.). Annandale, VA: National Communication Association.

Since its initial publication in 1978, *Communication Abstracts* has become the most widely used abstracting source in the field. Most of the major communication journals, related periodicals of allied fields, and books are represented in these volumes.

> *Communication Abstracts.* (1978–). Thousand Oaks, CA: Sage.
>
> ■   This bimonthly source comprehensively inspects the worldwide literature of communication and abstracts selected communication-related articles from over 200 periodicals, as well as relevant monographs, books, and research reports. *Communication Abstracts* includes paragraph-length summaries of journal articles or books, usually within the last year. More recent articles are not available in abstract form and must be located in the journals.
>
> Each abstract is listed alphabetically under the author's last name. A complete subject guide (referring to abstract numbers employed in the volume) is included in each issue. Among the many subjects covered are advertising, attitudes, broadcasting, broadcast regulation, communication technology, communication theory, consumer behavior, economic issues, group communication, health communication, information processing, intercultural communication, interpersonal communication, law, media effects, national development, news, organizational communication, political communication, public opinion, research methods, speech communication, and telecommunications.
>
> *Communication Abstracts* is published six times per year, in February, April, June, August, October, and December, with an annual bound **cumulation**. Cumulative subject and author indexes for each year appear in the December issue.

Although *Communication Abstracts* is not available as an on-line index, it is available on-line as a full-text periodical on at least one of the interdisciplinary indexes described later in this chapter. (In 1999 it could be searched on Ebsco's *Academic Search.*) The abstracts, titles, and subject headings are searchable by key word in this format. Because communication is an interdisciplinary field, you should also use indexes and abstracts that concentrate on the journals of other disciplines but selectively include several communication journals. For example, *Journal of Communication* and *Communication Monographs* are referenced in *Education Abstracts*, whereas the *Journal of Broadcasting & Electronic Media* and *Communication Research* are cited in *Humanities Abstracts*.

Humanities Abstracts [On-line]. (1984–). New York: Wilson.
Education Abstracts [On-line]. (1983–). New York: Wilson.
Social Sciences Abstracts [On-line]. (1984–). New York: Wilson.

■ Each of these indexes provides coverage of more than 400 English-language periodicals published in the United States and elsewhere, including several in communication. Each covers a wide range of interdisciplinary fields. Abstracts are included beginning with periodicals published in January 1994. These popular and useful indexes are available through several vendors. The full text and page image is available for a selected number of the periodicals indexed.

Researchers in psychology and sociology often publish communication-related articles, so the following are also essential sources for communication researchers:

PsycINFO [On-line]. (1967–). Arlington, VA: American Psychological Association.
PsycLIT [CD-ROM]. (1974–). Arlington, VA: American Psychological Association.
Psychological Abstracts. (1927–). Arlington, VA: American Psychological Association.

■ One of the oldest information services in the social and behavioral sciences, *Psychological Abstracts* surveys the world's literature in psychology and, selectively, related disciplines including communication. Journals, books, book chapters, conference papers, dissertations, and other materials are indexed and abstracted. Coverage is worldwide and includes references and abstracts to over 1300 journals in more than 20 languages. The subject headings used to index these tools are taken from the *Thesaurus of Psychological Index Terms*, which can be consulted either in print or on-line.

Sociofile [On-line]. (1974–). San Diego: Sociological Abstracts.
Sociological Abstracts. (1952–). San Diego: Sociological Abstracts.

■ *Sociofile* indexes and provides abstracts for articles from over 2000 journals in sociology and related disciplines, as well as dissertations, books and book chapters, and conference papers. It includes reviews of books and other media. The *Thesaurus of Sociological Indexing Terms* can be used to research terminology.

Communication researchers interested in education and related areas often turn to *ERIC*, a database produced with the aid of the Educational Resources Information Center (ERIC), a national system of clearinghouses, funded by the U.S. Office of Education. It includes two separate files, *Current Index to Journals in Education* (*CIJE*) and *Resources in Education* (*RIE*), both of which are also available in print format.

ERIC [On-line]. (1969–). Washington, DC: Educational Resource Information Center.

Current Index to Journals in Education. (1969–). Phoenix: Oryx Press.

Resources in Education. (1966–). Washington, DC: Government Printing Office.

■ *ERIC* contains the two indexes *RIE* and *CIJE*. Each of these can be searched as separate files on the database. The *CIJE* portion indexes over 800 periodicals, compared with the 427 indexed by *Education Abstracts*. Communication research journals such as *Human Communication Research* and *Communication Research* are more likely to be covered by *ERIC* than by *Education Abstracts,* although *ERIC*'s coverage of a particular journal is often selective rather than cover to cover. The *ERIC* thesaurus includes many terms specific to communication studies. The *RIE* portion of *ERIC* indexes and abstracts documents, which are generally locally published, is available only through the *ERIC* system. (The curriculum libraries of schools of education often subscribe to the entire collection.) These documents include research and project reports, bibliographies, curriculum materials, conference papers, and a variety of other materials.

Many additional discipline-specific indexes are available, and you may find it useful to consult indexes from other fields that provide information on communication-related topics. *Business Periodicals Abstracts*, for example, provides references to many articles in the area of organizational communication, as does *ABI/Inform*. Both of these are on-line tools found in many libraries. *Index to Legal Periodicals & Books* indexes the major legal journals in this country and a few foreign countries by author and subject. *America History and Life* covers the world's scholarly literature on the history and culture of the United States and Canada. These indexes and others are listed at the end of this chapter. We identify several indexes to government publications in Chapter 8.

There are, in addition, print abstracts on more specific topics. *Journalism & Mass Communication Abstracts* (1963–) is an example of a more narrowly focused abstracting service. It is a collection of abstracts of dissertations produced in departments of journalism or mass communication. You may find this source helpful when researching mass-communication topics. *Organizational Communication: Abstracts, Analysis, and Overview* (1976–1985) was another specialized publication that included abstracts of the annual literature pertinent to that subfield of communication through the mid-1980s. Other specialized abstracts are noted in the list at the end of the chapter.

■ GENERAL AND INTERDISCIPLINARY PERIODICAL INDEXES

Most libraries subscribe to a comprehensive, interdisciplinary index. (Few libraries can afford more than one, and they are similar in coverage.) At the present time, three companies compete in producing these indexes: University Microfilms International (UMI), Ebsco, and Information Access Corporation

(IAC). In a competitive marketplace, the indexes these companies supply tend to be repackaged and renamed with some frequency. In 1999 the databases of this type that students were likely to find in their library were:

Academic Search (Ebsco: EBSCOhost)
Expanded Academic Index (IAC: InfoTrac SearchBank)
Periodical Abstracts (UMI: ProQuest Direct)

These indexes provide access to a wide range of general-interest magazines and scholarly journals. They cover business, education, social sciences, humanities, medicine, and general science, as well as a few newspapers. Most index over 3000 periodicals. All provide abstracts and—for up to half of the periodicals indexed—the full-text or full-image articles. The full text is optionally searchable. The availability of full text and, sometimes, full image and their ease-of-use make these very convenient and popular tools.

Communication researchers will find these tools to be useful for a full range of projects, from a short speech to a substantial research study. Most index a fair number of the core communication journals, and they may include the full-text articles in communication journals to which your library does not otherwise subscribe. Their interdisciplinary nature makes them particularly worthwhile. Because these tools include popular as well as scholarly periodicals, students must distinguish between them to select sources appropriate for projects (see Chapter 7). Check to see if the index you are using has the capability of limiting search results to journals that are *peer reviewed*, one of the characteristics of scholarly journals. (Articles in peer-reviewed journals are evaluated by scholars in the field when being considered for publication.)

Communication researchers looking for an interdisciplinary approach that is even more comprehensive should be aware of *UnCover*, a periodical index (and document delivery service) that can be searched free of charge by anyone with access to the Internet <**http://uncweb.carl.org/**>. Based on the tables of contents of periodicals, it is an example of a particular type of periodical index, a *table-of-contents service*.

UnCoverWeb [On-line]. (1988–). Denver: UnCover.

■ This index covers more than 17,000 periodical titles in an extremely timely manner. Titles included are those subscribed to by libraries. Table-of-contents information is entered into the database as journals are received from the publisher, so issues are indexed on-line at about the same time that they arrive in libraries or on the newsstand. The table of contents of each journal issue can be displayed. Access points are key word, author/name, and journal title. There are real limitations: No subject headings are added, and there are no abstracts, unless they happen to appear in the table of contents. Thus, key-word searching does not generally provide an effective subject approach. However, *UnCover* covers communication journals comprehensively and is searchable by author. UnCover also offers a *journal alerting service* (or *current awareness service*). For a relatively modest fee, you can arrange to have the tables of contents of any of the journals it includes sent to you via e-mail, as they are added to the database. Some libraries have site licenses for this service.

■ LOCATING BOOK REVIEWS

Besides listing articles, many periodical indexes—including most of those discussed above—perform another service by referencing book reviews. Reviews appearing in the scholarly and professional journals covered by these and similar indexes are useful sources when you need to determine how scholars and other communication professionals have evaluated a particular work. You can find reviews of works of a more general or popular nature by using indexes that consist entirely of listings of book reviews, such as *Book Review Digest* (available both in print and on-line) or *Book Review Index*. Several other indexes of this type are listed at the end of the chapter. Not to be overlooked as a good source of reviews of both general and scholarly books are such interdisciplinary indexes as *Periodical Abstracts*, *Academic Search*, and *Expanded Academic Index*.

■ CITATION INDEXES

We've already discussed the valuable role that bibliographies play in research and their importance in a systematic search strategy. Often, our best leads come when we examine the bibliographies found at the ends of journal articles, books, book chapters, annual reviews, encyclopedias, and other reference books. This is where authors acknowledge their debt to prior research, helping you identify key authors and works. One disadvantage of bibliographies, of course, is that the items they cite must necessarily have an older publication date. Thus, we must update them using book catalogs and periodical indexes. To do so, we must first try to figure out just the right subject-heading and key-word searches. This process can be inexact, to say the least. Citation indexes provide an alternative way to do this updating that is in many ways more precise and direct.

Citation indexes simply compile the cited references from journal articles and selected books. When you use a citation index, you look up a reference to *a work that you know* to find articles *that have cited it*. For example, when researching political advertising you will find the following citation, which seems dated, in many bibliographies:

> Sears, D. O., & Freedman, J. L. (1967). Selective exposure to information: A critical review. *Public Opinion Quarterly, 31*, 194–213.

You look at the article and wonder what more recent information on the topic is available. It is likely that more current articles in this area will cite this work, so you consult a citation index under the first author's last name (Sears, D. O.). Here you find quite a few specific citations to this work, including:

> Kennamer, J. D. (1990). Self-serving biases in perceiving the opinions of others: Implications for the spiral of silence. *Communication Research, 17*, 393–404.

You determine that this is also an important work on your topic, so you look it up in the citation index to see where it has in turn been cited, and so on. This process can be quite productive in identifying works that are closely related to a topic.

The Institute for Scientific Information (ISI) publishes two citation indexes that cover most communication literature: *Arts & Humanities Citation Index* and *Social Sciences Citation Index*.

Social Sciences Citation Index. (1972–). Philadelphia: ISI.
Social Sciences Citation Index [On-line]. (1972–). Philadelphia: ISI.
Arts & Humanities Citation Index. (1976–). Philadelphia: ISI.
Arts & Humanities Citation Index [On-line]. (1980–). Philadelphia: ISI.

■   These multidisciplinary indexes cover the journal literature of the social sciences and the arts and humanities. The *Social Sciences Citation Index* covers over 1700 journals and the *Arts & Humanities Citation Index* over 1100. ISI citation databases are known collectively as *Web of Science*, which may be the way they are identified in your library's listing of databases.

Citations in these indexes are searched in an abbreviated format. For example, the article by J. D. Kennamer in *Communication Research* mentioned above would be searched in this format: KENNAMER JD COMM RES 17 393 90 R. There is no need to be intimidated by this extreme level of abbreviation, however. It is expected that you will enter the information you know and then browse indexes (or "word lists") to locate exact citations in the abbreviated form. A tutorial explaining procedures for using citation indexes is available on the ISI website <**http://www.isinet.com/**>. If you are using the print indexes, excellent instructions are available on the inside cover of each volume.

■ MEDIA INDEXES

Media indexes help you find newspaper materials, specific media sources, and reviews. Newspapers and media such as films and videotapes can provide communication students with useful information for research endeavors. They also often serve as important working tools for communication professionals.

Newspaper Indexes

Daily and weekly newspapers publish up-to-date information on current issues of local, national, and international scope. They also contain opinion columns, editorials, and media reviews that can be useful in the research process. For example, newspaper reports of Supreme Court decisions or regulatory agency actions can have a direct bearing on research about freedom of speech, broadcast programming, advertising, media law and regulation, and the like.

Like periodical indexes, **newspaper indexes** help you identify and find pertinent articles. Many on-line newspaper indexes are now available, some of which include the full text of the newspapers indexed. Newspaper indexes are often distributed by many of the same vendors that distribute indexes of magazines and journals. In fact, most of the comprehensive periodical indexes discussed above include indexing for a few national newspapers, such as the *New York Times,* the *Wall Street Journal,* and the *Christian Science Monitor*. Likewise, major business periodical indexes usually include indexing for the *Wall Street Journal* and a variety of regional business newspapers. Most college and university libraries make available one or more of the following newspaper indexes.

New York Times [On-line]. (1969–). New York: New York Times.
New York Times Ondisc [CD-ROM]. (1990–). New York: New York Times.
New York Times Index. (1913–). New York: New York Times.

■　This index provides subject access to and abstracts of news stories, editorials, letters to the editor, obituaries, and other features. Also included is material from the four wire services used by the *Times*: Associated Press, Bloomberg, Dow Jones, and Reuters. The full text of the most recent 90 days is available on-line through some vendors.

The "Prior Series" section of the print index provides coverage of the period 1851–1912.

Newspaper Abstracts [On-line]. (1989–). Ann Arbor, MI: UMI.

■　*Newspaper Abstracts* contains indexing and abstracting of significant articles appearing in 25 national and regional newspapers. National publications indexed include the *New York Times, Wall Street Journal, American Banker, Christian Science Monitor, Washington Post,* and *USA Today.* Coverage for most papers began in January 1989.

Additional databases that provide comprehensive coverage of newspapers include the *National Newspaper Index, Data Times EyeQ,* and *NewsBank.* In addition, comprehensive databases such as *NEXIS, NEXIS–LEXIS Academic Universe,* and *Dow Jones Interactive* index provide the full text of many newspapers. There are many options, but the situation will vary widely from library to library. Ask the reference staff at your library what access to newspaper indexing the library provides.

The World Wide Web provides another approach. Most newspapers now have websites, and a number provide searchable archives. Several comprehensive on-line directories to newspaper websites are available, including those maintained by the *American Journalism Review*'s *AJR NewsLink* <**http://www.newslink.org/menu.html**>. *Editor & Publisher* lists newspapers and magazines online at its MediaINFO site, as does the National Newspaper Association of America website. These sites do not necessarily indicate whether a newspaper's site includes archives, however. For this purpose, consult a listing maintained by the Special Libraries Association, "U.S. News Archives on the Web," at <**http://metalab.unc.edu/slanews/internet/archives.html#Ohio**>.

This site provides links to U.S. and international archives. One can link directly either to a newspaper's home page or to its searchable archives, if available. If a fee is charged to retrieve full-text articles, this is indicated. The Library of Congress also maintains a list of newspapers with searchable archives at <**http://lcweb.loc.gov/rr/news/oltitles.html**>.

A print directory, *Fulltext Sources Online* (semiannual), provides comprehensive coverage of the full-text offerings of 14 vendors, including DIALOG,

NEXIS, LEXIS, Westlaw, Dow Jones, Ovid, and Burrelle's. This source also indicates newspapers (and journals) that offer free Internet archives.

Retrospective newspaper indexing is more limited. Few of the 1500 daily newspapers in this country were indexed until fairly recently. *Newspaper Indexes: A Location and Subject Guide for Researchers*, Vols. 1 and 2 (1977–1982), provides a comprehensive list of newspaper indexes for a short time period. Newspapers that are not indexed sometimes have extensive library files that you can search on-site. Newspapers with smaller circulations, covering city, local, or regional news, can be located by using the *Gale Directory of Publications* (see Chapter 8). Occasionally, public libraries will index their own hometown newspapers, but college and university libraries seldom have time to do this.

If you are interested in investigating "nonestablishment" opinions on topics such as social movements, you might find articles in some newspapers to be important. Some publications with smaller circulations and specialized audiences are indexed in the following sources:

> *Alternative Press Index* [On-line and CD-ROM]. (1991–). Baltimore: National Information Services.
> *Alternative Press Index*. (1969–). Baltimore: Alternative Press Center.

> ■ This index covers most of the alternative and radical publications available in the United States. News of social issues and movements, as well as opinions on issues published in these magazines, journals, and newspapers, is accessible by combined author–subject listings. The print index is issued quarterly. Direct links to the websites of indexed publications are maintained on the Alternatives Press Center's website: <**http://www.altpress. org/**>. Entries indicate whether the full text is available on-line or via fax through UnCover's document delivery service.

> *Ethnic NewsWatch* [On-line and CD-ROM]. (1991–). Stamford, CT: SoftLine Information.

> ■ *Ethnic NewsWatch* is a full-text collection from 200 publications of the ethnic, minority, and native press. It includes newspapers, magazines, and journals published in the United States, United Kingdom, Africa, and Canada. English- and Spanish-language search options are available.

> *Disinformation* [On-line]. (No date). Available: http://www.disinfo.com.

> ■ *Disinformation*, much like *Alternative Press Index*, focuses on "radical" points of view and controversial issues. Topic subgroups such as censorship, propaganda, and newspeak contain references to articles in the press, media, and web sites that contain such points of view.

Broadcast Indexes

Information on other media, such as television, is also found in the collections of most libraries. (We discuss what is found in actual collections or archives in

Chapter 8.) The text of productions from CBS News through 1991 is available on microfiche for student use in libraries that subscribe to the *CBS News Index*. Similar services are provided for ABC News and public television. **Broadcast indexes** are useful for ascertaining perspectives on current events and for conducting content analyses of news programs. The *CBS News Index* provides guidance on where in the microfiche collection the desired transcript can be found. It remains useful for historical retrospective research.

> *CBS News Index*. (1975–1991). Ann Arbor, MI: University Microfilms International.
>
> ■ This index catalogs all daily news broadcasts, public affairs broadcasts, and programs (such as *60 Minutes* and *Face the Nation*) produced by CBS News from 1975 to 1991. Subject headings lead to descriptive phrases of the pertinent broadcasts, and locator information is given for the verbatim transcripts found in an accompanying microfiche collection.

Thus, many new access tools have become available with the advent of CD-ROM and on-line technology. Printed abstracts and indexes are becoming less useful now that searching electronic databases is possible in most libraries and many homes. If proper search techniques are used, searches should result in more valid citations for the researcher. In many cases, full-text documents are accessible (sometimes for a fee), and this saves researchers time and effort. Look through the list of additional access tools at the end of this chapter for more specialized tools.

SELECTED SOURCES

■ BIBLIOGRAPHIES

Aimiller, K., Lohr, P., & Meyer, M. (1989). *Television and young people: A bibliography of international literature, 1969-1989*. Munich: Saur.

Bibliographic Index. (1937–). New York: H. W. Wilson. (On-line, 1984–).

Blum, E., & Wilhoit, F. (1990). *Mass media bibliography: An annotated guide to books and journals for research and reference* (3rd ed.). Urbana: University of Illinois Press.

Carothers, D. F. (1991). *Radio broadcasting from 1920 to 1990: An annotated bibliography*. New York: Garland.

Catalog of Current Law Titles, Annual. (1991–). Buffalo, NY: Hein.

Communication Booknotes. (1969–1997). Washington, DC: Center for Telecommunications Studies, George Washington University.

Communication Booknotes Quarterly. (1998–). Mahwah, NJ: Erlbaum.

Cooper, T. W. (1988). *Television & ethics: A bibliography*. Boston: Hall.

Flannery, G. V. (1989). *Mass media: Marconi to MTV. A select bibliography of New York Times Sunday Magazine articles on communication 1900–1988*. Lanham, MD: University Press of America.

Gillmor, D. M., & Glasser, T. L. (1993). *Mass media law: Core readings in contemporary and historical media law. A selected bibliography* (3rd ed.). Minneapolis: University of Minnesota.

Gray, J. (1990). *Blacks in film and television: A Pan-African bibliography of films, filmmakers, and performers.* New York: Greenwood Press.

Greenberg, G. S. (1996). *Tabloid journalism: An annotated bibliography of English-language sources.* Westport, CT: Greenwood Press.

Horak, J. (Ed.). (1987). *Bibliography of film bibliographies.* New York: Saur.

Kelly, P. T. (1997). *Television violence: A guide to the literature.* Commack, NY: Nova Science.

Langham, J., & Chrichley, J. (Comps.). (1989). *Radio research: An annotated bibliography 1975–1988* (2nd ed.). Aldershot, VT: Aveburg.

Lent, J. A. (Comp.). (1991). *Women and mass communications: An international annotated bibliography.* Westport, CT: Greenwood Press.

McCavitt, W. E., Pringle, P. K., & Clinton, H. H. (1989). *Radio and television: A selected, annotated bibliography.* Metuchen, NJ: Scarecrow Press.

McCoy, R. E. (1968). *Freedom of the press: An annotated bibliography.* Carbondale: Southern Illinois University Press.

McCoy, R. E. (1979). *Freedom of the press, a bibliocyclopedia: Ten-year supplement, 1967–1977.* Carbondale: Southern Illinois University Press.

McCoy, R. E. (1993). *Freedom of the press: An annotated bibliography. Second supplement, 1978–1992.* Carbondale: Southern Illinois University Press.

National Union Catalog. (1953–). *N.U.C. U.S. Books.* Washington, DC: Library of Congress.

Northwest Regional Educational Laboratory. (1998). *Bibliography of assessment alternatives: Oral communication.* Portland, OR: Author.

Nuessel, F. (1992). *The image of older adults in the media: An annotated bibliography.* Westport, CT: Greenwood Press.

Performing arts books: 1876–1981. (1981). New York: Bowker.

Public Relations Society of America. (1996). *Bibliography for public relations professionals.* New York: Author.

Shiers, G. (1997). *Early television: A bibliographic guide to 1940.* New York: Garland.

Signorielli, N. (Ed.). (1993). *Mass media images and impact on health: A sourcebook.* Westport, CT: Greenwood Press.

Sloan, W. D. (Comp.). (1989). *American journalism history: An annotated bibliography.* New York: Greenwood Press.

WorldCat [On-line]. (1978–). Dublin, OH: Online Computer Library Center.

■ GUIDES TO THE LITERATURE

Aby, S. H. (1997). *Sociology: A guide to reference and information sources* (2nd ed.). Englewood, CO: Libraries Unlimited.

Asante, C. E. (1997). *Press freedom and development: A research guide and selected bibliography.* Westport, CT: Greenwood Press.

Awe, S. C. (1997). *ARBA guide to subject encyclopedias and dictionaries* (2nd ed.). Englewood, CO: Libraries Unlimited.

Balay, R., Carrington, V. F., & Martin, M. S. (1996). *Guide to reference books* (11th ed.). Chicago: American Library Association.

Baxter, P. M. (1993). *Psychology: A guide to reference and information sources.* Englewood, CO: Libraries Unlimited.

Block, E. S., & Bracken, J. K. (1991). *Communication and mass media: A guide to the reference literature.* Englewood, CO: Libraries Unlimited.

Bracken, J. K., & Sterling, C. H. (1995). *Telecommunications research resources: An annotated guide.* Mahwah, NJ: Erlbaum.

Butler, F. P. (1999). *Business research sources: A reference navigator.* Boston: Irwin McGraw-Hill.

Cabott, J. H. (1998). *Human psychology: Index of new information with authors, subjects, research categories, and references.* Washington, DC: Abbe.

Caswell, L. S. (1989). *Guide to sources in American journalism history.* New York: Greenwood Press.

Cates, J. A. (1997). *Journalism: A guide to the reference literature* (2nd ed.). Englewood, CO: Libraries Unlimited.

Chandler, Y. J. (1998). *Neal-Schuman guide to finding legal and regulatory information on the Internet.* New York: Neal-Schuman.

Cohen, M. L., Berring, R. C., & Olson, K. C. (1989). *How to find the law* (9th ed.). St. Paul: West.

Daniells, L. M. (1993). Business information sources (3rd ed.). Berkeley: University of California Press.

Day, A., & Walsh, M. (Eds.). (1994). *Walford's guide to reference material: Vol. 2. Social and historical sciences, philosophy, and religion* (7th ed.). London: Library Association Publishing.

Dyer, C. (Ed.). (1999). *The Iowa guide: Scholarly journals in mass communication and related fields* (7th ed.). Thousand Oaks, CA: Sage.

Elias, S., Levinkind, S., & Portman, J. (1998). *Legal research: How to find and understand the law* (6th ed.). Berkeley, CA: Nolo Press.

Greenfield, T. A. (1989). *Radio: A reference guide.* Westport, CT: Greenwood Press.

Herron, N. L. (1996). *The social sciences: A cross-disciplinary guide to selected sources* (2nd ed.). Englewood, CO: Libraries Unlimited.

Hill, S. M. (Ed.). (1989). *Broadcasting bibliography: A guide to the literature of radio and television* (3rd ed.). Washington, DC: National Association of Broadcasters.

Hoffman, F. W. (1995). *American popular culture: A guide to the reference literature.* Englewood, CO: Libraries Unlimited.

Jacobstein, J. M., Mersky, R. M., & Dunn, D. J. (1998). *Fundamentals of legal research* (7th ed.). New York: Foundation Press.

Martin, F. S., & Goehlert, R. (1996). *How to research Congress.* Washington, DC: Congressional Quarterly.

Morgan, J. (1996). *Film researcher's handbook: A guide to sources in North America, South America, Asia, Australasia and Africa.* New York: Routledge.

National Association of Broadcasters. (1996). *NAB legal guide to broadcast regulations* (2nd ed.). Washington, DC: Author.

Passarelli, A. B. (1989). *Public relations in business, government, and society: A bibliographic guide.* Englewood, CO: Libraries Unlimited.

Signorielli, N. (1991). *A sourcebook on children and television.* New York: Greenwood Press.

Sterling, C. H., Bracken, J. K., & Hill, S. M. (1998). *Mass communications research resources: An annotated guide.* Mahwah, NJ: Erlbaum.

Ward, J., & Hansen, K. A. (1997). *Search strategies in mass communication* (3rd ed.). New York: Longman.

Wick, R. L, & Mood, T. A. (1998). *ARBA guide to biographical resources, 1986–1997.* Englewood, CO: Libraries Unlimited.

York, H. E. (1990). *Political science: A guide to reference and information sources.* Englewood, CO: Libraries Unlimited.

■ PERIODICAL INDEXES AND ABSTRACTS

ABC Pol Sci. (1969–). Santa Barbara, CA: ABC-Clio Press.

ABC Pol Sci on Disc [CD-ROM]. (1984–). Santa Barbara, CA: ABC-Clio Press.

ABI/Inform Global [On-line]. (1971–). Ann Arbor, MI: University Microfilms International.

Academic Search [On-line]. (1984–). Ipswich, MA: Ebsco.

America History and Life. (1964–). Santa Barbara, CA: ABC-Clio Press.

America History and Life [On-line and CD-ROM]. (1969–). Santa Barbara, CA: ABC-Clio Press.

Arts & Humanities Citation Index [On-line]. (1980–). Philadelphia: Institute for Scientific Information. (Included in *Web of Science*)

ASHA [On-line]. (1998–). Washington, DC: American-Speech-Language-Hearing Association.

Book Review Digest. (1905–). New York: Wilson.

Book Review Digest [On-line]. (1983–). New York: Wilson.

Book Review Index. (1965–). Detroit: Gale Research.

British Humanities Index. (1962–1988). London: Library Association Quarterly. (CD-ROM version as *BHI Plus* after 1988)

Business Index ASAP [On-line]. (1988–). Foster City, CA: Information Access. (Available as part of InfoTrac SearchBank)

Business Periodicals Index [CD-ROM]. (1958–). New York: Wilson.

Business Source [On-line]. (1990–). Ipswich, MA: Ebsco.

Child Development Abstracts and Bibliography. (1927–). Chicago: Society for Research in Child Development/University of Chicago Press.

Child Development Abstracts and Bibliography [On-line]. (1990–). Chicago: Society for Research in Child Development/University of Chicago Press.

ComIndex [Computer diskette]. (1992–). Rochester, NY: Communication Institute for Online Scholarship. (Journals are indexed from inception)

Communication Abstracts. (1978–). Thousand Oaks, CA: Sage.

CommSearch (2nd ed.) [CD-ROM]. (1997). Annandale, VA: National Communication Association.

Contemporary Women's Issues [On-line]. (1992–). Beachwood, OH: Responsive Database Services.

CQ Researcher. (1992–). Washington, DC: Congressional Quarterly.

Current Index to Journals in Education. (1969–). Phoenix: Oryx Press. (Included in *ERIC*)

Current Law Index. (1980–). Los Altos, CA: Information Access.

Dissertation Abstracts International. (1938–). Ann Arbor, MI: University Microfilms International.

Dissertation Abstracts International [On-line]. (1980–). Ann Arbor, MI: University Microfilms International. (Coverage from 1861)

Education Index. (1929–). New York: Wilson.

Education Abstracts [On-line]. (1983–). New York: Wilson.

ERIC [On-line]. (1969–). Washington, DC: Educational Resource Information Center.

Ethnic NewsWatch [On-line and CD-ROM]. (1991–). Stamford, CT: SoftLine Information.

Expanded Academic Index [On-line]. (1980–). Foster City, CA: Information Access.

Film Literature Index. (1973–). Albany: State University of New York Press.

Historical Abstracts [On-line]. (1967–). Santa Barbara, CA: ABC-Clio Press.

Humanities Abstracts [On-line]. (1974–). New York: Wilson.

Humanities Index. (1974–). New York: Wilson.

Index to Journals in Mass Communication [Computer diskette]. (1988–1995). Riverside, CA: Carpelan.

Index to Legal Periodicals and Books. (1908–). New York: Wilson.

Index to Legal Periodicals and Books [On-line]. (1981–). New York: Wilson.

Journalism & Mass Communication Abstracts: M.A., M.S., Ph.D. Theses in Journalism and Mass Communication. (1963–). Columbia, SC: Association for Education in Journalism and Mass Communication.

Journalism Quarterly, cumulative index to volumes 1–40, 1924–1963. (1964). Columbia, SC: Association for Education in Journalism.

Journalism Quarterly, cumulative index to volumes 40–50, 1964–1973. (1974). Columbia, SC: Association for Education in Journalism.

Journalism Quarterly, cumulative index to volumes 51–60, 1974–1983. (1984). Columbia, SC: Association for Education in Journalism and Mass Communication.

Journal of Broadcasting: Author and topic index to volume 1 through 25 (Winter 1956/57 through Fall 1981). (1982). Washington, DC: Broadcast Education Association.

Legal Resource Index [On-line]. (1980–). Foster City, CA: Information Access.

Linguistics and Language Behavior Abstracts. (1967–). La Jolla, CA: Sociological Abstracts.

Linguistics and Language Behavior Abstracts [On-line]. (1973–). La Jolla, CA: Sociological Abstracts.

Matlon, R. J., & Ortiz, S. P. (Eds.). (1997). *Index to journals in communication studies through 1995* (2 vols.). Annandale, VA: National Communication Association.

Organizational Communication: Abstracts, Analysis, and Overview. (1976–1983). Beverly Hills, CA: Sage.

PAIS International [On-line]. (1972–). New York: Public Affairs Information Service.

Periodical Abstracts [On-line]. (1987–). Ann Arbor, MI: University Microfilms International.

Periodical Contents Index (PCI) [On-line]. (1996–). Alexandria, VA: Chadwyck-Healey. (Journals are indexed from inception to 1991)

Personnel Management Abstracts. (1955–). Ann Arbor: University of Michigan, Graduate School of Business.

Philosopher's Index. (1969–). Bowling Green, OH: Bowling Green State University.

Philosopher's Index [On-line]. (1990–). Bowling Green, OH: Bowling Green State University.

Psychological Abstracts. (1927–). Washington, DC: American Psychological Association.

PsycINFO [On-line]. (1967–). Washington, DC: American Psychological Association. (Coverage from 1887)

PsycLIT [CD-ROM]. (1974–). Washington, DC: American Psychological Association. (Coverage from 1887)

Public Affairs Information Service. (1915–). *Bulletin.* New York: Author.

Public Administration Abstracts. (1974–). Thousand Oaks, CA: Sage.

Readers' Guide Abstracts [On-line]. (1983–). New York: Wilson.

Readers' Guide to Periodical Literature. (1901–). New York: Wilson.

Resources in Education. (1966–). Washington, DC: Government Printing Office. (Included in the *ERIC* database)

Social Sciences Abstracts [On-line]. (1983–). New York: Wilson.

Social Sciences Citation Index [On-line]. (1972–). Philadelphia: Institute for Scientific Information. (Included in *Web of Science*)

Social Sciences Index. (1974–). New York: Wilson.

Sociofile [On-line]. (1974–). San Diego: Sociological Abstracts.

Sociological Abstracts. (1953–). San Diego: Sociological Abstracts.

Speech Index. (1935–). Metuchen, NJ: Scarecrow Press.

Topicator: Classified Article Guide to the Advertising/Communications/ Marketing/Periodical Press. (1965–). Golden, CO: Topicator.

UnCoverWeb [On-line]. (1988–). Denver: UnCover.

Web of Science [On-line]. (1987–). Philadelphia: Institute for Scientific Information. (*Web of Science* includes *Arts & Humanities Citation Index* and *Social Sciences Citation Index*. Available: http://www.webof science.com

Wilson Business Abstracts [On-line]. (1982–). New York: Wilson.

Women Studies Abstracts. (1972–). Rush, NY: Rush.

Women's Resources International [On-line]. (1972–). Baltimore: National Information Services.

Work Related Abstracts. (1950–). Warren, MI: Harmonie Park Press. (Formerly titled *Labor/Personnel Index*, 1950–1958, and *Employment Relations Abstracts*, 1959–1972)

■ MEDIA INDEXES

Alternative Press Center [On-line]. (1999). *Online directory.* Available: http://www.altpress.org/

Alternative Press Index. (1969–). Baltimore: Alternative Press Center.

Alternative Press Index [On-line and CD-ROM]. (1991–). Baltimore: National Information Services. Available: http://www.nisc.com

American Journalism Review [On-line]. (1999). *AJR NewsLink*. Available: http://www.newslink.org/menu.html

Black Newspaper Index. (1987–). Ann Arbor, MI: University Microfilms International. (Continues *Index to Black Newspapers*, 1977–1986)

Broadcast News [CD-ROM]. (1993–). Woodbridge, CT: Research Publications International.

CBS News Index. (1975–1991). Ann Arbor, MI: University Microfilms International.

Chicago Tribune Index. (1972–). Ann Arbor, MI: University Microfilms International.

Chicago Tribune Index. (1982–). New York: New York Times. (Continues *Chicago Tribune Newspaper Index*, 1972–1978, and *Bell & Howell Newspaper Index to the Chicago Tribune*, 1979–1981)

Christian Science Monitor Index. (1945–). Boston: Christian Science Monitor.

Christian Science Monitor Index. (1987–). Ann Arbor, MI: University Microfilms International. (Continues *Index to the Christian Science Monitor*, 1970–1978, and *Bell & Howell Newspaper Index to the Christian Science Monitor*, 1979–1986)

CNN News Transcripts [On-line]. (1991–). Oklahoma City: Data Times.

Data Times EyeQ [On-line]. (1996–). Oklahoma City: Data Times.

Dintrone, C. V. (1996). *Television program master index: Access to critical and historical information on 1002 shows in 341 books*. Jefferson, NC: McFarland.

Disinformation [On-line]. (No date.). Available: http://www/disinfo.com

Dow Jones News/Retrieval [On-line]. (1990–). New York: Dow Jones.

Editor & Publisher Interactive. (1999). *MediaINFO links: Online media directory* [On-line]. Available: http://www.mediainfo.com/emedia/

Ethnic NewsWatch [On-line and CD-ROM]. (1991–). Stamford, CT: SoftLine Information.

Film Index International [CD-ROM]. (1993–). Paris: Chadwyck-Healey.

Foreign Broadcast Information Service. (1995–). *WNC: World News Connection* [On-line]. Available: http://wnc.fedworld.gov/

Fulltext Sources Online: For Periodicals, Newspapers, Newswires & TV/ Radio Transcripts. (1989–). Bedford, NJ: Information Today.

Gale Database of Publications and Broadcast Media [On-line]. (1992–). Detroit: Gale Research.

Global NewsBank [On-line]. (1985–). New Canaan, CT: NewsBank.

Goble, A. (Ed.). (1999–). *Complete index to world film since 1895* [CD-ROM]. New Providence, NJ: Bowker.

Hanson, P. K., & Hanson, S. L. (Eds.). (1986). *Film review index, volume 1: 1882–1949*. Phoenix: Oryx Press.

Hanson, P. K., & Hanson, S. L. (Eds.). (1987). *Film review index, volume 2: 1950–1985*. Phoenix: Oryx Press.

Historical Index to the New York Times on CD-ROM [CD-ROM]. (1998–). Alexandria, VA: Chadwyck-Healey.

LEXIS-NEXIS Academic Universe [On-line]. (1998–). Miamisburg, OH: LEXIS-NEXIS.

Library of Congress. (1999). *Newspaper Indexes* [On-line]. Available: http://lcweb.loc.gov/rr/news/oltitles.html

Los Angeles Times Index. (1984–). Ann Arbor, MI: University Microfilms International. (Continues *Los Angeles Times Newspaper Index*, 1972–1978, and *Bell & Howell Newspaper Index to the Los Angeles Times*, 1980–1985)

Milner, A. C. (Ed.). (1977–1982). *Newspaper indexes: A location and subject guide for researchers* (3 vols.). Metuchen, NJ: Scarecrow Press.

National Information Center for Educational Media. (1998). *NICEM thesaurus*. Albuquerque: Author.

National Newspaper Index [On-line]. (1979–). Foster City, CA: Information Access.

NewsBank Electronic Information System [CD-ROM]. (1990–). New Canaan, CT: NewsBank.

Newspaper Abstracts [On-line]. (1989–). Ann Arbor, MI: University Microfilms International.

Newspaper Source [On-line]. (1995–). Ipswich, MA: Ebsco.

New York Times [On-line]. (1969–). New York: New York Times.

New York Times Index. (1851–). New York: New York Times.

New York Times Ondisc [CD-ROM]. (1990–). New York: New York Times.

NICEM Reference CD-ROM [CD-ROM]. (1967–). Albuquerque: National Information Center for Educational Media.

NICEM Reference Online [On-line]. (1967–). Albuquerque: National Information Center for Educational Media.

Official Index to the Times, 1906–1980 on CD-ROM [CD-ROM]. (1998–). Cambridge, UK: Chadwyck-Healey.

Palmer's Index to the Times on CD-ROM, 1790–1905 [CD-ROM]. (1994–1995). Cambridge, UK: Chadwyck-Healey.

Public Television Transcripts Index. (1973–). Woodbridge, CT: Research Publications International.

Riley, S., & Selnow, G. (Comps.). (1989). *Index to city and regional magazines of the United States*. New York: Greenwood Press.

Special Libraries Association, News Division. (1999, Feb. 8). *U.S. News archives on the Web* [On-line]. Available: http://metalab.unc.edu/slanews/internet/archives.html#Ohio

TV News Index and Abstracts [On-line]. (1980–). Available: http://tvnews.vanderbilt.edu

Wall Street Journal Index. (1955–). Ann Arbor, MI: University Microfilms International.

Washington Post Index. (1989–). Ann Arbor, MI: University Microfilms International. (Continues *Official Washington Post Index*, 1979–1988, and *Bell & Howell Newspaper Index to the Washington Post*, 1979–1981)

EXAMPLES

CHRIS decides to use *ComIndex* to find articles on ghostwriting. By entering the term "ghost," several relevant articles are identified.

FELECIA decides that it's time to look at some newspaper abstracts to find other reporters' stories on voice mail. *Newspaper Abstracts* seems to be a fairly general and far-reaching source, so that is a good place to start. This search reveals several recent articles on this phenomenon. She also decides to search some of the big papers, like the *New York Times* and *Wall Street Journal;* she can do this at the papers' websites or, better yet, by consulting *U.S News Archives On the Web.*

MARIA has now read several summary articles about attribution. Because the term originated in psychology, she decides to search the *PsycLIT* database. Looking only in the past 5 years for English-language journal articles, Maria finds there are 40 articles on this topic. She e-mails herself the search results along with the abstracts so that she can make an informed decision about which articles to read.

ORLANDO'S discovery that the term was coined by Horton and Wohl in 1956 allows for a *Social Sciences Citation Index* search. By entering the relevant information about this original article, Orlando can find out the citations of all articles that cited this original piece. This is especially fruitful to trace the research in this area over the years. Other relevant indexes and abstracts to search for this topic are *PsycINFO, Sociological Abstracts,* and *CommSearch.* By searching all of these, Orlando should have all articles needed for a thorough literature review of parasocial interaction.

KAT, CALVIN, ROCKY, and **MICHELLE'S** training program will undoubtedly benefit from the use of educational media. They consult the *NICEM Index* from the National Information Center for Educational Media and find several conflict-oriented videos. Calvin and Rocky volunteer to find some reviews and then preview those that are most appropriate.

EXERCISES

1. You are not having much luck with your literature search and notice that the few articles you have managed to find on your topic have appeared in journals in allied disciplines, mostly sociology. You turn to a guide to the literature of the social sciences, *The Social Sciences: A Cross-Disciplinary Guide to Selected Sources*, to identify sources in that discipline that may help you in your search. Use the subject index to:

   a. Find the entry number of the first literature guide listed under this discipline.

   b. Give the title of this guide.

2. By using the bibliographies of subject encyclopedias and other standard texts, you have found several references to a 1972 article by M. E. McCombs and D. Shaw published in *Public Opinion Quarterly*. It appears to be a key piece of research on your topic. Unfortunately, this study is several years old. To identify research done at a later time that you hope will update it, you turn to the on-line version of the *Social Sciences Citation Index*.

   a. Who is the author of the last article listed that cites your key article?

   b. In what journal and year did this appear?

   c. What is the title of this article?

3. You are doing research on interpersonal communication. Subject bibliographies have been useful, but you wish to find other sources for your literature search. To find summaries of research on your topic, you are now using *Communication Abstracts*. Locate the heading for your topic in the *Cumulative Subject Index* of the 1998 volume.

   a. What is the third entry number listed?

   b. Locate the abstract for this item and supply the complete citation in APA format (see Appendix A).

4. When doing research for a term paper in your Intercultural Communication class, you have been fortunate to find plenty of background information on your topic, multicultural training, but nothing about research done in this area since 1990. Because you feel the topic of interviewing is likely to be of interest to educators, you believe on-line searching of *ERIC* would be a good finding tool.

   a. Turning first to the thesaurus, what descriptors do you find used for your topic? In other words, to what descriptors are you referred? Choose the first one.

   b. Search the database from 1990 to the present. How many sources did you find?

   c. E-mail the results to your e-mail account.

5. Complete your search strategy sheet by adding sources from this chapter that will help lead you to primary sources. Have your instructor check your list before you begin examining each source for your topic.

6. Examine issues of *Communication Abstracts* in class and read some of the abstracts. Is your topic area a key word? If not, what key words lead you to articles in this area?
7. List the steps necessary for searching the *Index to Journals in Communication Studies Through 1995*. Try locating sources for your topic.

chapter 7

Communication Periodicals

I n previous chapters, we identified important books for researching communication topics and suggested how a book might be judged a standard or viable work. We've also described the tools used to identify periodical articles. In this chapter we focus on the periodicals containing these original research reports, articles on communication industry practices, and other original information.

We first discuss the major scholarly journals in the communication field. We describe the content and publisher of each journal. Any research study, literature review, or prospectus in communication typically references a number of the articles in these journals. Articles found in professional and trade magazines are less "scholarly" in nature in that they are usually not original research studies. These periodicals contain data on industry trends, along with industry news, opinion, and thought essays. They allow industry professionals to keep abreast of developments in their field. They contain useful information for communication students. For example, we could turn to them to find out about organizational management-training programs for dealing with the media.

Periodicals are publications with distinctive titles that are published on a regular basis. Communication periodicals are useful when researching any communication topic. Examine these sources during the research process and consider including them in research paper assignments. Be aware of their potential value in the future. In many careers, knowledge of these sources provides a means of networking and gives professionals a deeper understanding of the issues and research in the field.

SCHOLARLY JOURNALS

Scholarly journals are the major vehicles for reporting current studies conducted by academic and professional researchers. These journals are usually edited and published by a learned society, a professional association, an academic institution, or a commercial publishing firm. The **articles** are written by specialists and usually are critically evaluated by other scholars before being accepted for publication. They often represent well-designed, important, and current research efforts. A scholarly journal article may examine a topic that has not yet been studied and may never be treated in a book-length publication, or it may contain new information about a subject that has been researched and reported in the past. Many of these journals have web pages that contain submission information and often the table of contents for the past issue.

Although editorial practices differ, scholarly journals primarily publish unsolicited reports of research endeavors. This means that the researcher conducts an investigation and submits the report or manuscript to a journal editor. The editor then sends the manuscript to other communication researchers, who are specialists in a given area, typically for a blind review. Thus, the quality of unsolicited research articles is scrutinized before publication, and reviewers of the work are usually unaware of the author's identity. Articles that withstand this review process are generally rewritten once or twice before publication. Such revised manuscripts are often reviewed again before a publication decision. Most quality journals have a rather hefty manuscript-rejection rate. Sometimes scholarly journal editors solicit specific articles or opinion pieces from communication scholars. These pieces may also be reviewed by editorial board members to ensure their quality. Book reviews, notices of other publications, bibliographies, and general news about the field may also appear. But scholarly journals concentrate on publishing original theory and research articles.

As you examine scholarly journal articles, you will note that they are fairly standardized, especially the quantitative research articles. They begin with an introductory section analyzing past research about the conceptual issue or problem. This introduction includes a summary of previous related research, an explanation of gaps or contradictions found in studying the problem, an identification of the significance of the research problem, and the positing of research hypotheses or questions. The second section details the method of the investigation and how the information was observed or collected. It includes a description of the people, objects, or events studied. For survey research or experimental studies, for example, it would contain a summary of sample size, sample selection, and the devices used to measure the variables. Next, the results of the analysis are presented along with other findings. In quantitative research, this section describes the application of appropriate statistical tests to interpret the collected data. Finally, the last section presents a discussion of the meaning or implications of the results, the limitations of the study, and the future research needs in the problem area.

A several-sentence summary or paragraph-length abstract is usually found at the beginning of each article or in the journal's table of contents. These brief abstracts are often the basis of the synopses published in collections such as *Communication Abstracts*. They can be helpful in determining the article's utility for your own research project.

The references cited in footnotes or in the bibliography at the end of each article are usually the most up-to-date sources of material for that particular area of study at that time. Thus, both the content of the article and the references cited are valuable research aids. It is important to emphasize, though, that there are varied periods of delay between the time when the research study is initially conducted, when it is submitted for publication consideration, when it is eventually accepted for publication, and when the journal issue that contains the report is finally published. This lag time is often 2 years or even longer. Electronic journals have eliminated some of this lag.

An annotated list of some of the scholarly journals often used by communication students and researchers follows. These journals represent a selection of several major national scholarly journals in the communication field.

> *Communication Education*. (1952–). Annandale, VA: National Communication Association.

■   This quarterly journal publishes research and pedagogy articles about elementary, secondary, and higher education, primarily in speech communication. It has occasionally included reports that focus on organizational training or mass-communication instruction. Earlier volumes contained sections on innovative instructional practices, ERIC reports on specific communication topics, and reviews of print and nonprint resources for educators. Volumes contain reviews of books and other resources. *Communication Education* (formerly *Speech Teacher*) is published in January, April, July, and October, and an annual index appears in the October issue.

> *Communication Monographs*. (1934–). Annandale, VA: National Communication Association.

■   *Communication Monographs* publishes research reports and new theories about the processes of communication in several contexts. In general, the journal contains quantitative empirical research articles focusing on message, source, and receiver variables in interpersonal, group, organizational, and public communication. It is published quarterly in March, June, September, and December. An annual index appears in the year's final issue. (Volumes 1 through 42 were published under the title *Speech Monographs*.)

> *Communication Research*. (1974–). Thousand Oaks, CA: Sage.

■   This bimonthly journal focuses on models that explain communication processes and outcomes. Published articles report research in mass, international, political, organizational, and interpersonal communication. Some articles integrate interdisciplinary interests in human communication. There also are research and book-review essays. *Communication Research* is published in February, April, June, August, October, and December. Two of these issues each year are devoted to different themes. A yearly cumulative author index appears in the December issue.

> *Critical Studies in Mass Communication*. (1984–). Annandale, VA: National Communication Association.

■   *Critical Studies* publishes theoretical and critical essays about the evolution, economics, and organization of mass-communication systems; the form and structure of media content; the relationship between culture and mass communication; models of media processes; and mass-media criticism. There are review and criticism and booknotes sections. The journal is published quarterly in March, June, September, and December. A yearly cumulative article index appears in the December issue.

Human Communication Research. (1974–). Austin, TX: International Communication Association.

■ *HCR* offers a behavioral science approach to the study of human communication. Articles report original research, offer new methodological approaches, synthesize research literature, and present new theoretical perspectives on human interaction. The journal publishes research in interpersonal, organizational, and mass communication, as well as in methodology, information systems, and persuasion. Early volumes contained state-of-the-art pieces and a colloquy section presenting alternative ways of looking at communication issues. This quarterly journal is published in the fall, winter, spring, and summer. An annual index appears in the summer issue.

Journal of Broadcasting & Electronic Media. (1956/1957–). Washington, DC: Broadcast Education Association.

■ This quarterly journal, formerly the *Journal of Broadcasting*, publishes research articles about communication and the electronic media. Subject matter includes audience and media-effects research, communication policy and regulation, new technologies, broadcast history, international communication, media criticism, media content and programming, and economics. It also contains brief reports of research and book reviews. The journal is published in the winter, spring, summer, and fall, and yearly author and title indexes appear in the fall issue.

Journal of Communication. (1952–). Austin, TX: International Communication Association.

■ This quarterly journal focuses on the interdisciplinary study of communication theory, practice, and policy. Articles concentrate on mass-communication processes and the societal impact of communication. Also included are book reviews and review essays. The journal returned to being a publication of the International Communication Association in 1992. It is published in winter, spring, summer, and autumn. Title and author indexes appear annually in the autumn issue.

Journalism & Mass Communication Quarterly. (1924–). Columbia, SC: Association for Education in Journalism and Mass Communication.

■ This journal focuses on research in journalism and mass communication. Articles report on the conduct of news, mass-media effects, international communication, historical treatments of issues, and social and legal dimensions of the media. Also included are brief research reports, book reviews, mass-communication bibliographies, and annual convention summaries. It is published quarterly in the spring, summer, autumn, and winter.

Quarterly Journal of Speech. (1915–). Annandale, VA: National Communication Association.

■ *QJS* is the oldest journal in speech communication. Articles are generally historical or critical in nature, with an emphasis on rhetorical theory and criticism. The goal of the journal is to broaden awareness and understanding of speech communication from a humanistic viewpoint. Book-review and forum sections are included. The journal is published in February, May, August, and November. (Volumes 1–3 were published under the title *Quarterly Journal of Public Speaking*, and Volumes 4–13 were titled *Quarterly Journal of Speech Education.*)

Several other journals are also frequently consulted by communication researchers. Among these are journals published by different communication associations, such as the *Journal of Applied Communication Research* and *Text and Performance Quarterly* (National Communication Association); *Journalism & Mass Communication Educator* and *Journalism & Mass Communication Monographs* (Association for Education in Journalism and Mass Communication); *Communication Theory* (International Communication Association); and *World Communication* (World Communication Association). Besides the journals of several state associations, six journals are published quarterly by four regional communication associations:

Communication Quarterly. (1953–). Eastern Communication Association. (Formerly *Today's Speech*)

Communication Reports. (1988–). Western States Communication Association.

Communication Research Reports. (1984–). Eastern Communication Association.

Communication Studies. (1949–). Central States Communication Association.(Formerly *Central States Speech Journal*)

Southern Communication Journal. (1935–). Southern States Communication Association. (Formerly *Southern Speech Communication Journal* and *Southern Speech Journal*)

Western Journal of Communication. (1937–). Western States Communication Association. (Formerly *Western Journal of Speech Communication, Western Speech Communication,* and *Western Speech*)

Several electronic journals have begun recently. The *Journal of Computer-Mediated Communication,* the *American Communication Journal*, and the *Electronic Journal of Communication* publish articles of interest to communication scholars. We expect to see more of these emerging in the future. In assessing the quality of electronic journals, consider the editorial board and process, the quality of the articles, whether the journal referees manuscripts, the journal's acceptance rate, and the reputation of the authors.

Besides these scholarly communication journals, there are several related journals, such as *Public Opinion Quarterly* and the *Journal of Personality and Social Psychology,* that you may find useful. A list of scholarly journals is at the end of this chapter. Consult the library's catalog or serials list to determine whether these scholarly journals are available. Descriptions of many of these journals can be found in the following:

> Katz, W. A., & Katz, L. S. (1997). *Magazines for libraries* (9th ed.). New Providence, NJ: Bowker.

In addition, copies of the tables of contents of scholarly journals are available on the journal's home page or in the following:

> *Current Contents: Social and Behavioral Sciences.* (1961–). Philadelphia: Institute for Scientific Information.
>
> ■ This is a weekly publication of more than 1300 tables of contents. Each issue has a key-word subject index, author index, address directory, and publishers' addresses. Volumes related to the arts and humanities are also available.

An on-line table of contents service, such as UnCoverWeb, described in Chapter 6, might be more convenient: <**http://uncweb.carl.org**>.

PROFESSIONAL AND TRADE MAGAZINES

Professional and **trade magazines** are often important sources of information and insight into the communication field. They are used to lend perspective to practical applications of communication theory and research or to detail the issues, events, and trends facing the communication industry.

Generally, research reports are not the mainstay of professional and trade magazines, although the results of a study may sometimes be capsulized. These publications emphasize news of events, issues, and innovations in the field.

For example, they publish articles on new audio and video technologies, advertising campaigns, marketing and management strategies, communication-training programs in industry, public relations techniques, and in-house organizational publications. In addition, they often present news about people in the industry, upcoming professional events, and employment opportunities. Check the home pages of the organizations or publications for current news.

The following four publications are often consulted by students looking for information related to the professions of advertising, broadcasting, journalism, and public relations.

> *Advertising Age.* (1930–). Chicago: Crain Communications. Available: http://adage.com
>
> ■ This weekly magazine provides an extended review of news related to advertising and marketing. It includes summaries of current news about

advertisers, syndicators, agencies, and products; interactive media and technology reports; news about advertising professionals and businesses; analyses of media and marketing issues; data about products, market shares, and companies; viewpoints and letters to the editor; special reports on advertising and marketing; classified advertising; and a market index of marketing and media companies.

Broadcasting & Cable. (1931–). New York: Cahners. Available: http://www. broadcastingcable.com

■   This weekly trade publication offers broadcast industry news and special in-depth reports on major issues and developments in radio, television, and cable. It covers broadcast and cable news, programming, government actions, technology, the Internet, and business. Regular departments include brief broadcast-news summaries, industry-related meetings and events, commentaries, industry developments, station license approvals and transfers, Washington watch, Nielsen ratings, classified advertising, news about broadcast professionals, and a profile of an industry practitioner.

Columbia Journalism Review. (1962–). New York: Columbia University, Graduate School of Journalism. Available: http://www.cjr.com

■   This bimonthly magazine critically assesses the performance of the press. Articles focus on news professionals, journalistic practices, the media, press treatment of politics and contemporary issues, press news from around the world, and the operation of news organizations. Current issues and events in journalism are chronicled, and websites are highlighted. It also includes a publisher's note, editorials, "darts" and "laurels" for media performances, comments on industry and societal events, press treatment of news stories, book reviews and excerpts, letters to the editor, and a graphic presentation of errors in newspaper headlines and stories.

Public Relations Strategist. (1995–). New York: Public Relations Society of America. Available: http://www.prsa.org

■   This quarterly published magazine focuses on issues and trends for public relations practitioners. Features include an interview with a public relations CEO discussing public relations in organizations and articles on research, strategies, and issues. Articles have addressed feminism, alternative media, crisis public relations, getting the message across, moral reasoning, and corporate values.

Additional professional and trade magazines related to the communication field are listed in "Selected Sources," which follows. The articles in these publications are often indexed in the comprehensive, interdisciplinary indexes discussed in Chapter 6 (*Academic Search, Academic Index, Periodical Abstracts*). In the listings we include the earlier titles of scholarly journals in parentheses.

SELECTED SOURCES

■ SCHOLARLY JOURNALS

Communication

Argumentation and Advocacy (Journal of the American Forensic Association). (1964–). American Forensic Association.

Australian Journal of Communication. (1982–). Communication Institute.

Communication Education (Speech Teacher). (1952–). National Communication Association.

Communication Monographs (Speech Monographs). (1934–). National Communication Association.

Communication Quarterly (Today's Speech). (1953–). Eastern Communication Association.

Communication Reports. (1988–). Western States Communication Association.

Communication Research. (1974–). Sage.

Communication Research Reports. (1984–). Eastern Communication Association.

Communication Review. (1997–). Gordon & Breach.

Communication Studies (Central States Speech Journal). (1949–). Central States Communication Association.

Communication Theory. (1991–). International Communication Association.

European Journal of Communication. (1986–). Sage.

Health Communication. (1989–). Erlbaum.

Howard Journal of Communications. (1988–). Howard University.

Human Communication Research. (1974–). International Communication Association.

International Journal of Listening (Journal of the International Listening Association). (1987–). International Listening Association.

Journal-National Forensic League. (1991–). National Forensic League.

Journal of Applied Communication Research. (1973–). National Communication Association.

Journal of Asian Pacific Communication. (1991–). Ablex.

Journal of Communication and Religion (Religious Communication Today). (1978–). Religious National Communication Association.

Journal of Communication Inquiry. (1974–). Sage.

Journal of Health Communication. (1996–). Taylor & Francis.

Journal of International Communication. (1994–). International Association for Media & Communication Research, International Communication Section.

Journal of the Association for Communication Administration (Bulletin of the Association for Communication Administration, ACA Bulletin, Bulletin of the Association of Departments and Administrators in Speech Communication). (1972–). Association for Communication Administration.

National Forensic Journal. (1983–). National Forensic Association.

Philosophy and Rhetoric. (1968–). Pennsylvania State University Press.

Political Communication (Political Communication and Persuasion). (1980). American Political Science Association and International Communication Association, Political Communication Divisions.

Quarterly Journal of Speech (Quarterly Journal of Public Speaking, Quarterly Journal of Speech Education). (1915–). National Communication Association.

Rhetoric & Public Affairs. (1998–). Michigan State University Press.

Rhetoric Society Quarterly. (1971–). Rhetoric Society of America.

Southern Communication Journal (Southern Speech Communication Journal, Southern Speech Journal). (1935–). Southern States Communication Association.

Western Journal of Communication (Western Journal of Speech Communication, Western Speech Communication, Western Speech). (1937–). Western States Communication Association.

Women's Studies in Communication (ORWAC Bulletin: Women's Studies in Communication). (1977–). Organization for Research on Women and Communication.

World Communication (Communication). (1972–). World Communication Association.

Mass Communication

American Journalism. (1983–). American Journalism Historians Association.

Asian Journal of Communication. (1990–). Asian Mass Communication Research and Information Centre.

Canadian Journal of Communication (Media Probe). (1974–). E. Beattie.

Cinema Journal. (1966–). Society for Cinema Studies.

Communication Law and Policy. (1996–). Association for Education in Journalism and Mass Communication, Law Division.

Communications and the Law. (1979–). Rothman.

Critical Studies in Mass Communication. (1984–). National Communication Association.

Educational Technology Research and Development (Educational Communication and Technology Journal). (1953–). Association for Educational Communications and Technology.

Federal Communications Law Journal (Federal Communications Bar Journal). (1937–). Federal Communications Bar Association.

Film History. (1987–). Taylor & Francis.

Film Journal International (Film Journal). (1934–). Sunshine Group.

Film Quarterly (Quarterly of Film, Radio, and Television). (1945–). University of California Press.

Gazette. (1955–). Sage.

Hastings Communications and Entertainment Law Journal (COMM/ENT: A Journal of Communications and Entertainment Law). (1977–). University of California, San Francisco, Hastings College of Law.

International Journal of Public Opinion Research. (1989–). World Association for Public Opinion Research.

Journal of Broadcasting & Electronic Media (Journal of Broadcasting). (1956/1957–). Broadcast Education Association.

Journal of Communication. (1951–). International Communication Association.

Journal of Film and Video. (1949–). University Film and Video Association.

Journal of Mass Media Ethics. (1985–). Erlbaum.

Journal of Media Economics. (1988–). Erlbaum.

Journal of Popular Culture. (1967–). Bowling Green State University.

Journal of Popular Film & Television (Journal of Popular Film). (1972–). Bowling Green State University.

Journal of Radio Studies. (1992–). Broadcast Education Association.

Journalism & Mass Communication Educator. (1946–). Association for Education in Journalism and Mass Communication.

Journalism & Mass Communication Monographs. (1966–). Association for Education in Journalism and Mass Communication.

Journalism & Mass Communication Quarterly. (1924–). Association for Education in Journalism and Mass Communication.

Journalism History. (1974–). California State University Foundation.

Journalism Studies. (2000–). Sage.

Mass Communication & Society (Mass Comm Review). (1973–). Erlbaum.

Media, Culture & Society. (1979–). Sage.

Media Management Review. (1997–). Erlbaum.

Media Psychology. (1999–). Erlbaum.

Media Studies Journal (Gannett Center Journal). (1987–). Freedom Forum, Media Studies Center.

New Media & Society. (1999–). Sage.

Newspaper Research Journal. (1979–). Association for Education in Journalism and Mass Communication, Newspaper Division.

Nordicom Review of Nordic Research on Media & Communication. (1981–). Nordic Documentation Center for Mass Communication Research.

Public Opinion Quarterly. (1937–). American Association for Public Opinion Research.

Quarterly Review of Film and Video (Quarterly Review of Film Studies). (1976–). Harwood Academic Publishers.

Science Communication (Knowledge). (1979–). Sage.

Telecommunications Policy. (1976–). Butterworth Scientific.

Trends in Communication. (1997–). Boom.

Speech and Language

American Journal of Speech-Language Pathology. (1991–). American Speech-Language-Hearing Association.

American Speech. (1925–). American Dialect Society.

Applied Psycholinguistics. (1980–). Cambridge University Press.

Discourse & Society. (1990–). Sage.

Discourse Processes. (1978–). Society for Text and Discourse.

Discourse Studies. (1999–). Sage.

ETC.: A Review of General Semantics. (1943–). International Society for General Semantics.

Human Development. (1958–). Karger.

International Journal of American Linguistics. (1917–). Linguistics Society of America.

Journal of Communication Disorders. (1967–). Elsevier Science Publishing.

Journal of Language and Social Psychology. (1982–). Sage.

Journal of Linguistics. (1965–). Linguistic Association of Great Britain.

Journal of Memory and Language (Journal of Verbal Learning and Verbal Behavior). (1962–). Academic Press.

Journal of Psycholinguistic Research. (1971–). Plenum.

Journal of Speech, Language, and Hearing Research (Journal of Speech and Hearing Research). (1958–). American Speech-Language-Hearing Association.

Language & Communication. (1981–). Pergamon Press.

Research on Language and Social Interaction. (1968–). Erlbaum.

Semiotica. (1969–). International Association for Semiotic Studies.

Text and Performance Quarterly (Literature in Performance). (1980–). National Communication Association.

Written Communication. (1984–). Sage.

Advertising, Business, Marketing, and Public Relations

Academy of Management Journal. (1957–). Academy of Management.

Academy of Management Review. (1976–). Academy of Management.

Administrative Science Quarterly. (1956–). Cornell University.

Business Communication Quarterly (Bulletin of the Association for Business Communication, ABCA Bulletin, ABWA Bulletin). (1936–). Association for Business Communication.

Industrial & Labor Relations Review. (1947–). Cornell University.

Information Economics and Policy. (1983–). International Telecommunications Society.

International Journal of Advertising. (1983–). Advertising Association.

Journal of Advertising. (1972–). American Academy of Advertising.

Journal of Advertising History. (1977–). History of Advertising Trust.

Journal of Advertising Research. (1960–). Advertising Research Foundation.

Journal of Business. (1927–). University of Chicago Press.

Journal of Business and Technical Communication (Iowa State Journal of Business and Technical Communication). (1988–). Sage.

Journal of Business Communication. (1963–). American Business Communication Association.

Journal of Consumer Research. (1974–). University of California, Los Angeles, American Association for Public Opinion Research.

Journal of Current Issues and Research in Advertising (Current Issues and Research in Advertising). (1978–). CtC Press.

Journal of Marketing. (1936–). American Marketing Association.

Journal of Marketing Research. (1964–). American Marketing Association.

Journal of Public Relations Research (Public Relations Research Annual). (1989–). Association for Education in Journalism and Mass Communication, Public Relations Division.

Management Communication Quarterly. (1987–). Sage.

Organizational Behavior and Human Decision Processes (Organizational Behavior and Human Performance). (1966–). Academic Press.

Personnel Psychology. (1948–). Personnel Psychology.

Public Relations Quarterly (Quarterly Review of Public Relations). (1955–). American Public Relations Association.

Public Relations Review. (1975–). Foundation for Public Relations Research and Education.

Psychology, Sociology, and Social Psychology

American Behavioral Scientist. (1957–). Sage.

American Journal of Psychology. (1887–). University of Illinois Press.

American Journal of Sociology. (1895–). University of Chicago Press.

American Sociological Review. (1936–). American Sociological Association.

Child Development. (1930–). Society for Research in Child Development.

Cognitive Psychology. (1970–). Academic Press.

Cultural Studies. (1987–). Routledge.

Developmental Psychology. (1969–). American Psychological Association.

Family Relations (Family Coordinator). (1952–). National Council on Family Relations.

Group & Organization Management (Group & Organization Studies). (1976–). Eastern Academy of Management.

Human Organization (Applied Anthropology). (1941–). Society for Applied Anthropology.

International Journal of Intercultural Relations. (1977–). Society for Intercultural Education, Training, and Research.

Journal of Applied Psychology. (1917–). American Psychological Association.

Journal of Applied Social Psychology. (1971–). Winston.

Journal of Cross-Cultural Psychology. (1970–). International Association for Cross-Cultural Psychology.

Journal of Educational Psychology. (1910–). American Psychological Association.

Journal of Experimental Social Psychology. (1965–). Academic Press.

Journal of Humanistic Psychology. (1961–). Association for Humanistic Psychology.

Journal of Marriage and the Family (Living, Marriage and Family Living). (1939–). National Council on Family Relations.

Journal of Nonverbal Behavior (Environmental Psychology and Nonverbal Behavior). (1976–). Human Sciences Press.

Journal of Personality (Character and Personality). (1932–). Duke University Press.

Journal of Personality and Social Psychology (Journal of Abnormal and Social Psychology, Journal of Abnormal Psychology). (1906–). American Psychological Association.

Journal of Personality Assessment (Journal of Projective Techniques & Personality Assessment). (1936–). Society for Personality Assessment.

Journal of Research in Personality (*Journal of Experimental Research in Personality*). (1965–). Academic Press.

Journal of Sex Research. (1965–). Society for the Scientific Study of Sex.

Journal of Social and Personal Relationships. (1984–). Sage.

Personal Relationships. (1994–). International Society for the Study of Personal Relationships.

Personality & Social Psychology Bulletin. (1974–). Society for Personality and Social Psychology.

Small Group Research (*Small Group Behavior, International Journal of Small Group Research*). (1970–). Sage.

Social Forces. (1922–). Southern Sociological Society.

Social Psychology Quarterly (*Sociometry*). (1937–). American Sociological Association.

Symbolic Interaction. (1977–). Society for the Study of Symbolic Interaction.

History and Political Science

American Historical Review. (1895–). American Historical Association.

American Journal of Political Science (*Midwest Journal of Political Science*). (1957–). Midwest Political Science Association.

American Political Science Review. (1906–). American Political Science Association.

American Politics Quarterly. (1973–). Sage.

Comparative Political Studies. (1968–). Sage.

Comparative Politics. (1968–). CUNY Political Science Program.

Harvard International Journal of Press/Politics. (1996). Center on the Press, Politics, and Public Policy.

Journal of American History. (1914–). Organization of American Historians.

Journal of Conflict Resolution (*Conflict Resolution*). (1957–). University of Michigan, Center for Research on Conflict Resolution.

Journal of Politics. (1939–). Southern Political Science Association.

Journal of Social Issues. (1945–). Society for the Psychological Study of Social Issues.

Political Behavior. (1979–). Plenum.

Political Science Quarterly. (1886–). Academy of Political Science.

■ PROFESSIONAL AND TRADE PERIODICALS

Advertising Age. (1930–). Crain Communications.

Adweek. (1979–). Adweek.

American Cinematographer. (1920–). American Society of Cinematographers.

American Editor: Bulletin of the American Society of Newspaper Editors. (1970–). American Society of Newspaper Editors.

American Journalism Review (*Washington Journalism Review*). (1977–). University of Maryland, College of Journalism.

Audio-Visual Communications. (1967–). United Business Publications.

Billboard. (1894–). Billboard.

BPME Image. (1985–). Broadcast Promotion and Marketing Executives.

Broadcasting & Cable. (1931–). Cahners.

Broadcasting and the Law. (1970–). L & S Publications.

Broadcast Management/Engineering. (1965–). Mactier.

Business Horizons. (1958–). Indiana University, Graduate School of Business.

Columbia Journalism Review. (1962–). Columbia University, Graduate School of Journalism.

Corporate Television: The Official Magazine of the International Television Association. (1986–). International Television Association.

Daily Variety. (1933–). Daily Variety.

Editor & Publisher. (1901–). Editor & Publisher.

Educational Technology. (1966–). Educational News Service.

Electronic Media. (1982–). Crain Communications.

Feedback. (1959–). Broadcast Education Association.

Film Comment. (1962–). Film Society of Lincoln Center.

Folio: The Magazine for Magazine Management. (1972–). Merket Publications.

Harvard Business Review. (1922–). Harvard University, Graduate School of Business Administration.

Hollywood Reporter. (1930–). Wilkerson Daily.

Inside PR. (1990–). Editorial Media Marketing International.

Journal of Technical Writing and Communication. (1971–). Baywood.

Marketing News. (1967–). American Marketing Association.

Media & Methods (Teachers Guide to Media & Methods; Educators Guide to Media & Methods). (1964–). North America Publishing.

Mediaweek (Marketing & Media Decisions, Media Decisions). (1966–). A/S/M Communications.

Presstime. (1979–). American Newspaper Publishers Association.

Public Communication Review. (1981–). Boston University, School of Public Communication.

Public Relations Journal. (1945–). Public Relations Society of America.

Quill. (1912–). Society of Professional Journalists.

RTNDA Communicator. (1946–). Radio-Television News Directors Association.

Sight and Sound. (1932–). British Film Institute.

Technical Communication. (1954–). Society for Technical Communication.

Television Quarterly. (1962–). National Academy of Television Arts and Sciences.

Television/Radio Age. (1953–). Television Editorial Corporation.

Variety. (1905–). Variety.

Writer's Digest. (1920–). Writer's Digest.

■ ELECTRONIC JOURNALS

American Communication Journal [On-line]. (1997–). Available: http://www.americancomm.org/%7Eaca/acj/acj.html

Electronic Journal of Communication [On-line]. (1990–). Available: www.cios.org/www.ejcmain.htm

Journal of Computer-Mediated Communication [On-line]. (1995–). Available: http://www.ascusc.org/jcmc/index.html

EXAMPLES

CHRIS, in searching the indexes identified in Chapter 6, has found several journal articles on the ghostwriting topic. By reading articles such as the following, the issues start falling into place.

Bormann, E. G. (1961). Ethics of ghostwritten speeches. *Quarterly Journal of Speech, 47,* 262–267.

FELECIA has found a reference to an electronic journal, *Journal of Computer-Mediated Communication*, which might contain articles related to voice mail. She finds the site, searches for "voice mail," and finds several articles that contain these key words.

MARIA has now collected enough information from secondary sources to do a good job on her report on attribution. From the CIOS (Communication Institute Online Scholarship) search, she decides to look further at one article in the communication literature that sounds intriguing:

Berger, C. R. (1975). Proactive and retroactive attribution processes in interpersonal communications. *Human Communication Research, 2,* 33–50.

ORLANDO has amassed about 30 references on parasocial interaction. Many of these are articles from scholarly journals like *Journal of Broadcasting & Electronic Media, Communication Research,* and *Human Communication Research*. Now is the time to apply good reading and note-taking skills to them. Instead of photocopying them all, Orlando uses a notebook computer and takes notes on each article while reading it.

KAT, **CALVIN**, **ROCKY**, and **MICHELLE** found too much academic information on conflict in organizations and groups. They decide to split up the references and read those that might provide some guidance on how to train people to manage their conflict. They've found some good references in trade and professional periodicals. They decide to visit the American Society for Training and Development <**www.astd.org**> and look at the contents of their *Training and Development* magazine. The site allows visitors to read summaries of articles in each issue, and they find a feature in each issue that helps them become better trainers.

EXERCISES

1. During a literature search for a paper for your Communication Theory and Research class, you've examined bibliographies and indexes and found references to several scholarly journal articles. The abstracts suggest that these articles are pertinent to your topic, deception, so you search for these articles. You want to read them thoroughly to determine whether they lend insight to the paper and whether their references and footnotes can offer further help in your literature search.

   a. The first abstract leads you to *Human Communication Research*:

   > Brandt, D. R., Miller, G. R., & Hocking, J. E. (1980). The truth-deception attribution: Effects of familiarity on the ability of observers to detect deception. *Human Communication Research, 6,* 99–110.

   How was *judgmental accuracy* measured in this study?

   b. The second article is found in *Communication Monographs*:

   > Burgoon, J. K., Buller, D. B., Ebesu, A. S., & Rockwell, P. (1994). Interpersonal deception: V. Accuracy in deception detection. *Communication Monographs, 61,* 303–325.

   What three hypotheses were tested in this study?

   c. The third article is in *Communication Research*:

   > Stiff, J. B., Kim, H. J., & Ramesh, C. N. (1992). Truth biases and aroused suspicion in relational deception. *Communication Research, 19,* 326–345.

   What two procedures have researchers typically used to investigate detection of deception?

2. You are now working on a class report for your Media Law class and want to find recent developments in broadcast regulation. Starting with the most recent issue, you check the "Top-of-the-Week" news items in *Broadcasting & Cable* magazine for the most recent issue you can find. In one sentence, summarize the subject of the first "Top-of-the-Week" news item. Be sure to give the date of this issue.

3. In your Journalism class, your instructor suggests that you can find out about innovations in the field by examining the *Columbia Journalism Review*. You pick up a recent issue at a newsstand and scan the table of contents for interesting articles.

a. What is the title of the feature article in that issue?

b. What is the date of the issue you're reading?

4. Identify journals that might have articles on your topic. Look at the table of contents to be sure the topic is related. Examine recently published issues of these journals in your library's current periodicals section. Be sure to look at reference lists of articles on your topic.

5. Form topic-related discussion groups and talk about interesting articles found or sources valuable in searching the literature. Identify different facets of the topic so all of you will not be attempting to find the same sources.

chapter 8

Information Compilations

Y ou will often need to find recent facts to use in research reports, speeches, news stories, or presentations on current topics. For example, you might be preparing a public relations campaign and may need information on the cost of advertising in specific newspapers or magazines. Or the status of recent broadcast regulations may be required for a paper or television script on trends in broadcast law. Or you may have to lead a group discussion and want to consult a source about parliamentary procedure.

Several factual, quick-reference research sources can help with these and other related purposes. In addition, there are several collections and official publications of primary documents that are sometimes essential factual sources. In this chapter we focus on methods of finding facts to support viewpoints, finding sources of information outside the library, and locating current on-line information related to communication.

Collections and archives lead you to the text of speeches, editorials, television programs, communication regulations, and so on, which may be the focus of your analysis or may be used as supporting information for research reports or other projects. Statistical sources identify reference works and websites where census and other government and media statistics are reported. Because the statistical data cited in books and in journal articles are often not the most current, you should know where to turn to update such information.

Government documents are helpful when searching for up-to-date information on what is happening in Congress, the Supreme Court, or federal agencies such as the Federal Communications Commission. The U.S. government publishes so much information that a first-time user of government documents can be overwhelmed with the amount of available material. Many smaller libraries do not house all these documents, so you must find out how to request specific materials that you may need or find it on-line.

Yearbooks, directories, dictionaries, and manuals are also usually current. Yearbooks and directories are generally revised each year so that information is up-to-date. These sources provide names, addresses, and factual information about people, businesses, and clients and are vital tools for many types of communication professionals. They can be especially useful when you do not find needed information within library resources. These reference works can point the way to other information sources such as trade and professional organizations. If contacted directly, these organizations may be able to supply useful information to meet your particular needs. Dictionaries and manuals are desktop or on-line reference sources, helpful when you need quick, practical information.

COLLECTIONS AND ARCHIVES

Collections are compilations of documents of a similar type that either are gathered together in one location or published in periodical, book, or microform format. Materials such as speeches, editorials, historical documents, and media transcripts are often not easily accessible by the typical researcher, even though they may have appeared elsewhere in book, periodical, or original form. Thus, published collections of these materials allow you to examine important original materials to learn more about the content of the subject. They also enable you to use the materials as examples of communication events when supporting arguments in a position paper, research investigation, or other project. One reference source that allows the user to determine where collections and archives are located is Ash and Miller's (1993) *Subject Collections.*

■ SPEECH COLLECTIONS

If you are conducting critical or historical research, you may be interested in locating speeches given by important people or on newsworthy topics. Major newspapers such as the *New York Times* publish many newsworthy speeches shortly after they're given, but published collections make it easier to consult the original text of the speech without searching through back issues of these newspapers. They are especially helpful when the speech is old or when the newspaper account of the speech is not the original text but an edited version. Collections also contain speeches that are not published elsewhere. The collection of speeches used most often is the following:

> *Vital Speeches of the Day.* (1934–). New York: City News.
>
> ■   This collection of important recent speeches by government, industry, and other societal leaders usually includes the complete texts, but occasionally edited versions are presented. The many sides of issues are represented in the speeches selected for publication.
>
> *Vital Speeches* is published **semimonthly**. Annual author and subject indexes appear in the November issue. Speeches in this collection are ref-

erenced in the *Readers' Guide to Periodical Literature* and in comprehensive indexes such as *Academic Search*, which often include the full text of speeches indexed.

Speeches of the President of the United States are published in the *Weekly Compilation of Presidential Documents* (1965–). This source makes the speeches and other presidential documents accessible in a relatively short period of time. It is available on-line from 1993 through *GPO Access*, <**http://www.access.gpo.gov**>. An article by K. J. Turner (in the July 1986 issue of *Communication Education*, pp. 243–253) explains how to use presidential libraries to do research.

Collections of past presidential speeches are found in the following presidential libraries:

George Bush Presidential Library, College Station, TX
Jimmy Carter Library, Atlanta, GA
Dwight D. Eisenhower Library, Abilene, KS
Gerald R. Ford Museum, Grand Rapids, MI
Herbert Hoover Library, West Branch, IA
Lyndon B. Johnson Library, Austin, TX
John F. Kennedy Library, Boston, MA
Richard M. Nixon Library, Yorba Linda, CA
Ronald Reagan Library, Simi Valley, CA
Franklin D. Roosevelt Library, Hyde Park, NY
Harry S Truman Library, Independence, MO

These libraries contain speeches, other documents, and media accounts of events during each particular presidency. Most require you to visit the library to use the materials. A listing of library websites with current contact information is available through the National Archives and Records Administration, <**http://www.nara.gov**>. State of the Union addresses for Presidents Washington through Jackson are available on the White House web page: <**http://www. whitehouse. gov**>.

Other collections of speeches are listed at the end of this chapter. It is possible to locate in what collection the text of a speech appears by using the *Speech Index* (see Chapter 6). Many of these are available in a new on-line collection of American public speeches:

Douglass: Archives of American Public Address [On-line]. (1998, August). Available: http://douglass.speech.nwu.edu

■ This repository of American rhetoric and resources is searchable by title, date, speaker, or movement.

■ MEDIA COLLECTIONS

In addition to speeches, other media materials, such as those published in newspapers, are often compiled into collections. These are useful when you are interested in learning what journalists have said about a topic. *Editorials on File*, for example, is composed of newspaper editorials.

> *Editorials on File*. (1969–). New York: Facts on File.
>
> ■   Editorials for this collection are selected from more than 140 newspapers in the United States and Canada. Published twice per month, each issue includes the text of about 200 editorials chosen to represent newspaper positions on current issues. A cumulative subject index appears at the end of each annual volume. *Editorials on File* is available on-line through <**Facts.com**>.

Viewpoint (1976–), a similar type of periodical, brings together the work of newspaper and radio columnists with that of political cartoonists. A more complete microform edition is also available. *Facts on File* (1940–) differs from these works in that it is a weekly digest of national and foreign news prepared from the accounts published in selected major newspapers, periodicals, and other standard news sources.

The ability to publish in **microform** (**microfiche** or **microfilm**) has made it possible to assemble and make easily accessible collections of materials that would otherwise not be widely available. Articles from regional newspapers in all areas of the United States are made available in microfiche and are indexed through *NewsBank* (1970–). In addition, coverage of selected topics in specialized print media is provided by two microform collections, *Underground Newspaper Microfilm Collection* (Alternative Press Syndicate, 1963–1977) and *Herstory: Microfilm Collection* (Women's History Research Center, 1972–). The *Alternative Press Index* (described in Chapter 6) provides limited information on tapping these two sources.

Several historical collections of U.S. and British newspapers and periodicals are also available in microform. Many libraries are likely to own one or more of these collections. Because they may not be listed in library catalogs or periodical lists and their contents may be reviewed only by using special indexes, you'll need to ask a reference librarian about their availability.

Even though most of the collections just described consist of print media, electronic media collections are also available. Researchers often need to examine original broadcasts or their scripts, for example, to analyze their content or to conduct historical or critical research. Media professionals also consult archival materials when preparing news programs or documentaries. For example, the Television Script Archive at the University of Pennsylvania contains more than 24,000 television scripts from 1976 to the present.

In addition, printed transcripts in microformat are a convenient way to access some broadcasts. For example, many libraries subscribe to the *CBS News Television Broadcasts in Microform* (1975–). To use this source most efficiently, consult the *CBS News Index* (described in Chapter 6) for the listing of broadcasts. The National Archives will lend (for a fee) the CBS videotapes through interlibrary loan. These videotapes are also available for use at 13 regional archives.

As with the CBS broadcasts, actual collections of electronic media programs are generally available only in a few **archives** in the United States, such as the Museum of Television and Radio in New York City and Los Angeles and the Museum of Broadcast Communications in Chicago. Some are open to the general public. If they are, you'll still need to visit the archive to view or listen to the materials. Two exceptions are the Vanderbilt Television News Archive at Vanderbilt University (Nashville, TN) and the Public Affairs Video Archives at Purdue University (West Lafayette, IN); both rent videotapes and audiotapes. Vanderbilt lists its holdings in the *Television News Index and Abstracts* (1972–); it is searchable on-line at its website <**http://tvnews.vanderbilt.edu**>. This collection and others are described in the Television News Study Center's (1981) *Television News Resources: A Guide to Collections.*

C-SPAN (Cable-Satellite Public Affairs Network) programs are archived in the C-SPAN Archives. C-SPAN airs programs on Washington politics, proceedings of Congress, national events, world legislatures, conferences, and special topics that deal with communication, such as talk radio and political campaign commercials. These programs are cataloged, indexed, and distributed on videotape (about $30/hour) or through printed transcript (about $15/hour). Transcripts of Federal News Service materials (presidential speeches, daily briefings, congressional news conferences, Supreme Court decisions) are also available. For information, contact:

C-SPAN Archives
Purdue Research Park
PO Box 2909
West Lafayette, IN 47996-2909
Phone: (800) 277-2698
Internet: <http://www.pava.purdue.edu>

The Political Commercial Archive at the University of Oklahoma archives radio and television political advertisements. The archive includes commercials of candidates for political office, as well as those sponsored by political action committees, corporations, and special interest groups. Presidential debates, conventions, and significant televised speeches are also archived. You can use *WorldCat* to locate these materials, but archive staff must retrieve materials for users. More information is available on the Archive website <**http://www.ou.edu/pccenter/archives/archival.html**> where *A Catalog and Guide to the Archival Collections* may be consulted. For information, contact:

Political Commercial Archive
University of Oklahoma
610 Elm Avenue
Norman, OK 73019-0335
Phone: (405) 325-3114

Political speeches are also available in the MetaLab Internet archive at the University of North Carolina in Chapel Hill, which is available at <**http://metalab. unc.edu/metalab.shtml**>. You can read speech texts or send them to your e-mail address for downloading to your personal computer.

Although dated, other archives are identified in the "Review and Criticism" section of the March 1984 issue of *Critical Studies in Mass Communication* (see Chapter 7), where archives in mass communication, film, television, photography, and newspapers are described. Other indexes and directories of archive collections, including Godfrey's (1983) *A Directory of Broadcast Archives*, are listed at the end of this chapter. Note that these sources are useful in a historical sense but are now dated. Sterling, Bracken, and Hill's (1997) recent guide to the literature, *Mass Communications Research Resources* (see Chapter 6), also identifies more current electronic media archives. Other useful source materials are primary documents relating to the regulation of the electronic media industries. A useful but older compilation of such documents for those working in the area of broadcast law and freedom of expression is the following:

> Kahn, F. J. (Ed.). (1984). *Documents of American broadcasting* (4th ed.). Englewood Cliffs, NJ: Prentice Hall.

> ■ This sourcebook collects 43 primary documents about public policy, history, and issues in U.S. broadcasting. Documents include federal laws, commission regulations and notices, congressional reports and actions, court decisions, speeches, letters, and other documents from parts of the U.S. Constitution to cable access and radio deregulation.

> The book includes chronological and thematic tables of contents. The broad subject areas of these documents are broadcast-regulation development, freedom of expression, competition regulation, public broadcasting, and the public interest. Brief commentaries provide background, explanation, and interpretation. A few related readings follow each document. Also included are a glossary of legal terms, a brief identification of legal citations, an index to legal decisions, and a general index.

■ LEGAL COLLECTIONS

Loose-leaf reporting services assemble, organize, and digest topical legal reports on a single subject. These materials are collected in a binder, and regular supplements are distributed, often weekly. The major goal of these services is to keep the legal profession abreast of constantly evolving areas of law. These services are valuable for communication students interested in studying questions about policy, regulation, and freedom of speech. In particular, two of these services provide the text of legislative actions and court decisions that are significant for the mass media.

> *Pike & Fischer Radio Regulation*. (1946–). Bethesda, MD: Pike & Fischer.

> ■ This service consists of *Current Service*, *Digest*, and *Decision (Cases)* volumes. The *Current Service* volumes contain the text of current laws and regulations that affect broadcasting, including statutes, congressional committee reports, treatises, and international agreements, as well as rules and regulations of the Federal Communications Commission (FCC) for radio, television, and cable television.

The *Digest* volumes contain all FCC decisions, as well as selected Federal Radio Commission and federal and state court decisions, through July 1963. The *Decision* volumes contain FCC decisions and reports and court decisions prior to July 1963 in the first series and after that date in the second series. There also is a volume that provides a master index, finding aids, and FCC forms.

Media Law Reporter. (1977–). Washington, DC: Bureau of National Affairs.

■   This weekly service provides indexed coverage of all decisions of the U.S. Supreme Court and selected decisions of federal and state courts and administrative agencies that affect the electronic and print media. The full text is published for most opinions, including concurrences and dissents. Summary opinions are presented for some cases.

Decisions are classified in four major divisions: regulation of media content, regulation of media distribution, newsgathering, and media ownership. There is a topical index arranged alphabetically by major subjects (such as broadcast media or commercial speech) and subheads (such as regulation of advertising content). Also provided are tables of cases by plaintiff/defendant and by jurisprudence (such as U.S. Supreme Court or First Circuit Court of Appeals) and an index digest. There is an annual cumulation.

Besides the official report of the U.S. Supreme Court decisions, *United States Supreme Court Reports* (1790–), there are two useful and privately published editions of the Court's decisions, *United States Supreme Court Reports: Lawyers' Edition, Second Series* (1956–) and the *Supreme Court Reporter* (1882–). These unofficial reporting services reproduce the same text of the decisions as the official reports and include their own summary of cases and annotations written by the publishers' editorial staffs.

These official and unofficial reports of Court decisions can be useful when you are studying communication law, debate, or freedom of speech. They are available in law libraries and many university libraries. West Publishing also produces a *National Reporter System* of seven regional and two state *Reporters* that includes most of the decisions issued by the appellate courts of the 50 states each year. These are also available in law libraries.

■ MEASUREMENT COLLECTIONS

One other type of collection is a compilation of measures of communication attitudes and personality. Researchers find these collections useful when planning descriptive and experimental research studies. Robinson, Shaver, Wrightsman, and Andrews' (1991) *Measures of Personality and Social Psychological Attitudes* and McReynolds' (1968–1975) *Advances in Psychological Assessment* are often helpful to students conducting their own research projects. One additional work, Chun, Cobb, and French's (1975) *Measures for Psychological Assessment* indexes by author and subject the original sources and applications of 3000 psychological measures. For communication, consult the following:

> Rubin, R. B., Palmgreen, P., & Sypher, H. E. (Eds.). (1994). *Communication research measures: A sourcebook*. New York: Guilford Press.

■ This volume profiles over 60 often-used research measures in instructional, interpersonal, mass, and organizational communication. Besides presenting the actual measure and pertinent references to its use, each profile highlights the purpose, development, reliability, and validity of the measure. In addition, the editors and associate editors discuss measurement trends and issues within the four areas of communication research. A table of contents and an index provide ready access to each measure that is profiled.

Collections of measures are helpful for researchers conducting investigations because they provide not only the measure but information on the validity and reliability of the instrument.

STATISTICAL SOURCES

You will often need to locate statistical data to document research for a wide variety of projects, such as finding facts to support a debate case on social welfare, developing background material for a newspaper article on unemployment in a local area, doing research for a term paper on the history of broadcasting, or preparing for a speech or group discussion on trends in American television. Or when you are conducting research on a topic, you may find that the author of a book or article has cited data that are germane to your research but are now several years out of date. Thus, an important step in the research process is attempting to update such references by using **statistical sources**.

A major activity of governments at all levels is the collection, compilation, and publication of a wide variety of statistical data. The following statistical yearbook is often a good first place to check for data about the United States:

> U.S. Department of Commerce, Bureau of the Census. (1879–). *Statistical Abstract of the United States*. Washington, DC: Government Printing Office.

■ This annual compendium contains summaries of social, economic, and political statistics for the United States. "Communications and Information Technology" is one section of the *Abstract*. "Population," "Vital Statistics," "Education," and "Elections" are also included among the *Abstract*'s 30 sections. The source notes given for each table and the bibliography of sources at the end of the volume make this a handy guide to many statistics published by the U.S. government, as well as by trade associations and other organizations. A detailed subject index helps locate statistics on a specific topic. The table of contents is useful for researching broad subjects. This source is also available on CD-ROM and on the WWW at <**http://www.census .gov/statab/www/**>. The CD-ROM version includes additional data and direct links to all cited federal statistical sources.

The *American Statistics Index* (*ASI*) indexes statistical publications produced by all departments and agencies of the U.S. government, including the FCC and the Census Bureau. It can be quite helpful when conducting statistical research.

> *American Statistics Index: A Comprehensive Guide and Index to the Statistical Publications of the U.S. Government.* (1973–). Bethesda, MD: Congressional Information Service.
>
> ■ This commercially produced indexing and abstracting service provides comprehensive coverage of statistical publications of the federal government. It is issued monthly in two sections (indexes and abstracts) and is cumulated annually. Besides the index by subjects and names, the source contains indexes by title, by agency report numbers, and by geographic, economic, and demographic categories. The latter index is useful for researchers who are interested in statistics that are broken down in a particular way, such as by age, city, and so forth. Documents abstracted in *ASI* are available on microfiche in some libraries. *ASI* is available on-line as part of *Statistical Universe* and on CD-ROM as part of *Statistical Masterfile*. *Statistical Universe* provides links to the full text of many documents.

Because *ASI* provides excellent access to almost all statistical information published by the federal government, we won't cite all statistical publications that might be of interest to communication researchers. Some selected publications are listed at the end of this chapter, along with several statistical sources on the international level that are published by the United Nations. Later in this chapter, we discuss other U.S. government publications.

Governments and agencies are not, of course, the only sources of useful statistics. Many of the publications described or identified later in this chapter—in particular, the *Gale Directory of Publications and Broadcast Media*, the *Broadcasting & Cable Yearbook,* the *International Television and Video Almanac*, and the *Statesman's Yearbook*—include substantial amounts of statistical data drawn from a variety of sources.

Other important sources of statistical data include trade and professional associations such as the American Association of Advertising Agencies, the American Newspaper Publishers Association, the Association of American Publishers, the Electronic Industries Association, the National Association of Broadcasters, the Radio Advertising Bureau, and the Television Bureau of Advertising. These associations gather and report a variety of statistical data and materials about their respective industries. For example, the research department of the National Association of Broadcasters produces various booklets and reports about trends and developments in broadcasting. Statistical publications of many associations are indexed and abstracted in *Statistical Reference Index* (*SRI*), published by Congressional Information Service. It is available on-line as part of *Statistical Universe*.

Sources for some subject areas include several companies whose business it is to gather and market data, such as the Arbitron Ratings Company, the A. C. Nielsen Company, Standard Rate and Data, and the Gallup, Harris, and Roper polling organizations. These data are often summarized in separate publications, a few of which are listed at the end of this chapter. The Arbitron and Nielsen organizations produce a variety of materials such as detailed ratings reports for their client stations in radio and television markets, studies of the reliability of broadcast ratings, and pamphlets that detail trends in the electronic media or report specialty studies such as investigations of cable television and videocassette recorders.

One reference work that has compiled data from many of these sources provides a historical perspective on trends in the electronic media:

> Sterling, C. H. (1984). *Electronic media: A guide to trends in broadcasting and newer technologies 1920–1983*. New York: Praeger.

■ Data about quantitative trends in the electronic media industry since 1920 have been compiled from a variety of sources. About 150 tables are included in the book's eight sections: "Electronic Media Growth," "Ownership," "Economics," "Employment," "Content Trends," Audience," "International Aspects," and "Regulation." Each set of tables is accompanied by a narrative interpretation and by a discussion of the sources, reliability, and validity of the data. These features, as well as the additional references listed for each topic, make this a useful reference. A detailed table of contents lists each table included. The end of the volume contains a description of sources and references.

U.S. GOVERNMENT PUBLICATIONS

The U.S. government publishes periodicals, directories, handbooks, and bibliographies. You are probably already familiar with many of these documents. However, you may be less familiar with other common types of **government documents,** such as federal statutes, congressional hearings and reports, census materials, and government agency regulations and reports. This section describes some of these publications and special finding tools that can be used to identify and locate them. Many are listed on pp. 178–180.

Several government sources detail the rules and regulations of the United States. These sources help students and professionals keep abreast of changes in the law. For example, this information is important for preparing debate cases, analyzing media policy, understanding political campaign regulations, comparing the demographic composition of a sample, and the like. These materials are generally available in the government documents section of many libraries. Most are available on the WWW through *GPO Access* <**http://www.access.gpo.gov/**> and *Congressional Universe.* The general and permanent laws of the United States are codified in the United States Code.

> U.S. Congress, House of Representatives. (1994). *United States code* (1988 ed.). Washington, DC: Government Printing Office.

■ The Code includes the federal laws of this country. The text of the multitude of laws that existed in this country as of January 1989 are provided in the 50 titles or content areas of this 11th edition of the Code. For example, selected chapters of title 17, "Copyrights," include "Subject Matter and Scope of Copyrights," "Copyright Ownership and Transfer," "Duration of Copyrights," and the "Copyright Office." Title 47 of the code, "Telegraphs, Telephones, and Radiotelegraphs," includes the Communications Act of 1934, as amended. Other titles include "Census," "Commerce and Trade," "Education," "Labor," and "Money and Finance."

A new edition of the Code has been published every 6 years since 1926 by the Law Revision Counsel of the House of Representatives. A supplement is issued after each session of Congress. The Code is also available on-line through *GPO Access* and *Congressional Universe*.

The Federal Register publishes daily, on weekdays, regulations and legal notices issued by the executive branch and federal agencies.

U.S. General Services Administration, Office of the Federal Register. (1936–). *Federal Register*. Washington, DC: Government Printing Office.

■ The purpose of the *Federal Register* is to make regulations and notices, including presidential proclamations, executive orders, and federal agency documents and activities, available to the public. It is divided into several sections: rules and regulations, proposed rules, notices, and Sunshine Act meetings. For each of the rules or proposed rules, the agency, action, rule summary, effective dates, addresses, and supplementary information are included. Each notice announces hearings and investigations, committee meetings, delegations of authority, agency decisions and rulings, and agency statements of organization and function. For example, rule-making proceedings and hearings of the FCC and the Federal Trade Commission (FTC) are announced in the *Register*. The regulatory documents contained in the *Federal Register* are keyed to and codified in the *Code of Federal Regulations*. This publication of the U.S. General Services Administration contains the general and permanent rules of executive departments and federal agencies that are published in the *Federal Register*. The *Code of Federal Regulations* is indexed in the *Code of Federal Regulations: CFR Index and Finding Aids*. Both the *Federal Register* and the *Code of Federal Regulations* are available through *GPO Access* and *Congressional Universe*.

The FCC can be a particularly useful source of information if you are researching communication policy and regulation. Three of its publications are especially helpful. *FCC Rules and Regulations* contains the text of FCC rules in such matters as commission operation, frequency allocations, broadcast services, satellite communications, and cable television services. The weekly *Federal Communications Commission Reports* incorporates the FCC's current decisions, orders, policy statements, and public notices of hearings and rule-making proceedings. The *Reports* are cumulated yearly, and these volumes have a list of commission actions and documents. They also contain a subject digest that summarizes pertinent information on such topics as fairness, issues and program lists, and cellular communication systems. *The Annual Report of the Federal Communications Commission* provides a yearly comprehensive review of significant events in all areas of communication regulation, including broadcasting, cable television, common carriers (for example, satellites), spectrum management, and frequency allocations. These sources are also available through the FCC website, <**http://ftp.fcc.gov**>.

Also useful are the various reports of congressional committees, executive agencies, and other regulatory commissions such as the FTC. For example, if you are researching the topic of television violence, you might find references to the report of the Surgeon General's Advisory Committee (1972), *Television and Social Behavior*, to the congressional report of the House Committee on Interstate and Foreign Commerce (1977), *Violence on Television*, or to the report by the National Institutes of Mental Health (1982), *Television and Behavior*. These reports are widely cited, and because they sometimes contain the testimony of expert witnesses in addition to well-researched background material, they are useful resources for a research project.

One problem with locating government publications is that they are not included in some library catalogs. Many libraries shelve government publications in a special section, so they might be overlooked. You will need to investigate how such documents are handled in the library you are using. If they have not been included in the library catalog, you will need to discover what local access tools are available and how they are shelved and arranged. A reference librarian will be able to answer these questions for you.

Another difficulty in locating government publications is that they are also not included in most periodical indexes. The Public Affairs Information Service (PAIS) *Bulletin* (listed under "Periodical Indexes and Abstracts" at the end of Chapter 6) indexes some government publications. But even this source lists only about 1% of the federal documents published. Another source, though, the *U.S. Government Periodicals Index*, does index the publications of more than 100 agencies of the U.S. government. This source is also available on-line and on CD-ROM in some libraries.

In any library setting, the basic all-around tool used to identify the availability of U.S. government publications on a given topic, by a given author, or published by a given agency is the following:

U.S. Superintendent of Documents. (1895–). *Monthly Catalog of United States Government Publications.* Washington, DC: Government Printing Office.

■ The *Monthly Catalog* is the most complete catalog of publications of all branches of the federal government. It has semiannual and annual cumulative indexes by title, author/agency, and subject. Documents are listed only in the year they are published, so it is often necessary to search through several volumes to find information about a particular document.

Library of Congress subject headings have been used in the subject index since July 1976. The catalog is arranged alphabetically by issuing agency, with each entry assigned a number. It is to this number that the index refers. Information given in entries is similar to that found in most library catalog records, with the addition of the Superintendent of Documents number. This number is a classification number similar in function to a Library of Congress or Dewey decimal call number, and it is used in many libraries to arrange government documents on the shelf.

You should refer to the user's guide at the front of each volume to help identify the elements of each entry and decipher the abbreviations. The "Cumulative Subject Index" to the *Monthly Catalog of U.S. Government Publications, 1900–1971* should be used for retrospective searches.

The *Monthly Catalog* is available on-line from 1994 through *GPO Access* as the *Catalog of U.S. Government Publications* <**http://www.access. gpo.gov**>. This Web version includes direct links to electronic documents issued by many government agencies. Many libraries with government document collections subscribe to a CD-ROM version of this database.

One disadvantage of the *Monthly Catalog* as a tool for identifying relevant materials is that it does not include annotations or abstracts. However, such abstracts for two important types of government publications are available. For those published by Congress, consult the *CIS/Index to Publications of the United States Congress* (see below), and, as you recall, for those that are statistical in nature, the *American Statistics Index* is helpful.

The various committees of the U.S. Congress and their staffs investigate many current social, economic, and political issues and publish the results of these investigations either as hearings, committee prints, or reports. A hearing is simply a transcript of the testimony of witnesses before a committee or subcommittee. Because many of these witnesses are experts in their fields and collectively represent a broad range of views, hearings are often excellent resource materials for researching controversial topics, such as the effects of television on children. Committee prints are reports of background research done either by committee staffs or by the Congressional Research Service of the Library of Congress. House and Senate reports are the official committee reports to the entire House or Senate, summarizing the results of investigations or hearings and making recommendations. As of 1999 a limited number of congressional hearings were available through *GPO Access*.

All these publications, as well as the legislation that results from committee hearings and the like, are indexed and abstracted in the following:

CIS/Index to Publications of the United States Congress. (1970–). Washington, DC: Congressional Information Service.

■   This service provides complete indexing and abstracting for all the working papers of Congress, including committee hearings, prints, and reports. *CIS* appears monthly and is cumulated quarterly and annually. It is published in two parts, an index section and an abstract section. Entries in the index volume refer users to relevant abstracts by means of an entry number. Included in both the index and abstracts are entries for individual witnesses at hearings. The history of individual pieces of legislation is covered in annual cumulations. Some libraries own the complete microfiche collection of all documents that are abstracted. Access to this collection is by the entry number of the abstract.

This index is also available as part of *Congressional Universe* and on CD-ROM in some libraries. *Congressional Universe* provides access to the full text of many documents, including most congressional hearings.

Other useful publications for following current congressional deliberations are: *Congressional Index; Congressional Quarterly Almanac; Congressional Record: Proceedings and Debates of Congress; Congressional Record, Index to Daily Proceedings*; and *Congressional Quarterly Weekly Report. Congressional Quarterly* also produces useful guides for understanding the history and workings of Congress, the Supreme Court, and U.S. elections. These are listed at the end of this chapter.

The tools just described are useful only for finding publications of the U.S. government and for only a relatively recent time period. If you need to identify earlier documents or those at the local, state, or international levels, consult one or more of the finding aids for government materials listed at the end of this chapter, such as *Shepard's Acts and Cases by Popular Names: Federal and State* (1992). The Documents Center at the University of Michigan maintains a particularly comprehensive listing of sources of documents published on the WWW by state, federal, and international governments: <**http://www.lib.umich.edu/ libhome/documents.center/webdirec.html**>.

YEARBOOKS

Yearbooks and **annuals** contain current information on yearly developments in a specific field. They also provide excellent background information, statistics, narrative explanations, and listings, much like that found in directories and manuals. An excellent research tool for students in mass communication is the following:

> *Broadcasting & Cable Yearbook* (2 vols.). (1935–). New Providence, NJ: Bowker.
>
> ■   This comprehensive reference tool contains information about various elements of the radio, television, and cable industries. Volume 1 includes: a summary of relevant law and regulation; government agencies of relevance to broadcasting and cable in the United States and Canada; breakdowns of important data for every television and radio station, cable system, and satellite operator in the United States and Canada by state or province; Nielsen DMA (Designated Market Area) Atlas by television market; directories of advertising and marketing services, programming services, and equipment and professional services and suppliers; and listings of associations, events, education programs, books and periodicals, and awards.
>
> Volume 2 presents a brief year-in-review summary and the "Yellow Pages" of radio, television, and cable. It contains an alphabetical listing of

stations/companies and industry personnel. The *Yearbook* was originally issued as an annual supplement to *Broadcasting* magazine and then in two separate publications, *Broadcasting Yearbook* (1944–1979) and *Cable Sourcebook* (1972–1979). In 1980 the two were combined in the *Broadcasting/Cable Yearbook* (from 1982 to 1988 it was titled *Broadcasting/Cablecasting Yearbook*) and later called *Broadcasting Yearbook*, until 1992 when the R. R. Bowker Company began publishing it as *Broadcasting & Cable Marketplace* until 1993.

Other useful yearbooks, such as *Editor & Publisher International Year Book* (1959–), are listed at the end of this chapter.

DIRECTORIES

Directories provide basic information about people, companies, organizations, and publications. One directory that students in journalism and communication find helpful is the following:

Gale Directory of Publications and Broadcast Media (4 vols.). (1869–). Detroit: Gale Research.

■ Volumes 1 and 2 of this directory list newspapers, periodicals, and cable, radio, and television stations in the United States and Canada. Also included are economic descriptions of the states, provinces, cities, and towns of these media. The main section lists media by location. The descriptions for each listing include format of the medium, starting date, frequency of publication or operating hours for electronic media, key personnel, ownership, service area, subscription rates, and advertising rates.

Volume 3 provides summary information of industry activity (start-ups and cessations), industry statistics, broadcast and cable networks, news and feature syndicates, publisher and subject indexes, newspaper feature editors, and a master name and key-word index. Volume 4 provides maps of the United States, Puerto Rico, and Canada and regional market indexes for the different media, which refer to the main-section entries by entry number. Before 1987 this directory was known as the *Ayer Directory of Publications* and from 1987 to 1989, *Gale Directory of Publications*. This source is available on-line through *GaleNet* as the *Gale Database of Publications and Broadcast Media*.

Aside from the need to locate materials from newspapers and news programs, communication researchers occasionally need to find educational media when pursuing research projects dealing with the media—for example, historical or critical studies of film.

Educational or instructional media, including films, filmstrips, audiotapes, and videotapes, can be located in several reference sources. *The Video Source Book* is a handy way to find videotapes:

The Video Source Book (2 vols.). (1979–). Detroit: Gale Research.

■ This comprehensive annual lists videotapes available for purchase, rent/lease, off-air taping, free loan, or duplication. Coverage includes business and industry, entertainment, and instruction. Each entry contains a short description, credits, producer, audience/purpose, permissible uses (for example, broadcast television, in-home viewing), terms of availability (for example, loan, purchase, off-air record), television standards (for example, NTSC, PAL), distributor, and often, price. This source provides subject and credit indexes and a section on distributors.

A useful source for locating reviews assessing the content and quality of educational media is the following:

Media Review Digest. (1973–). Ann Arbor, MI: Pierian Press.

■ This annual publication indexes reviews of feature films and educational media such as educational films, videotapes, filmstrips, records, audiotapes, and miscellaneous productions. Items are arranged alphabetically by title within sections devoted to each form of media (for example, films and videotapes). Entries include a brief description of the item, followed by a listing of reviews that have appeared in periodicals. Among the indexes are a subject index by Library of Congress subject headings and an index of reviewers. The *Digest* also includes lists of film awards and prizes, bibliographies of media materials, and book reviews. From 1970 to 1972 this index was known as *Multi Media Reviews Index*.

Another type of media directory compiles facts about and synopses of television and radio programs. These are helpful when doing research about programming trends and the antecedents of contemporary programming. Descriptions usually include dates of airing, cast members, and brief summaries of program content. One such directory is:

Brooks, T., & Marsh, E. (Eds.). (1995). *The complete directory to prime time network and cable TV shows, 1946–present* (6th ed.). New York: Ballantine Books.

■ This volume lists and describes every regular television series (lasting 4 or more weeks) aired by the commercial networks during the 6 P.M. to sign-off period, as well as the top syndicated evening programs from 1946. News, sports, and movies are also included. Each entry provides the dates of the first and last telecasts, along with a history of the series, a list of cast members, and a synopsis of the program. Appendixes include the season ratings, season network schedules, major television awards, and other information. There is also a comprehensive index to cast members.

A general directory that may be useful to students of organizational or mass communication is the following:

Standard & Poor's Register of Corporations, Directors & Executives (3 vols.). (1928–). New York: Standard & Poor's.

■ This work is issued annually and contains information on location, telephone number, offices, products, sales, and number of employees of more than 37,000 U.S. and Canadian corporations.

A more specialized directory of corporations is *Working Press of the Nation* (1945–).

Some other directories of interest to communication students are at the end of this chapter. *Directories in Print* can help you find directories not given here. It lists more than 10,000 industrial, trade, and professional directories. It is available on-line as part of the *Gale Database of Publications and Broadcast Media*, offered through *GaleNet*.

DICTIONARIES

Academic disciplines use language and jargon that might confuse readers. The words may seem familiar, but often the meanings are not what we expect. There are sources that can help clarify your understanding of new or unique terms.

Dictionaries are usually thought of simply as alphabetic arrangements of words and their meanings. Although the denotative meaning of a word is typically sought when a dictionary is consulted, other information is available. This information often includes pronunciation, spelling, hyphenation, word etymology, syllabication, and synonyms.

There are four basic types of dictionaries. General dictionaries are the abridged and unabridged versions with which you are most familiar. You consult these when you need to find out the meaning of a word, how to pronounce a word, or where to divide a word into syllables. Language dictionaries give more attention to slang terms, the root and history of a word, and synonyms and antonyms. Foreign-language dictionaries translate words from one language to another and often provide a guide to pronunciation. Subject dictionaries, which are much more specialized, concentrate on one specific topic or discipline and will be our focus here.

Subject dictionaries list and define basic and specialized terms in a particular field. They also provide meanings for abbreviations, jargon, and slang. At times, subject dictionaries may resemble encyclopedias in that they give lengthy descriptions of and bibliographic references for terms. This is why we included one subject dictionary in Chapter 5 with encyclopedias. Less inclusive and more specialized dictionaries may be helpful when you encounter unfamiliar terms in communication and related areas. Two such dictionaries that define words and terms pertinent to the study of mass communication are the following:

Diamant, L. (Ed.). (1992). *Dictionary of broadcast communications* (new 3rd rev. ed.). Lincolnwood, IL: NTC Business Books.

■ This dictionary contains over 5000 technical, common, and slang words used by broadcasting, advertising, and communication professionals in Great Britain and the United States. Included are terms currently used in radio and television production and programming, network and station operations, broadcast engineering, audiotaping and videotaping, performing, advertising, research, and trade and government media. Definitions are not highly technical, and cross-references to comparable terms are given.

Wiechman, J. G., & Urdang, L. (Eds.). (1993). *NTC's dictionary of advertising* (Rev. ed.). Lincolnwood, IL: National Textbook.

■   This dictionary presents words and terms used in marketing, writing copy, art direction, graphics, media planning, research analysis and buying, consumer research, promotion, and public relations. Over 4000 entries explain special meanings of ordinary words, names of devices, services, organizations, and specialized initials and abbreviations. This is the seventh printing of a 1977 version published by Tatham-Laird & Kudner.

The dictionaries listed at the end of this chapter will help you find precise meanings for communication and research terms. The law dictionaries that we list will help when you need to know the legal sense or use of words. They are handy, quick-reference books, helpful in learning the language of a discipline.

MANUALS

A **manual**, or fact book, is a quick-reference handbook about a broad subject area. Usually, manuals present generally accepted data rather than the most recent information as in yearbooks and directories. They often provide statistical tables, bibliographies, glossaries, and limited directories. We list some examples of useful manuals in various facets of communication at the end of this chapter.

Students interested in publishing, writing, and editing also have several manuals and directories available for their use. The manuals provide tips on writing style and selling one's work. The directories reference publishing companies and other markets where work can be submitted. We also cite a few of these works in the list of "Selected Sources."

SELECTED SOURCES

■ COLLECTIONS

Alternative Press Center. (1963–). *Underground Press Collection*. Ann Arbor, MI: University Microfilms International.

Bearden, W. O., & Netemeyer, R. G. (1999). *Handbook of marketing scales: Multi-item measures for marketing and consumer behavior research* (2nd ed.). Thousand Oaks, CA: Sage.

Campbell, K. K. (Ed.). (1993). *Women public speakers in the United States, 1800–1925: A bio-critical sourcebook*. Westport, CT: Greenwood Press.

Campbell, K. K. (Ed.). (1994). *Women public speakers in the United States, 1925–1993: A bio-critical sourcebook.* Westport, CT: Greenwood Press.

CBS News Television Broadcasts in Microform. (1975–). Ann Arbor, MI: University Microfilms International.

Early American Newspapers. (1984–). New Canaan, CT: Readex Microprint.

Editorials on File. (1970–). New York: Facts on File. (Available on-line as part of Facts.com)

Executive Speeches. (1986–). Dayton, OH: Executive Speaker.

Facts on File. (1940–). New York: Facts on File.

Facts on File [CD-ROM]. (1980–). New York: Facts on File.

Facts.com [On-line]. (1999–). New York: Facts on File.

Federal Reporter. (1880–). St. Paul: West.

Historic Documents. (1972–). Washington, DC: Congressional Quarterly.

Media Law Reporter. (1977–). Washington, DC: Bureau of National Affairs.

National Reporter System. (1879–). St. Paul: West. (Includes the *New York Supplement* and the following *Reporters*: *Atlantic, California, North Eastern, North Western, Pacific, South Eastern, Southern,* and *South Western*)

NewsBank. (1970–). New Canaan, CT: NewsBank.

NewsBank InfoWeb [On-line]. (1991–). New Canaan, CT: NewsBank.

NewsBank [CD-ROM]. (1980–). New Canaan, CT: NewsBank.

Pike & Fischer Radio Regulation, Second Series. (1963–). Washington, DC: Pike & Fischer.

Podell, J., & Anzovin, S. (1988). *Speeches of the American presidents.* New York: Wilson.

Public Affairs Video Archives: The Education and Research Archives of C-SPAN Programming. (1987–). West Lafayette, IN: Purdue University.

Representative American Speeches. (1938–). New York: Wilson.

Robinson, J. P., Shaver, P. R., Wrightsman, L. S., & Andrews, F. M. (1991). *Measures of personality and social psychological attitudes: Vol. 1. Measures of social psychological attitudes.* San Diego: Academic Press.

Rubin, R. B., Palmgreen, P., & Sypher, H. E. (Eds.). (1994). *Communication research measures: A sourcebook.* New York: Guilford Press.

Salem, J. M. (Ed.). (1966–). *A Guide to Critical Reviews.* Metuchen, NJ: Scarecrow Press.

Shapiro, M. E. (1989). *Television network prime-time programming, 1948–1988.* Jefferson, NC: McFarland.

Shapiro, M. E. (1990). *Television network daytime and late-night programming, 1959–1989.* Jefferson, NC: McFarland.

Shepard's United States citations (8th ed.). (1994). Colorado Springs, CO: Shepard's/McGraw-Hill.

Signorielli, N. (Ed.). (1996). *Women in communication: A biographical sourcebook.* Westport, CT: Greenwood Press.

Supreme Court Reporter. (1882–). St. Paul: West.

Supreme Court Reporter [CD-ROM]. (1993–). St. Paul: West.

Television & Cable Factbook (3 vols.). (1983–). Washington, DC: Warren.

Television & Cable Factbook [CD-ROM]. (1996–). Washington, DC: Warren.

TV Facts, Figures & Film. (1986–). Syosset, NY: Broadcast Information Bureau.

United States Supreme Court Reports: Lawyers' Edition, Second Series. (1956–). Rochester, NY: Lawyers Co-operative.

Viewpoint. (1976–). Glen Rock, NJ: Microfilming Corporation of America.

Vital Speeches of the Day. (1934–). New York: City News.

Vital Speeches of the Day [CD-ROM]. (1990–). New York: City News.

Voices of multicultural America: Notable speeches delivered by African, Asian, Hispanic, and Native Americans, 1790–1995. (1996). Detroit: Gale Research.

Weekly Compilation of Presidential Documents. (1965–). Washington, DC: Government Printing Office.

West's General Digest: A Digest of All Current Decisions of the American Courts as Reported in the National Reporter System and Other Standard Reports. (1936–). St. Paul: West.

What They Said. (1969–). Beverly Hills, CA: Monitor.

Women's History Research Center. (1956–). *Herstory.* Berkeley, CA: Author.

Finding Tools for Collections

Ash, L., & Miller, W. G. (Comps.). (1993). *Subject collections* (7th ed., Rev. & enl., 2 vols.). New Providence, NJ: Bowker.

Black, S. (1990). *Thesaurus of subject headings for television: A vocabulary for indexing script collections.* Phoenix: Oryx Press.

Black, S., & Moersh, E. S. (Eds.). (1990). *Index to the Annenberg Television Script Archive.* Phoenix: Oryx Press.

Brady, A., Wall, R., & Weiner, C. N. (1984). *Union list of film periodicals: Holdings of selected American collections.* Westport, CT: Greenwood Press.

CBS News Index. (1975–). Ann Arbor, MI: University Microfilms International.

Chun, K., Cobb, S., & French, J. R. P., Jr. (1975). *Measures for psychological assessment: A guide to 3,000 original sources and their applications.* Ann Arbor: University of Michigan, Institute for Social Research.

Film and Television Index. (1975–). New Canaan, CT: NewsBank.

Godfrey, D. G. (Comp.) (1983). *A directory of broadcast archives.* Washington, DC: Broadcast Education Association.

Historic Documents: Cumulative Index. (1973–). Washington, DC: Congressional Quarterly.

Indexes to American Periodicals. (1992–). Indianapolis: Computer Indexed Systems.

Indexes to American Periodicals [CD-ROM]. (1998–). Indianapolis: Computer Indexed Systems.

Kellerman, L. S., & Wilson, R. A. (1990). *Index to Readex microfilm collection of early American newspapers.* New Canaan, CT: Readex.

Library of Congress, Copyright Office. (1891–). *Catalog of Copyright Entries.* Washington, DC: Author.

NewsBank Electronic Index [CD-ROM]. (1986–). New Canaan, CT: NewsBank.

NewsBank InfoWeb [On-line]. (1991–). New Canaan, CT: NewsBank.

Oral History Index. (1994–). Westport, CT: Meckler.

Oral History Sources. (1990–). Alexandria, VA: Chadwyck-Healey.

Rouse, S., & Loughney, K. (Comps.). (1989). *3 decades of television: A catalog of television programs acquired by the Library of Congress 1949–1979*. Washington, DC: Library of Congress, Motion Picture, Broadcasting, & Recorded Sound Division.

Rowan, B. G., & Wood, C. J. (1994). *Scholars' guide to Washington, D.C., media collections*. Baltimore: Johns Hopkins University Press.

Shamley, S. L. (Comp.). (1991). *Television interviews, 1951–1955: A catalog of Longine's chronoscope interviews in the National Archives*. Washington, DC: U.S. National Archives and Records Administration.

Smart, J. R. (Comp.). (1982). *Radio broadcasts in the Library of Congress, 1924–1941: A catalog of recordings*. Washington, DC: Library of Congress.

Television News Index and Abstracts: Annual Index. (1968–). Nashville, TN: Vanderbilt Television News Archive.

Television News Index and Abstracts: Annual Index [On-line]. (1968–). Available: http://tvnews.vanderbilt.edu

Television News Study Center. (1981). *Television news resources: A guide to collections*. Washington, DC: George Washington University, Gelman Library.

University of Oklahoma, Political Commercial Archive. (1996). *Political communication center: A catalog and guide to the archival collections*. Norman: University of Oklahoma, Political Communication Center.

Vanden Heuvel, J. (1991). *Untapped sources: America's newspaper archives and histories*. New York: Gannett Foundation Media Center.

■ STATISTICAL SOURCES

A. C. Nielsen Company. (1954–). *Nielsen Television Index*. New York: Author.

A. C. Nielsen Company. (1955–). *Nielsen Report on Television*. Northbrook, IL: Author.

A Matter of Fact: Statements Containing Statistics on Current Social, Economic, and Political Issues. (1984–). Ann Arbor: Pierian Press. (Available on-line as *FactSearch*)

American public opinion cumulative index, 1981–1985. (1987). Louisville: Opinion Research Service.

American Statistics Index: A Comprehensive Guide and Index to the Statistical Publications of the U.S. Government. (1973–). Bethesda, MD: Congressional Information Service.

American Statistics Index: A Comprehensive Guide and Index to the Statistical Publications of the U.S. Government [On-line]. (1973–). Bethesda, MD: Congressional Information Service. (Available as part of *Statistical Universe*)

Arbitron Radio. (1996). *Arbitron Radio market report reference guide: A guide to understanding and using radio audience estimates*. New York: Author.

Armstrong, C. J., & Fenton, R. R. (Eds.). (1996). *World databases in social sciences*. New Providence, NJ: Bowker-Saur/Reed Reference.

Dodd, D. (1991). *Historical statistics of the United States: Two centuries of the census, 1790–1990*. Westport, CT: Greenwood Press.

FactSearch [Database]. (1984–). Ann Arbor, MI: Pierian Press.

Index to International Statistics [On-line]. (1983–). Bethesda, MD: Congressional Information Service. (Available as part of *Statistical Universe*)

Kurian, G. (1994). *Datapedia of the United States, 1790–2000: America year by year.* Lanham, MD: Bernan Press.

Polling the Nations [CD-ROM and On-line]. (1998–). Bethesda, MD: SilverPlatter.

Radio Advertising Bureau. (1989–). *Radio Marketing Guide and Fact Book for Advertisers.* New York: Author.

Roper Organization. (1995). *America's watching: Public attitudes toward television.* New York: Network Television Association.

Schick, F. L., & Schick, R. (1994). *Statistical handbook on aging Americans: 1994 edition.* Phoenix: Oryx Press.

Simmons Market Research Bureau. (1979–). *Target Group Index: Study of Media and Markets.* New York: Author.

Standard Rate & Data Service. (1993–). *SRDS Consumer Magazine Advertising Source.* Des Plains, IL: Author.

Standard Rate & Data Service. (1993–). *SRDS Newspaper Advertising Source.* Des Plains, IL: Author.

Standard Rate & Data Service. (1993–). *SRDS Radio Advertising Source.* Des Plains, IL: Author.

Standard Rate & Data Service. (1994–). *SRDS TV and Cable Source.* Des Plains, IL: Author.

Statistical Reference Index. (1980–). Washington, DC: Congressional Information Service.

Statistical Reference Index [On-line]. (1980–). Washington, DC: Congressional Information Service. (Available as part of *Statistical Universe*)

Statistical Universe [On-line]. (1998–). Bethesda, MD: Congressional Information Service.

University of Michigan Library Documents Center. (1998, June 1). *Statistical resources on the Web* [On-line]. Available: http://www.lib.umich.edu/libhome/Documents.center/stats.html

U.S. Department of Commerce, Bureau of the Census. (1879–). *Statistical Abstract of the United States.* Washington, DC: Government Printing Office.

U.S. Department of Commerce, Bureau of the Census. (1952–). *County and City Data Book.* Washington, DC: Government Printing Office.

U.S. Department of Commerce, Bureau of the Census. (1963–). *Census Catalog & Guide.* Washington, DC: Government Printing Office. (Formerly *Bureau of the Census Catalog*)

U.S. Department of Commerce, Bureau of the Census. (1980). *Social indicators III.* Washington, DC: Government Printing Office.

U.S. Department of Commerce, Bureau of the Census. (1993–). *Population Profile of the United States.* Washington, DC: Government Printing Office.

■ U.S. GOVERNMENT PUBLICATIONS

Federal Communications Commission. (1934/1935–). *Annual Report of the Federal Communications Commission.* Washington, DC: Government Printing Office.

Federal Communications Commission. (1934/1935–). *Federal Communications Commission Reports*. Washington, DC: Government Printing Office.

Federal Communications Commission. (1982–). *FCC Rules and Regulations* (Rev. ed.). Washington, DC: Government Printing Office.

U.S. Administrative Office of the United States Courts. (1993–). *Judicial Business of the United States Courts*. Washington, DC: Government Printing Office.

U.S. Administrative Office of the United States Courts. (1993–). *Judicial Business of the United States Courts* [On-line]. Available: http://www.uscourts.gov

U.S. Congress. (1873–). *Congressional Record: Proceedings and Debates of the Congress*. Washington, DC: Government Printing Office.

U.S. Congress. (1873–). *Congressional Record: Proceedings and Debates of the Congress* [On-line]. Available: http://www.access.gpo.gov and through *Congressional Universe*

U.S. Congress, House of Representatives. (1995). *United States code* (1994 ed.). Washington, DC: Government Printing Office.

U.S. Congress, House of Representatives. (1995). *United States code* (1994 ed.) [On-line]. Available: http://www.house.gov, http://www.law.cornell.edu/uscode, and through *Congressional Universe*

U.S. General Services Administration, Office of the Federal Register. (1936–). *Federal Register*. Washington, DC: Government Printing Office.

U.S. General Services Administration, Office of the Federal Register. (1938–). *Code of Federal Regulations*. Washington, DC: Government Printing Office.

U.S. Supreme Court. (1790–). *United States Supreme Court Reports*. Rochester, NY: Lawyers Co-operative.

U.S. Supreme Court. (1998–). *United States Supreme Court Reports* [CD-ROM]. Rochester, NY: Lawyers Co-operative.

Finding Tools for Government Publications

AccessUN. (1997). Chester, VT: NewsBank.

American statistics index: User guide. (1992). Washington, DC: Congressional Information Service.

Barrett, R. E. (1994). *Using the 1990 U.S. census for research*. Thousand Oaks, CA: Sage.

CIS Index to Publications of the United States Congress. (1970–). Washington, DC: Congressional Information Service. (Available on-line and through *Congressional Universe*)

Congressional Index. (1938–). Chicago: Commerce Clearing House.

Congressional Quarterly Almanac. (1945–). Washington, DC: Congressional Quarterly.

Congressional Quarterly's guide to Congress (5th ed.). (1999). Washington, DC: Congressional Quarterly.

Congressional Quarterly's guide to U.S. elections (3rd ed.). (1994). Washington, DC: Congressional Quarterly.

Congressional Quarterly's guide to the U.S. Supreme Court (3rd ed.). (1997). Washington, DC: Congressional Quarterly.

Congressional Universe [On-line]. (1997–). Bethesda, MD: Congressional Information Service.

CQ Library [On-line]. (1998–). Washington, DC: Congressional Quarterly.

CQ Weekly (Congressional Quarterly Weekly Report). (1943–). Washington, DC: Congressional Quarterly. (Available on-line as part of *CQ Library*)

Declassified Documents Catalog. (1975–). Woodbridge, CT: Research Publications.

GPO on SilverPlatter, U.S. Superintendent of Documents Monthly Catalog of United States Government Publications [CD-ROM and on-line]. (1976–). Boston: SilverPlatter.

Guide to United States Supreme Court Reports, Lawyers' Edition. (1994). Rochester, NY: Lawyers Co-operative.

Hardy, G. J., & Robinson, J. S. (1996). *Subject guide to U.S. government reference sources* (2nd ed.). Englewood, CO: Libraries Unlimited.

Index to the Code of Federal Regulations. (1997). Bethesda, MD: Congressional Information Service. (Available through *Congressional Universe*)

Index to United Nations Documents and Publications [CD-ROM]. (1992–). New Canaan, CT: NewsBank/Readex.

Index to United Nations Documents and Publications [On-line]. (1992–). Available: http://infoweb.newsbank.com

Lesko, M., & Capretta, C. (Eds.). (1990). *Federal data base finder: A directory of free and fee-based data bases and files available from the federal government* (3rd ed.). Kensington, MD: Information USA.

Sears, J. L., & Moody, M. K. (1994). *Using government information sources: Print and electronic* (2nd ed., 2 vols.). Phoenix: Oryx Press.

Shepard's acts and cases by popular names: Federal and state (4th ed., 3 vols.). (1992). Colorado Springs, CO: Shepard's/McGraw-Hill.

Shepard's United States Citations: United States Supreme Court Reports (Lawyer's ed.). (1996–). Colorado Springs, CO: Shepard's/McGraw-Hill.

U.S. Congress. (1981–). *Congressional Record, Index to Daily Proceedings*. Washington, DC: Government Printing Office.

U.S. General Services Administration, Office of the Federal Register. (1963–). *Code of Federal Regulations: CFR Index and Finding Aids*. Washington, DC: Government Printing Office.

U.S. Government Information: Publications, Periodicals, Electronic Products. (1984–). Washington, DC: Government Printing Office.

U.S. Government Periodicals Index. (1993–). Bethesda, MD: Congressional Information Service. (Available on-line and on CD-ROM from 1993)

U.S. Library of Congress. (1984). *Popular names of U.S. government reports* (4th ed.). Washington, DC: Government Printing Office.

U.S. Superintendent of Documents. (1895–). *Monthly Catalog of United States Government Publications*. Washington, DC: Government Printing Office.

U.S. Superintendent of Documents. (1895–). *Monthly Catalog of United States Government Publications* [On-line]. Available: http://www.access.gpo.gov

■ YEARBOOKS

Barone, M., & Ujifusa, G. (1972–). *The Almanac of American politics*. Washington, DC: National Journal.

Broadcasting & Cable Yearbook (2 vols.). (1935–). New Providence, NJ: Bowker.

Cook, C. (Comp.). (1995). *World political almanac* (3rd ed.). New York: Facts on File.

Editor & Publisher International Year Book. (1959–). New York: Editor & Publisher.

Editor & Publisher International Year Book [CD-ROM]. (1994–). New York: Editor & Publisher.

Educational Media and Technology Yearbook. (1973–). Littleton, CO: Libraries Unlimited.

Facts on File Yearbook. (1942–). New York: Facts on File.

Information Please Almanac. (1947–). Boston: Information Please.

International Motion Picture Almanac. (1929–). New York: Quigley.

International Television & Video Almanac. (1956–). New York: Quigley.

World Almanac and Book of Facts. (1868–). Mahwah, NJ: World Almanac Books.

■ DIRECTORIES

Media

Andrew, G. (1990). *The film handbook*. Boston: Hall.

Audio Video Review Digest: A Guide to Reviews of Audio and Video Materials Appearing in General and Specialized Periodicals. (1989–). Detroit: Gale Research.

AV Market Place. (1984–). New Providence, NJ: Bowker. (Formerly *Audiovisual Market Place,* 1969–1983, and *Audio Video Market Place,* 1984–1988)

Brooks, T., & Marsh, E. (Eds.). (1995). *The complete directory to prime time network and cable TV shows 1946–present* (6th ed.). New York: Ballantine Books.

Brown, L. (1992). *Les Brown's encyclopedia of television* (3rd ed.). Detroit: Gale Research.

Cable advertising directory. (1980–). Washington, DC: National Cable Television Association.

Directory of Scholarly Electronic Journals, Newsletters, and Academic Discussion Lists (1991–). Washington, DC: Association of Research Libraries.

DWM: A Directory of Women's Media. (1972–). New York: National Council for Research on Women.

Educational film & video locator (4th ed., 2 vols.). (1990–1991). New York: Bowker.

Gale Database of Publications and Broadcast Media [On-line]. (1996–). Detroit: Gale Research.

Gale Directory of Publications and Broadcast Media (4 vols.). (1869–). Detroit: Gale Research.

Gianakos, L. J. (1978–). *Television drama series programming: A comprehensive chronicle.* Metuchen, NJ: Scarecrow Press.

Hammond, C. M. (1981). *The image decade: Television documentary, 1965–1975.* New York: Hastings House.

Literary Market Place: The Directory of the American Book Publishing Industry With Industry Yellow Pages. (1940–). New Providence, NJ: Bowker.

Literary Market Place: The Directory of the American Book Publishing Industry With Industry Yellow Pages [CD-ROM]. (1999–). New Providence, NJ: Bowker.

Literary Market Place: The Directory of the American Book Publishing Industry With Industry Yellow Pages [On-line]. (1999–). Available as *LMP Online*: http://www.literarymarketplace.com and http://lmp.bookwire.com

MacNeil/Lehrer News Hour: Broadcast Review and Index. (1979–). Sanford, NC: Microfilming Corporation of America.

Maltin, L. (1983). *The whole film sourcebook.* New York: New American Library.

Mayer, I. (Ed.). (1987). *The knowledge industry publications 200: America's two hundred largest media and information companies* (3rd ed.). Detroit: Gale Research.

McNeil, A. (1997). *Total television: A comprehensive guide to programming from 1948 to the present* (4th ed.). New York: Penguin Books.

Media Review Digest. (1973/1974–). Ann Arbor, MI: Pierian Press. (Formerly *Multi Media Reviews Index*, 1970–1972)

News Media Yellow Book: Who's Who Among Reporters, Writers, Editors, and Producers in the Leading National News Media. (1989–). New York: Leadership Directories.

PBS Video: Program Catalog. (1974–). Washington, DC: Public Broadcasting Service.

Reed, M. K., & Reed, R. M. (1999). *Career opportunities in television, cable, video, and multimedia* (4th ed.). New York: Facts on File.

Slide, A., Hanson, P. K., & Hanson, S. L. (Comps.). (1988). *Sourcebook for the performing arts: A directory of collections, resources, scholars, and critics in theatre, film, and television.* New York: Greenwood Press.

Terrace, V. (1981). *Radio's golden years: The encyclopedia of radio programs, 1930–1960.* San Diego: Barnes.

Terrace, V. (1991). *Fifty years of television: A guide to series and pilots, 1937–1988.* New York: Cornwall.

United Nations Department of Public Information. (1995). *World media handbook: Selected country profiles.* New York: Author.

Video Source Book (3 vols.). (1979–). Detroit: Gale Research.

Woolery, G. W. (1983). *Children's television: The first thirty-five years, 1946–1981: Part I. Animated cartoon series.* Metuchen, NJ: Scarecrow Press.

Woolery, G. W. (1985). *Children's television: The first thirty-five years, 1946–1981: Part II. Live, film, and tape series.* Metuchen, NJ: Scarecrow Press.

Working Press of the Nation (3 vols.) (1945–). New Providence, NJ: Bowker.

World Guide to Television. (1994–). Philadelphia: North American.

World Radio TV Handbook. (1947–). New York: Billboard.

Writer's and Artist's Yearbook: A Directory for Writers, Artists, Playwrights, Writers for Film, Radio and Television, Designers, Illustrators and Photographers. (1906–). London: Black.

Writer's Market: 8000 Editors Who Buy What You Write. (1930–). Cincinnati: Writer's Digest.

General

Directories in Print (2 vols). (1980–). Detroit: Gale Research. (Formerly *Directory of Directories*) (Available on-line as part of *Gale Database of Publications and Broadcast Media*)

Directory of Research Grants. (1975–). Phoenix: Oryx Press.

Federal Regulatory Directory. (1956–). Washington, DC: Congressional Quarterly.

Guide to American Directories. (1954–). Nyack, NY: Todd.

Information Industry Directory: An International Guide to Organizations, Systems, and Services Involved in the Production and Distribution of Information in Electronic Form (2 vols.). (1971–). Detroit: Gale Research.

International Who's Who. (1935–). London: Europa.

Martindale-Hubbell Law Directory (20 vols.). (1869–). New Providence, NJ: Martindale-Hubbell.

Martindale-Hubbell Law Directory [CD-ROM]. (1993–). New Providence, NJ: Martindale-Hubbell.

Martindale-Hubbell Lawyer Locator [On-line]. (1999). Available: http://lawyers. martingale.com/locator/home.html

Standard & Poor's Register of Corporations, Directors & Executives. (1928–). New York: Standard & Poor's.

United States Government Manual. (1974–). Washington, DC: Government Printing Office.

United States Government Manual [On-line]. (1995–). Available: http://www. access.gpo.gov/nara/nara001.html

Washington Information Directory. (1975–). Washington, DC: Congressional Quarterly.

Who's Who in Advertising. (1990/1991–). Wilmette, IL: Marquis Who's Who.

Who's Who in America (3 vols.). (1899/1900–). New Providence, NJ: Marquis Who's Who.

Worldbook of IABC Communicators. (1900–). San Francisco: International Association of Business Communicators.

■ DICTIONARIES

Appiah, K. A., Gates, H. L., & Vazquez, M. C. (Eds.). (1997). *The dictionary of global culture.* New York: Knopf.

Audi, R. (1995). *The Cambridge dictionary of philosophy.* New York: Cambridge University Press.

Bauml, B. J., & Bauml, F. H. (1997). *Dictionary of worldwide gestures* (2nd ed.). Lanham, MD: Scarecrow Press.

Bryant, D. C., Smith, R. W., Arnott, P. D., Holtsmark, E. B., & Rowe, G. O. (1968). *Ancient Greek and Roman rhetoricians: A bibliographical dictionary.* Columbia, MO: Artcraft Press.

Collin, P. H. (1998). *Dictionary of government & politics* (2nd ed.). Chicago: Fitzroy Dearborn.

Cross, W. (1995). *Prentice Hall encyclopedic dictionary of business terms.* Englewood Cliff, NJ: Prentice Hall.

Delson, D., & Jacob, S. (1990). *Delson's dictionary of motion picture marketing terms* (2nd ed.). Westlake Village, CA: Bradson Press.

Diamant, L. (Ed.). (1992). *Dictionary of broadcast communications* (new 3rd Rev. ed.). Lincolnwood, IL: NTC Business Books.

Ellmore, R. T. (1995). *NTC's mass media dictionary*. Lincolnwood, IL: National Textbook.

Fletcher, J. (1988). *Broadcast research definitions*. Washington, DC: National Association of Broadcasters.

Fox, R. W., & Kloppenberg, J. T. (1995). *A companion to American thought*. Cambridge, MA: Blackwell.

Garner, B. A. (Ed.). (1996). *Black's law dictionary* (Pocket ed.). St. Paul: West.

Garwood, A. N., & Hornor, L. L. (1991). *Dictionary of U.S. government statistical terms*. Palo Alto, CA: Information Publications.

Godfrey, D. G., & Leigh, F. A. (1998). *Historical dictionary of American radio*. Westport, CT: Greenwood Press.

Gregory, R. L., & Zangwill, O. L. (1998). *The Oxford companion to the mind* (2nd ed.). New York: Oxford University Press.

Honderick, T. (Ed.). (1995). *The Oxford companion to philosophy*. New York: Oxford University Press.

Hurwitz, L. (1985). *Historical dictionary of censorship in the United States*. Westport, CT: Greenwood Press.

Jary, D., & Jary, J. (Eds.). (1991). *HarperCollins dictionary of sociology*. New York: HarperPerennial.

Koocher, G. P., Norcross, J. C., & Hill, S. S. (Eds.). (1998). *Psychologists' desk reference*. New York: Oxford University Press.

Marriott, F. H., & Kendall, M. G. (1990). *A dictionary of statistical terms* (5th ed.). Burnt Mill, UK: Longman Scientific & Technical.

Marshall, G. (1998). *Dictionary of sociology* (2nd ed.). Oxford: Oxford University Press.

McBrien, J. L., & Brandt, R. S. (1997). *The language of learning: A guide to education terms*. Alexandria, VA: Association for Supervision and Curriculum Development.

McKerns, J. (1989). *Biographical dictionary of American journalism*. New York: Greenwood Press.

Penney, E. F. (1991). *The Facts on File dictionary of film and broadcast terms*. New York: Facts on File.

Plano, J. C., & Greenberg, M. (1997). *The American political dictionary* (10th ed.). Fort Worth, TX: Harcourt Brace.

Radio dictionary: A new testament of radio. (1993). Dublin, OH: Riverview Press.

Reed, R. M., & Reed, M. K. (1994). *The Facts on File dictionary of television, cable, and video*. New York: Facts on File.

Rosenberg, J. M. (1993). *Business dictionary of computers* (Rev. ed.). New York: Wiley.

Rosenberg, J. M. (1995). *Dictionary of marketing and advertising*. New York: Wiley.

Safire, W. (1993). *Safire's new political dictionary* (Rev. 3rd ed.). New York: Random House.

Schwandt, T. A. (1997). *Qualitative inquiry: A dictionary of terms*. Thousand Oaks, CA: Sage.

Shafritz, J. M. (1993). *The HarperCollins dictionary of American government and politics*. New York: HarperPerennial.

Slide, A. (1991). *The television industry: A historical dictionary*. New York: Greenwood Press.

Slide, A. (1998). *The new historical dictionary of the American film industry*. Chicago: Fitzroy Dearborn.

Stuart-Hamilton, I. (Ed.). (1996). *Dictionary of cognitive psychology* (Rev. ed.). London: Kingsley.

Sutherland, S. (1996). *The international dictionary of psychology*. New York: Crossroad.

Vogt, W. P. (1999). *Dictionary of statistics and methodology* (2nd ed.). Thousand Oaks, CA: Sage.

Watson, J., & Hill, A. (1997). *A dictionary of communication and media studies* (4th ed.). London: Arnold.

Weik, M. H. (1996). *Communications standard dictionary* (3rd ed.). New York: Chapman & Hall.

Weik, M. H. (1996). *Communications standard dictionary* (3rd ed.) [CD-ROM]. New York: Chapman & Hall.

Weiner, R. (1996). *Webster's New World dictionary of media and communications* (Rev. ed.). New York: Macmillan.

Wiechman, J. G., & Urdang, L. (Eds.). (1993). *NTC's dictionary of advertising* (Rev. ed.). Lincolnwood, IL: National Textbook.

Wolman, B. B. (1989). *Dictionary of behavioral science* (2nd ed.). San Diego: Academic Press.

Words and Phrases: All Judicial Constructions and Definitions of Words and Phrases by the State and Federal Courts from the Earliest Times (90 vols.). (1940–). St. Paul: West.

■ MANUALS

Baudot, B. S. (1989). *International advertising handbook: A user's guide to rules and regulations*. Lexington, MA: Lexington Books.

Belanger, S. E. (Comp.). (1989). *Better said and clearly written: An annotated guide to business communication sources, skills, and samples*. New York: Greenwood Press.

Berger, A. A. (1990). *Scripts: Writing for radio and television*. Newbury Park, CA: Sage.

Block, M. (1994). *Broadcast newswriting: The RTNDA reference guide*. Chicago: RTNDA/Bonus Books.

Christ, W. G. (1999). *Leadership in a time of change: A handbook for communication and media administrators*. Mahwah, NJ: Erlbaum.

Crawford, M. G. (1996). *The journalist's legal guide* (3rd ed.). Scarborough, Ontario: Carswell.

Dwyer, J. (1996). *The business communication handbook* (4th ed.). New York: Prentice Hall.

Ehrlich, E. H., Hand, R., Jr., & Bender, J. F. (1991). *NBC handbook of pronunciation* (4th ed., rev.). New York: HarperPerennial.

FindLaw [On-line]. Available: http://www.findlaw.com/

Goldstein, N. (1998). *Associated Press stylebook and libel manual* (Rev. & updated ed.). Reading, MA: Addison-Wesley.

Hamer, I. K. (1997). *Leading a group: A practical and comprehensive handbook* (5th ed.). Maroubra, N.S.W.: K. Hamer.

Henn, H. G. (1991). *Henn on copyright law: A practitioner's guide* (3rd ed.). New York: Practising Law Institute.

Henson, K. T. (1991). *Writing for successful publication*. Bloomington, IN: ERIC/RCS.

Kalbfeld, B., & Hood, J. R. (1987). *The Associated Press broadcast news handbook*. New York: Associated Press.

Kessler, L., & MacDonald, D. (2000). *When words collide: A media writer's guide to grammar and style* (5th ed.). Belmont, CA: Wadsworth.

Lippman, T. W. (Ed.). (1989). *The Washington Post deskbook on style* (2nd ed.). New York: McGraw-Hill.

MacDonald, R. H. (1994). *A broadcast news manual of style* (2nd ed.). New York: Longman.

Macnamara, J. R. (1996). *Public relations handbook for managers and executives* (Rev. ed.). New York: Prentice Hall.

McNeil, R. (1992). *UPI stylebook: The authoritative handbook for writers, editors & news directors* (3rd ed.). Lincolnwood, IL: National Textbook.

Nash, C. (1993). *The screenwriter's handbook*. New York: HarperPerennial.

Price, S. (1997). *The complete A–Z media & communication handbook*. London: Hodder & Stoughton.

Remocker, A. J. (1999). *Action speaks louder: A handbook of structured group techniques* (6th ed.). Edinburgh: Churchill Livingstone.

Robert, H. M. (1998). *Robert's rules of order newly revised* (9th ed., new & enl. ed.). Reading, MA: Addison-Wesley.

Weinberg, S. (Ed.). (1996). *The reporter's handbook: An investigator's guide to documents and techniques* (3rd ed.). New York: St. Martin's Press.

West's Law Finder: A Legal Resources Guide. (1959–). Eagan, MN: West.

Willis, E. (1993). *Writing scripts for television, radio, and film* (3rd ed.). Fort Worth, TX: Harcourt Brace Jovanovich.

Wren, C. G., & Wren, J. R. (1988). *The legal research manual: A game plan for legal research and analysis* (2nd ed.). Madison, WI: Adams & Ambrose.

EXAMPLES

CHRIS decides to check out some additional speech collections to see if speech authors are identified. At the *Douglass* site, they didn't seem to be given. Now it's time to check out the University of North Carolina site.

FELECIA'S initial investigation of voice mail has led to statistical sources. Just how many businesses out there have voice-mail systems? Felecia checks *A Matter of Fact* for an answer. Nine records are found for "voice mail." One of these articles is a press release about the University of Michigan's voice-mail system and provides good comparative data for the piece.

MARIA has now read several summary articles about attribution and the term seems to be used consistently in the literature. Just to be sure, she checks the *Dictionary of Behavioral Science* to see how the term is defined. A one-sentence definition adds nothing new, but a look at "Heider" revealed an entry for "Heider's theory of attribution." This paragraph presented the core of the theory in a nutshell.

ORLANDO'S paper on parasocial interaction is just about done. Throughout the journal articles there have been references to measurement techniques to measure the degree of parasocial interaction. Orlando decides to examine a measurement collection, *Communication Research Measures: A Sourcebook*, to see if the Parasocial Interaction Scale is profiled. It is! This source provides a double check on sources as well.

KAT and **CALVIN** have teamed up to find an audiovisual aid for the group project on conflict management. They decide to check *Media Review Digest*. In the alphabetical subject index under "conflict management," they are led to "mediation." The only film they find is *Breakthrough . . . Choosing a New Road*, a film meant for grades 4 to 9. Nothing is listed under "group conflict" or "interpersonal relations" either. **ROCKY** and **MICHELLE**, however, look at *Video Sourcebook* and find a film called *Conflicts, Conflicts!*, a 1985 management-training film that presents techniques for avoiding conflict, and it's geared to the adult viewer. They also find out that it can be rented from the University of Washington Educational Media Collection, so they ask their interlibrary loan staff for help in securing it for their project.

EXERCISES

1. In your Political Communication course, you have been studying the rhetoric of President Bill Clinton. To find verbatim texts of important speeches by national newsmakers, you consult *Vital Speeches of the Day*. Use the annual index

(printed in November) to locate his first Inaugural Address (called "American Renewal") delivered between October 15, 1992, and October 1, 1993. When was this speech delivered?

2. For your term paper in Mass Media Management, you will be using an article written in 1985 that cites statistical data, giving the Federal Communications Commission as its source. To see whether the FCC has updated these data, you use the on-line version of *American Statistics Index, Statistical Universe*. You find a reference under this agency to a publication that includes data on "TV station channel allocation." It sounds like this might be what you are looking for.

   a. What is the accession number for this item?

   b. Find the abstract for this publication. What is its title?

3. In your seminar on Issues in the Press, you are going to be giving a presentation on newspaper publishing. Although you have compiled a rather comprehensive bibliography on the topic, you find that you need additional facts and figures on circulation trends. You turn to the *Statistical Universe* to access the *Statistical Abstract of the United States* and find that an entire section of the volume is devoted to communications. Find the 1998 publishing section.

   a. Find a table in this section giving data on the number and circulation of daily and Sunday newspapers by states. What is the newspaper circulation per capita for the state of Hawaii?

   b. How does this figure compare with that given for the District of Columbia?

   c. What is the number of this table?

   d. These data are useful, but you would like to find a more comprehensive source. What is the title of the publication given as the source of these data?

4. You are studying the early development of radio in your Media History class. You come across a reference to an early radio station in Cleveland, Ohio, but the reference fails to mention the call letters of the station and when the station began. You consult the index of the most recent edition of the *Broadcasting & Cable Yearbook* and find a listing for a directory of U.S. and Canadian radio stations. Turning to this section, you discover that Cleveland has several radio stations.

   a. What are the call letters of the oldest radio station in Cleveland?

   b. In what year did that station go on the air?

   c. To whom is the station licensed?

5. You are interning as a communication-training specialist in a large company and have been asked to help develop an in-service human relations–training program. You've been given the task of identifying commercially available audiovisual materials that might be of use in this program. To identify existing videotapes and to determine their availability, you turn to the most recent edition of *The Video Source Book*. Looking in the subject index under the

heading "Personnel Management," you find a video with the title *Managing Diversity*. Find the full description of this video.

a. Is this video's level suitable for your audience?

b. Can the video be rented/leased?

c. What is the purchase price?

6. Identify projects or assignments that would require use of the sources listed in this chapter. Which sources would you keep near your desk? Why?

7. Meet in the library reference area and examine a selection of these sources. What interesting new things did you learn? How might you use these sources as a communication professional?

part three

Communication Research Processes

N ow that we've identified the basic search strategies and sources important for communication research, we will discuss the two processes next encountered by researchers: research and writing. Through the literature review, we determine questions that still need answers and formulate research strategies to uncover those answers. When conducting primary research, we seek to answer those questions. In writing, we determine the best way to present the information found during the literature search and, perhaps, the research investigation.

In Chapter 9 we focus on systematic procedures for conducting a research study. Our purpose in this chapter is to overview the major procedures used in communication research. We also provide several useful sources that you can consult when planning your own research project. Even if you will not be doing your own research, the information in the chapter will help you become an effective consumer of the research literature that you encounter.

Writing is just as systematic as searching and researching in that specific and rigorous conventions must be followed. In Chapter 10 we focus on basic writing principles, formatting styles, and copyediting. In Chapter 11 we discuss basic writing projects: abstracts, literature reviews, critical papers, research prospectuses, and research reports.

In Chapter 12 we invite you inside the research process to see the decisions and choices that researchers make. We take you through the conceptualization and execution of an actual study. You can find an abridged version of the original report of this study in Appendix B.

Part 3, then, identifies important processes in researching and writing about communication topics. We hope this section will whet your appetite for doing communication research.

chapter 9

Designing the Communication Research Project

Sometimes a literature review's summary and critical evaluation of past research is an end product of the research effort. In many instances, though, the literature review is only a beginning. We often need to go further to investigate new questions or problems we've uncovered. We'll need to conduct original research to answer the questions not already answered by past studies.

All researchers realize that many facets of communication are not fully understood. Because there are many questions that have yet to be answered adequately, the literature on a specific research topic is seldom complete. When this is the case, researchers must conduct their own investigations to answer the questions. In this chapter we overview research methods that can be used to bridge these gaps in our knowledge.

Our goal here is to introduce you to the conduct of research. This will help you understand much of the literature you encounter and, if needed, design your own research project. In either case, when reading research or doing research, it is important that you consult additional books about research methods, measurement, and analysis. We identify many useful sources at the end of this chapter.

THE RESEARCH PROCESS

Research is an objective, systematic, empirical, and cumulative process by which we seek to solve theoretical and applied problems. Such problems present obstacles to our understanding of communication. Research is *objective* because we try to be impartial when seeking the best solutions to the research problem. It is *systematic* because we move through a series of planned stages when conducting research. It is *empirical* because we look beyond ourselves to observe and to gather evidence. And, research is *cumulative* because it builds upon past knowledge. Research does not stand isolated from what others have done before.

193

If a question has already been answered in the literature, there is little need to duplicate the effort. However, many questions are unanswered and duplicating or replicating research is warranted if (a) there is reason to suspect the validity of the earlier studies, (b) another view would add to the diversity of knowledge about the problem, or (c) new information might bolster or alter previous findings in light of a changing communication environment. For example, the growth of VCRs and cable and satellite television in people's homes might change earlier findings about how television is used by the family.

DESCRIPTIVE AND EXPLANATORY RESEARCH

Researchers observe, describe, and often explain the relationships between variables or events. Research can be descriptive or explanatory. Our research question guides the choice of method. When doing **descriptive research**, we try to identify or describe events or conditions. We would conduct descriptive research if we were asking, "What is the present or past state of events?" When doing **explanatory research**, we look for underlying causes and explanations of events. We would conduct explanatory research if we were asking, "Why have these events happened in the manner that they did?"

Let's consider our example of media-related training programs for executives. If our research question is "How have these training programs changed during the past 3 decades?" our focus is descriptive. We would want to describe how the training programs have evolved over the years. If we ask, "Why is the information contained in these instructional methods effective?" our focus is explanatory. We would want to evaluate the content of past training programs on the basis of how we define *effective*—that is, our criteria to evaluate effectiveness (for example, the ability to field questions or credibility of response). Here, we would arrive at an informed judgment about *why* an instructional training method produces positive or negative, or expected or unexpected, results.

■ RESEARCH STAGES

The process of conducting original research consists of several stages:

1. Posing and developing a problem needing a solution
2. Reviewing past research and writings about that problem or subject
3. Identifying worthy questions previous investigators haven't answered
4. Devising the best method to seek answers to these questions
5. Gathering the necessary information to answer the research questions
6. Analyzing that information
7. Presenting the results of the inquiry
8. Considering the meaning and implications of these results to further knowledge of the subject or theory

Problem and Literature

We need to define and to describe our research problem precisely. Once we select and define the problem that we need to solve, we must go to the appropriate literature to see if others have already addressed similar issues. The literature will help clarify the current state of knowledge about our topic. It will also help us identify precise research questions about the problem that we need to answer. For example, suppose our problem concerns the role of nonverbal communication in the classroom. By reading what other researchers have written about the subject, we will be able to learn what they have discovered before us. This will help us focus on the precise questions we need to answer.

Research Question

We might narrow our focus to "How does nonverbal immediacy affect learning in the classroom?" Sometimes, if there's no theory or prior research to guide the study, the research question will suggest an *inductive* approach to the problem. We make our observations and then try to understand it and to develop a theory about the role of, in our example, immediacy and learning.

Or, if the research literature suggests, we might want to test a hypothesis. For example, we might predict that there will be a positive relationship between nonverbal immediacy and learning. Perhaps the literature suggests that, as we increase nonverbal immediacy in the classroom, learning will increase. A **hypothesis**, then, is an educated guess or prediction about the relationship between two or more variables. One of these variables is the **independent variable**. It is the antecedent, or the presumed cause, in the relationship. The other variable is the **dependent variable**. It is the consequent, or the presumed effect, in the relationship.

For example, if our hypothesis is "Communication training will improve a manager's media interview performance," training is our independent variable, and interview performance is our dependent variable. Or we might *predict* (in other words, hypothesize) that "Higher degrees of communication competence will result in better academic performance." Communication competence is our independent variable, and academic performance is our dependent variable. What we are predicting is that academic performance (the consequent) will vary *as a result* of a person's level of communication competence (the antecedent).

Whether we seek to answer a research question or to test a hypothesis, we must be sure that all elements, such as nonverbal immediacy and learning, are clearly defined so that we know precisely what answers we are seeking or what it is that we are testing. There are two types of definitions. A **conceptual definition** refers to terms used to describe a variable. For example, a conceptual definition of communication competence might be "being an effective communicator." A conceptual definition of academic performance might be "showing knowledge in the classroom."

An **operational definition**, on the other hand, describes the procedures we follow to observe or to measure the variables. For example, an operational definition of communication competence might be "the score obtained on the

Communication Competency Assessment Instrument." An operational defini- tion of academic performance might be "overall grade point average." It is important that an operational definition matches the conceptual definition of the concept being studied.

Method of Inquiry

Our method of inquiry is how we go about trying to answer the question or to test the hypothesis. Researchers have a wealth of possible methods available to them. We may, for example, choose to conduct an experiment or a survey, or we may want to use observational methods, or we may want to do a critical analy- sis. Sometimes the question itself suggests the most suitable approach, but often past research suggests the best approach. Past research, as described in the literature, can suggest a research method. In addition, different researchers are more comfortable working with one of the different **quantitative** (that is, deductive and statistical) or **qualitative** (that is, inductive and interpretive) research methods that we discuss in this chapter.

Data Gathering and Analysis

Once we select the most appropriate method, we need to gather our data. If we use observational methods, for example, we'll conduct our observations of non- verbal immediacy in selected classrooms in a systematic manner. If we use critical methods, we'll collect and examine written or visual examples. If we use experi- mental methods, we'll set up a more controlled environment in which we manip- ulate the amount of nonverbal immediacy and then measure the amount of learn- ing. After we collect our data, we need to analyze them to determine the answer to our research question. We might, for example, look for common themes in classroom discussions and examples or submit the data to statistical analysis.

Writing and Discussing

After completing our analysis, we need to write up our results and to consider the meaning and implications of our findings. Did our analysis support our hypothesis? What does it mean if nonverbal immediacy does lead to better learn- ing in the classroom? Do other factors also contribute to learning? Could we have improved our study in any manner? What does this suggest for future researchers to consider?

Let's return to our earlier investigation into the use of media-related train- ing programs for company executives. That study may have left several ques- tions unanswered. For example:

1. How long have these training programs been in existence?
2. How widespread are such media-training programs in this or other coun- tries today?
3. Are these training programs effective in improving an executive's ability to deal with the media?

4. Do training programs simply maintain the power structure of the organization?

After defining our problem and reading the literature, we will refine and seek to answer our research questions. We can probably find answers to questions 1 and 2 in the literature. The literature should also offer tentative but incomplete answers to questions 3 and 4, as well as disagreements among researchers. We might therefore need to design our own study or analysis to answer those questions. How we go about answering the questions reflects our method of approach to the investigation. We discuss various methods of communication research in the remainder of this chapter.

APPROACHES TO COMMUNICATION RESEARCH

We classify the method of communication research into two broad approaches. First, message- or artifact-oriented research looks at communication messages and attitudes associated with messages. It includes archival/documentary and survey/interview research. Second, people- or behavior-oriented research looks at communication behavior. It includes observational and experimental research. We will now briefly discuss these two approaches. Having this preliminary information, you should consult other books on research methods to determine the best procedures for a particular investigation.

■ MESSAGE- OR ARTIFACT-ORIENTED RESEARCH

Message- or **artifact-oriented research** focuses on examining and interpreting messages and related ideas, such as people's attitudes and opinions about messages, issues, or events. There are two principal types of message- and artifact-oriented research: archival/documentary and survey/interview research.

Archival/Documentary Research

Archival/documentary research centers on finding, examining, and interpreting messages that have been communicated. Common forms of archival/documentary research include library/documentary, historical, critical/rhetorical, and legal research, as well as secondary, conversation, textual, and content analysis. We'll briefly describe archival/documentary research forms. We'll explain one often-used form, content analysis, in slightly more detail.

Library/Documentary Research When conducting **library/documentary research**, we examine all relevant, published materials on our topic. These include printed materials such as published and collected documents (for example, chapters, articles, papers, speeches) and, perhaps, media materials such as films, audiotapes, and videotapes. In other words, when we do library/documentary research, we use many of the materials described in Chapters 5–8. We might use general sources, access tools, periodicals, and information compilations to examine a research problem or to answer a research question.

All original research begins with library/documentary research. That is, as we adjust our research questions to begin a study, we must first find out what others have learned about a subject.

Historical Research **Historical research** entails drawing conclusions and presenting new explanations about past communication events or communicators. Historical researchers work with *primary* documents, records, and artifacts, such as original speeches, letters, and recordings that are found in archives and libraries such as a presidential library or broadcast museum or archives. Original works are preferred to *secondary* sources, which provide another person's summary or explanation of the original sources.

Historical researchers also seek to collect testimony from authorities or others who can support or disconfirm the written and media materials. Interviews and oral histories are useful for gathering such testimony.

Historical researchers need to be as thorough as possible, examining all relevant and available records and artifacts. They seek to record accurately what transpired and to clarify relationships among societal institutions and conditions, people, events, and the like.

Historical studies may be biographical, movement or idea, regional, institutional, case history, selected, or editorial in nature (Phifer, 1961). For example, an institutional study might consider the societal forces that influenced the development of a news organization during the early 20th century. A biographical study might focus on the career of a government leader, business executive, or other personality. A movement study might examine the women's rights, civil rights, or antiwar movements during a certain period.

Critical/Rhetorical Research **Critical/rhetorical research** interprets and evaluates communication events and their consequences. Examples of critical research in communication might include applying Aristotle's concept of "invention" to political debate, doing a fantasy-theme analysis of organizational behavior, conducting a dramatistic analysis of a political campaign, examining the social and economic reasons for the decline in daily newspapers, and exploring how media help foster hegemony and maintain societal power structures. Critical/rhetorical research relies on thorough historical gathering of facts. It also relies on critical methods of choosing and applying appropriate criteria or standards of judgment to evaluate communication events.

For example, a president's televised news conferences might be evaluated by several criteria such as effective use of the medium, directness of response to reporters' questions, degree of control over the ground rules, rapport with members of the press, and the amount and quality of information disclosed. Which of these criteria would be used, of course, evolves from the research question. For example, a critical research project might evaluate how news media affected government policy during the past 25 years or how government policy restricted the flow of information via the media.

Marxism and cultural approaches are two major branches of critical theory in mass communication. In Marxist theories, the media are seen as powerful agents to restrain change for either ideological or economic reasons. The media are owned by a capitalist class and are organized to serve the interests of that class. Media messages depend on the underlying economic and ideological interests of the owners of the media. Marxist approaches direct us to examine critically the structure of media ownership, the operation of media market forces, and how ideological media messages intentionally influence culture by presenting distorted views of reality and class relationships. Cultural approaches focus our attention on understanding the meaning and role of popular culture for societal groups. They direct us to consider how mass culture subordinates deviant societal groups to nondeviant groups.

Legal/Policy Research   **Legal/policy research** is both historical and critical in nature. It seeks to clarify and to understand how law operates in society. It focuses on the evolution and application of legal doctrine such as First Amendment law and Federal Communications Commission (FCC) policy. Legal research centers on issues and cases in several areas: defamation, privacy, restraint of expression (such as censorship and obscenity), freedom of information and news access, newsperson privilege, free press and fair trial, and media regulation. Legal research often considers the origin and evolution of legal precedent, debate over such doctrine, and the role of societal agencies, groups, and the like in the status of the legal or policy issue. It relies heavily on primary documentation from legal codes, court cases, judicial opinions, and administrative rulings.

Secondary Analysis   The goal of **secondary analysis** is to shed new light on previous data and conclusions. Researchers sometimes work with previously gathered or archived data, and their purpose is to reconsider and to reinterpret those data in light of different ways of thinking. They may want to ask different questions—for example, about variables related to voting behavior—and use the same set of data previously used to answer other questions. They may want to reorder the data. For example, they may collapse continuous data such as ages ranging from 18 to 90 years into discrete categories such as younger, middle-age, and older. They may want to see if there are any trends over time by using several data sets. Or, they may use different statistical procedures to reanalyze relationships. These researchers seek new answers to new questions using not-so-new data.

Conversation Analysis   **Conversation analysis**, also termed *relational* and *interactional analysis* in the 1960s and 1970s, examines the structure, messages, function, rules, and content of conversations. Its purpose is to discover if and how people accomplish their goals when they interact. Interpersonal and small-group communication researchers primarily use this method.

Some researchers gather their data by surreptitiously eavesdropping on conversations. Others design experimental settings to record talk. Most, however, prefer to record the interaction in the most natural environment possible.

To do their analysis, researchers gather samples of conversation. They transcribe these samples into written text. Using a selected coding scheme, they categorize the messages and analyze message content and category structure. They then draw conclusions about the participants' goals, rules, and impact on the interaction.

There are two well-known types of conversation analysis. Rogers and Farace's Relational Control Coding Scheme is used to analyze the power and effects of talk on interpersonal relationships. Bales' Interaction Process Analysis is used to trace the stages of small-group interaction. More recently, researchers have been interested in the beginnings and endings of conversations and in the rules people develop and use in everyday conversation.

Textual Analysis **Textual analysis**, or *reception analysis*, is derived from literary criticism and focuses on "reading" media content or "text." It is interested in the text–audience relationship. Audience interpretations are compared to the media text to explain how meaning is socially constructed and variable. Researchers suggest that audience members "rework" the content.

Researchers generally use ethnography, including in-depth interviews and participant observation, to gather audience interpretations of discourse. They systematically record and categorize these audience reports of experiences with the selected media content, seeking explanations of how the meaning of such content is socially or culturally constructed. Such analyses have been done with television dramas, news, romance novels, and the like.

Content Analysis **Content analysis** looks at the characteristics of communication messages. The purpose is to learn something about the content and those who produced the messages. Our eventual interest might lie with the effects the content might have on receivers. However, we would need to link content analysis with another method such as survey or experimental research to address such effects. Speeches, news stories, and television programs are often subjected to content analysis to learn about underlying attitudes, biases, or repeating themes.

Doing a content analysis is a multistage process. Let's consider another research problem here: sex-role stereotyping on television. Here's the process. First, we select the titles we would want to sample, such as television comedy programs. Then, we select the dates to sample, say comedy programs in the 1990s. We might form two **composite weeks** that represent the entire year by randomly selecting two Mondays, Tuesdays, Wednesdays, and so on from throughout the year. We then select our units of analysis (for example, occupations of major characters on the TV shows) and assign these units to predetermined categories (for example, lawyer, physician, teacher, police officer). These categories must be *mutually exclusive* (that is, all categories must differ from one another) and *exhaustive* (that is, all possible categories are included in our analysis). We then compare whether more men or more women are presented in these different roles. We also might compare our findings with U.S. population statistics to see whether television presents an unfair or unflattering bias against women or men.

We will describe different sampling techniques in the next section when discussing survey research. As you can see, though, content analysis is a very systematic process.

Survey/Interview Research

Survey researchers seek to describe or to explain people's current attitudes, opinions, thoughts, and perhaps, reports of behavior (such as whether they voted) surrounding an issue or event (such as an election). Because survey research has been the most widely used method of communication research, we will explain it in more depth. We will also briefly identify other survey or interview forms: polls, ratings, interviews, and focus groups.

Survey Research   In our example research study we asked, "How widespread are media-training programs in this country today?" We can use survey research, sampling corporate leaders to answer the question. Survey researchers try to obtain the needed information systematically and efficiently (that is, in the shortest period of time and as inexpensively as possible). **Survey research** is an efficient means of gathering data from large numbers of people.

Before conducting a survey, we must first determine what it is we are trying to learn. Survey research can be used to measure attitudes and reported behaviors. It usually employs correlational designs, not looking for cause-and-effect connections but seeking to describe either the opinions of people or the relationships between two or more variables in hypotheses or research questions. Before we can construct the specific questions, we must determine how best to get this information (data-collection methods) and choose a sample of **respondents** (sampling).

There are four basic *data-collection methods*: personal interviews, telephone interviews, mail questionnaires, and self-administered surveys. *Personal interviews* are face-to-face encounters between the interviewer and selected respondents. *Telephone interviews* also require an interviewer but are conducted over the phone. *Mail questionnaires* are self-administered; a participant receives a survey in the mail and is asked to respond and return it. Besides mail questionnaires, respondents complete other *self-administered surveys* without prompting from interviewers, such as in a classroom or work setting. Each technique has its advantages and disadvantages. Consult one of the sources at the end of this chapter for additional information. They contain detailed descriptions of questionnaire design and methods of getting a high rate of return for completed questionnaires.

There are also standard methods of selecting a valid **sample** of people from a **population**. Samples are chosen because it is too costly, time-consuming, or unnecessary to conduct a census of the entire population. Sometimes, in fact, a sample can be better than a census of the whole population; if chosen randomly and care is taken to achieve a high return rate, a sample can better represent the population than could a census with a poor return rate. We use probability (random) and nonprobability (nonrandom) techniques to select samples.

Probability sampling allows us to generalize from the sample being observed to the entire population from which that sample is chosen. It uses random sampling techniques and assures us that the sample is representative of the population. These techniques include simple random, systematic, stratified, and cluster sampling.

- In a **simple random sample**, each person has an equal or known chance of being chosen. We might use a list of names to select a sample randomly and a table of random numbers to identify those who are chosen. This is not very efficient, though, when we have a large population.
- A **systematic sample** has us select every *n*th person from a current and complete list, or *sampling frame*. For example, we might choose every 10th name from a student directory.
- If we want to compare certain subgroups in the population, we can use a **stratified sample**. For example, to compare their responses, we can randomly select men and women for our sample in relation to how many of each group there are in the campus population. For example, we would select 55 women and 45 men if women comprise 55% and men 45% of the campus population.
- We could use a **cluster sample** if we find it impractical or impossible to compile a list of everyone in a population but can obtain lists of, say, housing units on campus. We could then draw a random or systematic sample of dorm residents from a random sample of dormitories.

All these probability sampling techniques assure us that the sample is representative of the population from which it is selected, so that we can generalize our findings from the sample to the population.

Sometimes, though, a probability sample isn't necessary. For example, we may be doing an exploratory, pilot study or assessing relationships between two variables to test a hypothesis. **Nonprobability sampling** does not permit us to generalize to other groups or situations, but it is valuable for studying particular groups of people. Its techniques include purposive, quota, and accidental sampling.

- With a **purposive sample**, we select a sample that contains either a variety of people (for example, to pretest a questionnaire before distributing it to our actual sample) or people who have a certain characteristic in which we're interested (for example, student leaders, reticent communicators, Internet users).
- A **quota sample** requires us to identify people with certain traits or who are members of known demographic groups (such as different college classes). If class standing is important to our research of a college population, we may want to sample 25 members of each undergraduate class (first-year to fourth-year students) for our 100-person sample. Quota sampling does *not* require random sampling among the different groups as does stratified sampling.
- An **accidental sample**, or a *convenience sample*, is based on sampling participants who happen to be available. Surveys done in college classes or with shoppers in malls are examples of this sampling technique.

Nonprobability sampling may lead to conclusions that differ from those we would have reached by using probability sampling. But nonprobability methods are still useful when investigating many research questions.

Survey research is a multistage process. Imagine, for example, that we want to learn about student attitudes toward parking on campus. Here's what we can do.

1. Identify our population of interest—say, the 10,000 students who attend the university.
2. Select a sample of that population to ask our questions. If our student directory is inclusive and up-to-date, we can systematically sample, say, 500 people from that directory. Because we know we won't reach everyone, we'll hope to end up with about 300 completed questionnaires.
3. Choose our method to collect the information. Here, we can use telephone interviewing because the survey is brief and we are working from a good phone directory.
4. Write the survey questions to gather the information. Our questions will be brief and focus on attitudes toward parking and other relevant information such as times of classes, work schedules, and so on.
5. Collect the information and analyze the responses.

How we present the questions is crucial for getting the information we seek. Here are some suggestions for constructing questionnaires.

- Instructions at the beginning of the questionnaire should relay the importance of the survey.
- Instructions for completing or skipping questions should be easily understood by participants and interviewers.
- The questions asked must be clear, precise, easily understood, logically arranged, and easily answered. Each question should ask for only one piece of information at a time.
- There should be effective transitions connecting different questions and parts of the questionnaire.
- If participants are given possible options to respond to, make sure that those choices are exhaustive (that is, include all possible options) and mutually exclusive (that is, the answers do not overlap).
- The questionnaire itself must be printed clearly and look professional. It should contain sufficient white space in margins and between questions.

We can use surveys for descriptive or explanatory purposes. As a descriptive technique, we can use survey research to identify current attitudes and opinions about issues or persons such as political candidates. Here, we need probability samples so that we can generalize from the smaller sample to the larger population.

As an explanatory technique, we can use survey research to examine the relationships between variables. We often use nonprobability samples when using surveys for explanation because we are interested in conceptual questions of relationships among variables, rather than in descriptive generalization. We can, for example, devise and use measures of nonverbal immediacy and of learning in an explanatory survey and see whether learning actually relates to nonverbal immediacy. Of course, it's best if our sample reflects the population.

When doing survey research, we need to consider, among other decisions, our sampling procedure, method of data collection, and questionnaire construction. Regardless of whether we use surveys for description or explanation, the choices for effective conduct of survey research, as you can see, are many.

Be sure to consult some of the sources at the end of this chapter for more complete information about survey research techniques.

Polls and Ratings   We use probability sampling techniques when doing polls and ratings research. Polls fit nicely with our discussion of surveys. **Polls** are a descriptive form of survey research whereby we try to learn about the attitudes or opinions of certain groups. Because these groups are usually large (for example, U.S. voters), we draw smaller, representative samples of the population and question those in the sample about our topic of interest. Typically, this has to do with attitudes about issues of importance or toward politicians. We constantly see results of such polls conducted by media organizations (for example, the *CBS News/New York Times* poll) or polling organizations (for example, the Gallup and Harris organizations).

Ratings are measures of reported behaviors of viewers or listeners of television or radio programs. They express the percentage of viewers or listeners who tune to a given program at a certain time. For example, a *rating* of 14 for *60 Minutes* means that 14% of all possible television households watched *60 Minutes* at that time. A *share* of 20 for the same program means that 20% of the television sets actually turned on at that time were tuned to that program. Ratings research is often conducted by companies such as A. C. Nielsen and Arbitron, although other organizations and individuals also do ratings research. These organizations use probability sampling procedures and, generally, either electronic data gathering (for example, people meters) or viewer/listener diaries.

Intensive Interviews and Focus Groups   Besides their use in survey research, **interviews** can be more in-depth. Such intensive interviews are used as qualitative techniques (that is, answering "why" and "how come" questions) by which we can gather information for several research methods such as oral histories and case studies. They might explore, for example, techniques of film directors or communicative behaviors of personnel directors in organizations. They can probe communication attitudes and behaviors such as views of television programs or reasons for interacting with others.

Interviews allow one-on-one contact between the researcher and the respondent for longer periods of time (for example, 1 or more hours). They are usually structured; that is, an interview schedule of questions and question order is prepared ahead of time. They do, though, allow flexibility to follow up and probe reasons for certain attitudes and responses.

The **focus group** is another qualitative technique widely used in marketing research but also gaining favor in some areas of communication research. Essentially, it is intensive group interviewing to understand consumer attitudes and behavior. Groups usually contain 6 to 12 participants, and researchers generally conduct at least two focus groups on a topic. A moderator or facilitator leads the group through a planned discussion of a topic such as attitudes about an organization, its programs, or policies.

Such groups are popular to test advertising product and broadcast-programming ideas. They require careful planning and recruiting of participants. Controlled group discussion is the key to successful focus groups so that all present get a chance to be heard.

We have included some sources at the end of this chapter that provide more detail about polls and ratings research and about interviews and focus groups.

■ PEOPLE- OR BEHAVIOR-ORIENTED RESEARCH

People- or **behavior-oriented research** focuses on actions and reactions of people that do not rely on self-reports of behavior. There are two primary types of this research: observational and experimental.

Observational Research

Observational research looks and sees how people act in different situations. Here, we don't rely on the self-reports of those being surveyed or interviewed (although we might want to interview people to check on our observations). Instead, we observe people in their typical or natural social settings and describe the actions (that is, behaviors) or messages of people or media being studied.

Suppose we are interested in studying communication between superiors and subordinates in organizations. We could devise a survey or interview selected people to get answers to our questions. But we might find that our questions are not answered sufficiently or that the response rate is low. The workers may feel that their employers might have access to their answers, or they may not respond in enough detail to offer insight into superior–subordinate communication. Observational techniques might be more effective for gathering this information.

There are at least five forms of observational research: ethnography, participant observation, unobtrusive observation, network analysis, and verbal and nonverbal coding.

Ethnography   **Ethnography** is used to form objective descriptions of social norms and events as they occur. When attending to the physical and social ecology of the communication setting, ethnographers try to explain behavioral regularities in social situations. In our superior–subordinate study, for example, a researcher might try to describe the rules of interaction by observing different participants in the organization. These would include the patterns of behavior and use of communication channels in that organization. The ethnographer might also interview employees or examine documents and artifacts to verify these observations. This observational technique often results in a *case study* such as describing the culture in a stadium at sporting events, the language used by police officers performing their jobs, conversations at a bar, or the family's social rules of television viewing.

Public relations campaigns are also suited to this case-study format. Here a problem has already been identified. Looking for behavioral norms and regularities, the researcher would observe and describe what the public relations practitioner did to solve the problem and then describe the consequences of this action. Ethnographies should include testimony from participants and examine available records and materials related to the case. Participant observation is often used in ethnographic research.

Participant Observation **Participant observation** is used to study social situations or organizations from an insider's perspective. Researchers participate in the social environment they are observing. They systematically record and classify their observations. The end result of the research is an analytic description of the social situation or organization, moving from specific observations to generalizations about the situation or organization.

Participant observers rely on their own observations, on information from group members, and on whatever records and materials are available and pertinent. For example, a participant observer may secure a job in an organization, observe superior–subordinate interactions, talk to colleagues who have worked there more than 2 years, examine memos, overhear conversations, and, perhaps, examine personnel files. From all these observations, the researcher would form conclusions about communication patterns in that organization.

Unobtrusive Observation **Unobtrusive observation** is used when researchers want to study communication in a natural setting, yet choose not to become participants in the group or organization. They may want to remain objective observers because they may feel their participation would contaminate the research setting they are studying or they may have ethical concerns about becoming a participant. They also feel that if those who they're observing knew they were being observed, they might behave differently.

Unobtrusive field observers also examine social situations or organizations in a systematic manner similar to participant observation, without becoming a group or social participant. For example, we might observe the use of persuasive sales tactics, the creative advertising process at an ad agency, gatekeeping in the newsroom, or the social climate of viewing television in public places.

Network Analysis **Network analysis** is the study of behavioral interactions among larger numbers of people. If, for example, we are interested in communication among all members of an organization, we can ask workers to keep a log of the people with whom they communicate, the length of these conversations, and the channels used (speech, memo, meetings, electronic mail, teleconferencing, fax, and so on). Then we can analyze the data to find out whether key individuals have open channels to those with whom they must communicate or what social or task roles different people fulfill in the organization.

Verbal and Nonverbal Coding Researchers have devised a variety of schemes to code verbal behavior (such as self-disclosure) and nonverbal behavior (for example, kinesics and facial expression). Also, others have developed systems to code marital, family, and group interaction. **Verbal and nonverbal coding** schemes seek to identify patterns of behavior found in the interaction.

Experimental Research

Like observational research, **experimental research** focuses on people and behavior. It is also more concerned with manipulating and controlling behavior to view reactions better. Experimental research is also markedly different in that observations are made under *controlled conditions*. Experimental research is causal. It is based on the premise that one event—let's say *Z*—will follow another event—let's say *Y*. If other factors are present (such as *A*, *B*, or *C*), then we could not be certain it is *Y* that produces *Z*. Thus, experimental researchers must **control** all relevant factors other than the one being studied. Laboratory settings provide the most control.

The researcher designs experiments to test hypotheses about the events. That is, if the researcher is examining the effect of variable *Y* on variable *Z*, she or he will have formed a hypothesis about the relationship. Evaluation and physiological research are done with experimental designs.

Let's say we want to answer the question "Is a training program effective in improving executives' abilities to deal with the media?" How can we design an experiment to give us an idea of the program's effectiveness? Experimental research employs several **experimental designs**, or blueprints, for the study.

Preexperimental Designs   We could design an experiment where the executives are given a training program, which we label **X**. We will measure an executive's ability to deal with the media through a simple test, which we label **O**. We will have the test consist of a question-and-answer session where we will rate the executives on various factors (for example, keeping cool when questioned intently, speed of answering after a question is asked, perceived honesty). We would use the resulting scores to measure the executives' abilities. This research design can be diagrammed like this:

$$\textbf{X} \qquad \textbf{O}$$

This design is known as a *One-Shot Case-Study Design*. It closely resembles descriptive survey or observational research. It is not, however, a controlled observation because many other variables can enter the situation. For example, we don't know what abilities these executives had before receiving the training program.

If we modify our original design and measure the executives' abilities before and after the training, we would be controlling for prior abilities and have a *One-Group Pretest–Posttest Design*:

$$\textbf{O} \qquad \textbf{X} \qquad \textbf{O}$$

This design allows us to say more about the effectiveness of the training program, **X**, but other variables still might be present. The executives might have improved their abilities on their own time, ability might be increased normally each time any executive deals with media questions, or the first measure of their abilities might cause the executives to become more receptive to training in this area.

Experimental Designs   What we need, then, is a group of executives who do not receive the training program so that we can be more certain that it is the program that influences the executives' abilities. The design that controls for these factors is known as the *Pretest–Posttest Control-Group Design*:

$$\textbf{R} \qquad \textbf{O} \qquad \textbf{X} \qquad \textbf{O}$$
$$\textbf{R} \qquad \textbf{O} \qquad \qquad \textbf{O}$$

In the diagram, **R** refers to the fact that we randomly assign individuals to one of the two groups so that some with higher and lower initial ability are presumably in each group. We give both groups an ability test but have only one group take the training program. The group that does not receive the training is called the **control group**. We then give the ability test again to both groups. We assume that any natural increase in ability from Test 1 to Test 2 would (because of random assignment to groups) occur in both groups. If ability improves more in the trained group, we can say that the training program had some effect.

What we still have not controlled, however, is the possibility that the group receiving the training program might be more sensitized and influenced by it as a result of the first ability test. We can see whether the initial ability test was influential in increasing sensitivity by dividing the executives into four groups instead of two. We would then give two of the groups the initial ability test and not give it to the other two groups. This is the *Solomon Four-Group Design*:

$$
\begin{array}{cccc}
\mathbf{R} & \mathbf{O} & \mathbf{X} & \mathbf{O} \\
\mathbf{R} & \mathbf{O} & & \mathbf{O} \\
\mathbf{R} & & \mathbf{X} & \mathbf{O} \\
\mathbf{R} & & & \mathbf{O}
\end{array}
$$

This design can help determine if the first test of ability increased executives' sensitivity to the training program. However, it does make our experimental research unnecessarily complicated. For one thing, it requires twice as many subjects as the other designs. It seems that an adaptation of this design, the *Posttest-Only Control-Group Design* might serve our initial purposes well enough:

$$
\begin{array}{ccc}
\mathbf{R} & \mathbf{X} & \mathbf{O} \\
\mathbf{R} & & \mathbf{O}
\end{array}
$$

In this design, we assign executives randomly to one of two groups. One group receives the training program; the other group does not. At the end, we measure the abilities of individuals in both groups. Now we have controlled for everything we could think of that would provide alternative explanations of our findings. Although we lack a pretest, we have also avoided the potential complications of sensitizing a group to the test and the unnecessary additional demands of the Solomon Four-Group Design. See Campbell and Stanley (1963/1981), Creswell (1994), and Spector (1981) for more information about experimental designs.

Control groups, which do not receive the experimental treatment that **experimental groups** do, then, are crucial for experimental designs. In these experimental designs, we randomly assign **subjects** (that is, participants in an experiment) to either the experimental group or the control group. Only those in the experimental group receive the experimental treatment (the independent variable) before we observe or measure the behavior (the dependent variable) of subjects in both groups.

In our media-training example, only those subjects assigned to the experimental group would be given communication training. We would measure the behavior or performance in media interviews for members of both the experimental and control groups. This enables us to see whether differences on the dependent measure (performance in media interviews) result from the experimental treatment (communication training) because only one of the two groups received that treatment.

Types of Experimental Research Experimental research is often subdivided into two main types, laboratory and nonlaboratory. In **laboratory research**, people are taken out of their natural surroundings so that more variables can be controlled (for example, noise, other people present, or the surroundings themselves). Sometimes, however, unrealistic results are achieved when people are moved from their normal social surroundings and when they perceive they are being observed. That is, they may communicate differently in a laboratory setting.

In **nonlaboratory** (or **field**) **research** settings (which are similar to those used in participant observation and case-study research), people are studied in their natural settings. The researcher, though, has less control over potentially influential variables.

For example, let's imagine you want to study the effects of violent cartoons on children's interactions with one another. In a laboratory study, you would randomly assign children to play groups where half the children view violent cartoons and the other half view nonviolent ones. You would then measure their aggression toward others. However, moving these children into "foreign" surroundings may in some way influence their behavior. They may realize they're being watched and curtail their aggression. But if you were to study them in a natural (or nonlaboratory) environment such as a day-care center, other factors might influence their behavior, such as already existing personality conflicts between certain children or the teacher's rules for proper behavior in the day-care center.

Obviously, your decision of where to study communication must take into account the other factors (or **intervening variables**) that could affect the research results. You must make choices about what elements of control can be sacrificed. What we are referring to here are questions of validity.

Measurement of variables must be valid. In general, **validity** refers to measuring what we intend to measure. If an index, test, or scale is used to measure a particular construct, the measure should include items or questions about all aspects of the construct (*content validity*), it should relate to other, similar measures or predict future behavior or attitudes (*criterion-related validity*), and should measure the construct it purports to measure (*construct validity*).

Measures also must be reliable. **Reliability** refers to how dependable, stable, consistent, and repeatable measures are in a study and across several studies. If we use a measure twice and the results are about the same both times, the measure has *test–retest reliability*. If all items in the measure seem to measure the same thing, we say the measure has *internal consistency*. If there are two forms for the same measure (say, a test) and people score the same on both, we'd say the forms are *parallel*. And if two or more raters/observers/coders agree on using some sort of scale for their observations, they are said to have *interrater reliability*.

Valid and reliable instruments increase the **internal validity** of a research study. They ensure that no one can derive other possible interpretations of the results. **External validity** refers to how generalizable the results are to people and contexts other than the experimental group and situation.

The various research methods we have described in this chapter are used to seek answers to research questions or to test hypotheses. Original research, then, is another important means of adding to our knowledge about communication. The sources listed at the end of this chapter describe more fully the types of communication research discussed here.

RESEARCH ETHICS

Now that we've considered how research is conducted, we should consider how researchers meet their ethical obligations to the participants in their research investigations and to their discipline. **Research ethics** concerns what is right and wrong in the conduct of research inquiries.

Researchers need to be responsible to their discipline, as well as to the participants in their research projects. Researchers must conform to their discipline's professional standards of conduct. It should go without saying that researchers need to be *accurate* and *honest* when conducting research. They examine primary sources of data and are honest and precise as to what their data reveal.

By now you can tell that research involves a series of choices about how to address research questions and to conduct such inquiries. Researchers must be careful to remain systematic and objective in the many choices they make when designing measures, selecting and observing participants, analyzing their data, and reporting the results of their studies.

In addition, especially because we involve people in so much of our research, communication researchers must constantly respect the rights of research participants. Researchers adhere to a basic rule: *Do no harm*. If you would not be willing to be a participant in your own research project, you probably shouldn't be doing that project with others. Researchers need to take steps to reduce or to eliminate the risk of physical or psychological discomfort. Toward this end, universities and many other organizations have Human Subjects Review Boards whose purpose is to balance the needs of the researcher and the rights of the research participants. Researchers who use human subjects need to obtain approval from this board before conducting their research. Primarily, Human Subjects Review Boards consider whether proposed research projects are of sufficient benefit to offset any potential costs or discomforts to the participants.

Researchers also consider several other ethical concerns. First, subjects or respondents should be voluntary participants in any research project. They should provide their *informed consent* and should not be coerced to participate. We should engage participants in research with their knowledge and consent. This, of course, is difficult for observational and field research in which observations may take place in crowded public places. This task is easier for survey and laboratory researchers to accomplish.

Second, researchers often withhold the true nature of the research project from the participants because knowing the purpose of the project may influence how participants act and answer questions. Sometimes, *deception* is even a necessary part of an experimental research project. Researchers, though, are obliged to inform participants about the goals and nature of the project at the project's conclusion. This is typically referred to as *debriefing*.

Third, researchers need to protect the *privacy* of their subjects or respondents by promising them anonymity or confidentiality. *Anonymity* means that participants take part in the research project without the researcher's knowledge of their identity (for example, no names are written on questionnaires). There are times when researchers need to be able to identify their participants, especially when they need to do follow-up questionnaires or interviews with the same people. *Confidentiality* means that researchers will protect and not reveal the names of participants.

We've just touched upon several important ethical concerns: honesty, harm, informed consent, deception, and privacy. In general, research participants must be treated fairly and shown courtesy and respect. Researchers must address these issues when they plan and conduct communication investigations.

SUMMARY

Research is an objective and systematic process to solve theoretical and applied problems. It can be descriptive or explanatory. It seeks to answer research questions not already answered by past research or to test hypotheses, which specify relationships among independent and dependent variables. The research process moves through several stages from developing a research problem to discussing the implications of the findings of a study. How we seek to answer questions reflects our method of inquiry.

One communication research approach is message- or artifact-oriented research, which includes archival/documentary and survey/interview research. Forms of archival/documentary research are library/documentary, historical, critical/rhetorical, and legal research and textual, secondary, conversation, and content analysis. Survey researchers primarily seek to describe or to explain attitudes. Decisions about sampling procedure, method of data collection, and questionnaire construction are crucial when doing survey research. Other survey or interview forms include polls, ratings, interviews, and focus groups.

Another communication research approach is people- or behavior-oriented research, which includes observational and experimental research. Forms of observational research are ethnography, participant observation, unobtrusive observation, network analysis, and verbal and nonverbal coding. Experimental research is conducted under controlled conditions and employs several designs. It can be done in the laboratory and in the field.

However research is done, measurement of variables must be valid and reliable. Researchers must also address several ethical issues when planning and conducting their studies.

SELECTED SOURCES

■ COMPREHENSIVE TEXTS

Anderson, J. A. (1987). *Communication research: Issues and methods.* New York: McGraw-Hill.

Babbie, E. (1998). *The practice of social research* (8th ed.). Belmont, CA: Wadsworth.

Barzun, J., & Graff, H. F. (1992). *The modern researcher* (5th ed.). Fort Worth, TX: Harcourt Brace Jovanovich.

Bostrom, R. N. (1998). *Communication research.* Prospect Heights, IL: Waveland Press.

Clark, R. A. (1991). *Studying interpersonal communication: The research experience.* Newbury Park, CA: Sage.

Frankfort-Nachmias, C., & Nachmias, D. (1996). *Research methods in the social sciences* (5th ed.). New York: St. Martin's Press.

Frey, L. R., Botan, C. H., Friedman, P. G., & Kreps, G. L. (1991). *Investigating communication: An introduction to research methods.* Englewood Cliffs, NJ: Prentice Hall.

Gudykunst, W. B., & Kim, Y. Y. (Eds.). (1984/1994). *Methods for intercultural communication research.* Ann Arbor, MI: UMI Books on Demand.

Judd, C. M., Smith, E. R., & Kidder, L. H. (1991). *Research methods in social relations* (6th ed.). Fort Worth, TX: Harcourt Brace Jovanovich.

Katzer, J., Cook, K. H., & Crouch, W. W. (1998). *Evaluating information: A guide for users of social science research* (4th ed.). Boston: McGraw-Hill.

Kerlinger, F. N. (1986/1992). *Foundations of behavioral research* (3rd ed.). Fort Worth, TX: Harcourt Brace College.

Reinard, J. C. (1998). *Introduction to communication research* (2nd ed.). Boston: McGraw-Hill.

Schutt, R. K. (1999). *Investigating the social world* (2nd ed.). Thousand Oaks, CA: Pine Forge Press.

Stacks, D. W., & Hocking, J. E. (1992). *Essentials of communication research.* New York: HarperCollins.

Watt, J. H., & van den Berg, S. A. (1995). *Research methods for communication science.* Boston: Allyn & Bacon.

■ CONTENT ANALYSIS

Holsti, O. R. (1969). *Content analysis for the social sciences and humanities.* Reading, MA: Addison-Wesley.

Krippendorff, K. (1980). *Content analysis: An introduction to its methodology.* Beverly Hills, CA: Sage.

Riffe, D., Lacy, S., & Fico, F. G. (1998). *Analyzing media messages: Using quantitative content analysis in research.* Mahwah, NJ: Erlbaum.

Weber, R. P. (1990). *Basic content analysis* (2nd ed.). Newbury Park, CA: Sage.

■ DESIGN AND MEASUREMENT

Camilli, G., & Shepard, L. A. (1994). *Methods for identifying biased test items*. Thousand Oaks, CA: Sage.

Campbell, D. T., & Stanley, J. C. (1963/1981). *Experimental and quasi-experimental designs for research*. Boston: Houghton Mifflin.

Carmines, E. G., & Zeller, R. A. (1979). *Reliability and validity assessment*. Beverly Hills, CA: Sage.

Cochran, W. G., & Cox, G. M. (1992). *Experimental designs* (2nd ed.). New York: Wiley.

Creswell, J. W. (1994). *Research design: Qualitative & quantitative approaches*. Thousand Oaks, CA: Sage.

Emmert, P., & Barker, L. L. (Eds.). (1989). *Measurement of communication behavior*. New York: Longman.

Hopkins, K. D. (1998). *Educational and psychological measurement and evaluation* (8th ed.). Boston: Allyn & Bacon.

Miller, D. C. (1991). *Handbook of research design and social measurement* (5th ed.). Newbury Park, CA: Sage.

Spector, P. E. (1981). *Research designs*. Beverly Hills, CA: Sage.

Sax, G. (1997). *Principles of educational and psychological measurement and evaluation* (4th ed.). Belmont, CA: Wadsworth.

Tardy, C. H. (1988). *A handbook for the study of human communication: Methods and instruments for observing, measuring, and assessing communication processes*. Norwood, NJ: Ablex.

Traub, R. E. (1994). *Reliability for the social sciences: Theory and application*. Thousand Oaks, CA: Sage.

■ MEDIA RESEARCH

Adams, R. C. (1989). *Social survey methods for mass media research*. Hillsdale, NJ: Erlbaum.

Berger, A. A. (1998). *Media research techniques* (2nd ed.). Thousand Oaks, CA: Sage.

Beville, H. M., Jr. (1988). *Audience ratings: Radio, television, cable* (Rev. ed.). Hillsdale, NJ: Erlbaum.

Fletcher, A. D., & Bowers, T. A. (1991). *Fundamentals of advertising research* (4th ed.). Belmont, CA: Wadsworth.

Hartshorn, G. G. (1991). *Audience research sourcebook*. Washington, DC: National Association of Broadcasters.

Hsia, H. J. (1988). *Mass communications research methods: A step-by-step approach*. Hillsdale, NJ: Erlbaum.

Lang, A. (Ed.). (1994). *Measuring psychological responses to media*. Hillsdale, NJ: Erlbaum.

Sharp, N. W. (Ed.). (1988). *Communications research: The challenge of the information age*. Syracuse, NY: Syracuse University Press.

Singletary, M. W. (1993). *Mass communication research: Contemporary methods and applications*. New York: Longman.

Startt, J. D., & Sloan, W. D. (1989). *Historical methods in mass communication*. Hillsdale, NJ: Erlbaum.

Stempel, G. H., & Westley, B. H. (Eds.). (1989). *Research methods in mass communication* (2nd ed.). Englewood Cliffs, NJ: Prentice Hall.

Ward, J., & Hansen, K. A. (1997). *Search strategies in mass communication* (3rd ed.). New York: Longman.

Webster, J. G., & Lichty, L. W. (1991). *Ratings analysis: Theory and practice*. Hillsdale, NJ: Erlbaum.

Williams, F., Rice, R. E., & Rogers, E. M. (1988). *Research methods and the new media*. New York: Free Press.

Wimmer, R. D., & Dominick, J. R. (1997). *Mass media research: An introduction* (5th ed.). Belmont, CA: Wadsworth.

■ QUALITATIVE AND APPLIED RESEARCH

Applied Social Research Methods. (1984–). Thousand Oaks, CA: Sage. (A series of over 45 monographs)

Berg, B. L. (1998). *Qualitative research methods for the social sciences* (3rd ed.). Boston: Allyn & Bacon.

Carter, K., & Spitzack, C. (Eds.). (1989). *Doing research on women's communication: Perspectives on theory and method*. Norwood, NJ: Ablex.

Creswell, J. W. (1998). *Qualitative inquiry and research design*. Thousand Oaks, CA: Sage.

Denzin, N. K., & Lincoln, Y. S. (Eds.). (1994). *Handbook of qualitative research*. Thousand Oaks, CA: Sage.

Fetterman, D. M. (1998). *Ethnography: Step by step* (2nd ed.). Thousand Oaks, CA: Sage.

Flick, U. (1998). *An introduction to qualitative research*. Thousand Oaks, CA: Sage.

Herndon, S. L., & Kreps, G. L. (1993). *Qualitative research: Application in organizational communication*. Cresskill, NJ: Hampton Press.

Krueger, R. A. (1994). *Focus groups: A practical guide for applied research* (2nd ed.). Thousand Oaks, CA: Sage.

Lindlof, T. R. (1995). *Qualitative communication research methods*. Thousand Oaks, CA: Sage.

Lofland, J. (1995). *Analyzing social settings: A guide to qualitative observation and analysis* (3rd ed.). Belmont, CA: Wadsworth.

Marshall, C., & Rossman, G. B. (1999). *Designing qualitative research* (2nd ed.). Thousand Oaks, CA: Sage.

Maxwell, J. A. (1996). *Qualitative research design: An integrative approach*. Thousand Oaks, CA: Sage.

Merton, R. K., Lowenthal, M. F., & Kendall, P. L. (1990). *The focused interview: A manual of problems and procedures* (2nd ed.). New York: Free Press.

Miles, M. B., & Huberman, A. M. (1994). *Qualitative data analysis: An expanded sourcebook* (2nd ed.). Thousand Oaks, CA: Sage.

Morgan, G. (Ed.). (1990). *Beyond method: Strategies for social research* (2nd ed.). Beverly Hills, CA: Sage.

Morris, R. A. (1997). *Doing legal research: A guide for social scientists and mental health professionals*. Thousand Oaks, CA: Sage.

Narula, U., & Pearce, W. B. (Eds.). (1990). *Cultures, politics, and research programs: An international assessment of practical problems in field research*. Hillsdale, NJ: Erlbaum.

O'Hair, D., & Kreps, G. L. (1990). *Applied communication theory and research*. Hillsdale, NJ: Erlbaum.

Qualitative Research Methods. (1986–). Thousand Oaks, CA: Sage. (A series of over 45 monographs)

Rossman, G. B., & Rallis, S. F. (1998). *Learning in the field*. Thousand Oaks, CA: Sage.

Shaffir, W. B., & Stebbins, R. A. (Eds.). (1991). *Experiencing fieldwork: An inside view of qualitative research*. Newbury Park, CA: Sage.

Stake, R. E. (1995). *The art of case study research: Perspectives on practice*. Thousand Oaks, CA: Sage.

Stewart, D. W., & Shamdasani, P. N. (Eds.). (1990). *Focus groups: Theory and practice*. Newbury Park, CA: Sage.

Strauss, A., & Corbin, J. (1998). *Basics of qualitative research: Grounded theory procedures and techniques* (2nd ed.). Thousand Oaks, CA: Sage.

Weitzman, E. A., & Miles, M. B. (1995). *Computer programs for qualitative data analysis*. Thousand Oaks, CA: Sage.

Wolcott, H. (1990). *Writing up qualitative research*. Thousand Oaks, CA: Sage.

Yin, R. K. (1994). *Case study research: Design and method* (2nd ed.). Thousand Oaks, CA: Sage.

■ RHETORICAL AND MEDIA CRITICISM

Brock, B. L., Scott, R. L., & Chesebro, J. W. (1989). *Methods of rhetorical criticism: A twentieth-century perspective* (3rd ed., rev.). Detroit: Wayne State University Press.

Foss, S. K. (1996). *Rhetorical criticism: Exploration & practice* (2nd ed.). Prospect Heights, IL: Waveland Press.

Hart, R. P. (1997). *Modern rhetorical criticism* (2nd ed.). Boston: Allyn & Bacon.

Phifer, G. (1961). The historical approach. In C. W. Dow (Ed.), *An introduction to graduate study in speech and theatre* (pp. 52–80). East Lansing: Michigan State University Press.

Rybacki, K. C., & Rybacki, D. J. (1991). *Communication criticism: Approaches and genres*. Belmont, CA: Wadsworth.

Vande Berg, L. R., & Wenner, L. A. (1991). *Television criticism: Approaches and applications*. New York: Longman.

■ STATISTICS

Bruning, J. L., & Kintz, B. L. (1997). *Computational handbook of statistics* (4th ed.). New York: Longman.

Cody, R. P., & Smith, J. K. (1997). *Applied statistics and the SAS programming language* (4th ed.). Upper Saddle River, NJ: Prentice Hall.

Cohen, J. (1988). *Statistical power analysis for the behavioral sciences* (2nd ed.). Hillsdale, NJ: Erlbaum.

Diekhoff, G. (1996). *Basic statistics for the social and behavioral sciences.* Upper Saddle River, NJ: Prentice Hall.

Flury, B. (1997). *A first course in multivariate statistics.* New York: Springer.

Flury, B., & Riedwyl, H. (1988). *Multivariate statistics: A practical approach.* London: Chapman & Hall.

Hair, J. F. (1998). *Multivariate data analysis: With readings* (5th ed.). Englewood Cliffs, NJ: Prentice Hall.

Healey, J. F. (1999). *Statistics: A tool for social research* (5th ed.). Belmont, CA: Wadsworth.

Kraemer, H. C., & Thiemann, S. (1987). *How many subjects? Statistical power analysis in research.* Newbury Park, CA: Sage.

Levin, J., & Fox, J. A. (1997). *Elementary statistics in social research* (7th ed.). New York: Longman.

Mantzopoulos, V. L. (1995). *Statistics for the social sciences.* Englewood Cliffs, NJ: Prentice Hall.

Mendenhall, W., Beaver, R. J., & Beaver, B. M. (1999). *Introduction to probability and statistics* (10th ed.). Pacific Grove, CA: Duxbury Press.

Monge, P. R., & Cappella, J. M. (Eds.). (1980). *Multivariate techniques in human communication research.* New York: Academic Press.

Ott, L. (1992). *Statistics: A tool for the social sciences* (5th ed.). Boston: PWS-Kent.

Ott, L., & Mendenhall, W. (1994). *Understanding statistics* (6th ed.). Belmont, CA: Duxbury Press.

Quantitative applications in the social sciences. (1976–). Thousand Oaks, CA: Sage. (A series of over 125 monographs on statistics and research methodology)

Sirkin, R. M. (1995). *Statistics for the social sciences.* Thousand Oaks, CA: Sage.

Stevens, J. (1996). *Applied multivariate statistics for the social sciences* (3rd ed.). Mahwah, NJ: Erlbaum.

Stevens, J. (1998). *SPSS for windows supplement: Applied multivariate statistics for the social sciences* (3rd ed.). Mahwah, NJ: Erlbaum.

Tacq, J. (1996). *Multivariate analysis techniques in social science research.* Thousand Oaks, CA: Sage.

Tatsuoka, M. M. (1988). *Multivariate analysis: Techniques for educational and psychological research* (2nd ed.). New York: Macmillan.

Walsh, A. (1990). *Statistics for the social sciences: With computer applications.* New York: Harper & Row.

Williams, F. (1992). *Reasoning with statistics* (4th ed.). Fort Worth, TX: Harcourt Brace Jovanovich.

■ SURVEY RESEARCH

Babbie, E. R. (1990). *Survey research methods* (2nd ed.). Belmont, CA: Wadsworth.

Converse, J. M., & Presser, S. (1986). *Survey questions: Handcrafting the standardized questionnaire*. Beverly Hills, CA: Sage.

Fink, A., & Kosecoff, J. B. (1998). *How to conduct surveys: A step-by-step guide* (2nd ed.). Thousand Oaks, CA: Sage.

Fowler, F. J., Jr. (1993). *Survey research methods* (2nd ed.). Thousand Oaks, CA: Sage.

Fowler, F. J., Jr. (1995). *Improving survey questions: Design and evaluation*. Thousand Oaks, CA: Sage.

Frey, J. H. (1989). *Survey research by telephone* (2nd ed.). Newbury Park, CA: Sage.

Lavrakas, P. J. (1993). *Telephone survey methods: Sampling, selection, and supervision* (2nd ed.). Thousand Oaks, CA: Sage.

Mangione, T. W. (1995). *Mail surveys: Improving the quality*. Thousand Oaks, CA: Sage.

Wilhoit, G. C., & Weaver, D. H. (1990). *Newsroom guide to polls and surveys*. Bloomington: Indiana University Press.

EXERCISES

1. Choose a research topic and identify one historical research question and one critical research question that are as yet unanswered by previous research.

2. Identify a research question for that topic that can be answered by content analysis. Describe the procedure you would use to conduct that content analysis.

3. How could you use participant observation to answer such a question on this topic? How would you function as a researcher in that environment, and what artifacts would you need to examine?

4. What research question relating to this topic could be answered by survey research? Explain the strengths and limitations of survey research to examine that question. Which observational technique would best lend itself to this project? Explain why.

5. Describe a possible experiment that could be conducted to provide more information on your topic. Develop two specific research questions about this topic and present an appropriate experimental design for each.

chapter 10

Writing Research Papers

W riting is an important part of any research endeavor. Without clear writing, readers cannot understand the writer's research ideas and findings. In this book it is impossible for us to provide a comprehensive overview of how to write well. Many books written specifically for that purpose contain comprehensive treatments of effective writing. In this chapter we present basic elements of good writing style, writing and bibliographic formats, and copyediting and proofreading techniques. In general, writers must use a clear, lucid style, adhere to the rules of grammar and spelling, and present the report in an accepted format.

BASIC ELEMENTS OF GOOD WRITING

Clear writing is smooth and consistent. That is, it has no shifts in topic or person and maintains consistent verb tense. A shift in topic or thought means that the writer begins writing about a particular subject and ends the paragraph or section with a different theme or idea. Writers must read through their drafts to avoid this. Shift in verb tense means that sentences vacillate between the past, present, and future tenses.

■ TENSE AND AGREEMENT

Most literature reviews and research reports should use a standard formula for verb tense. The *Publication Manual of the American Psychological Association* (APA, 1994), for example, advocates using the past tense (Miller [1983] showed . . .) or the present perfect tense (Miller [1983] has shown . . .) when reviewing the literature. Writers should also use the past tense to describe the procedures and the results of an already completed study. Thus, writers should use the past tense for any research finding, idea, or opinion that has already been published.

When they express their own conclusions or ideas about those results, writers should shift to the present tense to show the reader the difference between the two. The present tense is used to discuss the meaning and implications of the results of the study and to present conclusions. Writers should use the future tense for presenting future research ideas and in the method section of the research prospectus, before the study is actually done. Using this standard format helps ensure clear and consistent verb tense and smooth reading.

One problem writers face by adopting the APA rules is that they sometimes put everything into the past tense. But, as the following sentences show, the writer uses past tense in the first sentence to show that the study was conducted in the past. In the second sentence, however, the writer uses the present tense to discuss these results:

> Brown (1990) found that students who like their instructors asked more questions. Her results suggest that students learn more when teachers use immediacy behaviors in the classroom.

A shift in person means that there are inconsistencies in person and number (that is, between the noun and the singular or plural pronoun). One common mistake is to begin a sentence with a singular noun and shift to a plural pronoun, as in the following sentence:

> A person who has high communication satisfaction finds that they like conversing with other people.

The "they" in this example is incorrect because "person" is a singular noun. Writers often shift pronouns to the plural to avoid mistakes with noun–pronoun agreement or to avoid using the awkward "he/she" pronoun. They must remember to shift the subject also:

> People who have high communication satisfaction find that they like conversing with other people.

Actually, a more concise way of writing this sentence is to omit the words "find that they."

■ Voice

We sometimes confuse "past tense" with "passive voice." Writers should use the active, not the passive, voice in their writing whenever possible. When using the active voice, writers present the subject of the sentence first and avoid using prepositions. It makes writing more interesting and readable. Consider the following two sentences. The first is in the passive voice and the second in the active.

> In a study by Livingstone (1989), it was found that people had a clear understanding of the characters in *Coronation Street*.

> Livingstone (1989) found that *Coronation Street* viewers actively created a clear understanding of the program's characters.

■ TRANSITIONS

If we present our ideas in an orderly progression, we achieve continuity and smoothness. We should identify relationships between ideas and use transitions to maintain the progression of ideas. Transitions often help provide a time link (*then, next, after, while, since*); a cause–effect link (*therefore, so, thus, as a result*); an addition link (*besides, in addition, moreover, furthermore, similarly*); or a contrast link (*however, but, conversely, nevertheless, although, whereas*) (American Psychological Association, 1994, p. 24).

■ GRAMMAR

Of course, writers should follow standard rules of grammar throughout. Most scholars routinely consult a basic writing or grammar guide or handbook; keep one handy for your writing projects! Day (1998) provided "The Ten Commandments of Good Writing" that aptly illustrate grammatical problems:

1. Each pronoun should agree with their antecedent.
2. Just between you and I, case is important.
3. A preposition is a poor word to end a sentence with.
4. Verbs has to agree with their subject.
5. Don't use no double negatives.
6. Remember to never split an infinitive.
7. Avoid cliches like the plague.
8. Join clauses good, like a conjunction should.
9. Do not use hyperbole; not one writer in a million can use it effectively.
10. About sentence fragments. (p. 203)

■ PARAGRAPH STRUCTURE

Good writing also means writing strong paragraphs with clear thesis statements and complete sentences. A strong paragraph is one that focuses on only one idea. It begins with a *thesis* (that is, a brief condensation or overview of the paragraph) and uses explanation, elaboration, and supporting material to develop the thesis. Each sentence supports and develops that main idea. Often the paragraph ends with a transition to the next main idea.

Paragraphs can be too long or too short. Lengthy paragraphs (for example, a page long) often have two or more main ideas. They should be split into single-idea paragraphs. On the other hand, one or two sentence paragraphs lack adequate development of the thesis or main idea.

■ QUOTING AND PARAPHRASING

Plagiarism means using an author's words or ideas without giving credit. Credit for ideas usually is in the form of citing the author and year of publication in the text and reference list. Credit for actual words goes beyond this to giving the page number in the text and using quotation marks around the quoted material.

Babbie (1998) devised a system to help students see the difference between acceptable and unacceptable **citations**, and we've adapted it here. First, here is a paragraph from Rubin and McHugh's (1987) article on parasocial interaction:

> As Horton and Wohl (1956) hypothesized, parasocial interaction is similar to the establishment of social relationship with others. In this investigation, parasocial interaction was related strongly to social and task attraction towards the media personality, and to importance of relationship development with the personality. This supports previous contentions that media relationships can be seen as functional alternatives to interpersonal relationships (Rosengren & Windahl, 1972; Rubin & Rubin, 1985). Interpersonal and mediated relationships appear to follow a similar process of development. (p. 288)

Second, here are three acceptable citation methods:

Quotation	As Rubin and McHugh (1987) concluded, "interpersonal and mediated relationships appear to follow a similar process of development" (p. 288).
Paraphrase	Rubin and McHugh (1987) argued that interpersonal and media relationships follow a similar developmental pattern.
Idea	The way in which people develop relationships with others is very much like the way they develop relationships with television characters (Rubin & McHugh, 1987).

Note that all three methods give credit to the source. When we use a string of actual words, we must surround them with quotation marks and give the page number. Names of variables or constructs that authors use in their text need not be "quoted" because they are likely terms that others would use. The key here is a *string of words*.

Third, here are three unacceptable citations; we would term them "plagiarism."

Direct quotation, no citation	Interpersonal and mediated relationships appear to follow a similar process of development.
Edited quotation, presented as one's own	Media relationships can be seen as functional alternatives to interpersonal relationships and follow a similar process of development.
Paraphrased, but ideas presented as one's own	Media and interpersonal relationships follow similar developmental processes.

It is unethical to use another person's words or ideas and present them as your own. Universities and other organizations have specific rules about plagiarism that they expect people to follow.

Verb Choice

Often, when introducing quoted material or paraphrasing authors, we find we need a verb to tell the reader what the authors said, found, and so on. Many verbs are appropriate for scholarly reports, but choosing which one to use depends on the context of the paraphrasing or quotation. For example, the following sentence shows an active way of referring to a particular study (because the authors are listed as the subject instead of as a prepositional phrase):

Bell and Daly (1984) _____ four components of affinity seeking.

Now, which verb to use? Here are some commonly found in journal articles. Each has a specific meaning. Which one would be appropriate here?

argued	extended	proposed
assumed	explained	questioned
believed	found	reasoned
concluded	identified	replied
contended	investigated	reported
declared	maintained	showed
defined	noted	suggested
described	observed	thought
developed	presented	viewed

Many of these verbs would fit our sentence, depending on what meaning we want to convey. For example, we could use *proposed* to show that there may have been some controversy in the past about the number of components, and Bell and Daly's opinion is that there are four. We could use *presented* to introduce the four components. Or we could use *identified* to suggest Bell and Daly were among the first to see the four-part system; they may also have *described* and *found* them, but *identified* used in the thesis sentence helps us structure a paragraph about what the components of affinity seeking are and how the authors discovered them. Which verb to use depends on the paragraph's purpose.

■ STYLE

Writing style has many important elements. The following "Tips for Effective Writing" should help you improve your writing style.

1. Research papers are typically written in a formal style, often in the third person. Some scholarly journals, however, have relaxed this guideline and allow first-person writing. Avoid slang terms and colloquialisms.
2. Avoid an overly descriptive writing style—as in, "The subjects cowered nervously at the thought of spilling their souls to a stranger." That style may be appropriate for a creative writing assignment. It is not appropriate for a scholarly research project.

3. Use the active voice: "Johnson (1992) studied the effects of media viewing on adolescents." Avoid the passive voice: "The effects of media viewing on adolescents were studied by Johnson (1992)." Although you'll often encounter the passive voice in many published research articles, readers find the style tiresome. The tendency to use the third person sometimes encourages passive writing.

4. Avoid jargon in place of common terminology and be precise. You may be familiar with the terms, but your readers may not be. Kessler and McDonald (1996) provide a good example of scientific jargon: "Despite rigid re-examination of all experimental variables, this protocol continued to produce data at variance with our subsequently proven hypothesis" (p. 128). All the authors needed to say was that "the experiment didn't work."

5. Language should be gender neutral. Avoid using sexist language, sexist style, and language that makes the referent ambiguous—for example, *his* (when you intend *his* or *her*) and *men* (when you are referring to *people*). Also avoid language that stereotypes people—for example, the physician saw *his* patient, the *female* psychiatrist, or the police*man*. In many instances, we can avoid sexist language by using plural forms and being sensitive to stereotypes.

6. Be economical in expression. Say only what needs to be said. Wordiness does not improve comprehension. Yet, be sure to say enough so the reader can understand the point.

7. Make the conclusions drawn and the contradictions found in the literature clear in the report. We should not just assume that readers know our subject because we do. It is often wiser to assume that the reader knows little about the topic.

8. Be sure that the pronouns used (*its, this, that, these, those*) have clear references to their antecedents. Also, use pronouns to focus nouns—for example, this *test*, that *concept*, these *subjects*, those *results*.

9. Use short rather than elongated sentences. Avoid run-on expressions that will lose the reader's attention and comprehension.

10. Move from section to section without abruptness. Use transition sentences to help shift the reader's attention from one section to another. Provide appropriate headings and logical organization.

11. Use correct punctuation to support your meaning.

12. Use proper grammar and spelling. Never submit a manuscript or paper that isn't checked for spelling and typographical errors. *Proofread your work!*

13. Use consistent tense, topic, and person.

14. *Never plagiarize.* When you use sources closely in your writing, give credit to the original author. It is *never* acceptable to copy anything directly from another's materials without using quotation marks and citing the original source. As we have noted, even paraphrasing requires proper citation to that person's work.

15 . Do not quote from an abstract. Either summarize the original source (not the abstract) in your own words or quote the original author.

16. Pay attention to the structure and form of published articles. These articles are usually effective examples of how literature reviews can be written.

WRITING FORMATS

There are several different accepted writing and bibliographic formats. You may have become familiar with one style in high school and a different style in college. Commonly used formats in the humanities and social sciences are those of the Modern Language Association (MLA) and the University of Chicago (which is abstracted in Turabian):

> Gibaldi, J. (1995). *MLA handbook for writers of research papers* (4th ed.). New York: Modern Language Association of America.
>
> Turabian, K. L. (1996). *A manual for writers of term papers, theses, and dissertations* (6th ed.). Chicago: University of Chicago Press. (Revised by J. Grossman & A. Bennett)
>
> University of Chicago Press. (1993). *The Chicago manual of style* (14th ed.). Chicago: Author.

As of early 1999, only one main communication journal (*Text and Performance Quarterly*) requires the **MLA style** and only one (*Journalism & Mass Communication Quarterly*) requires the *Chicago Manual of Style*. All others allow or require submission of articles using the style of the American Psychological Association (APA). Most communication journals have adopted **APA style**:

> American Psychological Association. (1994). *Publication manual of the American Psychological Association* (4th ed.). Washington, DC: Author.

Because almost all our journals accept or require manuscripts in this style, we have used APA style throughout this book. We hope that, as you read the various chapters, you become familiar and adept with this style. We give an overview of the basics of APA style in Appendix A. This is not meant as a substitute for the APA *Publication Manual*, which presents much more information than we could here. In our overview, we summarize some of the technical aspects of APA style that are helpful in constructing literature reviews and research reports.

You should note that MLA style has become similar to APA style in recent years. For instance, in-text footnotes, prevalent in MLA and Turabian (an easy-to-follow guide to the *Chicago Manual of Style*), are now sometimes replaced by endnotes or endnote numbers (enclosed in parentheses), which refer to numbered "Works Cited" listed in the bibliography at the end of the manuscript. The MLA and Chicago (Turabian) footnote styles, however, are similar. For example, if we wanted to refer a reader to page 55 of this textbook or to page 260 of an article on symbolic convergence theory, the MLA footnotes and the Turabian endnotes would look like this (remember, the APA style does not use footnotes for references):

MLA   [1] Rebecca B. Rubin, Alan M. Rubin, and Linda J. Piele, *Communication Research: Strategies and Sources*, 5th ed. (Belmont: Wadsworth, 2000) 55.

        [2] Ernest G. Bormann, John F. Cragan, and Donald C. Shields, "In Defense of Symbolic Convergence Theory: A Look at the

Theory and Its Criticisms after Two Decades,"
Communication Theory 4 (1994): 260.

Chicago   1. Rebecca B. Rubin, Alan M. Rubin, and Linda J. Piele,
Communication Research: Strategies and Sources, 5th ed.
(Belmont, Calif.: Wadsworth, 2000), 55.
2. Ernest G. Bormann, John F. Cragan, and Donald C. Shields,
"In Defense of Symbolic Convergence Theory: A Look at the
Theory and Its Criticisms after Two Decades,"
Communication Theory 4 (November 1994): 260.

Chicago style permits references within the text (Rubin, Rubin, and Piele 2000, 55). MLA also allows citations in the text (Rubin, Rubin, Piele 55).

As mentioned, both MLA and Turabian use a Works Cited section for the bibliography, whereas the APA-style bibliography is simply called References. Chicago actually has two style formats, humanities and author-date. We present the author-date style here. To show how the three **bibliographic styles** differ, we present here one book and one article in each of the three styles:

MLA   Rubin, Rebecca B., Alan M. Rubin, and Linda J. Piele.
Communication Research: Strategies and Sources. 5th ed.
Belmont: Wadsworth, 2000.

Bormann, Ernest G., John F. Cragan, and Donald C. Shields. "In
Defense of Symbolic Convergence Theory: A Look at the
Theory and Its Criticisms after Two Decades." *Communication Theory* 4 (1994): 259-294.

Chicago   Rubin, Rebecca B., Alan M. Rubin, and Linda J. Piele. 2000.
Communication Research: Strategies and Sources. 5th ed.
Belmont, Calif.: Wadsworth.

Bormann, Ernest G., John F. Cragan, and Donald C. Shields.
1994. "In Defense of Symbolic Convergence Theory: A Look
at the Theory and Its Criticisms after Two Decades."
Communication Theory 4: 259-294.

APA   Rubin, R. B., Rubin, A. M., & Piele, L. J. (2000).
Communication research: Strategies and sources (5th ed.).
Belmont, CA: Wadsworth.

Bormann, E. G., Cragan, J. F., & Shields, D. C. (1994). In
defense of symbolic convergence theory: A look at the
theory and its criticisms after two decades. *Communication
Theory, 4,* 259-294.

Consult the manuals for more details on these styles.

A standard style for presenting your report or review is essential. (The APA and MLA manuals are helpful because they contain rules for writing.) The other important element is a suitable and consistent physical appearance. Anything that attracts negative attention—such as misspellings, typographic errors, tense shifts, nonparallel headings—will diminish the paper's effect. In short, your ideas may be lost in a maze of stylistic miscues.

PROOFREADING

Proofread all work before submitting it. Careless errors diminish its positive impact for the reader (for example, an employer, a professor, thesis committee, editor). When readers trip over careless word choices or blatant errors, they often lose sight of the important points made in the manuscript and, instead, start looking for other errors. When this happens, readers miss important thoughts and ideas. Use the following checklist to proofread your writing.

■ PROOFREADING CHECKLIST

1. Are all words spelled correctly? (Remember that word processing spelling checkers cannot tell the usage difference between correctly spelled homonyms or out-of-context typographic errors such as "that" instead of "than" or "not" instead of "note.")
2. Is the writing grammatically correct? Do subjects and verbs agree, is the form parallel, is the writing voice active, and is the past verb tense used when appropriate?
3. Are there any punctuation errors? Are all quotation marks outside the punctuation (except for semicolons and colons)? Question and exclamation marks go inside quotation marks only if they're part of the original quote.
4. Is one writing format used consistently throughout? Choose APA or MLA style and stick with it religiously.
5. Are any paragraphs overly long? If so, look for how many main thesis sentences appear in the paragraph and divide it accordingly.
6. Do all sentences flow together? If not, check the thesis sentence to be sure that all sentences are supporting or illustrating it.
7. Do all words have precise meanings? Is there any slang or casual language? Work on using short, clear, standard words rather than slang or technical jargon.
8. Are all quotations in proper form? Is proper credit given to other authors for all ideas and quoted material?

■ PROOFREADING SYMBOLS

Many researchers write at a computer. They can read and correct errors as they view their writing on the monitor. However, it is a good idea to print or type a copy to edit, before printing or typing the final version. Students and instructors find standard proofreading and copyediting symbols useful when proofreading and copyediting manuscripts. We've identified some of the main ones here:

Awk	Awkward
Cap	Use a capital letter
CF	Comma fault
Gr	Error in grammar

Ital	Italics (underlining)
Mng	Meaning not clear
Org	Faulty organization
Par	Paragraph problem (development, length, continuity)
//	Parallel-form problem
Pn	Punctuation problem
Pron	Error in pronoun form
Sp	Spelling error
T	Error in use of tense
Trans	Needs better transition
Wdy	Wordy
WW	Wrong word

Many other symbols are also used by journal and book editors when they edit manuscripts for publication. These are also useful for editing your own work before preparing the final copy to submit.

Symbol	Meaning	Example
ℓ	Delete character marked	journale
∩	Transpose	smybol
∧	Insert	manuscpt
ℓ	Delete; close up space	similair
○	Close up, no space	copy editing
#	Insert a space	andthe
≡	Capitalize	references
lc	Use lowercase	References
¶	Start paragraph	¶ Many other
no ¶	No paragraph	no ¶ At this point . . .
___	Italicize or underline	citation
∿	Boldface	citation

Most instructors use similar symbols or develop their own proofreading and copyediting systems. It's a good idea to ask if you don't understand the notations. Some journal editors and book publishers send their systems to authors during the proofreading stage. This involves authors in the process so they can be sure that what appears in print is what and how they want it to appear.

SUBMITTING MANUSCRIPTS

Occasionally, instructors will suggest that you submit your papers or research studies to be considered for publication or for presentation at a meeting of a professional association or conference. This means that you must pay special attention both to the writing style and to the guidelines for contributors that each journal or association publishes. Not only must the paper be flawless in writing, typing, and word choice, but it must also be appropriate for the particular journal or association to which it will be submitted.

We offer the following suggestions about what to avoid when submitting manuscripts. These are the sorts of things that guarantee failure:

- *Inadequate rationale.* The purpose of the study is not clear. A topic is not important to study just because we are interested in it or just because others have or haven't studied it before. We need to explain a rationale or guiding force for the study and to support the importance of the investigation. Authors have this burden of proof. Authors have an obligation to present clearly (a) the purpose for the study and (b) a solid rationale for the significance or importance of the study.
- *Uninteresting questions.* Authors must ask good questions. We must show that we are familiar with what others have written about our topic or problem in the literature. We need to present these questions in a compelling manner and build on the work that has been done before.
- *Sloppy procedures.* Whether the method is quantitative or qualitative in nature, sloppiness is not tolerated. Using questionable scales and measures, coders who cannot agree on their observations, and biased raters will result in measurement that is not valid or reliable. These can be "fatal flaws" in that the procedure does not allow us to address the research problem adequately.
- *Inappropriate sample.* The sample must be chosen with the study's purpose in mind. Convenience samples instead of probability samples need to be justified. The sample must sufficiently represent the population being studied. The size of the sample must be adequate. The number and kind of artifacts or primary documents examined must be appropriate for qualitative and historical research.
- *Inadequate analyses.* If we've asked good questions, established the significance of the study, and used sound methods, then we also need to analyze our observations appropriately. If all else is right, computing or reporting the wrong statistics or conclusions, or not providing a complete analysis, will not end the manuscript's future. Reviewers might suggest a different path for analysis. Following the suggestions of reviewers that make sense and revising and resubmitting the work can put the manuscript back on track.
- *Lack of contribution.* Overall, does the manuscript make an important contribution to our knowledge? Reviewers must see the significance of the study and how its publication is essential to furthering our understanding of the topic or problem. Often this comes out in the theory-development and discussion sections of the manuscript.
- *Inappropriate place of submission.* Occasionally, the manuscript is simply sent to the wrong place. Highly quantitative studies should not be submitted to *Quarterly Journal of Speech* or *Critical Studies in Mass Communication*. Oral interpretation studies should not be sent to the *Journal of Broadcasting & Electronic Media*. And, generally, mass-communication papers should not be sent to the Organizational Communication Division of either the NCA or ICA. Opinion essays would be more appropriate for a trade or professional periodical than for a scholarly journal. Discussing the paper with

professors, perusing the journals, and reading contributor submission guidelines in the journals can help place the manuscript in the right place.

For additional information on submitting manuscripts for publication, see:

Knapp, M. L., & Daly, J. A. (1993). *A guide to publishing in scholarly communication journals* (2nd ed.). Austin, TX: International Communication Association.

SUMMARY

Writers need to use a clear and lucid style, adhere to rules of grammar, spell properly, and present their reports in an appropriate format. The APA *Publication Manual* standardizes format by setting down rules for writing, bibliography form, and editorial style. It is often used by communication researchers when they are preparing research papers. There is no excuse for sloppy work that is not proofread and carefully edited. Any submitted work must conform to the basic standards of grammar, punctuation, spelling, and format or style. Failure to conform to these standards results in lower credibility and more negative evaluation.

REFERENCES

American Psychological Association. (1994). *Publication manual of the American Psychological Association* (4th ed.). Washington, DC: Author.

Babbie, E. (1998). *The practice of social research* (8th ed.). Belmont, CA: Wadsworth.

Brooks, B. S., Pinson, J. L., & Wilson, J. G. (1997). *Working with words: A concise guide for media editors and writers* (3rd ed.). New York: St. Martin's Press.

Day, R. A. (1998). *How to write & publish a scientific paper* (5th ed.). Cambridge: Cambridge University Press.

Gelfand, H., & Walker, C. J. (1997). *Mastering APA style: Instructor's resource guide* (4th ed.). Washington, DC: American Psychological Association.

Gibaldi, J. (1995). *MLA handbook for writers of research papers* (4th ed.). New York: Modern Language Association of America.

Harvard Law Review Association. (1996). *The bluebook: A uniform system of citation* (16th ed.). Cambridge, MA: Author.

Kessler, L., & McDonald, D. (1996). *When words collide: A media writer's guide to grammar and style* (4th ed.). Belmont, CA: Wadsworth.

Knapp, M. L., & Daly, J. A. (1993). *A guide to publishing in scholarly communication journals* (2nd ed.). Austin, TX: International Communication Association.

Owens, P. (1994). *Dr. Peter Owens' research paper writer* (Version 3.0) [CD-ROM and computer diskette]. Watertown, MA: Tom Snyder Productions.

Slade, C., Campbell, W. G., & Ballou, S. V. (1994). *Form and style: Theses, reports, term papers* (9th ed.). Boston: Houghton Mifflin.

Strunk, W., Jr., & White, E. B. (1979). *The elements of style* (3rd ed.). New York: Macmillan.

Turabian, K. L. (1996). *A manual for writers of term papers, theses, and dissertations* (6th ed.). Chicago: University of Chicago Press. (Revised by J. Grossman & A. Bennett)

University of Chicago Press. (1993). *The Chicago manual of style* (14th ed.). Chicago: Author.

EXERCISES

1. Check a paper you have written for effective writing style. Use the "Tips for Effective Writing" and "The Ten Commandments of Good Writing" as guidelines for this examination.

2. Select one recent single-authored communication book, one multiauthored communication book, one essay in an edited communication book, and one single-authored and one multiauthored article in scholarly communication journals. Construct the citations for each of these five sources using correct APA style (see Appendix A).

3. Choose two or three verbs (from page 222) for the following sentences. Compare and contrast the different meanings for those selected.

    a. Smith (1990)_____ verbal qualifiers as terms that connote a great degree of uncertainty.

    b. Smith (1990)_____ a method of measuring verbal qualifiers in speech.

    c. Smith (1990)_____ that women who use more verbal qualifiers are more likely to be perceived as weak.

    d. When Jones (1992) criticized Smith's (1990) new method of measuring verbal qualifiers, Smith _____ that the validity and reliability data were within the bounds of acceptability.

    e. Although Smith (1990)_____ that the method was acceptable, more current research (Jones, 1996; Miller, 1994; Williams, 1998) _____ that Smith's claim was premature.

    f. Smith (1990) _____ that future research should compare perceptions of both men and women as a result of qualifier use.

4. Another finding from the Rubin and McHugh (1987, p. 287) article discussed in this chapter follows. Write a paraphrased summary of this finding in one sentence.

    > The fifth hypothesis predicted a positive significant relationship between perceived relationship development importance and parasocial interaction. The correlation between these two variables was significant ($r = .52, p < .001$), supporting the fifth hypothesis.

5. Rewrite the following passive sentences in the active voice. Remember to use past tense when necessary.

   a. It was found by Graham (1986) that humor is used by people to get others to like them.

   b. When questionnaires were completed, subjects were allowed to leave the laboratory.

   c. Demographic characteristics of East Liverpool residents have been consistently found by researchers (Barbato, 1987; Offutt, 1990; Perse, 1986) to be representative of the general population.

   d. The scale was submitted to factor analysis to discover how many dimensions were contained in it.

6. Use proofreading and copyediting symbols to edit the following passage. Compare your editing with that of others and with that of your instructor.

   > We find that the notion of controlalso is very important when we think about and hypothesize about communication bheavior. Rubin (1986) argued that: "we need to consider whether locus of control, alone or in combination with other factors, produces variations in motives for and consequences of using personal and mediated information channels." (p. 135) Locus of control affects behavior (Rotter, 1954). "Internals" feel tehy control events in their lives, "externals" viewing life outcomes as dependent on luck, chance or powerful others. pointing to the reaserch of Williams, Phillips and Lum (1985) and Schoenbach and Hackforth (1987), Levy asked whether consumers use VCRs for control.

7. Find a copy of your college's or university's rules about writing and plagiarism. Read it carefully. What penalties are specified? Can you suggest any tips to avoid inadvertent plagiarism?

chapter 11

Preparing Research Projects

Communication students become involved in many different types of research projects during their careers. Many of these are theoretical and involve researching topics for the sake of increasing knowledge about the topic. Other projects are applied and are geared to solving a problem or answering a question. Often professional organizations have their own format and style for writing and presenting reports. Here we focus on the basic elements of preparing this information. These basics are also used by communication professionals.

We focus this chapter on five main academic projects students commonly undertake: abstracts, literature reviews, critical papers, research prospectuses, and original research reports. For each project, we define what it is, identify different types that exist, explain the format for preparing it, and highlight the steps involved in completing the project.

ABSTRACTS

An **abstract** is an abbreviated version or a condensation of a written work. Writers seem to agree that there are three main types of abstracts, identifiable by their internal purpose.

Indicative abstracts are used for screening, so readers can see if a document is pertinent to their interests. They give a description of the scope of the study, the main sections, and other relevant information found in the document. They are short paragraphs (usually 100 to 150 words), giving the purpose and results of the research. They guide the reader rather than informing. Abstracts that precede some journal articles or are in the journal's table of contents are often indicative, to give the reader a flavor for the piece, although many journals prefer shorter versions of informative abstracts.

Informative abstracts are used for information, so readers can identify the main findings and data in a document without having to reread the article. They are more detailed in nature, usually 150 to 400 words, and include information on the purpose and scope, methods, results, and conclusions. They should not contain references to previous literature or to unreported results. This type of abstract allows readers to identify the basic research concepts and findings and to determine whether the study is relevant to their interests. This is the type of abstract to use when preparing bibliography cards. *Communication Abstracts, Psychological Abstracts*, and *Dissertation Abstracts*, for example, publish informative abstracts.

Critical abstracts provide, in addition to main findings and information, a judgment or comment on the study's validity, reliability, or completeness. If a critical abstract becomes too critical, the abstract turns into a review. Often critical abstracts are 400 to 500 words long.

■ FORMAT

Abstracts, especially of empirical research articles, typically have four sections. The first is an orientation to the general nature of the study and what the research was about (for example, hypotheses and research questions). The second section describes the method, procedures, sample, and other specific information about how the study was done. The third section contains the results of the study. Those unfamiliar with statistics may have a difficult time understanding the elaborate statistical procedures used in many scholarly journal articles. It is important, though, that these results be read and noted, particularly as they relate to the hypotheses or research questions of the study. The last section of the abstract is typically the shortest. It condenses the author's discussion of the results, the relationship of the results to previous research findings, and proposed directions for further research.

■ STEPS

Cleveland and Cleveland (1990) and Collison (1971) have outlined the main steps involved in writing an abstract.

1. Ideally, read the article two or three times before writing the abstract.
2. Identify the main sections of the document and highlight, mark, or note important passages.
3. Write a draft of the narrative. Use complete sentences and your own words. Include the following:

    a. Objectives and scope: Why was the study done, and what does it include?

    b. Methodology: What procedures, subjects, instruments, and data analyses were used/performed? How was the study done?

    c. Results: What was found?

    d. Conclusions: What do we now know, and what implications does this have?

    e. Additional information: What interesting information doesn't fit into the above categories? What findings are incidental?

4. Edit and rewrite the draft.
   a. Check for brevity, reduce redundancy, and avoid repetition whenever possible.
   b. Use your own words.
   c. Clarify the lead sentence, or *thesis*. It contains vital information about the purpose of the study and should be clear, concise, and thorough.
5. Prepare and type the final abstract.
   a. Record the reference, accurately and completely, at the top of the abstract.
   b. Give your name at the bottom.

Keep in mind that informative and critical abstracts will be more detailed than indicative abstracts.

LITERATURE REVIEWS

You may be asked to find specific information in the communication literature, to review the research on a specific topic, and to write a literature review about that research. A **literature review** has two main purposes: to summarize research and to evaluate it. Pure summary is akin to objective and descriptive journalism, whereas evaluation contributes original ideas to our understanding and results in scholarship. Evaluation speaks to the validity of the research findings.

A literature review is a crucial part of the research process. First, it enables us to understand the current status of knowledge about a topic. Second, before you can conduct original research, you must know what scholarship already exists on the topic and evaluate the findings so that you can formulate new research questions to guide your study. As you begin to read original reports of communication scholarship, you will see that researchers explain to the reader how the literature was examined before the research question was formed. The literature review, then, acts as a guide for developing questions not yet answered by the published research literature.

There are two basic types of literature reviews: exemplary and exhaustive. An **exemplary,** or representative, **literature review** is similar to a preface in a research study. In the exemplary review, the writer assumes that the reader knows about the subject and so presents only key references to reacquaint the reader with representative works that relate to the research study.

Key references are those that have directly influenced the study being proposed or conducted. They will be cited and described as they relate to the topic, and they will provide the reader with a starting point for further information. However, the reader is to understand that other, perhaps more general, articles and books exist that may also be related to the subject. Missing key references is a sign of poor scholarship. Most scholarly journal articles begin with exemplary literature reviews; consult journal articles for examples of this type of literature review.

An **exhaustive literature review** is comprehensive. The writer attempts to find all the information pertinent to a topic (usually scholarly journal articles, book chapters, and books) and to summarize and evaluate the major findings. This type of review is typical of review essays in scholarly handbooks or year-books, theses and dissertations, and research papers required for communication classes. In an exhaustive review, the writer assumes that the reader has less knowledge of the area than is assumed with an exemplary review. The writer's goal is to emphasize pertinent findings, to review relevant methodological issues, to summarize major conclusions, and to evaluate the status of research on the topic. The reader of this type of review will assume that the writer has examined all the research and theory in the area and that most works on the topic will be referenced in the review.

■ FORMAT

You are probably familiar with writing *term papers*. The goal of a term paper is usually to summarize information from secondary sources and to make a statement about a particular topic. That is why instructors emphasize the need for creating a thesis statement and supporting it throughout the paper. Literature reviews are similar in this respect. A review of pertinent literature should also be cohesive (in other words, not choppy). Sources examined in the literature review, though, are usually primary rather than secondary. In each section of the literature review, the reader should see how the research helps clarify a specific aspect of the problem. The writer of such a review, consequently, must know exactly what that problem is before beginning the writing process.

The *thesis statement* is a way of clearly stating a position on the subject that you plan to support. It is not a personal opinion or belief. You must demonstrate the proposition with evidence from the research literature. Most often, an understanding of the problem emerges from the literature search process and discussions with others. Then, by organizing, integrating, and evaluating the published materials, you consider how adequately the research has clarified the problem. In short, you develop the thesis statement and support various arguments by summarizing and synthesizing those pertinent writings found during the literature search.

Introduction

This first part of a literature review orients the reader to the subject and indicates what is to follow. It is sometimes better to write the introduction after you have completed the paper because you may change your outline slightly during the writing process.

General Statement of the Problem

This second section describes the topic and explains its significance. Answer these questions: What do we mean by the topic? Why is it interesting? How is this topic a significant one in the communication field? Are there controversies that need to be resolved? Is this research area of special interest to a particular group of people?

You can establish the significance of the topic by arguing that this research fills a gap in the literature (in other words, no one else has adequately summarized this necessary or essential material), that it provides the possibility for fruitful exploration in the future, and that it relates to a problem that needs to be solved to make communication theory and practice more meaningful. By the end of this second section, then, the problem should be clearly defined and clarified for the reader.

Summary of Literature

The third section is the meat of the literature review. Here you summarize previous research, theory, and writings to inform the reader of the state of current knowledge in this area. You also should identify relationships, gaps, contradictions, and inconsistencies in the literature reviewed. There are several organizational strategies that can be used for this summary.

- *Topical order.* Here you present the main topics or issues, one-by-one, and emphasize the relationship of the issues to the main problem. For example, a topical order for a literature review on approaches to group leadership would include the trait approach, the situational approach, and the functional approach. Obviously, without transitions, the topics would appear as a sequence of minipapers and would not seem connected. Thus, you must keep the reader aware of the direction of this organizational scheme and the connections among the topics.
- *Chronological order.* This structure is most useful in historical research papers. It doesn't make much sense to describe, chronologically, research studies of group communication if you are emphasizing the need for more research on group cohesion. However, if you are arguing that group research has proceeded from an early emphasis on individual variables to a current emphasis on process variables, chronological order would be consistent with the problem being discussed. Again, this is why it is important that you know the problem before you begin to summarize the literature. The pattern of organization depends on knowing what the end of the paper will look like.
- *Problem–cause–solution order.* Another way to organize this section is to move from the problem to a solution. Several schemes exist for this purpose. The problem–cause–solution order is most typical of this format. You begin by fully describing the problem (for example, what is the influence of friends on decisions to purchase magazine subscriptions?). Then you identify and discuss the cause of the problem (for example, the impact of opinion leaders on newspaper reading has been examined, but the influence of friends on magazine subscriptions has not been investigated). Finally, you propose a solution—what type of research is needed to fill this gap in our knowledge?
- *General-to-specific order.* Here you would examine broad-based research first, then focus on specific studies that relate to the topic. For example, you may first look at writings that have addressed general issues about media effects, then review studies that have looked specifically at the influence of television viewing on children's aggressive behavior.

- *Known-to-unknown order.* Here you examine current literature about the problem and then identify, at the end, what is still not known.
- *Comparison-and-contrast order.* Here you show how studies and findings are similar to and different from each other.
- *Specific-to-general order.* Here you attempt to make some general sense out of specific studies so that conclusions can be drawn. For instance, you could describe three studies that have tried to measure interpersonal communication competence and then draw some conclusions about how competence should be defined or measured.

Critical Evaluation

A literature review typically ends with a critical evaluation of the literature. This section of the review carefully examines the research done to date by (a) critiquing the conduct and validity of the research on the topic and (b) proposing research questions that are still unanswered in the literature. Through this critical evaluation, the review becomes a piece of scholarship. It creates knowledge by adding new information to the already existing literature about the topic. Through the questions asked, it also sets forth an agenda for researchers to follow. By learning about research methodology, students can understand and evaluate the communication literature and add to the body of knowledge through their own scholarship.

■ STEPS

1. Choose and narrow the topic. How narrow the topic becomes depends on the purpose, scope, and type of project (see Chapter 2).
2. Formulate a working statement of the problem. According to Hubbuch (1996), it should begin with "What are the basic trends and developments in _____?"
3. Search the literature, employing either a general-to-specific or specific-to-general search strategy (see Chapter 2).
4. Once all sources have been abstracted, examine the bibliography cards for themes, topics, issues, patterns, and developments.
5. Write a thesis that summarizes these trends.
6. Refine your statement of the problem.
7. Choose an organizational strategy for the review and create an outline for the summary section.
8. Write each part of the summary section by focusing on the trends, themes, or ideas, citing studies you've read as illustrations or examples. Use the literature to develop your thesis or argument for each section. Do not merely give abstracts of your studies; show how the studies are connected and how they relate to the themes. Critique, where possible, the validity of the research.
9. Form conclusions about each main section and about the topic in general.
10. Identify gaps in the literature and propose questions for further study.

11. Write the introduction to the paper, orienting the reader to the subject, what will follow, and the significance of the topic. Make sure you define all terms in need of clarification.

12. Refine the summary section. Write transitions between the sections by pointing out common elements or referring to the thesis and minithesis statements.

13. Put the review aside for a few days and prepare the reference list, citing only those sources that actually appear in the review.

14. Reread the review, refine the grammar, and rewrite for clarity. Sometimes reading it aloud will help uncover mistakes.

15. Check the review carefully for spelling, typographic, and punctuation errors. Make necessary corrections.

16. Examine the review one last time with an APA manual (or whatever manual you are following) in hand to be sure all stylistic conventions are followed. Make necessary corrections.

17. Print or type the final version of the literature review. Proofread it.

CRITICAL PAPERS

As we just explained, a critical evaluation is often considered a part of any literature review. Sometimes, however, your goal may be to conduct an exemplary literature review, rather than an exhaustive one, and draw conclusions about the subject based on pertinent evidence. This, then, is a critical paper. **Critical papers** may range from a few pages to **monograph** length; their size depends on how narrowly defined the topic is and how much pertinent literature exists on it. Article-length critical papers can be found in journals such as *Critical Studies in Mass Communication* and *Quarterly Journal of Speech*.

A key feature of a critical paper is the strong thesis statement. You test the thesis by gathering facts and other evidence and analyzing these materials for authenticity, validity, and relevance. You may change the thesis as you proceed because you want to let the facts guide the paper rather than select only those facts that support a predetermined opinion.

No set format exists for critical papers. The topic, data, and author's perspective determine the format and structure.

■ STEPS

1. Choose and narrow the topic. Consult with people who have written critical papers to adjust the topic to the size appropriate for your specific purpose or goal.

2. Search the literature and archives for relevant data/facts, transcripts, opinions, recordings, research reports, and so on.

3. Develop a working thesis statement.

4. Test the thesis with previously gathered data. Adjust as necessary.

5. Search for and gather additional data. Adjust the thesis as the data suggest.

6. Check for appropriate grammar and sentence structure.

7. Critically evaluate the clarity of the paper's ideas.

8. Check for spelling, typographic, punctuation, and stylistic errors. Make necessary corrections.
9. Print or type the final version of the critical paper. Proofread it.

RESEARCH PROSPECTUSES

Some assignments (such as a senior thesis, master's thesis, doctoral dissertation, or independent study project) will require you to move beyond a summary and critical evaluation of the literature to suggest the next step or steps that should be taken to solve the problem. At this point, statements of hypotheses or research questions should clearly and logically emanate from the literature review. Proposed research methods to answer these questions (see Chapter 9) must also be consistent with those used and critically discussed earlier in the paper. These are the basic elements of a research **prospectus.**

Typically, the type of research project proposed will influence which type of literature review one writes. Some institutions, for example, require that the literature review be exhaustive for thesis and dissertation prospectuses, whereas others require only exemplary reviews. An independent study project prospectus may include only several paragraphs or a couple of pages of literature review. So, the purpose of the project and the guidelines of the institution influence the extent of the prospectus. Be sure to ask before proceeding.

■ FORMAT

Many formats exist for organizing research prospectuses. Most often the format depends on the project being proposed. Many times the format for people- or behavior-oriented studies differs slightly from that used for artifact- or message-oriented studies. The outline that follows contains basic elements of the prospectus and questions that research prospectuses should answer. Depending on the nature of the proposed project, you may not need to include answers to all these questions. Note that some entries in the outline are more relevant for some forms of research (that is, message or behavior) than for others. The main difference among these is in the Method section. Also, you may want to shift the order of some sections to reflect your own project. In any case, this outline will guide you to provide a complete prospectus for an adviser or a committee to examine.

   I. COVER PAGE
       A. Title
       B. Author
       C. Date
       D. Purpose of Submission
  II. ONE-PAGE ABSTRACT
 III. RESEARCH PROBLEM (Introduction, Questions, and Overview)
       A. What is the goal of the research project?
       B. What is the problem, issue, or critical focus to be researched?

C. What are the important terms to be defined?

D. What is the significance of the problem?

   1. Do you want to test a theory?

   2. Do you want to extend a theory?

   3. Do you want to test competing theories?

   4. Do you want to replicate a previous study?

   5. Do you want to correct previous research that was conducted in an inadequate manner?

   6. Do you want to resolve inconsistent results from earlier studies?

   7. Do you want to solve a practical problem?

   8. Do you want to test a method or methodology?

E. What are the limitations and delimitations of such a study?

IV. REVIEW OF LITERATURE

A. What is the theoretical framework for the investigation?

B. Are there complementary or competing theoretical frameworks?

C. What does previous research reveal about the different aspects of the problem?

D. What research questions and hypotheses have emerged from the literature review?

V. METHOD

A. What will constitute the data for the research?

B. What materials and information are needed to conduct the research?

   1. How will they be obtained?

   2. What special problems can be anticipated in acquiring needed materials and information?

   3. What are the limitations in the availability and reporting of materials and information?

C. Who will provide the data for the research?

   1. What is the population being studied?

   2. Who will be the subjects or respondents for the research?

      a. What is the sample size?

      b. What are the characteristics of the sample?

   3. Which sampling technique will be used?

D. What questionnaire or measures will be used?

   1. If previously developed:

      a. How reliable and valid are the measures?

      b. Why use these measures rather than others?

   2. If developing a measure for the research:

      a. Why develop a new measure?

      b. How will items be developed?

      c. What format will be used for the items?

d. How will reliability and validity be assessed?
E. What methods or techniques will be used to collect the data?
   1. What are the variables?
   2. How will the variables be manipulated, controlled, measured, and/or observed?
F. What procedures will be used to apply the methods or techniques?
   1. What are the limitations of this methodology?
   2. What factors will affect the study's internal and external validity?
   3. How will plausible rival hypotheses be minimized?
   4. What sources of bias will exist? How will they be controlled?
G. Will any ethical principles be jeopardized? How will subjects be debriefed?
VI. DATA ANALYSIS
A. How will the data be analyzed?
B. What criteria will be used to determine whether the hypotheses are supported?
C. What was discovered (about the goal, data, method, and data analysis) as a result of doing a pilot study (if conducted)?
D. What statistics will be used, if any?
VII. CONCLUDING INFORMATION
A. How will the final research report be organized? (Outline)
B. What sources have you examined thus far that pertain to your study? (Reference List)
C. What measures, questions, credentials, or data must be made available? (Appendixes of Materials and Instruments)
D. What time frame (deadlines) have you established for collecting and analyzing the data and for writing the report? (Timetable/Schedule)

These questions suggest that planning is vital to any research project. You must have a clear plan of action and stick to it throughout the project. Remember, research is systematic, and objective methodological conventions must be followed.

■ STEPS

We will not repeat, here, all the steps involved in conducting a literature review or critical essay, even though they are pertinent. Instead, we will focus on the main steps in constructing the research prospectus.

1. Determine what it is that you want to study. Discuss the topic with an adviser who is interested in this topic and willing and able to advise your research.
2. Review the literature and develop specific research questions that you want to answer or hypotheses that you want to test.

3. Consult with your adviser on the feasibility of conducting such research. Your adviser may want to see your literature review before this meeting. If you need to have a prospectus committee, now is the time to begin to set it up.
4. Construct the research problem section and orient the literature review to your particular problem area.
5. Determine which procedures or methods will best answer your questions or test your hypotheses. Explain these thoroughly and review other research that has used these procedures/methods.
6. Submit the plan to your adviser and discuss the wisdom of proceeding as planned.
7. Polish (rewrite, edit, proofread) the prospectus and submit it.

ORIGINAL RESEARCH REPORTS

Original **research reports** are comprehensive summaries of what happened when a research project was carried out. Besides the literature review, they include information on what was planned and what was discovered.

Reports differ slightly depending on the type of research conducted. Archival and documentary research reports emphasize support for arguments and procedures for analyzing the contents of documents. Survey research reports focus on sampling procedures, questions asked, and statistical analysis of results. Observational research reports detail methods for observing behavior and the findings of the observations. Experimental reports emphasize controlled procedures and statistical analysis of results.

■ FORMAT

As previously outlined, the research process involves careful planning and execution. A specific convention for reporting research results should also be followed. Although research reports vary depending on the type of research project conducted, some elements are common to all research reports.

In the first section, the *introduction*, develop the problem and its significance and provide background information on the study. You should include the rationale for the study, the purpose of the investigation, and a review of the most pertinent literature. If the report will be submitted to a journal for publication, this review should be exemplary (briefer than that required for a classroom literature review). If the report will be a thesis or dissertation, the review should be exhaustive.

In the second section, detail the *method* and materials used in the study. Include in this section the sample you studied, the research design, the measures you used, and the specific procedures you followed in conducting the study. In other words, how did you examine, observe, or measure your data? These details should be precise so that another researcher could reproduce or replicate your study.

In the third section, present your *results*. This might be the shortest section of an experimental research report because you are limited here to just the results of your investigation. It could, however, be the longest section of a report if the study is archival/documentary in nature. You may find tables and figures helpful for relating complicated or summary data here, especially for survey and experimental research.

The last section of the report is the *discussion*. In this section *discuss* (not recapitulate) the results that you found. Point out where expected results were not found. Show how your results agreed or disagreed with previous research. Discuss the theoretical meaning/implications or the practical applications of your results. Identify the limitations of your study and point to future directions for investigation. It is your job here to make sure that the meaning of the results and the significance of the study are clear.

■ STEPS

We outlined the basic steps in conducting research in Chapter 9. In Chapter 10 we summarized some basic concerns of reviewers when they read a submitted manuscript. Keep these concerns in mind both as you prepare to conduct a research study and as you write the research report about that project. Earlier, in the literature review and prospectus sections of this chapter, we detailed the steps for writing research reports. Here, we'll take you through the steps that follow a completed prospectus.

1. Conduct the research study.
2. Analyze the data and summarize the results.
3. Review the findings in relation to what you expected to find and in relation to what has been found before. Generate important ideas that need further explanation or elaboration in the discussion section.
4. Write the discussion section, pulling together the main themes or issues that are important and the new findings from your study. Also include ideas for new research projects that emerged from your findings.
5. Check the research report for coherence and clarity.
6. Submit the report to your professor or committee, for convention presentation, or for publication.

The last step can be very involved. Students submit projects to their instructors, and researchers often consider submitting literature reviews and research reports to professional associations for convention presentation and for publication in scholarly journals. Each year the professional associations publish a "Call for Papers" for the next year's convention. Contact the organization for further information (see Chapter 1).

The choice of where to submit a completed research report to be considered for publication largely depends on the nature of the work. To find the right place for your manuscript, scan *Current Contents* (see Chapter 7) and examine the contents of recent issues of a variety of journals. Look at the prefaces and the "Instructions to Authors" or "Manuscript Submission Guidelines" in the journals to see which one is most likely to consider your paper for publication.

Two other publications offer detailed descriptions of communication journals and may help you decide where to submit your articles:

Dyer, C. S. (Ed.). (1998). *The Iowa guide: Scholarly journals in mass communication and related fields* (7th ed.). Thousand Oaks, CA: Sage.

Knapp, M. L., & Daly, J. A. (1993). *A guide to publishing in scholarly communication journals* (2nd ed.). Austin, TX: International Communication Association.

It is of course important to consider the prestige of publishing in a quality journal, but you also must consider where the article will have the most impact for the audience you have in mind. A small-scale study, a study focused on a state or regional issue, or a study looking at links between two or three variables might be more appropriate in a state or regional journal, whereas a study having national implications or seeking to add to our theoretical knowledge would be better placed in a national journal. Discussions with colleagues and professors can help you decide on the best market for your paper.

Each journal details its policies and procedures for submitting manuscripts for consideration. These guidelines explain the journal's review policy, the appropriate manuscript style (such as APA or MLA), and the number of copies to send. Most journals do not ask you to send the original typed or printed copy and do not return copies if the manuscript is not accepted for publication. So be sure to keep a copy for yourself before you send the paper out for review. Address inquiries about specific journal policies and procedures to the editor whose name is listed on the inside cover or first pages of each journal. Because most editors change every 3 or so years, be sure to consult the most recent issue of the journal.

Typically, you would send three or four copies of a manuscript to the editor of the selected journal. It is important that the paper be written in the style acceptable to that journal. You will often have to provide an abstract with your manuscript. Examine the journal to decide whether to send an indicative or an informative abstract.

The editor will decide whether the manuscript is of sufficient quality and within the purview of the journal. If it is not, you will receive a letter saying so. If it is, the editor will send you an acknowledgment of receipt and send the manuscript, usually with author identity removed, to two or three reviewers chosen for their expertise about the paper's content or methodology. These reviewers will send their recommendations to the editor. After receiving all recommendations, the editor will evaluate the manuscript and the reviews and send you a letter. The letter will advise you whether the editor has accepted the paper for publication. He or she will usually include copies of the reviews. The review process typically takes about 3 months (sometimes longer).

To be publishable a study has to investigate significant research questions in a rigorous and methodologically sound manner. It should extend knowledge in one's field. Most seminar papers and many convention papers do not meet these criteria.

The editor's decision letter may accept or reject the paper or ask you to resubmit a revision after you have incorporated the editor's and reviewers' suggestions. Don't be disheartened by a less than enthusiastic review. A vast majority of manuscripts (often up to 85% or 90% in the best journals) are either rejected or in need of revision. Very few initial submissions are accepted. If you're asked for a revision, follow the specific editor and reviewer suggestions and rewrite. The process may be time-consuming and demanding, but often the results are rewarding. If a paper is rejected and you feel the manuscript really does have merit, use the editor and reviewer comments to revise the paper and submit it to a different journal. Most journal editors will tell you that they want to see only your best work, and reviewer comments help you make the manuscript better.

SUMMARY

Abstracts are condensations of research reports. They indicate what can be found in a document or what the major findings are; sometimes critical comments are added. Taking notes by abstracting articles on bibliography cards saves researchers time and energy.

Literature reviews, the bases of most research projects, have standard patterns of organization: an introduction to the subject, a general statement of the problem, a summary of previous research to inform the reader of the state of current knowledge, and a critical review of the literature. An exemplary, or representative, literature review is similar to the introductory section of a research study. In an exhaustive literature review, the writer attempts to summarize all major investigations on a topic. Both types of reviews require the writer to select and narrow a topic and to search the relevant literature for appropriate sources.

Critical papers include a literature review but concentrate on developing new understandings or conclusions about the literature. The thesis of such papers is supported by the literature and information reviewed.

A literature review is also part of a research prospectus. After identifying the problem, thoroughly reviewing the pertinent literature, and posing the research questions, the prospectus writer describes the method, sample, and procedures for the study. A list of reference sources, appendixes of the instruments (that is, the questionnaire, scales, or coding system) used in the study, and a timetable for the investigation are all included with the prospectus.

A research report must also be systematically organized. The first section is an introduction that provides background information, the rationale, and the purpose of the investigation, as well as a review of the pertinent literature. The second section contains the method and procedures used in the study. The third section describes the results or findings. In the final section, the author discusses the meaning and significance of these findings.

When you submit research reports to be considered for convention presentation or for publication, they must follow the association's or the journal's guidelines. Journals follow systematic procedures for reviewing manuscripts. Manuscripts must address important questions, advance knowledge, be methodologically and stylistically appropriate, and include abstracts to help readers quickly identify the purpose, findings, and relevance of the research. The following sources can help guide you through these writing projects.

REFERENCES

American Psychological Association. (1994). *Publication manual of the American Psychological Association* (4th ed.). Washington, DC: Author.

Barzun, J., & Graff, H. F. (1992). *The modern researcher* (5th ed.). Fort Worth, TX: Harcourt Brace Jovanovich.

Cleveland, D. B., & Cleveland, A. D. (1990). *Introduction to indexing and abstracting* (2nd ed.). Littleton, CO: Libraries Unlimited.

Collison, R. L. (1971). *Abstracts and abstracting services*. Santa Barbara, CA: ABC-Clio Press.

Day, R. A. (1998). *How to write & publish a scientific paper* (5th ed.). Cambridge: Cambridge University Press.

Dyer, C. S. (Ed.). (1998). *The Iowa guide: Scholarly journals in mass communication and related fields* (7th ed.). Thousand Oaks, CA: Sage.

Glatthorn, A. A. (1998). *Writing the winning dissertation: A step-by-step guide*. Thousand Oaks, CA: Sage.

Henson, K. T. (1995). *The art of writing for publication*. Boston: Allyn & Bacon.

Hubbuch, S. M. (1996). *Writing research papers across the curriculum* (4th ed.). Fort Worth, TX: Harcourt Brace College.

Knapp, M. L., & Daly, J. A. (1993). *A guide to publishing in scholarly communication journals* (2nd ed.). Austin, TX: International Communication Association.

Locke, L. F., Spirduso, W. W., & Silverman, S. J. (1993). *Proposals that work: A guide for planning dissertations and grant proposals* (3rd ed.). Newbury Park, CA: Sage.

Madsen, D. (1992). *Successful dissertations and theses: A guide to graduate student research from proposal to completion* (2nd ed.). San Francisco: Jossey-Bass.

Roth, A. J. (1999). *The research paper: Process, form, and content* (8th ed.). Belmont, CA: Wadsworth.

EXERCISES

1. Choose a scholarly journal article and write informative, indicative, and critical abstracts of it. After writing these, compare them with one about that same article in *Communication Abstracts.*

2. Prepare an outline of a research prospectus for a topic of interest.

3. Examine a thesis or dissertation and an article that has been written and published based on that work. Look at the scope of the literature covered and depth of coverage. When comparing the two, identify what was omitted, condensed, changed, or added.

4. Compare the publication submission guidelines for three or four different journals. What do they have in common? What elements differ?

5. Prepare a critical review of a research article that you read this semester.

chapter 12

Conducting a Research Study

N ow that you're well versed in the strategies and sources for searching and researching communication topics, we thought you might like a behind-the-scenes look at the research process. The best way for us to provide this inside look is to explain how we conducted one research study. We'll talk about how we conceptualized the study, chose the procedures, and analyzed the data. The actual research report can be found in:

> Rubin, A. M., & Rubin, R. B. (1989). Social and psychological antecedents of VCR use. In M. R. Levy (Ed.), *The VCR age* (pp. 92–111). Newbury Park, CA: Sage.

We have included an abbreviated version of the research report in Appendix B.

CONCEPTUALIZATION

In a study we did several years ago, we began to understand how confinement in a hospital affected the television-viewing habits of patients (A. Rubin & Rubin, 1981). Before entering the hospital, younger and older people had different reasons for watching television. Once within the confines of the hospital room, however, their reasons became very much alike—both younger and older patients watched television for companionship and to fill time. This may seem like common sense (actually, much research supports common sense), but it led us to wonder whether confinement was the only factor that diminished chronological- or biological-age differences.

After reading through much of the relevant social gerontology literature, we concluded that other important elements also affect aging and communication. We decided we should examine age, not as the number of years a person has lived, but as a constellation of factors that define a person's position in life. These *life-position* elements were physical health, mobility, social activity, interpersonal interaction, life satisfaction, and economic security. We named this *contextual age* and created a scale to measure the various aspects of this construct (A. Rubin & Rubin, 1982a).

We received a small grant from the ABC television network and began to look at how life position affected the way people used television. We published a few reports of research studies in which we used these contextual-age measures to examine viewing patterns of older and younger people (for example, A. Rubin & Rubin, 1982a, 1982b; R. Rubin & Rubin, 1982). One theoretical perspective helped guide our research: uses and gratifications.

Uses-and-gratifications theory is based on several basic principles. First, a person's behavior is motivated or goal directed. Second, people (for example, media audiences) actively seek communication sources (for example, television or friends) to satisfy their needs or wants. Third, people select from among different communication sources when trying to satisfy these needs. Fourth, people are influenced by social and psychological factors (such as age, education, personality, and life position) when they communicate. Fifth, people can identify their own reasons for communicating.

At about the same time, we began to look carefully at how interpersonal and mass communication might interface within uses and gratifications and other theoretical perspectives. We developed an agenda for research (A. Rubin & Rubin, 1985). All the while, we saw *contextual age* as an important antecedent to communication because the literature we read and our own research suggested that life position strongly influences how we communicate. We generated several research questions in that article and focused on the links among personal and mediated communication theory and research.

Our research then took separate paths to try to answer some of the questions posed in the research agenda. Among other topics, we looked at how lonely people have a sense of interpersonal interaction (called parasocial interaction) with television newscasters (A. Rubin, Perse, & Powell, 1985), how involved viewers are when they watch soap operas (A. Rubin & Perse, 1987), and why people use videocassette recorders (VCRs) (A. Rubin & Bantz, 1987). The VCR was an expanding home communication technology at the time, and the popular and scholarly literature began to emphasize the need to understand why people use VCRs. (We found much of this literature by using computerized searching techniques that we will describe later in this chapter.) We found eight major reasons why people use their VCRs: for library storage, time shifting, socializing, critical viewing, occupying children, and watching music videos, exercise tapes, and rented movies. As you can see, some of these reasons are closely entwined with interpersonal communication.

Other lines of our research looked at parasocial relationships with television characters (Perse & Rubin, 1989; R. Rubin & McHugh, 1987) and why people talk interpersonally with others (R. Rubin, Perse, & Barbato, 1988). In this last study, we created a scale to measure the motives people have for conversing with others. This interpersonal motives scale was modeled after uses-and-gratifications scales that looked at why people use media such as television. We found several primary interpersonal motives: communicating for pleasure, affection, inclusion, control, relaxation, and escape.

At the conceptual level, based on uses-and-gratifications theory, we expected a link between using media (here, the VCR) and communicating interpersonally. We felt it was time to look at this part of the theory. We wanted to study this problem: What are the relationships between motives for using the media and motives for communicating interpersonally with others? This is the general problem statement that guided our research.

COMPUTER SEARCH

We were aware of the uses-and-gratifications literature in communication because we had worked closely with it over the years. We were not, though, up to date on the VCR literature that had appeared in print since the earlier VCR study had been completed. So we decided to update our knowledge of this area through a limited (in terms of years) computer search.

We first searched *ABI/Inform* to find articles focusing on business aspects of VCRs. We used such key words (derived from the database's glossary) as "videocassette" AND-ed to "recorder" AND "home use," but NOT "instruction" (because we didn't want articles dealing only with using VCRs to teach classes). We asked for articles published from 1986 (a similar computer search for the earlier VCR article covered the period through 1985) to 1988 (when we did the study). This resulted in 10 hits. The articles came from sources we may not have found on our own: *Marketing News, Incentive Marketing, Marketing & Media Decisions, Marketing, Advertising Age, IEEE Spectrum, Discount Merchandiser, Journal of Advertising Research*, and *Consumer Electronics*. These articles gave more of a "trade" than a theoretical perspective on VCR use.

We also used *PsycINFO* to update our search of *Psychological Abstracts*. We used "videotape recorders" as our key word and excluded education-related articles by NOT-ing the key words "educational television," "teaching," and "videotape instruction." This resulted in three hits for the 1986–1988 period, including articles from the *British Journal of Occupational Therapy; Behavior Research Methods, Instruments, & Computers*; and *Journal of Fluency Disorders*. These were interesting but not highly useful sources.

We then searched *ERIC*. Here our key words were "videotape cassettes" AND "videotape recorders" NOT "educational television," "television curriculum," OR "teaching." There were 10 hits for the 2-year period. These included articles from *Clearing House, Computing Teacher, Communication Quarterly*, and *Library Hi Tech* and six convention papers (from the Research in Education section).

We also updated our earlier search of *Sociological Abstracts*, using such key words as "videotape" AND "cassette" AND "recorder." There were no hits for 1986–1988. We then used the library's CD-ROM of *Dissertation Abstracts* to see what dissertations may have looked at VCRs during this time. We located three and printed their citations and abstracts at the terminal.

MODEL

We used the abstracts found in the computer database searches to determine which articles might be relevant for our study. Besides the earlier literature we had read about personal and mediated communication, life position, and VCRs, we also read these newly found articles. Based on this review of the pertinent literature and our earlier research, we created a model to represent the relationships among the variables we expected to influence how VCRs are used (Figure 12-1).

In our model we expected that (a) locus of control and demographic characteristics such as age and gender would influence a person's life position, (b) life position would affect reasons people communicate with others, (c) these interpersonal motives would influence why people use VCRs, and (d) these VCR motives would affect how often someone uses his or her VCR. This conceptual model guided our investigation.

Thus, by now we had identified our research problem and searched the relevant literature. We had developed a model and were focused on the following research question: What are the social and psychological antecedents of VCR use? Now we were ready to plan the method of our study to answer this research question.

QUESTIONNAIRE

We decided to use survey research to answer the research question. Recall that survey research is an efficient means of gathering information from large groups of people. We felt that a self-administered questionnaire was the most appropriate survey technique. Uses-and-gratifications research typically uses

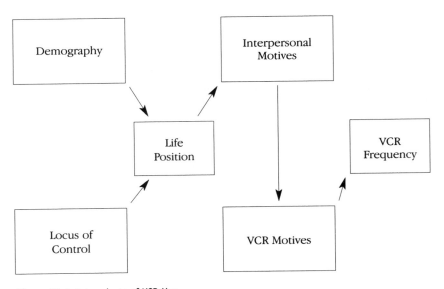

Figure 12-1 Antecedents of VCR Use

questionnaires for data gathering. Remember that one assumption of uses and gratifications is that people can report their reasons for communicating. Also, we felt that they can best provide information on their own life position, sense of control in their lives, and demographic information. These variables have been measured with survey questionnaires in the past. The study also was correlational in nature, making survey research an appropriate choice.

So we aimed to conduct a survey that included several scales to measure the variables in our model. First, we had to devise *demographic questions* to tap social elements that are known to influence communication behavior. Respondents anonymously filled in their age and the number of people who lived in their home or apartment (household size). They circled responses to indicate their gender (male or female), their highest level of completed education (elementary school, some high school, high school graduate, some college, college graduate, or advanced degree), and their current employment status outside the home (full time, part time, or unemployed).

As is the convention in survey research, we placed these demographic questions on the last page of the questionnaire. This is done so that important information would have already been gathered if someone feels these questions are too personal and chooses not to respond to them.

Second, we needed a measure of personality. During our literature search and past research, one personality variable often seemed to influence communication: *locus of control*. This construct refers to how much people feel in command of their lives. Externally controlled people feel that others or luck determines how events in their lives turn out. Those who are internally controlled feel that their own actions influence their destinies.

One scale, developed in 1966, to measure this construct had become a standard in the psychology literature, but our literature search suggested that another scale might be more precise. We turned to the *Social Sciences Citation Index* to see how many others had used Levenson's (1974) scale since its development. We found impressive data supporting the scale's validity and reliability. Valid scales measure what they intend to measure, and reliable scales are dependable and used consistently by respondents. So we chose to go with the more recent scale, citing some supporting research.

Third, we needed measures of life position, interpersonal motives, and VCR motives. In our own research, we had already developed such measures. Based on some of our previous research mentioned earlier in this chapter, we were able to use slightly shortened but still valid and reliable versions of the scales so that the questionnaire would not become too long. Lengthy questionnaires are tedious and troublesome. Respondents can become fatigued when trying to answer all the questions. Respondents also are volunteers who have limits on their available time.

We adapted the *life-position* scales from our contextual-age measures of physical health, mobility, interaction, life satisfaction, and economic security (A. Rubin & Rubin, 1982a; R. Rubin & Rubin, 1982). So we asked respondents how much they agreed with questions about their physical health (for example, "I usually feel in top-notch physical condition"), mobility (for example, "I have to rely on other people to take me places"), life satisfaction (for example, "I find a great deal of happiness in my life"), and so on.

And, we adapted the communication-motives scales from our *interpersonal-motives* research (R. Rubin et al., 1988) and *VCR-motives* research (A. Rubin & Bantz, 1987). So we asked respondents how much certain statements were like their own reasons for talking with other people (for example, "to get something I don't have" and "because I need someone to talk to or be with") or for using a VCR at home (for example, "because I want to entertain people who come over" and "because it gives you more choice over what to watch"). In Figure 12-2 we've included examples of a few VCR-motivation items from the original questionnaire.

Fourth, we needed a measure of how often people use their VCRs. For years, media researchers have struggled with the problem of how to measure media exposure. For example, merely asking people one question—how many hours they usually watch television—may result in a socially desirable underestimation. Because VCRs are not used in the same manner every day, we needed two different questions. One question asked respondents to fill in the number of days each week they use a VCR. The other question asked them to fill in the number of hours they use a VCR on those days. We created an index of *VCR frequency* by multiplying the number of days by the number of hours.

We constructed the questionnaire so that it began with a brief introduction to the study. Each section included basic instructions about completing

---

HERE ARE SEVERAL REASONS OTHER PEOPLE HAVE GIVEN FOR WHY THEY USE A VCR AT HOME. FOR EACH REASON, PLEASE CIRCLE THE NUMBER TO INDICATE HOW MUCH EACH REASON IS LIKE YOUR OWN REASONS FOR USING A VCR AT HOME.

If the reason is **exactly** like your own reason, circle a **5**.

If the reason is **a lot** like your own reason, circle a **4**.

If the reason is **somewhat** like your own reason, circle a **3**.

If the reason is **not much** like your own reason, circle a **2**.

If the reason is **not at all** like your own reason, circle a **1**.

I Use a VCR at Home Because	Exactly	A Lot	Some-what	Not Much	Not at All
1. I like to have movies or programs that can be viewed many times.....	5	4	3	2	1
2. It is convenient to rent tapes.	5	4	3	2	1
3. I like to have tapes available for members of the family.	5	4	3	2	1
4. I like the freedom to set my own schedule.	5	4	3	2	1
5. I want to entertain others at parties...	5	4	3	2	1
6. I want to re-watch a program and review it critically.	5	4	3	2	1
7. I like to have the ability to view programs any time.	5	4	3	2	1

Figure 12-2 VCR Study Questionnaire Example

the questions. We systematically arranged the sections to prevent earlier questions from biasing answers to later questions. We presented the sections in the following order: interpersonal motives, interspersed contextual-age and locus-of-control items, VCR frequency, VCR motives, and demographics. We prepared the pages so that instructions for answering questions were clear, transitions between sections were smooth, questions were not crammed together, and the questionnaire could be professionally reproduced.

PROCEDURE

The multivariate statistics that we used to analyze the collected information required a sample size of about 300 respondents. However, we know that some surveys are lost, others are not usable (for example, incomplete or unreadable), and some people surveyed would not even use VCRs. So we had almost 500 questionnaires printed and distributed about 450 of these, hoping to end up with 300 usable surveys.

We were concerned about how to get responses from a sufficiently broad sample. We did not have the funds to hire a survey research team to conduct door-to-door interviews or a marketing firm to conduct telephone interviews. Yet we wanted to survey a wide range of people of varied backgrounds and interests.

We decided to use purposive, quota-sampling procedures (see page 202) and to have the students in our upper-division communication research classes serve as research assistants. We trained these assistants in data-collection techniques and in the ethics of conducting surveys (for example, the voluntary and anonymous nature of questionnaire completion). We gave the assistants specific instructions about when and how to collect the data. They were told to choose a wide variety of people to represent the general population and to solicit one man and one woman of various educational backgrounds from each of four age groups: 18 to 34 years, 35 to 49, 50 to 64, and 65 years and older.

The demographic questions in the survey allowed us to check the breadth of the sample. For example, the average age of our sample was 43 years. The descriptive statistics about the sample are reported in the method section of the research report.

Our assistants collected these data during spring break in 1988. Some students took the surveys home or on vacation to other states, but most (85%) respondents were from Ohio. We received 428 completed questionnaires; 299 respondents owned or used a VCR. These 299 VCR users became the sample for our study.

Once our assistants returned the surveys to us, we had to "clean" all questionnaires. This means we went through each questionnaire to (a) place numeric codes on certain questions that needed them, (b) declare "missing" for the data analysis any questions that were not answered, (c) write answers clearly in the margins for any questions where the handwriting was not sufficiently legible to prevent errors when entering the data into the computer, and (d) make sure, in general, the survey was usable.

When the questionnaires were clean, we entered the data into a file on the computer. We then prepared the data for statistical analysis. Before proceeding with the analysis, though, we first checked 10% of the data to see whether any typing errors had occurred in data entry. Finding only a single error (in the 3200 numbers we checked), we felt reassured that our data were ready for analysis.

ANALYSIS

The analysis for the study was systematic and straightforward but complex. As is true for any quantitative study, our conceptual model and the level of measurement of our variables dictated the nature of our statistical tests. We used a standard statistical software package, SPSS, for our analyses (SPSS, 1988).

We first ran a *frequency analysis* on each measure. This gave us summary statistics (such as means and standard deviations) of all our variables. It also allowed us to find possible errors in our data. For example, we used 5-point scales to measure locus of control, life position, and communication motives. In other words, a question would ask whether the respondent "strongly agreed" (coded 5), "agreed" (4), "agreed some and disagreed some" (3), "disagreed" (2), or "strongly disagreed" (1) with the item. The frequency analysis could not tell us if a 3 was entered on the computer for a response when a 4 should have been entered. However, it could tell us if a 0 or 6 was entered by mistake (remember, the responses had to range from 1 to 5). Fortunately, all our data complied with expectations.

We included several variables for each component of the model. For example, *locus of control* included internal control, powerful-others external control, and chance external control. *Life position* consisted of physical health, interaction, mobility, life satisfaction, and economic security. And *interpersonal motives* included relaxation, pleasure, control, inclusion, affection, and escape.

In addition, a survey often includes several questions for each variable to measure different aspects of that variable and to ensure the reliability of the measure. We followed this practice. So, for example, we asked three questions to measure internal locus of control, another three questions to measure life satisfaction, another three questions to measure the inclusion interpersonal motive, and so on. We added the numeric responses to all three questions together to create the scales to measure each variable. As suggested by past research, we did this for the locus-of-control, life-position, and interpersonal-motive variables.

Because past research was not as clear about VCR motives, we could not simply add up the answers to the different questions. Instead, we used a statistical procedure known as *factor analysis*, which determines the different dimensions of motivation that might exist. In this way, we could identify five primary motives for using the VCR: library storage, social interaction, freedom of choice, learning, and time shifting.

After creating our scales for each variable in this manner, we were ready to try answering our research question. We employed several other statistical procedures in the analysis. These included partial correlation, multiple regression, and canonical correlation.

EPILOGUE

So what did we find? Well, we did identify specific social and psychological antecedents of the different motives for using VCRs and for how often a VCR is used. For example, we found that we could predict social-interaction reasons for using a VCR from specific interpersonal motives—seeking companionship and affection and putting off doing something else—and from restricted mobility but a tendency to interact with others.

We went on to discuss the implications of our results. We observed that "the VCR is a convenient and economical mechanism for communication storage and retrieval" (A. Rubin & Rubin, 1989, p. 106). And we pointed to how our findings support the principles of uses and gratifications and how our reasons for communicating with others help predict how and why we use VCRs.

Having read this book, you are now ready to read the results for yourself. They are found in Appendix B. We have great faith in your ability to understand the literature and basics of research methodology.

We have tried to infuse you with our love for discovery and hope you'll extend your own literature reviews and research papers into do-able research projects. If you fear venturing out on your own the first time (the second time will be a breeze!), ask a fellow student or professor to work with you on the research project. By conducting research, you'll gain even more insight into the strategies and sources of communication research than we can provide here. We wish you the best!

REFERENCES

Levenson, H. (1974). Activism and powerful others: Distinctions within the concept of internal-external control. *Journal of Personality Assessment, 38*, 377–383.

Perse, E. M., & Rubin, R. B. (1989). Attribution in social and parasocial relationships. *Communication Research, 16*, 59–77.

Rotter, J. B. (1966). Generalized expectancies for internal versus external control of reinforcement. *Psychological Monographs, 80*(1), 1–28.

Rubin, A. M., & Bantz, C. R. (1987). Utility of videocassette recorders. *American Behavioral Scientist, 30*, 471–485.

Rubin, A. M., & Perse, E. M. (1987). Audience activity and soap opera involvement: A uses and effects investigation. *Human Communication Research, 14*, 246–268.

Rubin, A. M., Perse, E. M., & Powell, R. A. (1985). Loneliness, parasocial interaction, and local television news viewing. *Human Communication Research, 12*, 155–180.

Rubin, A. M., & Rubin, R. B. (1981). Age, context and television use. *Journal of Broadcasting, 25*, 1–13.

Rubin, A. M., & Rubin, R. B. (1982a). Contextual age and television use. *Human Communication Research, 8*, 228–244.

Rubin, A. M., & Rubin, R. B. (1982b). Older persons' TV viewing patterns and motivations. *Communication Research, 9*, 287–313.

Rubin, A. M., & Rubin, R. B. (1985). Interface of personal and mediated communication: A research agenda. *Critical Studies in Mass Communication, 2*, 36–53.

Rubin, A. M., & Rubin, R. B. (1989). Social and psychological antecedents of VCR use. In M. R. Levy (Ed.), *The VCR age* (pp. 92–111). Newbury Park, CA: Sage.

Rubin, R. B., & McHugh, M. P. (1987). Development of parasocial interaction relationships. *Journal of Broadcasting & Electronic Media, 31*, 279–292.

Rubin, R. B., Perse, E. M., & Barbato, C. A. (1988). Conceptualization and measurement of interpersonal motives. *Human Communication Research, 14*, 602–628.

Rubin, R. B., & Rubin, A. M. (1982). Contextual age and television use: Reexamining a life-position indicator. *Communication Yearbook, 6*, 583–604.

SPSS, Inc. (1988). *SPSS-X user's guide* (3rd ed.). Chicago: Author.

appendix A

APA Style Basics

The *Publication Manual of the American Psychological Association* (1994) contains seven main sections: content and organization of a manuscript, expression of ideas, APA editorial style, manuscript preparation and sample paper, manuscript acceptance and production, journals program of the American Psychological Association, and bibliography. Here we are going to highlight some of the basic principles of the APA style that are most important to consider when writing literature reviews, prospectuses, and research papers. First, we will explain the basic bibliographic format used for references. Then, we will present some basic elements of the editorial style for the text of the paper.

BIBLIOGRAPHIC FORMAT

A **bibliography** is a list of sources compiled on a specific topic. It is not just the end product of communication research; it is a necessary component of any project. Bibliographies sometimes include citations for sources in addition to those sources actually cited in a paper. However, the reference list attached to research reports, literature reviews, review articles, term papers, and the like includes only those works that were consulted (that is, actually read) during research and that are cited in the paper. No extraneous sources should be included. The purpose of a reference list is not to show all the works you've found but to give necessary information so that readers can identify and retrieve those sources that were actually used. In APA style, the reference list is given the heading References.

The APA *Publication Manual* suggests that reference lists be double-spaced when typed. However, to save paper, your instructor may allow you to single-space the entries and double-space between them. As you may have noticed by now, the second and succeeding lines of each citation are indented three spaces when they are typeset. This allows a reader to distinguish more easily between the entries when looking for a specific source. When you type the references, however, type each entry like a miniparagraph, with the first line indented five to seven spaces, using the tab key.

As an experienced researcher, you will find that the more you consistently use any style, the easier it is to organize your findings for the final product, be it a research paper, seminar paper, speech, editorial, newspaper article, debate, or report.

■ BOOKS

Learning the APA style for books is not difficult. For a single-authored book (Example 1), the first element in the citation is the author's last name, followed by a comma, and then the author's initial(s). Next, place in parentheses, followed by a period, the year the book was published. Then give the title of the book. Capitalize only the first letter of the first word (except for proper nouns), and underline the entire title. End the title with a period. The final elements in the citation include the city (and state postal abbreviations for smaller cities) where the book was published, followed by a colon and the name of the publisher. End the citation with a period. Note that only single spaces are used to separate each element in all citations. For example:

Example 1: Single-Authored Book

Perloff, R. M. (1995). <u>The dynamics of persuasion.</u> Hillsdale, NJ: Erlbaum.

Underlined words are typeset in italics. Thus, every time you see italics in our text (or others), read it as underlining in typed manuscripts. If only a specific part of a source such as a chapter is used, this is indicated in the text citation itself. For example: (Perloff, 1995, chap. 3). Typeset, the preceding citation would appear like this:

Perloff, R. M. (1995). *The dynamics of persuasion*. Hillsdale, NJ: Erlbaum.

If a book has been reissued since its first edition, that should be indicated in the citation:

Example 2: Reissued Book

Newcomb, H. (Ed.). (1995). <u>Television: The critical view</u> (5th ed.). New York: Oxford University Press.

Note the abbreviations used. The lowercase (ed.) is an abbreviation of edition. When this term is capitalized (Ed.), it is an abbreviation of editor. If the book has two authors, use a comma and an ampersand between the names (Example 3). If the reference is an essay (or chapter) in an edited book, the essay's title is not underlined, but the book's title is (see Example 4). Inclusive pages of the essay in an edited book should be indicated in the reference. Doctoral dissertations

(Example 5), films (Example 6), and television programs (Example 7) are stylistically similar.

Example 3: Dual-Authored Book

> Baran, S. J., & Davis, D. K. (1995). <u>Mass communication theory: Foundations, ferment and future.</u> Belmont, CA: Wadsworth.

Note the use of the ampersand before the name of the last author in a series of authors. Also use the ampersand in the text of the paper, but only when the names appear as a citation in parentheses—for example, (Baran & Davis, 1995). We could have eliminated the state in this reference if it were a one-of-a-kind city (such as Chicago or Boston, see Example 2). Had this been an edited book, (Eds.) would have been inserted between the last editor's name and the year of publication.

Example 4: Essay in an Edited Book

> Bryant, J. (1989). Messages features and entertainment effects. In J. J. Bradac (Ed.), <u>Message effects in communication science</u> (pp. 231-262). Newbury Park, CA: Sage.

As you can see, the page numbers of the essay are included in parentheses following the book's title. If an edited book has two editors, use an ampersand between the two names; if there are three or more editors, separate all names with commas and use an ampersand before the last name.

Example 5: Doctoral Dissertation

> Rodgers, R. V. P. (1991). An analysis of rhetorical strategies in the recruitment literature directed to prospective black student populations at The Pennsylvania State University (Doctoral dissertation, The Pennsylvania State University, 1991). <u>Dissertation Abstracts International, 52,</u> 4147A.

If you read the dissertation on microfilm, you would also include the University Microfilms number in parentheses at the end of the entry. When an unpublished doctoral dissertation does not appear in *Dissertation Abstracts International,* underline the title. Follow the title with the words "Unpublished doctoral dissertation," a comma, the name of the university where it was completed, another comma, the city where the university is located, and the state or country if the city is not well known. The year when the dissertation was completed sometimes is 1 year earlier than when the abstract appears in *Dissertation Abstracts International*. If that is the case, both dates are slashed (for example, 1991/1992) when the dissertation is cited in the text. Also note that the first letters in The Pennsylvania State University are capitalized because it is a proper noun.

■ NONPRINT MEDIA

The style for nonprint media is explained in the APA *Publication Manual* (pp. 216–222). The producer is the first author (Example 6); sometimes the director is listed as second author. Example 7 also shows the producer as the first author for a series in the first citation, and a writer as the author for an episode in that series for the second citation.

Example 6: Film

Lehman, E. (Producer), & Nichols, M. (Director). (1966). Who's afraid of Virginia Woolf? [Film]. Burbank, CA: Warner Brothers.

Example 7: Telecast (Series and Episode)

Lasiewicz, C. (Producer). (1995). 48 hours [Telecast]. New York: CBS.

Kandra, G. (1995). Stopping the clock (E. Shapiro, Director). In C. Lasiewicz (Producer), 48 hours. New York: CBS.

The APA *Publication Manual* provides other examples for broadcast programs and other electronic media. As in any referencing style, it is most important to be accurate, complete, and consistent.

■ GOVERNMENT PUBLICATIONS

The style used for government publications is not fully explained in the APA *Publication Manual*. If the report is available from the National Technical Information Service (NTIS) or from the U.S. Government Printing Office (GPO), use the style shown in Example 8. If the report is not available from these agencies, do not include it in the bibliography but treat it as a footnote along with other not widely or easily accessible material.

Technical reports of nongovernment organizations that are available to the public are treated like books (Example 9).

Example 8: Government Document

U.S. Senate, Special Committee on Aging. (1980). How old is "old"? The effects of aging on learning and working (DHHS Publication No. NIH 78-1446). Washington, DC: Government Printing Office.

Example 9: Technical Report

Balkema, J. B. (Ed.). (1972). A general bibliography on aging. Washington, DC: National Council on the Aging.

Note that in Example 8 the primary government body is identified as the document's author, followed by the subsidiary agency (in this case, a committee). The reference also includes the issuing department's report number. This report is issued by the National Institutes of Health (NIH) of the Department of Health and Human Services (DHHS). It can be purchased by the public from the U.S. Government Printing Office. Example 9 is very much like a single-authored book reference (Example 1), except that the author is an editor (Ed.) of the work and the publisher of the report is an agency.

The APA *Publication Manual* (pp. 201–215) presents bibliographic formats for books and nonprint materials not discussed here. Consult the *Publication Manual* for assistance when the preceding examples do not fully apply.

■ PERIODICALS

The format for periodicals is slightly different from that used for books. Capitalize the first letter of each word (except prepositions that are three letters or less, conjunctions, and articles) in the name of the periodical. (Capitalize only the first letter of the first word of the article's title.) Underline the name of the periodical, not the title of the article, and the volume number of the journal in which the article appears. The page numbers of the article come after the periodical's volume number. The standard format for a journal article with one author is shown in Example 10 and that for a coauthored article is given in Example 11.

Example 10: Single-Authored Article

Garramone, G. M. (1985). Effects of negative political advertising: The roles of sponsor and rebuttal. Journal of Broadcasting & Electronic Media, 29, 149-159.

Example 11: Dual-Authored Article

Suzuki, S., & Rancer, A. S. (1994). Argumentativeness and verbal aggressiveness: Testing for conceptual and measurement equivalence across cultures. Communication Monographs, 61, 256-279.

If each issue of a particular journal starts with a page 1, include the issue number in parentheses after the volume number to make locating the article easier (Example 12).

Example 12: Issues Beginning With Page 1

Turow, J. (1994). Hidden conflicts and journalistic norms: The case of self-coverage. Journal of Communication, 44(2), 12-31.

In Example 12, the number 2 in parentheses indicates that the article appears in Volume 44's second issue.

Example 13: Book Review

> Benjamin, L. (1982). [Review of Telecommunications, mass media, and democracy: The battle for the control of U.S. broadcasting, 1928-1935]. Journal of Broadcasting & Electronic Media, 38, 241-242.

Similar to a journal article title, if the review had its own title, the title would follow the date. The information in the brackets indicates the title of the book being reviewed.

Articles appearing in general-interest or trade periodicals and magazines, such as *Advertising Age* or *Time*, are identified by date and by volume number. If the article begins in one place and is continued elsewhere, give all page numbers but use a comma to separate the page numbers. Similar to journal articles, do not use "Vol." before a volume number or "p." before a page number.

Example 14: Magazine Article

> Bell, N., & Amdur, M. (1994, January 24). NBC Super Channel looks to make mark in Europe. Broadcasting & Cable, 124(4), 112.

When the author is unknown, begin the citation with the name of the article and alphabetize it according to the first significant word in the title (not "a," "an," "the," and so on). Bibliographic format for newspaper articles is similar to that of general-interest periodicals but omits the volume number and uses "p." or "pp." before the page numbers. Consult the APA *Publication Manual* (pp. 194–201) for other examples of periodical citations.

■ Unpublished Papers, Reports, Personal Communications, and Speeches

Professional convention papers or other reports are often available though the ERIC Document Reproduction Service. Example 15 shows how these are referenced. However, not all convention papers are submitted to or accepted by ERIC. When unpublished papers and reports are available for use in a research project, they are cited as in Examples 16 and 17.

Example 15: Eric Report/Paper

> Feeser, T., & Thompson, T. L. (1990). A test of a method of increasing patient question asking in physician-patient interactions. Paper presented at the annual meeting of the Speech Communication

Association, Chicago. (ERIC Document Reproduction Service No. ED 325 887)

Example 16: Unpublished Convention Paper

Thomas, S., & Gitlin, T. (1993, May). <u>Who says there's a dominant ideology and what happens if that concept is falsified?</u> Paper presented at the annual meeting of the International Communication Association, Washington, DC.

Example 17: Unpublished Convention Poster Session

Sharkey, W. F., & Kim, M. (1994, November). <u>The effect of embarrass-ability on perceived importance of conversational constraints.</u> Poster session presented at the meeting of the Speech Communication Association, New Orleans.

Do not list oral interviews, personal conversations, memos, letters, and unpublished speeches with the references because the text is not permanently stored for others to examine. They are, however, referenced in the text. Be sure to include the name, type of communication, and date. An example is: (R. Jacobs, personal communication, March 27, 1995).

■ LEGAL REFERENCES

The field of law has its own conventions for citing work in legal periodicals. In most legal periodicals, citations of court cases, statutes, and such are placed in footnotes. In the APA style, legal references are placed in the reference list along with the other references.

In the text of a manuscript, cite the legal materials in the same way as other references. Begin with the first few words of the reference list entry, then give the date. This information will help the reader identify the citation in the references. Underline the names of court cases, but not statutes. The APA *Publication Manual* (pp. 223–234) offers examples of typical citations of legal materials but refers the user to *The Bluebook: A Uniform System of Citation* for more information.

■ ELECTRONIC SOURCES

Citations to works on the Internet or on CD-ROM are treated similarly. Generally, the citation begins with the author of the work (if known), the title of the work, the medium [in brackets], year of creation, title of the work, and publisher and location. Example 18 is the style used for a CD-ROM and Examples 19 and 20 show Internet sites. Note that it might be appropriate to cite the last date of visiting the site. The style for electronic sources is still evolving.

Example 18: CD-ROM

> Polling the nations [CD-ROM]. (1998–). Bethesda, MD: SilverPlatter.

Example 19: On-line With Author

> U.S. Congress, House of Representatives. (1995). United States code (1994 ed.)[On-line]. Available: http://www.law.cornell.edu/uscode (1999, February 14)

Example 20: On-line Without Author

> Polling the nations [On-line]. (1998–). Available: http://webspirs. silverplatter.com:8000/ucb2

CITING SOURCES IN THE PAPER

You have probably seen APA style used in many sources you've already examined. It is easily recognizable. First, books or other publications are generally not cited in footnotes or notes. There are usually only a few, if any, notes in an article. When the work of an author is referred to in the text of the paper, it is cited by using the author's last name and year the source was published. For example:

> Scott (1992) identified . . .
> Several researchers (Anthony, 1990; Gregory & Jacobs, 1985; Polk et al., 1980) reported . . .
> Douglass (1986) concluded: "The research findings clearly indicate support for the hypotheses" (p. 55).

These sources are then fully listed at the end of the article or chapter. This eliminates the need for most footnotes in the text.

As the preceding examples suggest, there are rules governing where in the sentence the citation occurs. As the first example shows, if an author's (or authors') name is used in the sentence, the year of publication directly follows the name. If an author (or authors) has two or more works published in the same year that are cited in the reference list, the works are alphabetized in the list by the first significant word in the title of the article or book. The first receives an "a" after the year, the second a "b," and so on. The "a" and "b" are also used in the text reference so the reader can find the exact source being referenced. See Chapter 12 for an example of this.

In the second example, several specific researchers are being identified, so their names (alphabetically arranged by first author) and years are enclosed in parentheses and works are separated by semicolons. When a source has two authors, always give both names (joined by an ampersand). When there are three to five authors, list all names the first time the reference is mentioned in the text—for example, (Polk, Erickson, Adams, & Johnson, 1980)—and abbreviate, as in the second example, for the next and subsequent mentions (Polk et al., 1980). Whenever a source has six or more authors, always use this abbreviated convention (et al.) in the text, even the first time the reference is mentioned.

The third example shows how sources of quotations are cited. Note the page number of the quotation is given at the end of the sentence before the period. Had the author's name not been integrated into the sentence as it was here, it would be placed, along with the year, with the page number, as follows:

> "The research findings clearly indicate support for the hypotheses" (Douglass, 1986, p. 55).

MANUSCRIPT STYLE

■ TYPING

Using standard 8 1/2-inch by 11-inch paper, create margins of at least 1 inch on the top, bottom, and sides. This allows a maximum 6 1/2-inch typed line (65 characters in pica [10 pitch] and 78 characters in elite [12 pitch]). Do *not* justify the right margin or hyphenate words, even if your software program wants to do it automatically for you. Double space everything. Just set your typewriter or computer software to double space and everything should conform to APA style. Put no more than 27 lines of text on a page. Check with your instructor, adviser, or graduate school for possible alterations to these standard typing instructions.

■ FORMAT

APA style suggests a standard system of setting up and ordering the pages of a manuscript. See pp. 7–21 and the sample paper on pp. 258–272 of the APA *Publication Manual*.

Title Page

Papers begin with a title page. Type a *page header* (the first few words of the title) in the upper right-hand corner, with the page number several spaces to its right. Page headers should be consistent on every page of the manuscript. Then, starting flush left across the top of the page (but below the page header), type "Running head:" and insert a shortened title in the space. This would be the abbreviated title appearing at the top of published pages (50 characters or less, all in capital letters). Then, about centered in the middle of the page are the paper's complete title (in uppercase and lowercase letters), below which are the author's name and institutional affiliation. Double-space between lines of the title, as well as between title, author, and affiliation.

Abstract

On the next page (page 2), comes the abstract. In one double-spaced paragraph, concisely summarize what the paper or study is about: the problem, method, findings, and conclusions. Do not indent the first line of the abstract as you would normally indent paragraphs. The abstract should be 100 to 120 words for empirical papers and 75 to 100 words for review or conceptual papers.

Text

The text begins on the next page (page 3). Most research reports are broken into sections, and headings help the reader see where the different sections begin and end. Headings and subheadings also help readers see the flow of the text and orient them to the thesis of each area.

Most journal articles have two or three levels of headings; longer manuscripts might use more than three levels. The headings should be precise and clearly worded and their format standardized throughout the paper. The form of the heading depends on how many levels you need throughout the paper. For example, if you need three levels of headings beyond the title, center the first level and type in both uppercase and lowercase letters. Position the second level flush left and type in both uppercase and lowercase letters and underline. Indent (as you would a normal paragraph) and underline the third level heading; type the heading in lowercase letters (with the first letter of the first word capitalized) and end the heading with a period. The paragraph begins one space after that period. This format is as follows:

First-Level Heading

<u>Second-Level Heading</u>

<u>Third-level heading.</u> Begin text of paragraph . . .

Because the entire manuscript is double spaced when typed, the text is double spaced before and after the first- and second-level headings (extra space is not used above and below headings). Pages 92–93 of the APA *Publication Manual* contain examples of headings when more than or fewer than three levels are needed.

References

These begin on a new page following the end of the text of the manuscript. Center the heading References at the top of the page and begin typing them, after a normal double space. Check with others to see if there might be a different style operating at your university.

Appendix

If you have appendixes, they come next. Center Appendix A at the top of the first appendix and center the title in uppercase and lowercase under it. Remember to double space before the title.

Notes

Author notes and content footnotes follow any appendixes. Content footnotes are used sparingly in APA style. They are occasionally used to add important information to the points made in the text. Use footnotes only when the flow of the discussion would be broken by incorporating this information directly into the text.

Center the heading Footnotes at the top of the page and then sequentially number and enter each note, using a five- to seven-space paragraph indentation for the first line of each; place the footnote number slightly above and to the left of the first word of each note. In the text, number all notes consecutively and type the numbers (called superscripts) slightly above the end of the line of text (following any punctuation marks except a dash).

Tables, Figure Captions, and Figures

Place tables, figure captions, and figures at the end of the manuscript. Tables and figures require a very specific format. Quantitative tables contain exact values of data (usually statistics) in columns and rows. Qualitative tables contain words instead of numbers. Figures are charts, graphs, pictures, or drawings that extend and clarify the content of the paper.

APA style suggests that you use tables and figures sparingly. If you have only a few statistics to report, incorporate them into the text of the paper. For a large number of statistics, use a quantitative table and do not duplicate the numbers in the text. Tables need descriptive headings and clear labels for the variables in the columns and rows. Headings for both tables and figures should clearly identify the content. Table 1 is an example of how to present a table. Again, the APA *Publication Manual* provides more specific information on how to format tables (pp. 120–141) and present figures (pp. 141–163).

Table 1 Percentage of Employed U.S. College Students

WORK HOURS PER WEEK	REGION			
	SOUTHEAST	NORTHEAST	MIDWEST	WEST[a]
0	25	20	21	22
1–10	35	39	40	37
11–20	19	20	30	30
21–30	10	12	6	9
31–40	8	8	3	2
Over 40	3	1	0	0

Note. These are fictitious data created just for this book.
[a] Includes Alaska and Hawaii.

REFERENCES

American Psychological Association. (1994). *Publication manual of the American Psychological Association* (4th ed.). Washington, DC: Author.

Harvard Law Review Association. (1996). *The bluebook: A uniform system of citation* (16th ed.). Cambridge, MA: Author.

appendix B

Social and Psychological Antecedents of VCR Use

The videocassette recorder (VCR) has become a socially significant communication technology as it moved into the home in the 1980s. VCRs provide expanded content and context options over traditional media. They accentuate choice, involvement, and control, and highlight the active and interactive nature of personal and mediated communication. Research about the nature and impact of VCRs, however, is limited even though over 60% of all U.S. households now have VCRs.

We take a uses and gratifications (U&G) approach to studying VCRs. U&G is based on the tenet that social and psychological factors influence people's motives to communicate, choices of communication alternatives, behavior, and communication effects. An underlying U&G assumption is that people choose to communicate purposely to satisfy felt needs; this behavior produces gratifications. . . .

U&G is especially appropriate for studying VCRs, which invite active audience participation by allowing greater control over viewing choices than traditional media. . . . Our goal is to explain social and psychological antecedents of VCR use, and to consider the interplay of personal and mediated communication. We test a model by which we expect VCR motives to complement interpersonal communication motives, which are influenced by life position, which is affected by personality and demographic factors.

Motives for Using VCRs

Harvey and Rothe (1985–1986) identified six basic reasons to use VCRs: to zap commercials, to time shift, to establish an environment for children, to increase viewing choices, to increase noncommercial viewing by building a library of programs, and to fast view by zipping through programs. Time shifting and increasing viewing choices were the most important uses. . . .

This chapter is condensed from Rubin, A. M., & Rubin, R. B. (1989). Social and psychological antecedents of VCR use. In M. R. Levy (Ed.), *The VCR age: Home video and mass communication* (pp. 92–111). Newbury Park, CA: Sage. Copyright 1989 by Alan M. Rubin and Rebecca B. Rubin. Reprinted by permission of the authors.

Rubin and Bantz (1987, 1988) . . . found eight interrelated motives for using VCRs [and] . . . proposed that VCR use is active behavior that complements and extends other modes of communication. VCR use is a functional alternative to interpersonal communication. They argued that we need to examine VCR use in relation to interpersonal communication and to examine the social and psychological antecedents of VCR use, including how an individual's life position and sense of life control affect VCR use. . . .

Personal and Mediated Communication

Although U&G typically has been used in mass communication, we have proposed its relevance for interpersonal communication (A. Rubin & Rubin, 1985). Interpersonal channels are need-gratification alternatives, which may be coequal to mediated channels. For example, one can gratify companionship needs by conversing with a friend or by listening to talk radio. Social and psychological antecedents affect both interpersonal and media motives. . . .

The social nature of VCR use requires consideration of interpersonal and social interaction. Schoenbach and Hackforth (1987) found that West German video households have more leisure-time activities, and that nonusers of VCRs are not more physically active than VCR users. In a study of interpersonal communication and media consumption in Saudi Arabia, Al-Attibi (1986) found that interpersonal communication fulfills adolescents' affective, entertainment, and escape needs, whereas the media gratified information needs. . . .

Life Position and Communication

Life position affects both personal and mediated communication. We have conceptualized life position as "contextual age," a constellation of social, psychological, economic, health, and communication indicators of age (A. Rubin & Rubin, 1982). We developed contextual age as an alternative to chronological age because the latter improperly assumes homogeneity along such life-position dimensions as life satisfaction, mobility, and interaction (A. Rubin & Rubin, 1986). . . .

Life position affects how people use media (A. Rubin & Rubin, 1982; R. Rubin & Rubin, 1982). For example . . . those low in life satisfaction and economic security tend to watch television for companionship and escape. Wenner (1976) found that . . . socially mobile elderly, for example, use television to avoid social contact with others, but socially isolated elderly use television content to facilitate interaction with others. . . .

Locus of Control

The notion of "control" also is important when addressing communication behavior. . . . Locus of control affects behavior (Rotter, 1954). "Internals" feel they control events in their lives, whereas "externals" view life outcomes as dependent on luck, chance, or powerful others. Pointing to the research of Williams, Phillips, and Lum (1985) and Schoenbach and Hackforth (1987), Levy (1987) asked whether consumers use VCRs for control.

Locus of control commonly refers to a person's mastery of his or her environment and life. Locus of control is consistent with U&G's active audience concept. Active audience members seek to gratify their needs and control their actions. According to Brenders (1987), "internals should be motivated to seek out, exert greater effort in, and derive greater satisfaction from situations allowing personal control" (p. 96). . . .

Demographic Characteristics

Demography affects life position and communication behavior. For example, we have found . . . age to relate positively to economic security and life satisfaction but negatively to health and mobility (A. Rubin & Rubin, 1986). Demography also affects VCR use. When examining the social context of VCR viewing in Great Britain, Gunter and Levy (1987) found male/female differences and that most VCR playback is done alone. A. Rubin and Bantz (1987) identified age and gender differences in why VCRs were used. And, Dobrow (1987) linked VCR use with education, income, and ethnic background. . . .

Model of VCR Use

In this study, then, we employed a U&G orientation to examine antecedents of VCR use. . . . The model outlines an expected sequence to the social and psychological antecedents of VCR use: demography and locus of control influence a person's social and psychological well-being or life position, life position affects motives for interpersonal communication, interpersonal motives lead to VCR motives, and VCR motives affect the frequency of VCR use.

Method

Sample and Procedures

Similar to past survey-research studies (e.g., A. Rubin & Bantz, 1987; R. Rubin, Perse, & Barbato, 1988), we included a wide range of people in the sample by using purposive quota sampling. Students enrolled in two undergraduate communication research classes at Kent State University were given specific age and gender sampling quotas. We trained these assistants in data collection and research ethics, and instructed them to solicit one male and one female of various educational backgrounds from each of four age groups to represent the general population: 18–34, 35–49, 50–64, and 65 years and over. Questionnaires were anonymous and individually self-administered. . . . A total of 428 completed questionnaires were returned; 299 of these respondents

(69.9%) owned or used a VCR at home. The latter group constituted the sample for this study.

Respondents in the VCR sample ranged in age from 18 to 75 ($M = 42.99$, $SD = 15.39$); 52.8% were male (0 = male, 1 = female), 67.6% were presently married, and 79.4% were employed outside the home. . . .

Measurement

Locus of control. We measured locus of control (LOC) with Levenson's (1974) scale. . . . Respondents reported their agreement with 12 statements (1 = *strongly disagree*, 5 = *strongly agree*). Four summed and averaged items represented each of three LOC dimensions: *Powerful Others Control* ($M = 2.43$, $SD = 0.69$, alpha = .70), *Internal Control* ($M = 3.69$, $SD = 0.57$, alpha = .64), and *Chance Control* ($M = 2.46$, $SD = 0.66$, alpha = .66). . . .

Contextual age. Contextual age (CA) reflects life position rather than just chronological age (A. Rubin & Rubin, 1986). Respondents stated their agreement with 18 statements (1 = *strongly disagree,* 5 = *strongly agree*). Three summed and averaged items were used for each of four CA dimensions: *Physical Health* ($M = 3.66$, $SD = 0.77$, alpha = .62), *Mobility* ($M = 4.11$, $SD = 0.85$, alpha = .65), *Life Satisfaction* ($M = 3.66$, $SD = 0.71$, alpha = .72), and *Economic Security* ($M = 3.10$, $SD = 0.92$, alpha = .81). To improve reliability, we combined the six interpersonal interaction and social activity items into a fifth CA dimension of *Interaction* ($M = 3.31$, $SD = 0.63$, alpha = .62). . . .

Interpersonal communication motives. We used the Interpersonal Communication Motives scale to measure interpersonal (IP) motives (R. Rubin et al., 1988). Respondents reported how much each of 18 statements was like their own reasons for talking to people (1 = *not at all*, 5 = *exactly*). Three summed and averaged items were used for each of six IP motives: *Relaxation* ($M = 3.02$, $SD = 0.85$, alpha = .75), *Pleasure* ($M = 3.48$, $SD = 0.87$, alpha = .80), *Control* ($M = 2.47$, $SD = 0.88$, alpha = .69), *Inclusion* ($M = 2.99$, $SD = 0.97$, alpha = .77), *Affection* ($M = 3.75$, $SD = 0.76$, alpha = .74), and *Escape* ($M = 2.25$, $SD = 0.87$, alpha = .66). . . .

VCR motives. We adapted earlier measures of . . . VCR use (A. Rubin & Bantz, 1987) to assess motives for using a VCR. Respondents stated how much each of 22 reasons for using a VCR at home was like their own reasons (1 = *not at all*, 5 = *exactly*). Given the exploratory level of this analysis compared with the previous established scales, responses were subjected to principal components factor analysis with iterations and oblique rotation (SPSS, 1988). The factor solution explained 63.9% of the total variance. . . . There were five factors [*Library Storage, Social Interaction, Freedom of Choice, Learning,* and *Time Shifting*]. . . . Freedom of choice and time shifting were the two most salient VCR motives.

VCR frequency. We asked respondents to estimate . . . how many days each week they usually use a VCR at home, and, on those days they use a VCR, how many hours each day they usually use the VCR to watch or record programs or tapes. . . . Daily VCR use averaged 2.51 hours ($SD = 1.64$) on an average 2.29 days ($SD = 1.77$) each week. We multiplied the days per week and hours per day of VCR use to create an index of weekly VCR frequency ($M = 6.63$ hours, $SD = 8.49$).

Results

Correlates of VCR Motives and Frequency

We first looked at the partial correlates of VCR motives and frequency. Several conclusions are evident from the data. . . . First, VCR motives were interrelated. The strongest associations were between using the VCR for: library storage and both time shifting and social interaction, and freedom of choice and time shifting. Second, VCR motives correlated more with interpersonal motives than with other antecedents. . . . Third, VCR frequency of use was linked more to motives for using VCRs than to other variables. VCR frequency correlates were: library storage, freedom of choice, time shifting, and social interaction VCR motives; less education; LOC external, powerful others, and chance control; and IP control.

Predictors of VCR Motives and Frequency

Next, we asked which antecedent variables best explained VCR motives. We regressed each VCR motive on blocks of antecedent variables, which were entered into the equation based on the conceptual model: (a) demography, (b) locus of control, (c) contextual age, and (d) interpersonal motives. . . . To locate predictors of VCR frequency, we also regressed frequency on the same blocks of antecedent variables with the addition of VCR motives on a fifth step. . . . Five of the six equations were significant. . . .

Significant final predictors of the library storage VCR motive were: communicating interpersonally for control, larger household size, and male gender. The measures explained 11.7% of the library storage variance. . . .

Significant final predictors of the social interaction VCR motive were: communicating interpersonally for inclusion, escape, and affection, CA interaction, CA immobility, and younger age. The measures explained 31.1% of the social interaction variance. . . .

At the conclusion of the analysis, the only significant predictor of the freedom of choice VCR motive was LOC internal control. The measures explained 12.6% of the freedom of choice variance. . . .

Although communicating interpersonally for control predicted the learning VCR motive, the regression equation was not significant. The predictors explained only 8.3% of the learning variance. . . .

Significant final predictors of the time shifting VCR motive were: communicating interpersonally for control, CA life dissatisfaction, and younger age. The measures explained 12.8% of the time shifting variance. . . .

Significant final predictors of VCR frequency were: VCR library storage and freedom of choice motivation, LOC external control, and less education. The measures explained 21.1% of the VCR frequency variance.

Multivariate Relationships: VCR Use and Antecedents

In the last stage of the analysis, we used canonical correlation to assess the multivariate relationships among the set of antecedents to VCR use and the set of VCR motives and frequency. We included only those antecedents that were significant contributors in the regressions. . . . The analysis identified two significant roots.

The first canonical root (R_C = .58, lambda = .47, p < .001) explained 33.1% of the common variance between the variates. . . . Across the sets, younger, interactive, but less mobile persons, who communicated with others for reasons of inclusion, escape, and affection, used VCRs primarily for social interaction, and to store tapes, for convenient choice, and to time shift.

The second canonical root (R_C = .39, lambda = .70, p < .001) explained 14.9% of the common variance between the variates. . . . Across the sets, less educated and externally controlled persons, who were less satisfied with their lives, were more frequent users of VCRs primarily to shift time rather than for convenient choice.

Discussion

The VCR is an evolutionary technology that is more than an appendage to television. VCRs allow us to use traditional channels of communication, such as television and interpersonal interaction, in different ways. . . .

Our results reinforce previous U&G notions. First, communication motives are interrelated. . . . The VCR is a convenient and economical mechanism for communication storage and retrieval. Convenience, choice-making ability, time restructuring, and social utility are central to VCR use. Such components reinforce earlier contentions that "VCR use is indeed active behavior" (A. Rubin & Bantz, 1988, p. 191).

Second, motives to communicate interpersonally predict motives for using a VCR. Communicating interpersonally for reasons of inclusion, affection, and escape predicted social interaction motives for using the VCR. . . . VCR use links interpersonal and mass communication (A. Rubin & Bantz, 1987); and VCR use increases time spent with family and friends (Harvey & Rothe, 1985–1986; Roe, 1987). . . .

In addition, communicating interpersonally to achieve control (i.e., getting others to do something) predicted several VCR motives: time shifting, library storage, and learning. This supports Schutz's (1966) notion that control is an interpersonal communication need, yet further suggests that those who seek to achieve control can do so in both personal and mediated contexts. . . .

Third, there are social and psychological antecedents to communication motivation, which explain VCR use. External locus of control and less education predicted frequency of VCR use. Perhaps the externally controlled use VCRs as a way to increase feelings of control in their lives. . . . Internal locus of control was the best predictor of the VCR freedom of choice motivation, which was a personal control factor emphasizing choice over what to watch, freedom to set one's own schedule, and multiple viewing options. . . .

We found support, then, for U&G assumptions that there are social and psychological antecedents to communication motives and behavior, which must be examined and understood. In this study, social demography, psychological predispositions, and life position contribute to our understanding of VCR motives and behavior.

There are several directions for future research. Beyond motives, we need to consider . . . what is being taped or replayed by VCR users and . . . to examine the consequences of VCR use for social interaction and interpersonal relationships. How do VCRs alter family interaction and the home environment? . . . Do VCRs compensate for interpersonal communication deficiencies of the immobile or media dependent? Consequences also extend to societal structures. For example, how do VCRs affect network television programming and . . . the music industry?

References

Al-Attibi, A. A. M. (1986). Interpersonal communication competence and media consumption and needs among young adults in Saudi Arabia (Doctoral dissertation, Ohio State University, 1986). *Dissertation Abstracts International, 47*, 10A.

Brenders, D. A. (1987). Perceived control: Foundations and directions for communication research. *Communication Yearbook, 10*, 86–116.

Dobrow, J. R. (1987). The social and cultural implications of the VCR: How VCR use concentrates and diversifies viewing (Doctoral dissertation, University of Pennsylvania, 1987). *Dissertation Abstracts International, 48*, 03A.

Gunter, B., & Levy, M. R. (1987). Social contexts of video use. *American Behavioral Scientist, 30*, 486–494.

Harvey, M. G., & Rothe, J. T. (1985–1986). Video cassette recorders: Their impact on viewers and advertisers. *Journal of Advertising Research, 25*(6), 19–27.

Levenson, H. (1974). Activism and powerful others: Distinctions within the concept of internal-external control. *Journal of Personality Assessment, 38*, 377–383.

Levy, M. R. (1987). Some problems of VCR research. *American Behavioral Scientist, 30*, 461–470.

Roe, K. (1987). Adolescents' video use. *American Behavioral Scientist, 30*, 522–532.

Rotter, J. B. (1954). *Social learning and clinical psychology*. Englewood Cliffs, NJ: Prentice Hall.

Rubin, A. M., & Bantz, C. R. (1987). Utility of videocassette recorders. *American Behavioral Scientist, 30*, 471–485.

Rubin, A. M., & Bantz, C. R. (1988). Uses and gratifications of videocassette recorders. In J. Salvaggio & J. Bryant (Eds.), *Media use in the information age* (pp. 181–195). Hillsdale, NJ: Erlbaum.

Rubin, A. M., & Rubin, R. B. (1982). Contextual age and television use. *Human Communication Research, 8*, 228–244.

Rubin, A. M., & Rubin, R. B. (1985). Interface of personal and mediated communication: A research agenda. *Critical Studies in Mass Communication, 2*, 36–53.

Rubin, A. M., & Rubin, R. B. (1986). Contextual age as a life-position index. *International Journal of Aging and Human Development, 23*, 27–45.

Rubin, R. B., Perse, E. M., & Barbato, C. A. (1988). Conceptualization and measurement of interpersonal communication motives. *Human Communication Research, 14*, 602–628.

Rubin, R. B., & Rubin, A. M. (1982). Contextual age and television use: Reexamining a life-position indicator. *Communication Yearbook, 6*, 583–604.

Schoenbach, K., & Hackforth, J. (1987). Video in West German households. *American Behavioral Scientist, 30*, 533–543.

Schutz, W. C. (1966). *The interpersonal underworld*. Palo Alto, CA: Science and Behavior Books.

SPSS, Inc. (1988). *SPSS-X user's guide* (3rd ed.). Chicago: Author.

Wenner, L. (1976). Functional analysis of TV viewing for older adults. *Journal of Broadcasting, 20*, 77–88.

Williams, F., Phillips, A. F., & Lum, P. (1985). Gratifications associated with new communication technologies. In K. E. Rosengren, L. A. Wenner, & P. Palmgreen (Eds.), *Media gratifications research: Current perspectives* (pp. 241–252). Beverly Hills: Sage.

appendix C

Glossary

abstract   (a) A paragraph-length or longer summary or condensation of an *article,* book, or other work. (b) A *periodical* composed of summaries of scholarly *research reports* and theoretical articles that have been published in *journals* and books. Some abstracts also include summary descriptions of books and dissertations.

abstracting service   (a) An organization that produces *abstracts.* (b) Abstracts supplied to subscribers by an organization.

access point   Any searchable field in a record in a *computerized database*. Access points in most *bibliographic databases* include author, article title, journal title, *subject headings* or *descriptors*, and *key words* in each of these fields as well as in the abstract field. Access points in searchable full-text documents include, in addition, all the words in the text. *Stop words* are not access points.

access tool   Bibliographic work or *computerized database* that can be used to locate sources of information on a topic. Examples include *periodical index, abstracting service, bibliography, catalog, on-line* or *computerized database*, and *directory.*

accidental sample   A *nonprobability sampling* technique in which those people who happen to be available are chosen for the *sample.*

almanac   A yearly compendium of factual information.

annotated bibliography   A list of writings or other materials that includes short descriptions or evaluations in addition to citations.

annotation   A short description of a published work. Critical annotations also evaluate the works described.

annual   A publication that appears once a year.

annual review   An *annual* that provides summaries of scholarly research activities in a particular content area.

APA style (format)   The style recommended by the American Psychological Association for referencing information in scholarly publications and for arranging information in *citations* and *bibliographies*.

NOTE: Terms appearing in *italics* are included in this glossary.

appended bibliography   A list of writings or other materials that appears at the end of a book, *article*, or other work.

archival/documentary research   Inquiry that centers on finding, examining, and interpreting messages. Common forms include *library/documentary research, historical research, critical/rhetorical research*, and *legal research*, as well as *textual analysis, secondary analysis, conversation analysis*, and *content analysis*.

archive   (a) An organized body of public records or historical documents. (b) An institution that collects, preserves, and provides services related to the use of stored materials.

article   A manuscript published in a *journal*, other *periodical*, or an *encyclopedia*.

artifact-oriented research   See *message-* or *artifact-oriented research*.

audience   The target of a class project: the class members, the general public, the instructor, or a specific societal group.

behavior-oriented research   See *people-* or *behavior-oriented research*.

bibliographic database   A *computerized database* that consists primarily of *citations* to publications and sometimes includes *abstracts*.

bibliographic style   The style used for arranging information in a *citation* or a *bibliography*. Examples: *APA style* and *MLA style*.

bibliography   A list of writings or other materials, usually compiled on the basis of topic, author, or some other element common to the entries and systematically arranged. Types of bibliographies include *annotated, appended, current, general, retrospective,* and *selective topical*.

bibliography card   A note card on which the complete *citation* for a publication is entered by a researcher as a record-keeping and record-finding device. It includes a brief summary of the contents of the publication.

bibliography-management program   Software program that facilitates the development and maintenance of personal *bibliographic databases*. Examples include EndNote, Reference Manager, and ProCite. These programs allow the user to create records or to download them directly from bibliographic databases, to add notes and *key words*, and to format the output in a variety of *bibliographic styles*, including APA and MLA. Some can be integrated into standard word processing programs.

bimonthly   A publication that appears every other month.

book stacks   Library book shelves or floors of the library containing retrievable books.

Boolean operator   See *logical (Boolean) operator*.

bound periodicals   Older *periodicals* in a library collection. Recent issues of periodicals normally accumulate until an entire volume can be collected together for binding.

broadcast index   A list of programs archived via audiotape or videotape that can be searched by title or subject.

browser   Software that provides an interface to the *World Wide Web*.

catalog   A systematic list of books and other materials that records, describes, and indexes the resources of one or more libraries or *collections*. Some library catalogs are still available on cards; some are published in book format or on *microfilm* or *microfiche*. Most library catalogs now allow *on-line* access.

CD-ROM   An abbreviation for "compact disk-read-only memory," this term usually refers to a small laser disk that stores electronic *data*.

citation   A reference note on the source of facts, quotations, and opinions. A complete citation contains sufficient bibliographic information to enable a researcher to locate the item.

citation index   A list of works that have been cited by subsequently published works. The listing is usually by cited author, enabling one to locate later works that have cited that author's *research*.

client   A computer or program that requests a service of another computer or program (called the *server*).

cluster sample   A *probability sampling* technique in which subgroups of a *population* are identified in stages, and then the *sample* is drawn randomly from the final subgroup.

collection   A compilation of documents or media of a similar type that are gathered together and published as *periodicals*, books, or in *microform*.

communications software   A software program that enables a computer equipped with a *modem* to communicate with another computer over telephone lines.

composite week   In *content analysis,* when a week is created by randomly selecting one Monday, one Tuesday, one Wednesday, and so on from all possible Mondays, Tuesdays, Wednesdays, and so on for the year.

computerized database   A *database* stored on a magnetic or optical medium so that it can be accessed by computer. Types of computerized databases include *bibliographic*, *directory*, *statistical*, *full-text*, *image,* and *source*.

Comserve   An electronic information service for the communication field available through e-mail.

conceptual definition   Terms used to describe the true meaning of a *variable*.

content analysis   Examination of the structure and content of messages, particularly those in the media.

control   (a) One aim of science (in addition to theory, explanation, understanding, and prediction). (b) To test or verify by means of conducting an experiment in a contained atmosphere.

control group   The group of individuals that does not receive the experimental treatment.

controlled vocabulary   The set of *subject headings* or *descriptors* used by a particular *index, abstracting service, catalog*, or *computerized database* to describe listed works.

conversation analysis   Examination of the structure, messages, function, rules, and content of conversations.

critical paper   A treatise that analyzes and evaluates literature and draws conclusions about the subject.

critical/rhetorical research   Selection and application of appropriate criteria to interpret and to evaluate a communication event and its consequences.

cumulation   The contents of successive volumes of a title incorporated into one volume. The current issues of printed *periodical indexes*, for example, are usually cumulated into volumes covering a longer time period.

current bibliography   A list of writings or other materials that is updated on a regular basis.

data   Information that is observed or gathered in the conduct of *research*.

database   A collection of information organized in such a way that specific items can be retrieved.

database producer   An organization that compiles and publishes *computerized databases*.

dependent variable   The consequent or presumed effect in a relationship between two or more *variables*.

descriptive research   An identification and description of events or conditions.

descriptor   A word or phrase under which publications dealing with a particular *subject* are listed in a *periodical index*. See also *subject headings*.

dictionary   A book or *computerized database* containing a collection of words, together with their meanings, equivalents, derivation, syllabication, and other useful information. *Subject dictionaries*, which define terms in a particular *discipline* or of a highly specialized nature, often include relatively extended *encyclopedia*-type entries.

directory   A systematically arranged list of individuals, institutions, or organizations, giving addresses, activities, publications, and other information.

directory database   A *computerized database* that contains references to organizations, people, grants, research projects, contracts, and so forth. See also *web directory*.

discipline   A branch of knowledge and the individuals who teach and *research* in it.

document delivery service   A service offered by *database vendors*, allowing users to order publications *on-line* for delivery through the mail.

documentary research   See *archival/documentary research*.

domain   Portion of an *Internet* address that specifies the location of the addressee.

downloading   The practice of transferring *data* from a larger computer to a smaller one.

e-mail   Electronic mail or messages that are sent via computer networks.

encyclopedia   A comprehensive compilation of information, usually arranged alphabetically by topic in essays and providing overviews that typically include definitions, descriptions, background, and bibliographic references. General encyclopedias attempt to encompass all branches of knowledge, whereas subject encyclopedias limit coverage to a specific *discipline*.

ethnography   *Observational research* used to describe social norms and events as they occur.

exemplary literature review   An examination and description of only those materials that pertain most closely to the topic.

exhaustive literature review   An examination and description of all materials on a topic.

experimental design   A plan or blueprint for the conduct of *experimental research*.

experimental group   The group in an experiment that receives the experimental treatment or manipulation.

experimental research   An investigation of communication events under *controlled* conditions. Usually, the goals are to explain and to predict relationships among *variables*.

explanatory research   Inquiry that looks for underlying causes and explanations of events.

external validity   The results of an empirical *research* study that are generalizable to other people, situations, times, and so forth.

field   Part of a *record* used in a *database* to hold particular information about each document. *Bibliographic databases* include such fields as title, author, journal name, publication year, *abstract*, and *subject heading* or *descriptor*.

field research   See *nonlaboratory research*.

finding tool   See *access tool*.

focus group   Intensive group interviewing used to understand consumer attitudes and behaviors.

free-text searching   A method of searching *computerized databases* in which all words in a *record* or *citation* can be searched. Free-text searching uses *natural language* rather than a *controlled vocabulary*. This type of searching is often called *key-word searching*.

full-image database   See *image database*.

full-text database   A *computerized database* that contains the complete text of publications such as *journals,* newspapers, books, and so forth. Every word of the entire text of these publications can be searched.

full-text periodicals   Publications that contain complete articles.

general bibliography   A list of writings or other materials that includes *citations* of materials on a variety of topics.

goal   The aim of a particular project: to inform, persuade, or inform and persuade.

gopher   A menu-driven information system that transparently connects users to other *Internet* sites. Gopher was the predecessor to the *World Wide Web*, and some resources accessed through the web are still on a gopher system.

government document   Any printed matter originating from or printed at the expense or with the authority of an office of a legally organized government. Types include hearings, committee prints, and reports.

guide to the literature   A type of reference that lists and annotates available sources (for example, *directories, indexes*, and *journals*) for a specific *discipline* or subject area. Guides sometimes offer descriptions of the literature in a field, recommend effective *search strategies*, and identify organizations that may provide additional information to researchers.

handbook   A compact book of facts, sometimes called a *manual*. Scholarly or subject handbooks organize, summarize, and make readily accessible a body of information about a field of study.

historical research   An examination of past observations to understand the events that occurred.

hit   A record that the computer has found containing the *descriptor* or *key word* that is used with a *computerized database* search. It is sometimes termed a "posting."

home page   The default document *World Wide Web* users see when connecting for the first time to a particular WWW server. From the home page, the user goes to other *web pages* on the *website*.

html (hypertext markup language)   The language used to write *hypertext* documents for the *World Wide Web*.

http (hypertext transport protocol)   The program that establishes connections between *hypertext* documents on *World Wide Web*.

hyperlink   A connection on *World Wide Web* documents to another Web resource that can be activated by clicking. Textual hyperlinks are usually underlined and/or highlighted in color. They may also be an icon, image, or button.

hypertext   A document that includes links to other documents.

hypertext markup language See *html*.

hypertext transport protocol See *http*.

hypothesis   An educated guess or prediction about the relationship among two or more *variables*.

identifier   A type of *controlled vocabulary* used by ERIC for subject retrieval.

image database   A *computerized database* that contains graphic images such as photographs, reproductions of artworks, and textual material.

implied Boolean symbol   A symbol used in a search *query* to designate *records* to be included (+) or excluded (−).

independent variable   The antecedent or presumed cause in a relationship between two or more *variables*.

index   A list (usually alphabetical) giving the location of materials, topics, names, and so forth in a work or group of specified works. Also, a shortened form of *periodical index*.

interface   The particular screen design and features used by a search system to facilitate communication between a user and a *computerized database.*

interlibrary loan system   A cooperative arrangement between libraries and groups of libraries by which one library may borrow material for its patrons from another.

internal validity   Indicates that the results of a study cannot be explained in any other way. That is, little or no fault can be found with the study's sampling method, measuring instruments, and *research* design.

Internet   An international network of computer networks used to access *computerized databases*, communicate with others, and retrieve document files.

Internet protocol (IP) address   An *Internet* address expressed numerically.

intervening variable   A factor other than the *independent variable* that can affect the *dependent variable*.

interview   A qualitative technique used to probe *respondents'* attitudes and behaviors.

journal   A *periodical* containing *research reports* and *review articles* in a specific scholarly field or *discipline*.

key word Any word in a *database record* that can be searched to retrieve search results. In most *bibliographic databases*, any word in the title, *abstract*, and subject-heading *fields* is a key word. In a *full-text database*, any word in the body of the text may be a key word. Key words are not part of a *controlled vocabulary*. Therefore, searching that does not rely on *subject headings* or *descriptors* is often called *key-word searching*.

key-word searching A method of searching *computerized databases* in which the words in most or all *fields* in a *record* can be searched. Key-word searching uses *natural language* rather than a *controlled vocabulary*.

laboratory research Investigations conducted in surroundings that are new to the individuals being studied. Usually, laboratory research is conducted to strengthen the *control* of extraneous *variables*.

LC Abbreviation for the Library of Congress. *Library of Congress subject headings* are often called LC subject headings.

legal/policy research Inquiry into how law operates in society.

Library of Congress classification A system of subject classification of materials developed by the Library of Congress for its *collection*. It is widely used by college and university libraries in the United States to arrange and locate materials on shelves. Call numbers are composed of letters and numbers.

Library of Congress subject headings *Subject headings* developed by the U.S. Library of Congress. These are used in the *catalogs* of most academic and public libraries in the United States.

library/documentary research A review of existing documents or written, printed materials such as those found in a library.

listserv An electronic discussion group on a particular topic, which uses a mailing list software program to distribute messages to all members' *e-mail* boxes.

literature review A summary, synthesis, and evaluation of previous *research* about a topic. Two types are *exemplary* and *exhaustive*.

literature search Systematically seeking published material on a specific subject.

logical (Boolean) operators A word such as AND, OR, or NOT, which is used in *database* searching to combine words and concepts.

magazine A type of *periodical* intended for general reading or for a particular profession.

manual A compact book of facts. Manuals are similar to *handbooks,* but the term "manual" more specifically denotes how-to guides for accomplishing specific tasks.

media index A finding tool for newspaper materials, films, television videotapes, and reviews of these.

message-/artifact-oriented research Scientific inquiry that examines messages and attitudes associated with messages. Types include *archival/documentary* and *survey research*.

metasearch engine A *search engine* that automatically submits a search *query* to several other search engines.

microfiche   Positive or negative sheet film (usually 4 inches by 6 inches) used for compact storage of information.

microfilm   Positive or negative roll film, loose or in a cartridge, which is used for compact storage of information.

microform   The general term for either *microfiche* or *microfilm*.

MLA style (format)   The style recommended by the Modern Language Association for referencing information in scholarly publications and for arranging information in *citations* or *bibliographies*.

modem   Equipment used with computers to translate digital computer signals into analog telephone signals, making it possible to transmit *data* between computers over telephone lines.

monograph   A book that treats a single subject within a single volume.

multimedia database   A collection of *data* that includes media such as audio, graphic images, and video.

natural language   (a) Words and phrases, in no particular order or arrangement, used to conduct *natural language searches*. (b) A term used in *computerized-database* searching to distinguish between the vocabulary available for *key-word searching* and a *controlled vocabulary*, consisting of *descriptors* or *subject headings* listed in a *thesaurus*.

natural language searching system   Search system that allows *queries* to be entered informally, using *natural language* terms, phrases, and syntax. Queries can be stated in the form of a question. This type of search system contrasts with Boolean search systems.

network analysis   The study of behavioral interactions among organizational members.

newsgroup   An electronic discussion group on *Usenet*.

newspaper index   A list of articles, editorials, and reviews that have been published in a newspaper.

newsreader   A program that allows the user to access and participate in *Usenet* newsgroups.

noncirculating collection   A *collection* of library materials that may not be checked out for use outside the library. The *reference collection* of a library is usually noncirculating.

nonlaboratory research   An investigation conducted in naturalistic surroundings. The subjects may or may not be aware that *research* is being done.

nonprobability sampling   The nonrandom selection of members of a *population* for a *sample*.

observational research   A *nonlaboratory research* procedure where trained observers describe the behaviors or messages of the people or media being studied. Observational research includes *ethnography, participant observation, unobtrusive observation, network analysis,* and *verbal and nonverbal coding.*

on-line   A term used in on-line *database* searching, designating the direct interactive process of retrieving computer *data* while a search is in progress.

on-line catalog   A *bibliographic database* consisting of the holdings of a particular library.

Online Computer Library Center (OCLC) This service is used by many libraries to automate their cataloging and *interlibrary loan* procedures. OCLC makes the resulting *WorldCat* database available through their FirstSearch service. *WorldCat* includes the holdings of most academic and public libraries in the United States.

on-line search service A service offering access to *on-line databases* using search *protocols* usually specific to the service *vendor.*

operational definition A procedure followed to observe or to measure a *variable.*

operator A word or symbol used to create logical sets that can then be used to retrieve terms in various combinations. *Boolean operators* include AND, OR, and NOT. *Implied Boolean symbols* (operators) include "+" and "−".

participant observation An *observational research* technique used to study social situations or organizations where researchers participate in the observed environment.

people-/behavior-oriented research Scientific inquiry that examines people's behavior. Types include *observational* and *experimental research.*

periodical A publication with a distinctive title intended to appear at some specified interval (for example, daily, weekly, monthly, or *quarterly*). See also *journal* and *magazine.*

periodical index An *index* to *articles* published in many different *periodicals,* often including *abstracts* of articles. This term is often shortened to *index.*

plagiarism Using an author's words or ideas without giving credit.

poll *Survey research* used to describe the attitudes or opinions of a *sample.*

population People or objects that have some common characteristic. Researchers often draw a *sample* of this group to investigate for the purpose of generalizing to the larger population.

portal A *World Wide Web* site that offers a variety of resources and services, such as *e-mail*, a *search engine*, and shopping.

primary source A document, manuscript, record, recording, or an original published report of *research.* Primary sources are often written about or reworked, resulting in *secondary sources.* Legal primary sources include statutes, court decisions, executive orders, and treaties.

probability sampling The random selection of members of a *population* for a *sample.* The purpose is to generalize observations from that sample to the population.

professional magazine See *magazine.*

prospectus A proposal for a research study in which the author thoroughly reviews the supporting literature, sets up *hypotheses* or research questions, and details the methods that will be followed to answer the questions or test the hypotheses.

protocol The particular commands and techniques used in *on-line search* systems to create *search statements* to retrieve *citations* and other types of information.

proximity operator A word or symbol used to specify the closeness of *natural language* terms in *free-text* or *key-word searching* of *computerized* or *on-line databases.*

purposive sample   A *nonprobability sampling* technique in which the *sample* is selected to represent either a variety of *respondents* or respondents who possess a certain trait.

qualitative research   Inductive, interpretive methods of scientific inquiry.
quantitative research   Deductive, statistical methods of scientific inquiry.
quarterly   A publication that appears four times a year.
query   A request for information entered by a user of *computerized databases* that instructs the search system to retrieve a specified *set* of documents. Also termed a *search statement*.
quota sample   A *nonprobability sampling* technique in which members of a *sample* are chosen because they have a certain characteristic.

ratings   Measures of the size of broadcast audiences.
record   An entry in a *computerized database* that provides sufficient information about a publication or other information source to permit its identification and retrieval. Records include standardized *fields*, such as title, author, journal name, publisher, and *subject headings* or *descriptors*.
reference   See *citation*.
reference book   A book that forms part of the *reference collection* in a library. Reference books are generally meant to be consulted rather than read in their entirety. Examples include *encyclopedias, dictionaries, almanacs, yearbooks,* and *directories*. They are normally *noncirculating*.
reference collection   A library collection that houses *reference books*. This is normally a *noncirculating collection*.
reference librarian   A librarian who staffs the reference desk and can assist library patrons in locating suitable materials.
relevance ranking   The order used to list the results of a *database* search when the most relevant results are listed first and the least relevant are listed last. Relevance is determined automatically by a ranking algorithm that takes into account such factors as the number of search terms that appear in each document and where they appear. *Search engines* and *natural language search systems* usually rank results by relevance.
reliability   A measure's stability, consistency, and repeatability.
research   Objective, systematic, empirical, and cumulative inquiry into a subject.
research ethics   What is right and wrong in the conduct of *research*. Issues include honesty, harm, deception, informed consent, and privacy.
research report   A summary of an original *research* study typically consisting of four main sections: introduction, method, results, and discussion.
respondent   A participant in *survey research*.
retrospective bibliography   A list of writings or other materials that appears at a particular point in time and is not updated.
review article   A published manuscript that thoroughly examines the literature on a particular topic and presents original conclusions about the strength, sufficiency, or consistency of the information.
rhetorical research   See *critical/rhetorical research*.

sample   A subgroup of a *population* that is examined in a *research* study. Two methods of sampling are *probability* and *nonprobability*.

scholarly journal   See *journal*.

scope The breadth of a project; narrow, moderate, or broad. This is determined by amount of time allowed (for oral projects) or length of final copy (for written projects).

search engine   A *key-word searching* system that creates its own *database* of *World Wide Web* resources, and facilitates searches of this database through its own search interface. Most search engines allow the use of *Boolean*, *implied Boolean*, and adjacency *operators*. Some also allow *natural language searching*.

search statement   A request for information entered by a user of *computerized databases* that instructs the search system to retrieve a specified *set* of documents. Often called a search *query*.

search strategy   The organized plan by which a person conducts a *literature search*. In *computerized database* searching, it refers to a set of planned search statements that are to be entered into the search system to retrieve the desired records.

secondary analysis   Examination of previously gathered or archived *data*.

secondary source   A work that consists of information compiled from *primary*, or original, sources. Examples include *annual reviews, dictionaries*, document sourcebooks, *encyclopedias,* and *textbooks*.

selective topical bibliography   A list of writings or other materials that includes only *citations* to those materials judged to be most pertinent or valuable to a particular topic. It is not comprehensive.

semiannual   Published twice each year at 6-month intervals.

semimonthly   Published twice each month.

series   Separate works usually related by subject, author, or format that are assigned a collective series title and issued successively by a publisher.

server   A computer whose software allows it to store *data* and make it available to network users; users employ *client* software on their own workstations to access the *data*.

set   A group of *records* retrieved from a *computerized database* as the result of a particular *search statement*.

simple random sample   A *probability sampling* technique in which each person has an equal or known chance of being chosen for the *sample*.

source database   A *computerized database* that includes sufficiently complete information to satisfy an information need. *Full-text, statistical*, and *image databases* are examples.

statistical database   A *computerized database* that consists primarily of numerical or other statistical *data*.

statistical source   A reference work where census and other government or media statistics are reported.

stratified sample   A *probability sampling* technique in which the *sample* is selected from certain subgroups of the *population* to ensure adequate representation of those groups.

subject   A participant in *experimental research*.

subject dictionary A *dictionary* that resembles an *encyclopedia* in that it contains elongated meanings for the terminology of one subject area or discipline.

subject heading A word or group of words under which publications dealing with a particular subject are listed in a *catalog, periodical index, computerized database, abstracting service,* or *bibliography*. Subject headings are usually arranged alphabetically. See also *descriptor*.

survey research A *research* procedure used to collect information about conditions, events, opinions, people, organizations, and so forth. Survey researchers question members of a *sample* often to describe a *population*.

systematic sample A *probability sampling* technique in which every *n*th person or event is chosen for the *sample* from a list of persons or events.

textbook An overview and explanation of one or more topics presented in an easy-to-understand manner.

textual analysis Examination of media content or text in relation to *audience* interpretation.

thesaurus (a) A list of *descriptors* or *subject headings* and their related terms that accompanies a particular *computerized* or printed *index, abstracting service,* or *catalog* to indicate the specific indexing terms used in that source. (b) A book of synonyms and antonyms.

topical bibliography A list of *references* on one specific topic or theme.

trade magazine See *magazine*.

uniform resource locator (URL) A standardized way of representing the addresses of many types of resources on the *World Wide Web*, including *servers*, documents, media, *databases*, and network services.

union catalog A list of library contents for multiple libraries.

unobtrusive observation *Nonlaboratory research* where the researcher observes participants without their being aware that they're being observed.

Usenet A worldwide network of electronic discussion groups, or *newsgroups,* that can be accessed on most college and university campuses through a *newsreader* program.

validity Measuring what one intends to measure.

variable Something that can assume different values. A concept to which numbers are attached and that changes in value. For example, television viewing can be a variable with values that range from 0 to 24 hours each day; eye color can be a variable (blue = 1, green = 2, brown = 3, hazel = 4, and so forth).

vendor An organization supplying *on-line databases* to other organizations or individuals. Vendors are essentially retailers of on-line *databases*.

verbal and nonverbal coding Application of schemes to describe messages systematically.

web directory Listings of web resources arranged hierarchically by subject or type of resource. Directories may be searchable by *key word*. Directories may be called "virtual libraries," "meta" websites, "clearinghouses," and "subject guides." Some directories are devoted to a single subject area, others attempt to evaluate, select, and list sites (and other directories) from many subject areas.

web page   A single document, written in *html*. It may be thought of as a single screen, although the user may have to scroll to view the entire document.

website   A collection of web pages that are linked to each other and focused on a single subject. A website consists of a *home page* and other *web pages* and resources. The term may more generally refer to any *World Wide Web* resource.

World Wide Web   A system based on *hypertext* and other *hyperlinks* that allows the user to explore and connect to other *Internet* resources. Often abbreviated to "Web" or "WWW."

yearbook   An annual volume describing current developments in a specific field. Information may be given in narrative or statistical form.

Subject Index

CIOS, 49, 56, 120
Citation indexes, 125–26, 280
Citing sources, 264–65
Cluster sample, 202, 280
Coding, verbal and nonverbal, 206
Collections
    defined, 157, 158
    legal, 163
    measurement, 163–64
    media, 159–62
    selected finding aids, 176–77
    selected list, 174–176
    speech, 158–59
Comgrads, 56
Committee print, Congressional,
        169–170
Communication discipline, 2–9
Communication Institute for Online
        Scholarship (CIOS), 57
Comparison-and-contrast order, 236
Composite week, 200
Conceptual definition, 195–196, 280
Congressional Information Service, 165
Consequent, 195
Content analysis, 200, 280
Content footnote, 267
Contexts, communication, 3
Control groups, 208, 280
Controlled conditions, 207
Controlled vocabulary, 70–72, 280
Convenience sample, 202
Conversation analysis, 199, 280
Copy-editing symbols, 226–227
Critical abstract, 233
Critical papers, 238–39
Critical theory, 198
Critical/rhetorical research, 198–199,
        280
CRTNET, 54
C-SPAN archives, 161

D
Data gathering and analysis, 196
Databases
    bibliographic, 67–68, 278
    directory, 68, 281
    evaluation, 119
    full-text, 68, 282
    image, 283
    multimedia, 69, 286
    producers, 118–119, 281
    searching, 69–82

source, 68, 289
statistical, 68, 289
types, 66–69
vendors, 118–119
web-based, 69
Data-collection methods, 201
Dependent variable, 195, 281
Descriptive research, 194, 281
Descriptors, 281
DIALOG searches, 85
Dictionaries
    media, 173–174
    selected, 183–185
    subject, 98
Directories
    communication, 49–52
    media, 181–182
    selected list, 183
Directory databases, 68
Discipline, communication, 3–9
Doctoral dissertations, bibliographic
        format, 259
Document delivery services, 85

E
Eastern Communication Association
        (ECA), 8
Editorial study, 198
Educational Resources Information
        Center (ERIC), 6, 122–123
Electronic discussion groups, 54–57
Electronic Industries Association, 165
Electronic media collections, 159–162
Electronic sources, bibliographic
        format, 263–264
EMPATHY, 54
Empirical research, 193
Encyclopedias
    defined, 97, 281
    selected list, 104–105
    subject, 97
    types, 97
Endnotes, 218–223
ERIC, 6, 122–123
Ethics, research, 210–211
Ethnography, 200, 205, 281
Evaluation of sources, 28–30, 52–53
Experimental design, 209, 281
Experimental group, 282
Experimental research, 206–210, 282
Explanatory research, 194, 282
External validity, 210, 282

F

Federal Communications Commission (FCC), 162
Federal Radio Commission, 163
Field experimental settings, 211
Field research, 209
Field-specific online searching, 76–78
FirstSearch, 76, 113, 118
Focus groups, 204
FOI-L, 54
Footnotes, 224–25
Full-text databases, 24, 68, 118, 282

G

Gallup, 166
General search-record card, 35
General-to-specific order, 236
General-to-specific search strategy, 26
Government publications
  defined, 166–70, 282
  selected finding aids, 168–170
  selected list, 178–179
Grammar, 220
Guides to the literature
  defined, 113, 282
  selected list, 130–132
  types, 113–115

H

Handbooks
  defined, 93–94, 282
  selected list, 100–102
  types, 94–96
Harris (poll), 166
Hearings, congressional, 166, 169–170
Historical research, 198, 282
H-FILM, 54
Hypotheses, 10, 201, 283

I

Image databases, 69, 283
Independent variable, 195, 283
Indicative abstract, 232
Informative abstract, 232
Institutional study, 198
Interaction Process Analysis, 200
Interactional analysis, 199
Interlibrary loan system, 28, 84, 283
Internal validity, 210, 283
International Association of Business Communicators, 8

International Communication Association (ICA), 5
International Listening Association, 8
Internet
  communication research
  access to, 45
  addresses, 46
  evaluating sources, 52–53
Interpersonal communication, 3
Intervening variable, 209, 283
Interviews, 201, 204, 283

J

Jargon, 223
Journals, scholarly
  advertising, business, marketing, and public relations, 150–151
  communication, 146–148
  electronic, 153
  history and political science, 152
  psychology, sociology, and social psychology, 151–152
  speech and language, 149–150
  submitting manuscripts, 243–245
  types, 140–144
JOURNET, 54

K

Key-word searching, 26, 70–72, 285
Known-to-unknown order, 236

L

Laboratory research, 209, 285
Lambda Pi Eta, 8
Language and symbol systems, 3
Legal
  collections, 163
  encyclopedias, 97
  research, 115–116
Legal references, bibliographic format, 263
Legal/policy research, 199, 285
Library of Congress
  catalog, 113
  classification system, 285
  subject headings, 24, 285
Library procedures, 15–17
Library/documentary research, 197, 285
Listservs, 54–56, 285
Literature reviews
  defined, 234–235, 285
  exemplary, 234

exhaustive, 234
non-linear search process, 14
organizing strategies, 236–237
outline, 37
parts, 235–236
steps, 237–238
research questions, 22–23, 194
search strategies, 17–35
tips, 35
topics, 14, 18–19
writing, 35–37, 235–238
Logical (Boolean) operators, 72–75, 285
Loose-leaf reporting services, 162–163

M
Magazine, 285
Manuals
defined, 174, 285
selected list, 185–186
Manuscript style, APA, 229, 265–67
Marxist theories, 198
Mass communication, 4
Measurement collections, 163–164
Media
collections, 159–162
dictionaries, 173–174
directories, 181–182
indexes, 136, 126–129, 285
instructional, 171–172
Message-oriented research, 197, 285
MetaLab Internet archive, 161
Meta-search engines, 53, 285
Microform collections, 160–161
MLA format or style, 224–225
Monograph, 286
Movement study, 198
Multimedia databases, 69, 286
Museum of Broadcast Communications, 161
Museum of Television and Radio, 161

N
Narrowing a topic, 18–19, 22–23
National Association of Broadcasters, 8, 165
National Communication Association (NCA), 5
National Forensic Association, 8
National union catalogs, 113
Natural language searching, 81–82, 286
Network analysis, 206, 286
Newsgroups, Usenet, 56–57

Non-laboratory research, 209, 286
Non-print media, bibliographic format, 260
Nonprobability sampling, 202, 286
Nonverbal coding, 211
Note taking, 31–34

O
Observational research, 205, 286
OCLC, 113, 287
Online Computer Library Center (OCLC), 113, 287
Online catalogs, 24
Online search techniques, 69–82
Operational definition, 195, 287
Operators, logical, 72–75, 287
Organizational communication, 3
Original research reports, 242–245

P
Paragraph structure, 220
Paraphrasing, 220–21
Participant observation, 206, 287
pdf format, 46
People-oriented research, 205–210, 287
Periodical indexes
abstracts, 117
communication, 120–121
defined, 117, 287
full-text, 118
general and interdisciplinary, 123–124
selected list, 132–134
types, 117–124
Periodicals, bibliographic format, 261–262
Personal communications, citing, 263
Phrase searching, 76
Pi Kappa Delta, 9
Plagiarism, 57, 220–21, 223, 287
Political Commercial Archive, 161
Polls, 204, 287
Population, 201, 287
Posttest-only control-group design, 208
Preexperimental designs, 207
Presidential libraries, 159
Pretest-posttest control-group design, 207
Primary sources, 198, 287
Print media collections, 159–160
Probability sampling techniques, 202, 204, 287

Problem-cause-solution order, 236
Professional and trade magazines
    types, 145–146
    selected list, 152–153
Professional communication organiza-
    tions, 6–7
Proofreading
    checklist, 226
    symbols, 226–227
Prospectus, research, 242, 239–242, 287
Proximity operators, 75–76, 287
Public Affairs Video Archives, 161
Public communication, 4
Public Relations Society of America, 8
Publishers' series, 99
Purposive sample, 202, 288

Q

Qualitative research methods, 196, 288
Quantitative research methods, 196,
    288
Questionnaires, 203
Quota sample, 202, 288
Quoting, 220–221

R

Radio Advertising Bureau, 165
Radio-Television News Directors
    Association, 8
Ratings research, 204, 288
Reading research, 30–31
Regional study, 198
Relational analysis, 199
Relational Control Coding Scheme, 200
Relevance ranking, 83, 288
Reliability, 209, 288
Religious Communication Association, 9
Reports, congressional, 169–170
Research
    approaches, 10, 197–211
    archival/documentary, 197–200, 278
    artifact-oriented, 197–204, 278
    behavior-oriented, 205–210, 278
    critical/rhetorical, 198–99, 280
    defined, 1, 193
    descriptive, 194
    empirical, 193
    ethics, 210–211
    ethnography, 200, 205
    experimental, 206–210, 282
    explanatory, 194, 282
    field, 209

historical, 198, 282
laboratory, 209, 285
legal/policy, 199, 285
library/documentary, 197, 285
message oriented, 197–204, 285
non-laboratory, 209, 286
observational, 205–206, 286
people-oriented, 205–210, 287
problem, 195
process, 193–94
projects, 9–10, 14
prospectus, 239–242
questions, 22–23, 36, 195–196
reports, 242–245
stages, 194
survey/interview, 201–205, 290
systematic nature, 1
texts, selected list, 217
topics, 14
Respondents, 201, 210, 288
Retrospective bibliography, 288
Rhetoric, 2, 4
Rhetorical research, 288
Roper, 166

S

Samples and sampling, 204, 289
Sampling frame, 202
Scholarly journals, 140–44
Search engines, 52–54
Search procedures, online, 23–28
Search records, 34–35
Search strategy, 17–35,116
Search strategy sheet, 24
Search techniques, online
    Boolean operators, 72–75
    controlled vocabulary, 70–72
    field-specific searching, 76–78
    key words, 70–72
    mediated, 85
    narrowing and broadening, 22–23
    natural language, 81–82
    phrase searching, 76
    proximity operators, 75–76
    subject headings, 70–72
    truncation, 78
    word/phrase indexes, 78–79
    World Wide Web, 82–84
Secondary analysis, 199, 289
Secondary sources, 198, 289
Selected study, 198
Series, 99–100, 106–107, 289

Sexist language, 223
Simple random sample, 202, 289
Small group communication, 3
Society of Professional Journalists, 8
Sociocultural approaches, 200
Solomon four-group design, 208
Source databases, 68, 289
Southern States Communication
    Association (SSCA), 8
Specific-to-general order, 236
Specific-to-general search strategy, 26
Speech collections, 158–159
Speech Communication Association, 5
Standard Rate and Data Service, 166
Statistical databases, 68, 289
Statistical sources, 164–166, 177–78
Stratified sample, 202, 289
Subject
    dictionaries, 98, 290
    encyclopedias, 97
    handbooks, 94–96
    headings, Library of Congress, 20–21
    headings list, 34
    heading searches, 26
Subjects
    ethical treatment, 210
    random assignment, 208
Submitting research papers, 243–245
Supreme Court decisions, 163
Survey/interview research, 201–205, 290
Systematic inquiry, 1
Systematic sample, 290

T
Tables, APA format, 267
Technical reports, bibliographic format,
    260
Television Bureau of Advertising, 165
Textbooks
    defined, 96–97, 290
    research methods, selected list,
        212–217
    selected list, 102–104
Textual analysis, 200, 290
Thesaurus, 290
Thesis statement, 235
Topical bibliography, 290
Topical order, 236
Topic, selecting and narrowing, 21–25
Trade magazines
    types, 145–146

selected list, 152–153
Transitions, 220
Truncation, 78
Turabian style, 225–228

U
U. S. Government publications,
    166–170
Uniform resource locator (URL), 45–46,
    290
Union catalog, 290
Unobtrusive observation, 206, 290
Unpublished papers, bibliographic
    format, 262–263
URL, 45–46, 290
Usenet newsgroups, 56–57

V
Validity, 282–283, 290
Vanderbilt Television News Archive, 161
Variable
    defined, 10, 290
    dependent, 195, 281
    independent, 195, 283
    intervening, 209, 283
Vendor, database, 290
Verb choice, 222
Verb tense, 218–219
Verbal and nonverbal coding, 211, 290
Voice, active and passive, 219

W
Web rings, 51
Western States Communication
    Association (WSCA), 8
Women in Communications, 8
Word/phrase indexes, 78–79
World Communication Association
    (WCA)., 8, 51
World Wide Web
    browsers, 46–47
    copyright, 57
    databases, 69
    directories, 49–52, 290
    ethical issues, 57
    evaluation, 52–53
    origin, 42–43
    research resource, 26
    research uses, 43–44
    search engines, 52–54
    searching, 82–84

troubleshooting, 48

Writing style
  basic elements, 223
  formal, 222

tips, 222–223

Y

Yearbooks, 180–181, 292

Source Index

FROM THE WADSWORTH SERIES IN MASS COMMUNICATION AND JOURNALISM

GENERAL MASS COMMUNICATION

Biagi *Media/Impact: An Introduction to Mass Media*, Fourth Edition
Biagi *Media/Reader: Perspectives on Media Industries, Effects, and Issues*,
　Third Edition
Day *Ethics in Media Communications; Cases and Controversies*, Third Edition
Fortner *International Communications: History, Conflict, and Control of the
　Global Metropolis*
Jamieson/Campbell *The Interplay of Influence*, Fourth Edition
Lester *Visual Communication*, Second Edition
Lont *Women and Media: Content, Careers, and Criticism*
Straubhaar/LaRose *Media Now: Communications Media in the Information Age*,
　Second Edition
Surette *Media, Crime, and Criminal Justice: Images and Realities*, Second Edition
Whetmore *Mediamerica, Mediaworld: Form, Content, and Consequence of Mass
　Communication*, Updated Fifth Edition
Zelezny *Communications Law: Liberties, Restraints, and the Modern Media*,
　Second Edition

JOURNALISM

Bowles/Borden *Creative Editing for Print Media*, Third Edition
Hilliard *Writing for Television, Radio & New Media*, Seventh Edition
Kessler/McDonald *The Search: Information Gathering for the Mass Media*
Kessler/McDonald *When Words Collide*, Fifth Edition
Klement/Matalene *Telling Stories/Taking Risks: Journalism Writing at the Century's
　Edge*
Parrish *Photojournalism: An Introduction*
Rich *Writing and Reporting News: A Coaching Method*, Third Edition
Rich *Workbook for Writing and Reporting News*, Third Edition

PHOTOJOURNALISM AND PHOTOGRAPHY

Parrish *Photojournalism: An Introduction*
Rosen/DeVries *Introduction to Photography*, Fourth Edition

PUBLIC RELATIONS AND ADVERTISING

Hendrix *Public Relations Cases*, Fourth Edition
Jewler/Drewniany *Creative Strategy in Advertising*, Sixth Edition
Marlow *Electronic Public Relations*
Mueller *International Advertising: Communicating Across Cultures*
Newsom/Carrell *Public Relations Writing: Form and Style*, Fifth Edition
Newsom/Turk/Kruckeberg *This Is PR: The Realities of Public Relations*, Seventh
　Edition
Sivulka *Soap, Sex, and Cigarettes: A Cultural History of American Advertising*
Woods *Advertising and Marketing to the New Majority: A Case Study Approach*

RESEARCH AND THEORY

Babbie *The Practice of Social Research*, Eighth Edition
Baran/Davis *Mass Communication Theory: Foundations, Ferment, and Future*,
　Second Edition
Rubenstein *Surveying Public Opinion*
Rubin/Rubin/Piele *Communication Research: Strategies and Sources*,
　Fifth Edition
Wimmer/Dominick *Mass Media Research: An Introduction*, Sixth Edition

FROM THE WADSWORTH SERIES IN SPEECH COMMUNICATION

Babbie *The Basics of Social Research*
Babbie *The Practice of Social Research*, Eighth Edition
Barranger *Theatre: A Way of Seeing*, Fourth Edition
Braithwaite/Wood *Case Studies in Interpersonal Communication: Processes and Problems*
Campbell *The Rhetorical Act*, Second Edition
Campbell/Burkholder *Critiques of Contemporary Rhetoric*, Second Edition
Cragan/Wright *Communication in Small Groups: Theory, Process, Skills*, Fifth Edition
Crannell *Voice and Articulation*, Fourth Edition
Freeley/Steinberg *Argumentation and Debate: Critical Thinking for Reasoned Decision Making*, Tenth Edition
Govier *A Practical Study of Argument*, Fourth Edition
Hamilton *Essentials of Public Speaking*
Hamilton/Parker *Communicating for Results: A Guide for Business and the Professions*, Fifth Edition
Jaffe *Public Speaking: Concepts and Skills for a Diverse Society*, Second Edition
Kahane/Cavender *Logic and Contemporary Rhetoric: The Use of Reason in Everyday Life*, Eighth Edition
Larson *Persuasion: Reception and Responsibility*, Eighth Edition
Littlejohn *Theories of Human Communication*, Sixth Edition
Lumsden/Lumsden *Communicating with Credibility and Confidence*
Lumsden/Lumsden *Communicating in Groups and Teams: Sharing Leadership*, Third Edition
Miller *Organizational Communication: Approaches and Processes*, Second Edition
Peterson/Stephan/White *The Complete Speaker: An Introduction to Public Speaking*, Third Edition
Rubin/Rubin/Piele *Communication Research: Strategies and Sources*, Fifth Edition
Rybacki/Rybacki *Communication Criticism: Approaches and Genres*
Samovar/Porter *Intercultural Communication: A Reader*, Ninth Edition
Samovar/Porter/Stefani *Communication Between Cultures*, Third Edition
Trenholm/Jensen *Interpersonal Communication*, Fourth Edition
Ulloth/Alderfer *Public Speaking: An Experiential Approach*
Verderber *The Challenge of Effective Speaking*, Eleventh Edition
Verderber *Communicate!*, Ninth Edition
Verderber/Verderber *Inter-Act: Using Interpersonal Communication Skills*, Eighth Edition
Wood *Communication Mosaics: A New Introduction to the Field of Communication*
Wood *Communication in Our Lives*, Second Edition
Wood *Communication Theories in Action: An Introduction*, Second Edition
Wood *Gendered Lives: Communication, Gender, and Culture*, Third Edition
Wood *Interpersonal Communication: Everyday Encounters*, Second Edition
Wood *Relational Communication: Continuity and Change in Personal Relationships*, Second Edition